Developments in
Japanese Economics

GP 8900192

Developments in Japanese Economics

Edited by

RYUZO SATO
The Center for Japan-U.S.
Business and Economic Studies
New York University
New York, New York

TAKASHI NEGISHI
Faculty of Economics
University of Tokyo
Tokyo
Japan

ACADEMIC PRESS
Harcourt Brace Jovanovich, Publishers
Tokyo Boston San Diego
New York Berkeley London
Sydney Toronto

ACADEMIC PRESS JAPAN, INC.
Ichibancho Central Bldg., 22-1 Ichibancho,
Chiyoda-ku, Tokyo 102

United States Edition published by
ACADEMIC PRESS, INC.
1250 Sixth Avenue, San Diego, CA 92101

United Kingdom Edition published by
ACADEMIC PRESS, INC. (LONDON) LTD.
24/28 Oval Road, London NW1 7DX

Library of Congress Cataloging–in–Publication Data

Developments in Japanese economics/Ryuzo Sato, Takashi Negishi
  [editors].
     p. cm.
  Bibliography: p.
  Includes index
  Contents: Rules of thumb in expectations formation and stability
of growth dynamics/Hajime Hori—Balance of payments adjustment
under price rigidity/Michihiro Ohyama—Market equilibrium and
optimum social welfare in a two-region economy/Noboru Sakashita—
Economic expansion, industrialization, and Dutch disease economics
in the context of international monetary economics/Akira Takayama—
Expenditure patterns and international trade in Quesnay's Tableau
economique/Takashi Negishi—Progress of Japanese national
accounts in an international perspective of the SNA review/
Yoshimasa Kurabayashi and Hiroshi Matsuura—Revaluation of durable
capital stock in Japanese manufacturing and its application for the
measurement of potential growth rate during the OPEC decade/
Shunsuke Mori and Takamitsu Sawa—Why is Japan's private saving
rate so high?/Charles Yuji Horioka—Labor market segmentation,
human resource utilization, and economic development/Koji Taira—
A comparative study on financial development/Keimei Kaizuka—
Internationalization of Japanese commercial banking and the yen/
Masahiro Fujita—Estimations of self-dual demand functions/Ryuzo
Sato and Masahiro Matsushita.
  ISBN 0-12-619845-4
  1. Economics—Japan. I. Satō, Ryūzō, Date- . II. Negishi.
Takashi, Date- .
HB126.J2D48 1988   87-34806
330′.O952—dc19   CIP

Printed in the United States of America
89 90 91 92   9 8 7 6 5 4 3 2 1

Contents

Part II
THEORY AND APPLICATIONS

Part III
COMPARATIVE ANALYSIS

Contributors

Numbers in parentheses refer to the pages on which the authors' contributions begin.

Masahiro Fujita (p. 217), *The Research Institute for Economic and Business Administration, Kobe University, Rokko-dai-machi, Nada-ku, 657, Japan*

Hajime Hori (p. 3), *Department of Economics, Tohoku University, Kawauchi, Sendai 980, Japan*

Charles Yuji Horioka (p. 145), *Institute of Social and Economic Research, Osaka University, 6-1, Mihogaokam Ibaragi-shi, Osaka-ku 567, Japan*

Keimei Kaizuka (p. 197), *Department of Economics, The University of Tokyo, 7-3-1, Hongo Bunkyo-ku, Tokyo 113, Japan*

Yoshimasa Kurabayashi (p. 99), *Hitotsubashi Institute of Economic Research, Hitotsubashi University 2-1, Naka, Kunitachi-shi, Tokyo 186, Japan*

Masahiro Matsushita (p. 253), *Department of Economics, Aoyama Gakuin University, 4-25 Shibuya 4-chrome, Shibuya, Tokyo 150, Japan*

Hiroshi Matsuura (p. 99), *Economic Research Institute, Economic Planning Agency, 3-1-1, Kasumigaseki, Chiyoda-ku, Tokyo 100, Japan*

Shunsuke Mori (p. 125), *Kyoto Institute of Economic Research, Kyoto University, Yoshida Honmachi, Sakyo-ku, Kyoto 606, Japan*

Takashi Negishi (p. 85), *Department of Economics, The University of Tokyo, 7-3-1, Hongo Bunkyo-ku, Tokyo 113, Japan*

Michihiro Ohyama (p. 31), *Department of Economics, Keio University, 2-15-45, Mita, Minato-ku, Tokyo 108, Japan*

Noboru Sakashita (p. 43), *Institute of Socio-Economic Planning, The University of Tsukuba, Sakura, Ibaraki 305, Japan*

Ryuzo Sato (p. 253), *The Center for Japan-U.S. Business and Economics Graduate School of Business Administration, New York University, 100 Trinity Place, New York, New York 10006*

Takamitsu Sawa (p. 125), *Kyoto Institute of Economic Research, Kyoto University, Yoshida Honmachi, Sakyo-ku, Kyoto 606, Japan*

Koji Taira (p. 181), *Department of Economics, University of Illinois, Urbana-Champaign, Illinois 61829*

Akira Takayama (p. 59), *Department of Economics, Southern Illinois University Carbondale, Illinois 62901*

Preface

In the past "Japanese Economics" often meant either "regional analysis," (in particular, that applicable only to Japan) or "purely mathematical generalizations and refinements" of basic economic theories developed by non-Japanese economists.

The first category refers to the work of "Japanologists," a group of economists, sociologists, political scientists, historians, and other related disciplines. Their strength lies in their proficiency in language and deep appreciation of Japanese culture. But most western economists consider the studies by Japanologists to lack the analytic rigor characteristic of American and European contributions.

Burmeister and Dobell, in the preface to the Japanese edition of *Mathematical Theories of Economic Growth* (Translated by R. Sato and E. Ohsumi, Keio-Shobo Publishing Co., Tokyo, 1976), expressed their admirations of the Japanese contributions to mathematical economics. Others have been less kind. Japanese economics is frequently given the deprecatory connotation of n-dimensional extensions that does not add substantially to the economic insight provided by the two-dimensional results developed by non-Japanese predecessors.

This perception of Japanese economics is similar to the prevailing view of Japanese contributions in science and technology. It is generally understood that the Japanese are the so-called "process innovators" rather than "products innovators."[1] Hence the mathematical refinements of Japanese economics represent the "process innovative" aspect of Japanese science and technology.

These extreme views, in addition to being wrong, also mislead others on the role of the Japanese economist in policy making. This book is an attempt to present the mainstream "Japanese Economics" and to entice the serious attention of the non-Japanese audience by summarizing the studies conducted by prominent contemporary Japanese economists.

The twelve chapters of the book are divided into three parts: the first part deals with economic theory, the second with theory and application, and the third with comparative analysis. In Part 1, there are four papers. In the paper entitled "Rules of Thumb in Expectations Formation and Stability of Growth Dynamics," Hajime Hori demonstrates that the steady state of a heterogeneous capital goods model is stable even with an infinitely short forecast if people supplement their forecast of the future with suitable rules of thumb. If the forecast horizon cannot be extended into the indefinite future for some reason, then empirical rules of thumb that contain necessary information in a condensed form should be used in its place. This is a stabilizing force in growth dynamics. Michihiro Ohyama's paper on "Balance of Payments Adjustment under Price Rigidity" is of particular interest to those who are concerned with balance of payments equilibrium. Using a simple dynamic model, he shows that the supply of domestic money must assume a unique value if the economy is to achieve the long run equilibrium. If the supply of money falls short of the appropriate level, the economy may experience the early symptom of the paradoxical J-curve effect that seems to have hindered the improvement of the U.S. balance of payments since the Plaza Accord in 1985. If, on the other hand, the supply of money is greater than the appropriate level, the economy will suffer from a chronic balance of payments deficit in the long run.

People migrate from one region to another region for different reasons. The present-day Japan is no exception. In fact, the Japanese pattern of regional migration is getting more and more complicated. Noboru Sakashita attempts to explain these complexities by examining the discrepancy between the market equilibrium and the social optimum and discussing policy measures in his paper "Marketing Equilibrium and Optimum Social Welfare in a Two-Region Economy." Akira Takayama's theoretical paper on "Economic Expansion, Industrialization, and Dutch Disease Economics in the Context of International Monetary Economics" is developed "in the hope of explaining some experiences in Japan and other countries." The section on Dutch Disease Economics, which is concerned with the general equilibrium effects of a secular boom like the North Sea oil boom for Britain in the 1970s, the

---

[1] See C. Freeman, *Economics of Industrial Innovations*, 2nd Edition, MIT Press, Cambridge, MA, 1982.

Schlochteren natural gas boom for the Netherlands in the 1960s, and the manufacturing goods boom for Japan in the 1960s, should be particularly appealing to both theoretical and applied economists, because this is one of the best examples of the uses of economic analysis in real world problems. The reader will learn much from Takayama's elaborate footnotes.

In Part 2, Takashi Negishi demonstrates his wide range of interests. In the paper entitled "Expenditure Patterns and International Trade in Quesnay's Tableau économique," he shows that, in addition to the traditional and the new interpretations of Quesnay's Tableau économique, there is yet another interpretation. The introduction of international trade makes the type of expenditure a matter of indifference, because any change in it can always be adjusted by a corresponding change in international trade so that there is no change in the production and the revenue (rent) of the nation. It is also emphasized that it is not the mere changes in expenditure pattern but changes in capital accumulation that are relevant for economic growth and decline. Thus in an open economy the expenditure pattern need not matter as much as capital accumulation.

The paper by Yoshimasa Kurabayashi and Hiroshi Matsuura is one of the best examples of how Japanese economists apply theory to empirical endeavors. One of the present authors is directly responsible for the ground work of the "new Japanese system of national accounts," which attracted attention from international economists and statisticians for its special merit. The present paper attempts to review this system in the light of past experiences and to present a simplified and integrated system of national accounts. The paper by Shunsuke Mori and Takamitsu Sawa on "Revaluation of Durable Capital Stock...," represents a very serious work undertaken by econometricians using the Berndt and Wood method. The authors revaluate the durable capital stock of the Japanese manufacturing industries, which may have become obsolete due to drastic changes in energy prices in the 1970s. They also propose alternative revaluation procedures and evaluate the potential production capacity of the Japanese manufacturing sector to compare it with realized output.

Charles Yuji Horioka's study on "Why is Japan's Private Saving Rate so High" is most timely and welcomed. Born and educated in the United States, but having the experience of teaching in Japanese Universities, Horioka's understanding of the Japanese system and Japanese economics is quite unique and should be greatly appreciated. An analysis of the determinants of inter-country differences in private saving rates is conducted using data from the period of 1957–1984 for twenty-one OECD countries. It is found that Japan's exceptionally high private saving rate is due to the peculiarities of the age structure of its population—the much lower ratio of the aged and the somewhat lower ratio of the young. The rapid aging of the Japanese population will cause the private saving rate to decline moderately until 1989 and much more sharply thereafter, becoming negative by about the year 2012. Although this conclusion may sound provocative, there is a lot to learn from this paper.

The first paper in Part 3, by Koji Taira, deals with labor market segmentation in Japan. The author utilizes "institutional" analysis rather than conventional labor economics to develop a comprehensive view of labor market behavior. The source of this approach is the stage theory of labor market characteristics. The author applies the U.S. stage analysis of "proletarianization" and "homegenization" to the Japanese labor market. He explores the hypothesis that the deficient proletarianization and homogenization of the Japanese labor force before World War I resulted in a much pronounced labor market segmentation in later years in Japan than in the United States.

Keimei Kaizuka's paper, entitled "A Comparative Study on Financial Development," is particularly timely, as the world economy today depends more than ever on the sound functioning of financial markets. Today's global financial structure is characterized by two types of financial transactions, namely, transactions in open and competitive markets and bilateral transactions. The author first studies the new topology of financial structure and then applies it to four countries: Great Britain, the United States, West Germany, and Japan. The paper concludes that, roughly speaking, the United States and Great Britain are similar, while West Germany and Japan are comparable in the sense that the banking sector played the dominant role, contrasting with the U.S.—Great Britain case where an open economy and a bond market had been firmly established before the banking system was consolidated.

The paper entitled "Internationalization of Japanese Commercial Banking and Yen," by Masahiro Fujita, presents the results of a survey conducted to study how Japanese city banks are dealing with internationalization. The internationalization of finance has three aspects: internationalization of domestic currency, transactions of both domestic and foreign currencies with non-residents and residents, and internationalization of money and capital markets. From this work the reader can gain some historical background and some insights regarding the present and future developments of the Japanese banking industry in the world market.

The last paper of the volume is by Ryuzo Sato and Masahiro Matsushita on "Estimation of Self-Dual Demand Functions: An International Comparison." The authors begin with a summary of the theoretical work done in this area by Hicks, Houthakker, Samuelson, Sato, and others, and then attempt to investigate the validity of the theory by using both the U.S. and Japanese data. The self-dual demand functions are of particular interest, because the underlying direct utility functions are a "mirror image of indirect utility functions which can be easily derivable from the self-dual demand functions. In fact, most of the known types of demand functions used for empirical analysis are 'self-dual'. The study shows that this class of demand functions fits U.S. and Japanese data very well, though different elasticities are applicable to different countries. For instance, demand for housing in the two countries differs drastically. An average household in Japan is not as sensitive to price changes as an average household in the United States. This may indicate that Americans move from one place to another more often seeking better housing conditions. Japan, in a sense, is a more rigid society in that respect.

The editors naturally owe a lot to the contributors of the volume, but they also owe much to the publisher for patiently waiting for the final version. The wait has been so long that at least one contributor has "forgotten" about his work. The editors are, nevertheless, very proud of all the works included in this volume because the volume, when it is published, will be new to many scholars of Japanese economics. It is hoped that these papers will endure the passage of time. The authors wish to thank President Junichiro Minagawa for his encouragement and the privileges he allowed us during the course of the preparation of this volume.

Ryuzo Sato
Takashi Negishi

Part 1

ECONOMIC THEORY

1

Rules of Thumb in Expectations Formation and Stability of Growth Dynamics

HAJIME HORI*

Department of Economics
Tohoku University
Kawauchi, Sendai
Japan

1.

It is well known that the steady states of growth models with myopic perfect foresight usually show saddle-point instability (see R. M. Solow [1959] and D. W. Jorgenson [1960] for dynamic Leontief models; F. H. Hahn [1966] and K. Kuga [1977] for neoclassical heterogeneous capital goods models; and K. Nagatani [1977] for monetary growth models). The essence of such instability is rather simple and is roughly as follows. A relatively high price of an asset is compatible with portfolio balance only if the expected rate of change of that price is relatively high, because the ratio of these two quantities is one of the components of the expected rate of return on the asset. Therefore, if the expected rate of change is equal to the actual, a relatively high price brings about a relatively high rate of price increase, hence instability.

The myopic perfect foresight assumption, however, has some undesirable features that make us skeptical about the reality of the instability conclusion. Firstly, prices are regarded as state variables and, therefore, as given at each moment of time. Thus, what adjusts to equate supply and demand at each moment of time is not the prices at that moment but the prices at the next

*The author wishes to thank Professor K. Inada for useful discussions.

3

moment. Since this means that each momentary equilibrium is established by relegating disequilibrating factors to the next moment, the instability result may not be surprising. Secondly, the expected price changes are simply assumed to equal the actual without any explanation concerning the mechanisms by which expectations are formed and equated to the actual price changes. Thirdly, in a class of models where multiple assets compete with each other in terms of their rates of return, one of the asset prices becomes negative in finite time on every nonconvergent growth path, as was shown by Solow [1959] and Shell and Stiglitz [1967]. But this is impossible if the assets consist of equity capital and debt of limited liability corporations, as in most of today's advanced economies.

There have appeared a few attempts to reinstate stability by eliminating some of these undesirable features. Shell and Stiglitz [1967] showed that a long-run (instead of myopic) perfect foresight, together with free disposal of assets, might find the right initial prices which would lead to the saddle-point type steady state, because vanishing of one of the asset prices on a non-convergent growth path would cause excess demand for the asset and this disequilibrium would be foreseen. Sargent and Wallace [1973] also argued that correct expectations of the events of the infinite future would establish the right initial prices leading to the steady state. Although these works assume a perfect foresight with an infinitely long forecast horizon, Hori [1982] showed that, for a dynamic Leontieff-type model similar to the one analyzed by Solow [1959] and Jorgenson [1960], the stability conclusion was robust with respect to the length of the forecast horizon in the sense that the economy converges to a neighborhood of the steady state if the forecast horizon is finite but long.

The present paper is concerned with the stability implications of another aspect of expectations formation. If the forecast horizon cannot be extended into the indefinite future for some reason, people will try to supplement their future forecast by some empirical rules of thumb which, they suppose, contain necessary information in a condensed form. Does this tend to stabilize the economy?

Since what we aim at in this paper is not generality but the demonstration of an idea, we will employ the simplest heterogeneous capital-goods model, namely an Uzawa-type two-sector growth model (see Uzawa (1961)) modified by the nonshiftability of capital, which introduces the heterogeneity of capital goods. Available assets are the two kinds of equity capital with limited liability, and the nonnegativity of their prices plays an important role. In such a model simple but powerful rules of thumb are available, and, even with an apparent myopia, the dynamics of the model are stable.

The analysis proceeds in the following order. Section 2 specifies the real aspect of the model. Section 3 specifies the mechanism of expectations formation and the rules of thumb which supplement the expectations formation, and defines equilibrium asset prices. A discrete-time formulation is employed. Section 4 analyzes the growth paths of the basic discrete-time model and of the limiting continuous-time model which is reached as the length of the unit period of the discrete-time model contracts to zero. Section 5 contains a summary and some concluding remarks. The appendix proves some of the propositions stated without proof in the main text.

2.

The technological structure of the model is that of a nonshiftable-capital, two-sector growth model with a couple of additional simplifying assumptions.

There exist two productive sectors in the economy, the investment-goods sector denoted by 1 and the consumption-goods sector denoted by 2. Their production technologies are represented by Cobb-Douglas production functions which relate the amounts of labor and capital employed at time t, $L_i(t)$, and $K_i(t)$ to the rate of production at that time, $Y_i(t)$,

$$Y_i(t) = [L_i(t)]^{a_i}[K_i(t)]^{1-a_i}, \qquad 0 < a_i < 1, \qquad i = 1, 2. \tag{1}$$

Since $Y_i(t)$ is the rate of production, the amount of the ith goods produced by using $L_i(t)$ and $K_i(t)$ during the interval $[t, t + h]$ is $Y_i(t)h$. (The reference to t may be omitted when there is no possibility of confusion.)

Let h denote the length of the unit period in our discrete-time model. Labor force grows according to

$$L(t + h) = (1 + \lambda)^h L(t), \qquad t = 0, h, 2h, \ldots, \tag{2}$$

where λ is a positive constant.

Labor is inelastically supplied and mobile between the two sectors, and perfect competition prevails in the labor market. Thus total labor force is employed, and the uniform wage rate is equal to the marginal value product of labor in both sectors. Let p and w denote the price of the investment goods and the wage rate, respectively, both in terms of the consumption goods. Then,

$$w = a_2 \left(\frac{K_2}{L_2}\right)^{1-a_2} \tag{3}$$

and

$$p = \frac{a_2 \left(\dfrac{K_2}{L_2}\right)^{1-a_2}}{a_1 \left(\dfrac{K_1}{L_1}\right)^{1-a_1}}. \tag{4}$$

The classical savings behavior prevails, namely, all the wage income is consumed and all the profit income is saved. This, together with (3), implies that the fractions of labor employed in the two sectors are constant over time. Namely,

$$\frac{L_1(t)}{L(t)} = 1 - a_2, \qquad \frac{L_2(t)}{L(t)} = a_2, \qquad t = 0, h, 2h, \ldots \qquad (5)$$

A central feature of the technological side of our model is that capital equipment, once installed in one sector, cannot be shifted to the other, although newly produced investment goods can be installed in either sector. This nonshiftability of capital introduces heterogeneous assets in the simplest way, namely, capital in the first sector with total amount K_1 and capital in the second sector with total amount K_2. In view of the institutional arrangements of today's advanced economies, we will interpret these assets as *limited liability equity*. Let $q_i(t)$ denote the price of the ith equity capital and $r_i(t)$ the flow of dividends to a unit of the ith equity capital at time t. Because of the limited liability assumption, the q_i's are nonnegative. The r_i's are given by

$$r_1 = p(1 - a_1)\left(\frac{L_1}{K_1}\right)^{a_1}, \qquad r_2 = (1 - a_2)\left(\frac{L_2}{K_2}\right)^{a_2}. \qquad (6)$$

Note that the amount of the dividend paid at the end of period $[t, t + h]$ to the holder of a unit of the ith equity capital is $r_i(t)h$.

Concerning the relation between the q_i's and p, it is assumed that

$$\max[q_1(t), q_2(t)] = p(t), \qquad t = 0, h, 2h, \ldots \qquad (7)$$

The rationale is as follows. If $q_i > p$, it will be profitable to buy investment goods, install them in the ith sector, and issue equity securities correspondingly, the extra profit to a unit of such an operation being equal to $q_i - p$. Such extra profits will generate excess demand for the investment goods. If both q_1 and q_2 are smaller than p, then it will cause losses to buy investment goods and issue corresponding equity securities. Thus excess supply of investment goods will result. Therefore (7) has to hold in order for the investment-goods market to be cleared.

This consideration also suggests how to formulate the mechanism of allocation of newly produced investment goods. In fact, it does not pay to invest in the first sector if $q_1 < q_2$ and vice versa. Thus

$$K_i(t + h) = K_i(t) + b_i(q(t))Y_1(t)h, \qquad i = 1, 2, \qquad t = 0, h, 2h, \ldots, \qquad (8)$$

where $q(t) = (q_1(t), q_2(t))$,

$$0 \le b_1(q(t)) \le 1, \qquad b_2(q(t)) = 1 - b_1(q(t)), \qquad (9)$$

and

$$b_1(q(t)) = \begin{cases} 1 & \text{if } q_1(t) > q_2(t) \\ 0 & \text{if } q_1(t) < q_2(t) \end{cases}. \tag{10}$$

Let us define new state variables $x_i(t)$ by

$$x_i(t) = K_i(t)/L(t), \qquad i = 1, 2, \qquad t = 0, h, 2h, \ldots \tag{11}$$

and let $x(t) = (x_1(t), x_2(t))$. Then equations (4), (6), and (8) can be rewritten:

$$p = g(x) \equiv \left[\frac{a_2^{a_2}(1 - a_2)^{1 - a_1}}{a_1} \right] \left[\frac{x_2^{1 - a_2}}{x_1^{1 - a_1}} \right] \tag{12}$$

$$r_1 = f_1(x) \equiv \left[\frac{(1 - a_1)(1 - a_2)a_2^{a_2}}{a_1} \right] \left[\frac{x_2^{1 - a_2}}{x_1} \right] \tag{13}$$

$$r_2 = f_2(x) \equiv \frac{(1 - a_2)a_2^{a_2}}{x_2^{a_2}}$$

$$x_i(t + h) = u_i(x(t), b_1(q(t)))$$

$$\equiv \frac{x_i(t) + b_i(q(t))(1 - a_2)^{a_1} x_1(t)^{1 - a_1} h}{(1 + \lambda)^h},$$

$$i = 1, 2, \qquad t = 0, h, 2h, \ldots \tag{14}$$

3.

Equations (9) through (14) show that a momentary equilibrium is established once the capital stocks and asset prices are given (except when $q_1(t) = q_2(t)$). Since the capital stocks are given physically at each moment of time, what remains to be considered is the asset prices.

Our assumptions relevant to the determination of asset prices (and the formation of expectations which affect asset prices) are as follows:

(1) *Identical expectations.* All the portfolio holders have identical expectations.

(2) *Availability of information.* People know the technological structure of the economy, i.e., they know the relation between p and the q_i's given in (7), and the functions $b_i(\cdot)$, $g(\cdot)$, $f_i(\cdot)$, and $u_i(\cdot)$.

(3) *Consistency of expectations.* People expect that, as long as the non-negativity constraint remains ineffective, present and future asset prices will be consistent in the sense that the rates of return to the two assets will be equal.

(4) *Inertia in asset price determination.* Expected asset prices for time t formed at time $t - 1$ are actually realized at time t if there exists a sequence

of expected asset prices for time $t + 1$ through the forecast horizon (looked at from time t, not from time $t - 1$) which are nonnegative and consistent in the above sense.

The assumption of identical expectations is quite standard and does not require particular explanation. The information availability assumption[1] is made so that we can focus our attention on the analysis of the implication of *finite* forecast horizons. The consistency assumption can be regarded as an assumption of people's belief that competition among portfolio holders will equate the rates of return. The inertia assumption is designed to represent a probably psychological force which picks, among an infinite number of candidate pairs, one pair of asset prices to be realized. The need for an assumption like this comes from the fact that there is no physical constraint on the values asset prices can take except their nonnegativity and equation (7), which leave the level of the lower price undetermined[2].

There is another essential assumption concerning the expectations formation, which will be stated later.

Now, for each $\xi = (\xi_1, \xi_2) \gg 0^3$ and $\pi = (\pi_1, \pi_2)$ satisfying $\max(\pi_1, \pi_2) = g(\xi)$, define a *consistent sequence of N terms* by requiring a sequence of four-dimensional vectors $\{(\xi(n), \pi(n))\}_{n=0}^{N} = \{(\xi_1(n), \xi_2(n), \pi_1(n), \pi_2(n))\}_{n=0}^{N}$ to satisfy the following for $n = 0, 1, \ldots, N - 1$:

$$\xi(0) = \xi, \qquad \pi(0) = \pi, \tag{15}$$

$$\pi_2(n)[\pi_1(n + 1) + f_1(\xi(n + 1))h] = \pi_1(n)[\pi_2(n + 1) + f_2(\xi(n + 1))h], \tag{16}$$

$$\xi_i(n + 1) = u_i(\xi(n), b_1(\pi(n))), \text{ and} \tag{17}$$

$$\max[\pi_1(n + 1), \pi_2(n + 1)] = g(\xi(n + 1)). \tag{18}$$

Existence of a consistent sequence for any N and any suitable (ξ, π) is easy to see.

Let $\tilde{x}(t + nh; t, \xi, \pi)$ and $\tilde{q}(t + nh; t, \xi, \pi)$ denote the expectations of $x(t + nh)$ and $q(t + nh)$ formed at time t when capital stocks and asset prices are ξ and π. According to our consistency assumption, *people form expectations for the coming N periods based on a consistent sequence of N terms* in the sense that a sequence of expectations $\{(\tilde{x}(t + nh; t, \xi, \pi), \tilde{q}(t + nh; t, \xi, \pi))\}_{n=1}^{N}$ carries with

---

[1] This terminology is due to Friedman [1979], who distinguished between the information availability assumption and the information exploitation assumption which make up the rational expectations hypothesis.

[2] In models with myopic perfect foresight, this indeterminacy of asset prices shows up as arbitrariness of initial asset prices.

[3] We adopt the following inequality symbols: $(\xi_1, \xi_2) \geqq 0$ if both ξ_1 and ξ_2 are nonnegative; $(\xi_1, \xi_2) > 0$ if $(\xi_1, \xi_2) \geqq 0$ and $(\xi_1, \xi_2) \neq 0$; $(\xi_1, \xi_2) \gg 0$ if both ξ_1 and ξ_2 are positive.

it a consistent sequence $\{(\xi(n), \pi(n))\}_{n=0}^{N}$ such that $\xi(0) = \xi$, $\pi(0) = \pi$,

$$\tilde{x}(t + nh; t, \xi, \pi) = \xi(n), \qquad n = 1, 2, \ldots, N, \tag{19}$$

and

$$\tilde{q}_i(t + nh; t, \xi, \pi) = \max(\pi_i(n), 0), \qquad i = 1, 2, \qquad n = 1, 2, \ldots, N.^{4} \tag{20}$$

What is to be noted about the sequence of expectations $\{(\tilde{x}(t + nh; t, \xi, \pi), \tilde{q}(t + nh; t, \xi, \pi))\}_{n=1}^{N}$ is that the equal rates-of-return condition (16) is violated for this sequence when the nonnegativity condition (20) becomes effective. In fact suppose, for example, that $\pi_1(n) > 0, \pi_2(n) > 0$, and $\pi_1(n + 1) < 0$ for some $0 < n < N$. Then

$$\frac{\tilde{q}_1(t + (n + 1)h; t, \xi, \pi) + f_1(x(t + (n + 1)h; t, \xi, \pi))h}{\tilde{q}_1(t + nh; t, \xi, \pi)}$$

$$> \frac{\pi_1(n + 1) + f_1(\xi(n + 1))h}{\pi_1(n)} = \frac{\pi_2(n + 1) + f_2(\xi(n + 1))h}{\pi_2(n)}$$

$$= \frac{\tilde{q}_2(t + (n + 1)h; t, \xi, \pi) + f_2(x(t + (n + 1)h; t, \xi, \pi)h)}{\tilde{q}_2(t + nh; t, \xi, \pi)}$$

by (16), (18), (19), and (20). This inequality still holds even if $\pi_1(n) = 0$, because in that case the extreme left-hand side becomes infinite. Clearly, π cannot be an equilibrium asset price vector at time t, if such an inequality is expected for the future. Thus, in order for π to be an equilibrium asset price vector at time t, there must exist a sequence of expectations $\{(\tilde{x}(t + nh; t, \xi, \pi), \tilde{q}(t + nh; t, \xi, \pi))\}_{n=1}^{N}$ for which the nonnegativity constraint is ineffective.

But existence of such a sequence may not yet be sufficient for equilibrium because, even though N may be fixed at some finite level, there is an alternative way of extending the forecast horizon qualitatively.

In fact, define two sets S_1 and S_2 of perverse sign patterns between $f_1(\xi) - f_2(\xi)$ and $\pi_1 - \pi_2$ by

$$S_1 = \{(\xi_1, \xi_2, \pi_1, \pi_2) | \xi \gg 0, \quad f_1(\xi) \geqq f_2(\xi), \quad \pi_1 < \pi_2\},$$
$$S_2 = \{(\xi_1, \xi_2, \pi_1, \pi_2) | \xi \gg 0, \quad f_1(\xi) \leqq f_2(\xi), \quad \pi_1 > \pi_2\}. \tag{21}$$

Then the S_i's *predict a future negativity of one of the prices in a consistent sequence* in the sense that *if* $\{(\xi(n), \pi(n))\}_{n=0}^{\infty}$ *is consistent and if* $(\xi(n'), \pi(n')) \in S_i$

---

[4] Given ξ and π, a sequence of expectations formed at time t may not be unique, firstly because the $b_i(s)$'s satisfying (9) and (10) are not unique when $q_1(s) = q_2(s)$, and secondly because the $\pi_i(n + 1)$'s satisfying (17) and (19) are not unique when $\pi_1(n)$ or $\pi_2(n)$ is negative. In spite of this, we let $\tilde{x}(t + nh; \xi, \pi)$ and $\tilde{q}(t + nh; \xi, \pi)$ denote one set of expectations since it is immaterial, as long as the expectations of all the portfolio holders coincide, to which of all the possible sets of expectations they refer, as will be seen in the following.

*for an $n' \in \{0, 1, \ldots\}$ and an i, then $\pi_i(n'') < 0$ for the same i and for some $n'' \in$
$\{n', n' + 1, \ldots\}$*. Moreover, the S_i's are *invariant with respect to a consistent
sequence in the sense that if $\{(\xi(n), \pi(n))\}_{n=0}^{\infty}$ is consistent and if $(\xi(n'), \pi(n')) \in$
S_i for an $n' \in \{0, 1, \ldots\}$ and an i, then $(\xi(n), \pi(n)) \in S_i$ for the same i and all $n \in$
$\{n', n' + 1, \ldots\}$ as long as $\pi(n - 1) > 0$.*

The invariance of the S_i's readily follows from (10), (16), and (17) and the
detailed proof is omitted.

To see that the S_i's predict a future negativity, suppose that

$$(\xi(n), \pi(n)) \in S_i, \qquad \pi(n) > 0. \tag{22}$$

If $\pi_j(n) = 0$, then $\pi_j(n + 1) < 0$ by (16). If $f_1(\xi(n)) = f_2(\xi(n))$ and $\pi_i(n) > \pi_j(n)$,
then $f_i(\xi(n + 1)) < f_j(\xi(n + 1))$ by (10) and (17), and $\pi_i(n + 1) > \pi_j(n + 1)$ by
(16). Therefore we can safely assume, instead of (22), that

$$f_i(\xi(n)) > f_j(\xi(n)) \qquad \text{and} \qquad 0 < \pi_i(n) < \pi_j(n). \tag{23}$$

It will suffice to see that (23) implies the existence of a positive constant C such
that for any integer $k \geq n$ satisfying $\pi(k) \gg 0$,

$$\frac{\pi_i(k + 1)}{\pi_j(k + 1)} - \frac{\pi_i(k)}{\pi_j(k)} < -Ch. \tag{24}$$

(24) implies that $\pi_i(k)$ will be negative for some k because, by the invariance of
the S_i's, $\pi_i(k) = g(\xi(k))$ for all $k > n$ as long as $\pi(k - 1) \gg 0$.

To see the existence of a positive C satisfying (24), first note that for all $k \geq n$
with $\pi(k) \gg 0$,

$$\frac{\pi_i(k + 1)}{\pi_j(k + 1)} - \frac{\pi_i(k)}{\pi_j(k)} < \left[1 - \frac{f_i(\xi(n))}{f_j(\xi(n))}\right] \frac{h}{\dfrac{g(\xi(k + 1))}{f_j(\xi(k + 1)) + h}}. \tag{25}$$

In fact, by virtue of (10), (16), (18), (23), and the invariance of the S_i's, it holds for
all $k \geq n$ with $\pi(k) \gg 0$ that

$$\frac{\pi_i(k + 1)}{\pi_j(k + 1)} - \frac{\pi_i(k)}{\pi_j(k)} < \left[1 - \frac{f_i(\xi(k + 1))}{f_j(\xi(k + 1))}\right] \frac{h}{\dfrac{g(\xi(k + 1))}{f_j(\xi(k + 1)) + h}}.$$

But $f_i(\xi(k + 1))/f_j(\xi(k + 1)) = \text{constant} \times \xi_j(k + 1)/\xi_i(k + 1)$, which increases
monotonically as k increases as long as $\pi_j(k + 1) > \pi_i(k + 1)$. Thus $f_i(\xi(k + 1))/f_j(\xi(k + 1)) > f_i(\xi(n))/f_j(\xi(n))$, from which (25) follows.

Now, for the case where $(i, j) = (2, 1)$, we can write

$$\frac{g(\xi)}{f_1(\xi)} = \frac{\xi_1^{a_1}}{(1 - a_1)(1 - a_2)^{a_1}},$$

and $\xi_1(k + 1)$ has an upper bound (see (14)). Thus (24) holds.

For the case where $(i, j) = (1, 2)$, we have

$$\frac{g(\xi)}{f_2(\xi)} = (a_1(1 - a_2)^{a_1})^{-1} \times \frac{\xi_2}{\xi_1^{1 - a_1}}.$$

Since $b_1(\pi(k)) = 0$ for all $k \geq n$, it follows that

$$\frac{\xi_2(k + 1)}{\xi_1(k + 1)^{1 - a_1}} = (1 + \lambda)^{-ha_1}\left[\frac{\xi_2(k)}{\xi_1(k)^{1 - a_1}} + (1 - a_2)^{a_1}h\right] \qquad (26)$$

Thus $\xi_2(k)/\xi_1(k)^{1 - a_1}$ converges to some finite limit because $(1 + \lambda)^{-ha_1} < 1$. Thus $g(\xi(k + 1))/f_2(\xi(k + 1))$ has an upper bound and again (24) holds. This completes the proof that the S_i's predict a future negativity.

In view of the relation between the nonnegativity constraint and unequal expected rates of return, this property of the S_i's means that if $(\xi, \pi) \in S_i$, then, due to the inertia assumption, the ith asset will bring a larger rate of return in the future. Thus there is enough incentive for portfolio holders to learn and exploit this property of the S_i's. Since the structure of the S_i's is simple enough to be learned through experience by portfolio holders, we will adopt the following assumption:

(5) *Availability of rules of thumb.* People know that the S_i's predict a future negativity of one of the prices and utilize this knowledge as rules of thumb in forming expectations and making portfolio decisions.

Now, to define an equilibrium asset price vector suitably, let us call $\{(\xi(n), \pi(n))\}_{n=0}^N$ a *permissible sequence of N terms* if it is consistent and, for each $n = 0, 1, \ldots, N, (\xi(n), \pi(n))$ is strictly positive and satisfies

$$(\xi(n), \pi(n)) \in (S_1 \cup S_2)^c \qquad (27)$$

where the superscript c denotes the complement. Then, for a given $\xi \gg 0$, π is *an equilibrium asset price vector with forecast horizon N* if there exists a permissible sequence of N terms $\{(\xi(n), \pi(n))\}_{n=0}^N$ such that $\xi(0) = \xi$ and $\pi(0) = \pi$. Note that $\pi_i > \pi_j$ implies $f_i(\xi) > f_j(\xi)$ if π is an equilibrium asset price vector for ξ.

With this definition, it can be shown that *for any $\xi \gg 0$ and for any positive integer N, there exists an equilibrium asset price vector with forecast horizon N.* The proof, however, is rather lengthy and relegated to the appendix.

4.

The basic feature of the present growth dynamics, which are composed of the sequences of actual capital stocks, actual asset prices, expected capital stocks, and expected asset prices, lies in that when unequal rates of return are expected to accrue in the future, this expectation acts upon the current asset prices and investment allocation. The questions which naturally arise in relation to this feature of the model are the following.

(1) In view of the fact that, in many myopic perfect foresight models, the non-negativity constraint on asset prices becomes effective in finite time on every divergent growth path, as was noted in Section 1, and the fact that unequal rates of return arise when the nonnegativity constraint becomes effective, as was noted in Section 3, the above feature of the present model seems to provide a stabilizing force. Is this conjecture correct?

(2) Expectations in the present model are usually different from the actually realized values as long as the forecast horizon N is finite, because the possible events at time $t + N + 1$, which affect the equilibrium asset prices at time $t + 1$, are not taken into account when expectations for time $t + 1$ are formed at time t, $t - 1$, and so on. But then, how much do expectations differ from the realized?

This section is concerned with these questions. For convenience, the analysis will proceed in the following order: (1) movements of actual capital stocks, (2) movements of expected capital stocks, (3) some properties of the expectational sequences that are needed for the analysis of actual and expected asset prices, and (4) movements of actual and expected asset prices.

a.   Movements of Actual Capital Stocks

(10), (13), (14), (16), and (27) imply that if $f_i(x(t)) > f_j(x(t))$, then $b_i(q(t)) = 1$ and $b_j(q(t)) = 0$ unless

$$f_1(u(x(t), b)) = f_2(u(x(t), b)) \qquad \text{for some } b \in [0, 1] \qquad (28)$$

because negation of (28) implies that $q_i(t) > q_j(t)$. Such an investment allocation will reduce or reverse the profit differential because, by (13) and (14),

$$\frac{f_i(x(t + 1))}{f_j(x(t + 1))} = \text{constant} \times \frac{x_j(t + 1)}{x_i(t + 1)} < \text{constant} \times \frac{x_j(t)}{x_i(t)} = \frac{f_i(x(t))}{f_j(x(t))}.$$

Geometrically, define the *equiprofit curve* to be the locus of x satisfying

$$f_1(x) = f_2(x) \qquad (29)$$

and note that $x(t)$ is close to the equiprofit curve if (28) holds, because (28) means that the profit differential at time t is small enough to be wiped out by one period's investment. Thus $x(t)$ *will first move towards the equiprofit curve and then stay within its neighborhood*, which depends upon h because the magnitude of one period's investment is roughly proportional to h.

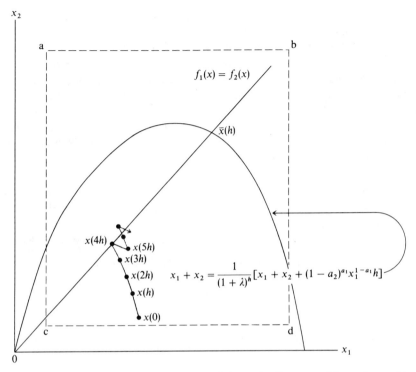

Figure 1. Starting from $x(0)$, $x(t)$ first moves toward the equiprofit curve and then, after reaching its neighborhood, toward the steady state $\bar{x}(h)$. As long as $0 < h \leq \bar{h}$, $x(t)$ never leaves the rectangle abcd which is bounded away from the origin.

To find the overall trend of the movements of $x(t)$ along the equiprofit curve, sum (14) over $i = 1, 2$ to obtain

$$x_1(t + h) + x_2(t + h) = \frac{x_1(t) + x_2(t) + (1 - a_2)^{a_1} x_1(t)^{1 - a_1} h}{(1 + \lambda)^h}. \tag{30}$$

Hence $x_1(t) + x_2(t)$ increases over time if

$$x_1(t) + x_2(t) < \frac{x_1(t) + x_2(t) + (1 - a_2)^{a_1} x_1(t)^{1 - a_1} h}{(1 + \lambda)^h}$$

and decreases if a reversed inequality holds. As can be seen from Figure 1, this implies that, *after reaching a neighborhood of the equiprofit curve, $x(t)$ will zigzag around the curve toward the steady state $\bar{x}$ given by*

$$f_1(\bar{x}) = f_2(\bar{x})$$

$$\bar{x}_1 + \bar{x}_2 = \frac{\bar{x}_1 + \bar{x}_2 + (1 - a_2)^{a_1} \bar{x}_1^{1 - a_1} h}{(1 + \lambda)^h}. \tag{31}$$

It should be noted that recurrent deviation of $x(t)$ from the equiprofit curve is due to the assumed discontinuous investment allocation in a discrete-time setting. Since the situation is the same in a neighborhood of the steady state, $x(t)$ will not usually converge to the steady state but oscillate around it after reaching its neighborhood. But, since the deviation of $x(t)$ from the equiprofit curve is basically of the magnitude of one period's investment, which is proportional to h = length of the unit period, *it will decrease as h decreases and, in the limiting continuous-time model, $x(t)$ will, after reaching the equiprofit curve, move along it and converge to the steady state.*[5] *Therefore the steady state is stable in the limiting continuous-time model.*

Note that this conclusion has been reached without an explicit reference to the expectations, and therefore without any restriction on the length of the forecast horizon, except that the rules of thumb concerning the future movements are utilized.

To obtain a formal description of the limiting continuous-time model, let

$$n(h) = \min\{n \in \{0, 1, \ldots\} \,|\, (28) \text{ holds at } t = nh\},$$

$$T = \lim_{h \to 0} n(h)h$$

for a given $x(0)$. Then in the limiting model,

$$\frac{f_1(x(t))}{f_2(x(t))} \equiv \frac{1 - a_1}{a_1} \frac{x_2(t)}{x_1(t)} = 1 \qquad \text{for all } t \geq T.$$

Thus, if we let

$$k(t) \equiv x_1(t) + x_2(t),$$

then

$$x_1(t) = (1 - a_1)k(t), \qquad x_2(t) = a_1 k(t), \qquad t \geq T. \tag{32}$$

On the other hand, by (30), $k(t)$ satisfies

$$\frac{k(m(t/h)h + h) - k(m(t/h)h)}{h} = \frac{1}{(1 + \lambda)^h} [(1 - a_2)^{a_1} x_1(m(t/h)h)^{1 - a_1}$$

$$- \frac{(1 + \lambda)^h - 1}{h} k(m(t/h)h)], \tag{33}$$

where $m(a)$ denotes the minimum integer not smaller than a[6] and can be shown to satisfy

$$\lim_{h \to 0} m(t/h)h = t.$$

---

[5] It is interesting to note that the movement of $x(t)$ is exactly the same as when static expectations are assumed. For the latter, see Hori [1977].

[6] For $\xi_i(t)$ to be well defined for an $h > 0$, t has to be an integral multiple of h.

Let h go to zero in (33) to obtain

$$\dot{k} = (1 - a_2)^{a_1} x_1^{1 - a_1} - \mu k \tag{34}$$

where

$$\mu \equiv \lim_{h \to 0} \frac{(1 + \lambda)^h - 1}{h} = \log(1 + \lambda)$$

Finally, from (32), (34), and the consideration of the movements of $x(t)$ for $t < T$, we obtain

$$\dot{x}_i(t) = b_i(t)(1 - a_2)^{a_1} x_1(t)^{1 - a_1} - \mu x_i(t), \qquad i = 1, 2 \tag{35}$$

where

$$b_1(t) = \begin{cases} 1 & \text{if } 0 \leq t < T \quad \text{and} \quad f_1(x(0)) > f_2(x(0)) \\ 0 & \text{if } 0 \leq t < T \quad \text{and} \quad f_1(x(0)) < f_2(x(0)) \\ 1 - a_1 & \text{if } t \geq T \end{cases}$$

and

$$b_2(t) = 1 - b_1(t) \qquad \text{for all } t \geq 0.$$

b.   Movements of Expected Capital Stocks

Let $\tilde{x}(t, s)$ denote the expectations of $x(t)$ formed at time s. Then, for each fixed s, both $x(t)$ and $\tilde{x}(t, s)$ start from the same point (i.e., $\tilde{x}(s, s) = x(s)$ for all $s \geq 0$) and obey the same dynamic constraint (14). Moreover, if we let $\tilde{q}(t, s)$ denote the expectations of $q(t)$ formed at time s, then $\tilde{x}(t, s)$ and $\tilde{q}(t, s)$ also satisfy (10) and (27). Therefore $\tilde{x}(t, s)$ can deviate from $x(t)$ only when $\tilde{x}(t, s)$ reaches a neighborhood of the equiprofit curve so that $f_1(u(\tilde{x}(t, s), b)) = f_2(u(\tilde{x}(t, s), b))$ for some $b \in [0, 1]$. After then, $\tilde{x}(t, s)$ will usually deviate from $x(t)$ because an exact estimation of b will be impossible. Even then, however, since both $\tilde{x}(t, s)$ and $x(t)$ will stay within a neighborhood of the equiprofit curve, and since the size of the neighborhood decreases as h decreases, the deviation of $\tilde{x}(t, s)$ from $x(t)$ will decrease to zero as h decreases to zero. Therefore $\tilde{x}(t, s)$, as well as $x(t)$, will first approach the equiprofit curve and then stay within its neighborhood. Since the size of the neighborhood decreases as h decreases, the deviation of $\tilde{x}(t, s)$ from $x(t)$ will decrease as h decreases.

In interpreting this result, however, we need to be careful. In fact, if the forecast horizon N is finite and independent of h, then the length of the forecast horizon, Nh, converges to zero as h converges to zero. Therefore, in the limit, $\tilde{x}(t, s)$ is defined only for the trivial case of $t = s$. One might try to see if the expected rate of change of $x(t)$ is equal to the actual in the limit. But if the rates of change of capital stocks are defined in the usual way by

$$\frac{\xi_i(m(t/h)h + h) - \xi_i(m(t/h)h)}{h},$$

then, for $t \geq T$, they do not coverge (as h decreases to zero) because of the discontinuous jumps of b_i and $\tilde{b}_i$ between 1 and 0.

In order to have a meaningful $\tilde{x}(t, s)$ even in the limiting continuous-time model, let us consider the case where $N = N(h)$ depends on h in such a way that

$$\lim_{h \to 0} N(h)h = H > 0 \tag{36}$$

In this case, the closeness between $\tilde{x}(t, s)$ and $x(t)$ implies that

$$\lim_{h \to 0} \tilde{x}(m(t/h)h, m(s/h)h) = \lim_{h \to 0} x(m(t/h)h) \quad \text{for all } s \geq 0 \text{ and all } t \tag{37}$$

$$\text{such that } 0 \leq t - s < H.$$

Namely, *the medium-run forecast of capital stocks becomes more and more exact as the unit period becomes shorter and, in the limiting continuous-time model, it becomes perfect.*

In order to have a concept of the rates of change which is meaningful in the limiting continuous-time model, note that the time-derivative in the right-hand side of (35) is a double limit of the discrete-time formulation in the sense that

$$\dot{x}_i(t) = \lim_{t' \to t} \frac{\lim_{h \to 0} x_i(m(t'/h)h) - \lim_{h \to 0} x_i(m(t/h)h)}{t' - t}, \qquad i = 1, 2. \tag{38}$$

Thus, if the forecast horizon $N = N(h)$ is long enough to satisfy (36), then (37) implies that the expected rate of change of capital stocks in the sense of (38) is well defined and is equal to the actual.

Actually, however, (36) is not necessary in order to define the expected rate of change in a meaningful way. Note that the double limit in (38) is well defined because the first limiting operation averages out the kinks of $x(m(t/h)h)$, by increasing the number of periods between t and t' to infinity. Thus assume that

$$\lim_{h \to 0} N(h) = \infty$$

$$\lim_{h \to 0} N(h)h = 0 \tag{39}$$

and consider if it is possible to define the expected rate of change of captial stocks by

$$(\dot{x}_i(t))^e = \lim_{h \to 0} R_i(t, h), \qquad i = 1, 2, \tag{40}$$

where

$$R_i(t,h) \equiv \frac{\tilde{x}_i(m(t/h)h) + N(h)h, m(t/h)h) - x_i(m(t/h)h)}{N(h)h}.$$

If $0 \leq t < T$, (40) is well defined because $\lim_{h \to 0} b_1(m(t/h)h)$ exists for such a t. To see if it is defined for $t \geq T$, note that the difference between $\tilde{x}_2(\tau,s)/\tilde{x}_1(\tau,s)$ and the slope of the equiprofit curve, and the difference between $x_2(s)/x_1(s)$ and the slope of the equiprofit curve are both of a magnitude proportional to h. This is because (1) the distance between $\tilde{x}(\tau,s)$ and the equiprofit curve, and the distance between $x(s)$ and the equiprofit curve are both of the magnitude of one period's investment, which is proportional to h, and (2) both $\tilde{x}(\tau,s)$ and $x(s)$ lie in a compact set which is bounded away from both axes. Thus the difference between $\tilde{x}_2(\tau,s)/\tilde{x}_1(\tau,s)$ and $x_2(s)/x_1(s)$ is of a magnitude proportional to h. Therefore there exists a constant C such that

$$\frac{\left| \frac{\tilde{x}_2(m(t/h)h + N(h)h, m(t/h)h)}{\tilde{x}_1(m(t/h)h + N(h)h, m(t/h)h)} - \frac{x_2(m(t/h)h)}{x_1(m(t/h)h)} \right|}{N(h)h} \leq \frac{C}{N(h)}$$

for all $t \geq n(h)h$,

which implies that

$$x_2(m(t/h)h)R_1(t,h) - x_1(m(t/h)h)R_2(t,h) = \varepsilon(h) \qquad \text{for all } t \geq n(h)h, \quad (41)$$

where $\varepsilon(h) \to 0$ as $h \to 0$. On the other hand, since $\tilde{x}_i(\tau,s)$ has to satisfy (14), it follows that

$$R_1(t,h) + R_2(t,h)$$

$$= - \sum_{i=1}^{2} x_i(m(t/h)h) \times \frac{(1+\lambda)^{N(h)h} - 1}{N(h)h} \times (1+\lambda)^{-N(h)h} \qquad (42)$$

$$+ (1 - a_2)^{a_1} \times \sum_{n=1}^{N(h)} \frac{\tilde{x}_1(m(t/h)h + N(h)h - nh, m(t/h)h)^{1 - a_1}h/(1+\lambda)^{nh}}{N(h)h}.$$

Solving (41) and (42) for $R_i(t,h)$, we find that $\lim_{h \to 0} R_i(t,h)$ exists and is equal to (35). Thus we can conclude that *if the forecast horizon satisfies* (39), *then, in the limiting continuous-time model, the expected rate of change of capital stocks in the sense of* (40) *is well defined and equal to the actual.*

c.   Some Properties of the Expectations Sequences

In order to facilitate the analysis of the movements of actual and expected asset prices, let us make explicit the constraints imposed on them by (16), (18), and (27).

(i) Let $\tilde{q}(s + nh, s) = \pi(n)$ and $\tilde{x}(s + nh, s) = \xi(n)$ for convenience. If

$$\left[\frac{\pi_2(n)}{\pi_1(n)} - 1\right]\left[\frac{\pi_2(n + 1)}{\pi_1(n + 1)} - 1\right] \leq 0 \qquad \text{for some } n \in \{0, \ldots, N - 1\},$$

then, for this n, it holds that

$$1 + \frac{f_i(\xi(n + 1)) - f_j(\xi(n + 1))}{g(\xi(n + 1))}h \leq \frac{\pi_j(n + 1)}{\pi_i(n + 1)} \leq 1$$

for $(i, j) = (1, 2)$ or $(i, j) = (2, 1)$. This is because $\{(\xi(n), \pi(n))\}_{n=0}^{N}$ satisfies (16) and (18), as can be easily verified.

(ii) With the same notation as in (i), if

$$\pi_i(n) \geq \pi_j(n) \qquad \text{for all } n \in \{n_1, n_1 + 1, \ldots, n_2\},$$

then

$$\frac{\pi_j(n_2)}{\pi_i(n_2)} = \frac{\pi_j(n_1)}{\pi_i(n_1)} \times \prod_{n=n_1+1}^{n_2}\left[1 + \frac{f_i(\xi(n))}{g(\xi(n))}h\right] - h \sum_{n=n_1+1}^{n_2}\left[\frac{f_j(\xi(n))}{g(\xi(n))}\right]$$

$$\times \prod_{l=n+1}^{n_2}\left(1 + \frac{f_i(\xi(l))}{g(\xi(l))}h\right)\right],$$

where $\Pi_{n_1+2}^{n_1+1}(\cdot) = 1$ for convenience. This also follows from (16) and (18), as can be verified by induction on n_2.

(iii) For each $l \geq n(h)$, there exists an integer $\bar{N}$ satisfying the following:

(a) If $N \geq \bar{N}$, there exist integers $n_0 = l, n_1, \ldots, n_m, n_{m+1} = l + N$ such that

$$0 < n_{i+1} - n_i \leq \bar{N}, \qquad i = 0, 1, \ldots, m$$

and

$$[\tilde{q}_1(n_i h, lh) - \tilde{q}_2(n_i h, lh)][\tilde{q}_1((n_i + 1)h, lh) - \tilde{q}_2((n_i + 1)h, lh)] \leq 0$$

$$i = 1, 2, \ldots, m.$$

(b) $\bar{N}$ is independent of h provided that $0 < h \leq \bar{h}$ for some $\bar{h} > 0$.

In other words, there is an integer, $\bar{N}$, independent of h, such that, unless the forecast horizon is shorter than $\bar{N}$, the ranking of the two expected asset prices alternates within $\bar{N}$ periods. This basically follows from (27) but the proof is relegated to the appendix.

d. Movements of Actual and Expected Asset Prices

What is special about the movements of (actual and expected) asset prices is that there is no physical constraint, like equation (17) for capital stocks, which tends to make the movements smooth. Thus, $q(t)$ and $\tilde{q}(t + s, t)$ may show quite violent movements as time proceeds and unforeseen prospects develop. As a result, $\tilde{q}(t, s)$ may not be close to $q(t)$ even if t is close to s because, although $\tilde{q}(t, s)$ is close to $\tilde{q}(s, s) = q(s)$ by (16), (17), and (18), if t is within the forecast horizon and is close to s, $q(t)$ may be very different from $q(s)$.

If the forecast horizon covers a certain number of periods, however, this situation can be avoided and the movements of prices show some regularity. In fact, suppose

$$N \geq \bar{N} \tag{43}$$

and, for an arbitrary $n \geq n(h)$, let v be such that $n \geq v \geq n(h)$ and $n - v \leq N$. Then, by the third property of the expectations sequences, there exists an integer m such that $|m - n| \leq \bar{N}, 0 \leq m - v \leq N$, and such that people expect at time vh that a change in the ranking of the two asset prices will take place at time mh. For these m and v, $\tilde{q}_1(mh, vh)/\tilde{q}_2(mh, vh)$ is close to unity if h is small, by the first property of the expectations sequences. Hence $\tilde{q}_1(nh, vh)/\tilde{q}_2(nh, vh)$ is close to unity if h is small, by the second property of the expectations sequences, because $|m - n| \leq \bar{N}, \bar{N}$ is independent of h, and the expected and actual capital stocks lie in a compact set bounded away from both axes. More precisely, there is a $D > 0$ such that if $n \geq v \geq n(h)$ and $n - v \leq N$, then

$$\left| \frac{\tilde{q}_1(nh, vh)}{\tilde{q}_2(nh, vh)} - 1 \right| \leq Dh. \tag{44}$$

By further taking (18) into consideration and noting that $\tilde{x}(nh, vh)$ is close to $x(nh)$, we see that both $\tilde{q}_1(nh, vh)$ and $\tilde{q}_2(nh, vh)$ are close to $g(x(nh))$ if h is small. Furthermore, we see that $q_1(nh)$ and $q_2(nh)$ are also close to $g(x(nh))$ if h is small, because $q(nh) = \tilde{q}(nh, nh)$ also satisfies (44). In summing, we can conclude that *if $N \geq \bar{N}$, $n \geq v \geq n(h)$, $n - v \leq N$, and if h is small, then the expected asset prices $\tilde{q}(nh, vh)$ are close to the actual, which in turn are close to each other.*

In the limiting continuous-time model, it follows from the above that for all $t \geq T$, where T is defined by (32)

$$q_1(t) = q_2(t) = g(x(t)). \tag{45}$$

Since $x(t)$ converges to the steady state $\bar{x}$ as time proceeds, as was shown before, $q(t)$ also converges to the steady state $\bar{q}$, where $\bar{x}$ and $\bar{q}$ are given by

$$\bar{x}_1 + \bar{x}_2 = \frac{(1 - a_2)^{a_1} \bar{x}_1^{1 - a_1}}{\log(1 + \lambda)},$$

$$f_1(\bar{x}_1) = f_2(\bar{x}_2), \tag{46}$$

$$\bar{q}_1 = \bar{q}_2 = g(\bar{x}).$$

The first equality in (46) is obtained by letting h go to zero in (31). Therefore *the steady state of the limiting continuous-time model is stable in terms of both the prices and quantities if N satisfies* (43).

Next *suppose that $N = N(h)$ satisfies* (39). *Then the expected rate of change of asset prices in the sense of* (40) *is well defined and equal to the actual for all* $t \geq T$. In fact, consider the following identity:

$$\frac{\tilde{q}_i(m(t/h)h + N(h)h, m(t/h)h) - q_i(m(t/h)h)}{N(h)h}$$

$$\equiv \frac{\tilde{q}_i(m(t/h)h + N(h)h, m(t/h)h) - g(\tilde{x}(m(t/h)h + N(h)h, m(t/h)h)}{N(h)h}$$

$$+ \frac{g(\tilde{x}(m(t/h)h + N(h)h, m(t/h)h)) - g(x(m(t/h)h))}{N(h)h}$$

$$+ \frac{g(x(m(t/h)h)) - q_i(m(t/h)h)}{N(h)h}, \qquad i = 1, 2. \tag{47}$$

By (18) and (44), the first and the third terms of the right-hand side of (47) vanish for all $t \geq T$ as h goes to zero and $N(h)$ goes to infinity. Since we know that $(\dot{x}_i(t))^e = \dot{x}_i(t)$, the second term in the right-hand side of (47) converges to $g'\dot{x}_i(t)$, which in turn is equal to $\dot{q}_i(t)$ by (45), proving the assertion.

A notable feature of the limiting continuous-time model for the case where (39) holds is that the steady state defined by (46) is stable even though expectations are perfect and seemingly myopic in the sense that they cover only the current rates of change. The reason for this result becomes clear if we go back to the original discrete-time model: the expectations are not really myopic, because people know that the S_i's predict a future negativity and utilize this knowledge to qualitatively extend the forecast horizon.

Finally suppose that $N = N(h)$ satisfies (36). Since (44) still holds for $n = m(t/h)$ and $v = m(s/h)$ if $0 \leq t - s < H$ and if h is sufficiently small, and since (37) holds in this case, we can conclude, in the same way as for capital stocks, that $\tilde{q}_i(m(t/h)h, m(s/h)h)$ *is close to* $g(x(m(t/h)h))$ *and therefore to* $q_i(m(t/h)h)$ *if* $t \geq s > n(h)h$, $t - s < H$, *and if h is small. In the limiting continuous-time model, medium-run price expectations $\tilde{q}(t, s)$ are perfect if $t \geq s > T$ and $t - s < H$.* Movements of actual prices are qualitatively the same as under (43) because (36) implies (43).

5.

Assuming that asset holders form expectations for a finite future by using the knowledge of the economy's technological structure and supplement them by some rules of thumb, I have shown the following concerning the stability of the steady state of a nonshiftable-capital, two-sector growth model:

(1) There is a neighborhood of the steady-state per-capita capital stock vector which the per-capita capital stock vector approaches and stays in after reaching. This neighborhood contracts as the length of the unit period becomes shorter and, in the limiting continuous-time model, coincides with the steady-state point. Thus the steady-state per-capita capital stock vector in the limiting continuous-time model is globally asymptotically stable.

(2) The same holds true concerning the asset prices if the number of periods to be forecast is not smaller than a certain constant which is independent of the length of the unit period.

Although expectations are imperfect in the basic discrete-time model due to the finiteness of the forecast horizon, it is not the sluggishness of the revision of expectations, as in many adaptive expectations models, which contributes to the above stability result. In fact I have shown that, in the limit, seemingly myopic perfect foresight is compatible with stability. Rather, the basic factors contributing to the stability are as follows: (1) The non-negativity constraint on the asset prices becomes effective and, as a result, the equality of the rates of return is violated on every divergent growth path. (2) Unequal rates of return, when foreseen, react upon the present asset prices and push the economy onto another growth path on which unequal rates of return are not yet foreseeable. (3) People try to extend the forecast horizon by the use of some rules of thumb.

Before concluding, let me remark on the restrictiveness of some of the assumptions adopted in the paper.

(1) There is not much excuse for the use of Cobb-Douglas functions and the classical savings behavior, except that they facilitate the exposition of the basic idea. It may be worthwhile to note that the feature of these assumptions which is crucial for the negativity-predictiveness of the S_i's and for the zigzagging movement of $x(t)$ along the equi-profit curve is that an exclusive allocation of all the newly produced investment goods to one of the sectors always decreases that sector's profit relative to the other sectors.

(2) Although I believe that the discontinuous investment allocation represented by equation (10) has an element of reality, it may be too much of a simplification under certain circumstances. For example, if the act of investment itself is costly, as in the case of the quarter-circle investment technology in Caton and Shell [1971], or if not all the asset holders agree in forecast so that there is some positive investment even in the sector whose capital commands a lower price, then the perverse relationships between asset prices and proifts which are predictive of future unequal rates of return will take a more complicated form than the S_i's.

(3) The nonnegativity constraint on asset prices, which plays a crucial role in guiding the economy towards the steady state in the present approach, is

effective because different assets compete with each other solely in terms of the expected rates of return as expressed in equation (16). Thus, if the risks of return, as well as the expected rates of return, come to play a role in the demand for assets, it seems possible that the nonnegativity constraint becomes everywhere ineffective.[7] It remains to be seen how probable such cases are, and whether, in such cases, there is any economically meaningful force which tends to push the economy onto the convergent growth path.

Appendix

This appendix contains proofs of two propositions given in the text.

a.   *Existence of an Equilibrium Asset Price Vector (Section 3)*

We have to show that for any $\xi \gg 0$ and for any integer $N > 0$, there exists a permissible sequence $\{(\xi(n)), \pi(n))\}_{n=0}^{N}$ such that $\xi(0) = \xi$. Since $\pi(n) \gg 0$ for all $n = 0, 1, \ldots, N$ if $\{(\xi(n)), \pi(n))\}_{n=0}^{N}$ is consistent and $\pi(N) \gg 0$, as can be seen from (16) and (18), it suffices to show, by virtue of the invariance of the S_i's, that there exists a consistent sequence such that (27) holds for the last date N. But then it suffices to show that there exists a consistent sequence $\{(\xi(n), \pi(n))\}_{n=0}^{N}$ such that $\xi(0) = \xi$ and $\pi_1(N) = \pi_2(N)$.

First suppose that the following two propositions hold.

(i) *Given $\xi \gg 0$, $\pi \geq 0$, and $\{b^n\}_{n=0}^{M-1}$, where $0 \leq b^n \leq 1$ and $\max(\pi_1, \pi_2) = g(\xi)$, define a sequence $\{\pi(n)\}_{n=0}^{M}$ recursively by (15), (16), (17) and (18) with $b_1(\pi(n))$ replaced by b^n (and letting $\pi_i(n + 1) \leq 0$ if $\pi_i(n) \leq 0$.) If we let*

$$\pi_i(n) = v_i^n(\xi_1, \xi_2, \pi_1, \pi_2, b^0, b^1, \ldots, b^{n-1}), \qquad i = 1, 2, \qquad n = 1, 2, \ldots M$$

$$(\text{A-1})$$

denote this functional relation, then the v_i^n's are continuous functions.

(ii) *For each $\xi \gg 0$ and each integer $M \geq 1$, let $S^M(\xi)$ denote a set of $(M + 2)$-dimensional vectors $(\pi_1, \pi_2, b^0, \ldots, b^{M-1})$ such that $\pi \geq 0$ and such that the sequence $\{(u(\xi(n-1), b^{n-1}), v^n(\xi, \pi, b^0, \ldots, b^{n-1}))\}_{n=1}^{M}$ is consistent, where $u(\cdot) = (u_1(\cdot), u_2(\cdot))$ and $v^n(\cdot) = (v_1^n(\cdot), v_2^n(\cdot))$. Then $S^M(\xi)$ is nonempty and connected.*

---

[7] For example, in Sargent and Wallace [1973], where a logarithmic demand function for real balances is assumed, the nonnegativity constraint never comes into picture. Although Sargent and Wallace conclude that, with long-run perfect foresight, the price level converges to the steady state value, the bare essence of the mechanisms which lead to this result is the assumption that "the public expects that … a process of ever-accelerating inflation or deflation would eventually come to an end." But apparently this assumption begs the question.

If (i) and (ii) hold, then, for each given $\xi \gg 0$, $v_1^N(\xi, \cdot) - v_2^N(\xi, \cdot)$ is well defined and continuous on a nonempty connected set $S^N(\xi)$. Now it is easy to see that

$$(0, g(\xi), 0, \ldots, 0) \in S^N(\xi)$$
$$(g(\xi), 0, 1, \ldots, 1) \in S^N(\xi). \tag{A-2}$$

It is also easy to see that

$$v_1^N(\xi_1, \xi_2, 0, g(\xi), 0, \ldots, 0) - v_2^N(\xi_1, \xi_2, 0, g(\xi), 0, \ldots, 0) < 0$$
$$v_1^N(\xi_1, \xi_2, g(\xi), 0, 0, \ldots, 0) - v_2^N(\xi_1, \xi_2, g(\xi), 0, 1, \ldots, 1) > 0. \tag{A-3}$$

From (A-3) we can conclude, by using the intermediate value theorem, that there exists a $y \in S^N(\xi)$ such that

$$v_1^N(\xi, y) - v_2^N(\xi, y) = 0.$$

By construction, this y determines the desired consistent sequence. Therefore it suffices to prove (i) and (ii).

Proposition (i) is easy to see. Nonemptiness of $S^M(\xi)$ in proposition (ii) has already been shown in (A-2). Thus it remains to show that $S^M(\xi)$ is connected. For this purpose, it is also necessary to show that $S^M(\xi)$ is compact.

Compactness of $S^M(\xi)$ results if it is shown to be closed.

Let $(\pi_1^j, \pi_2^j, b^{0j}, \ldots, b^{M-1,j}) \in S^M(\xi)$, $j = 1, 2, \ldots$, and let them converge to $(\bar{\pi}_1, \bar{\pi}_2, \bar{b}^0, \ldots, \bar{b}^{M-1})$. Clearly $\max(\bar{\pi}_1, \bar{\pi}_2) = g(\xi)$ and $0 \leqq \bar{b}^n \leqq 1$ for each n, and therefore, for each $i = 1, 2$ and $n = 1, \ldots, M$, $\bar{\pi}_i(n) \equiv v_i^n(\xi_1, \xi_2, \bar{\pi}_1, \bar{\pi}_2, \bar{b}^0, \ldots, \bar{b}^{n-1})$ is well defined and satisfies

$$\bar{\pi}_i(n) = \lim_{j \to \infty} \pi_i^j(n), \qquad n = 1, 2, \ldots, M \tag{A-4}$$

by the continuity of $v_i^n(\xi, \cdot)$, where $\pi_i^j(n) \equiv v_i^n(\xi_1, \xi_2, \pi_1^j, \pi_2^j, b^{0j}, \ldots, b^{n-1,j})$. Since the $\pi_i^j(n)$'s and the b^{nj}'s satisfy (10), the $\bar{\pi}_i(n)$'s and the $\bar{b}^n$'s also satisfy (10) by (A-4) and therefore $(\bar{\pi}_1, \bar{\pi}_2, \bar{b}^0, \ldots, \bar{b}^{M-1}) \in S^M(\xi)$.

Connectedness of $S^M(\xi)$ will be shown by induction on M. Since

$$S^1(\xi) = \{\pi_1, g(\xi), 0) \mid 0 \leqq \pi_1 \leqq g(\xi)\} \cup \{(g(\xi), g(\xi), b) \mid 0 \leqq b \leqq 1\}$$
$$\cup \{g(\xi), \pi_2, 1) \mid 0 \leqq \pi_2 \leqq g(\xi)\},$$

which is homeomorphic to a compact interval $[0, 1]$, $S^1(\xi)$ is connected.

Suppose $S^M(\xi)$ is connected but $S^{M+1}(\xi)$ is not. Then there exist two nonempty disjoint subsets of $S^{M+1}(\xi)$, denoted by G_1 and G_2, which are closed relative to $S^{M+1}(\xi)$ (and thus compact since $S^{M+1}(\xi)$ is compact) and whose union is $S^{M+1}(\xi)$. Let

$$\Psi: R^{M+3} \to R^{M+2}, \qquad \Psi(z_1, \ldots, z_{M+2}, z_{M+3}) = (z_1, \ldots, z_{M+2})$$

be a projection. It is easy to see that

$$\Psi(S^{M+1}(\xi)) = S^M(\xi). \tag{A-5}$$

Now consider $\Psi(G_1)$ and $\Psi(G_2)$. They are nonempty and compact because they are continuous images of nonempty compact sets G_1 and G_2. They also satisfy

$$\Psi(G_1) \cup \Psi(G_2) = \Psi(G_1 \cup G_2) = S^M(\xi)$$

where the second equality follows from (A-5). Hence, connectedness of $S^M(\xi)$ implies that

$$\Psi(G_1) \cap \Psi(G_2) \neq \phi.$$

Let

$$(\pi_1, \pi_2, b^0, \ldots, b^{M-1}) \in \Psi(G_1) \cap \Psi(G_2)$$

and let β_1 and β_2 be such that

$$(\pi_1, \pi_2, b^0, \ldots, b^{M-1}, \beta_i) \in G_i, \qquad i = 1, 2.$$

Disjointness of G_1 and G_2 implies that $\beta_1 \neq \beta_2$, which in turn implies that $\pi_1(M) = \pi_2(M)$ by (10). But then we clearly have

$$H \equiv \{(\pi_1, \pi_2, b^0, \ldots, b^{M-1})\} \times [0,1] \subset S^{M+1}(\xi),$$

where H is closed and connected. Now let

$$G_i' = G_i \cap H, \qquad i = 1, 2.$$

Then G_1' and G_2' are nonempty, closed relative to H, disjoint because G_1 and G_2 are disjoint, and their union is equal to H. This contradicts the connectedness of H, and this contradiction proves the connectedness of $S^{M+1}(\xi)$.

b. Existence of A Uniform $\bar{N}$ Within Which The Ranking of The Two Asset Prices Is Expected To Change (Section 4)

In order to prove the proposition in Section 4 of the text, which we shall call Proposition A, we consider the following two propositions:

Proposition B. *For each $l \geq n(h)$, there exists an integer $\bar{N}$ satisfying the following.*
   (a) *If $N \geq \bar{N}$, there exist integers $n_0 = l, n_1, \ldots, n_m, n_{m+1} = l + N$ such that*

$$0 < n_{i+1} - n_i \leq \bar{N}, \qquad i = 0, 1, \ldots, m$$

and

$$[f_1(\tilde{x}(n_i h, lh)) - f_2(\tilde{x}(n_i h, lh))] \times [f_1(u(\tilde{x}(n_i h, lh), b^i))$$
$$- f_2(u(\tilde{x}(n_i h, lh), b^i))] \leq 0 \qquad \text{for some } b^i \in [0,1], \qquad i = 1, 2, \ldots, m.$$

   (b) *$\bar{N}$ is independent of h provided that $0 < h \leq \bar{h}$ for some $\bar{h} > 0$.*

Proposition C. *For an* $x_1(0) > 0$, *which is the initial per-capita capital stock of the first sector (implicitly given in Propositions A and B), let* $\{\zeta(n)\}_{n=0}^{M}$ *be a sequence such that*

(i) $\qquad 0 < \zeta_1(0) \leq \bar{x}_1 \equiv \max\left[x_1(0), \sup_{0 < h \leq \bar{h}} \left\{ \frac{(1 - a_2)^{a_1} h}{(1 + \lambda)^h - 1} \right\} \right],$

(ii) *there is an accompanying sequence* $\{b_1(n)\}_{n=0}^{M}$ *for which* $f_i(\zeta(n)) > f_j(\zeta(n))$ *implies* $b_i(n) = 1$ *unless* (28) *holds, and*

(iii) (17) *holds with* $b_1(\pi(n))$ *replaced by* $b_1(n)$.

Then there exists an $\bar{N}$, *independent of* $\zeta(0)$ *and of h as long as* $0 < h \leq \bar{h}$, *such that if* $M \geq \bar{N}$ *and if*

$$[f_1(\zeta(0)) - f_2(\zeta(0))][f_1(u(\zeta(0), b^0)) - f_2(u(\zeta(0), b^0))] \leq 0 \qquad \text{(A-6)}$$

for some $b^0 \in [0, 1]$, *then*

$$[f_1(\zeta(n)) - f_2(\zeta(n))][f_1(u(\zeta(n), b^n)) - f_2(u(\zeta(n), b^n))] \leq 0 \qquad \text{(A.7)}$$

for some $n \in \{1, \ldots, \bar{N}\}$ *and some* $b^n \in [0, 1]$. *(Note that* $\bar{x}_1$ *is an upper bound of the values which* $x_1(t)$ *or* $\tilde{x}_1(t, s)$ *can take.)*

We will prove Proposition A by showing that B implies A, that C implies B, and finally that C holds.

$B \Rightarrow A$. For simplicity, we let $\tilde{x}(nh, lh) = \xi(n)$ and $\tilde{q}(nh, lh) = \pi(n)$. Suppose B holds. We will show that the same $\bar{N}$ and n_i's serve the purpose of A. Since the relevant inequality holds for an n_i if $\pi_1(n_i) = \pi_2(n_i)$, and since $\pi_1(n_i) = \pi_2(n_i)$ by (27) if $f_1(\xi(n_i)) = f_2(\xi(n_i))$, the case remaining to be considered is where $f_j(\xi(n_i)) > f_k(\xi(n_i))$, $\pi_j(n_i) > \pi_k(n_i)$, and $f_j(u(\xi(n_i), b^i)) \leq f_k(u(\xi(n_i), b^i))$ for some $b^i \in [0, 1]$. Now, $\pi_j(n_i) > \pi_k(n_i)$ implies that $b_j(n_i h, lh) = 1$ by (10), which, together with the assumed existence of a $b^i \in [0, 1]$ such that $f_j(u(\xi(n_i), b^i)) \leq f_k(u(\xi(n_i), b^i))$, implies that $f_j(\xi(n_i + 1)) \leq f_k(\xi(n_i + 1))$ by (13) and (14). Therefore $\pi_j(n_i + 1) \leq \pi_k(n_i + 1)$ by (27), which completes the proof.

$C \Rightarrow B$. Let $\{\xi(n)\}_{n=0}^{l - n(h) + N}$ denote a sequence given by

$$\xi(n) = \begin{cases} x(n(h)h + nh), & n = 0, 1, \ldots, l - n(h) \\ \tilde{x}(n(h)h + nh, lh), & n = l - n(h) + 1, \ldots, l - n(h) + N. \end{cases}$$

Then one can show that for any integer $\bar{u} \leq l - n(h) + N - \bar{N}$, a sequence $\{\zeta(n)\}_{n=0}^{l - n(h) + N - \bar{n}}$ defined by $\zeta(n) = \xi(\bar{n} + n)$ satisfies the three conditions of Proposition C. Since

$$[f_1(\xi(0)) - f_2(\xi(0))][f_1(u(\xi(0), b^0)) - f_2(u(\xi(0), b^0))] \leq 0$$

for some $b^0 \in [0, 1]$ by the definition of $n(h)$, we can apply Proposition C recursively to $\{\xi(n)\}_{n=0}^{l - n(h) + N}$ to obtain the desired sequence $\{n_0, \ldots, n_{m+1}\}$.

Proof of Proposition C. Suppose that a sequence $\{\zeta(n)\}_{n=0}^{M}$, together with an accompanying sequence $\{b_1(n)\}_{n=0}^{M}$, satisfies the three conditions and (A-6) of Proposition C. Further suppose, without loss of generality, that $f_1(\zeta(1)) \neq f_2(\zeta(1))$. I will prove the existence of the asserted $\bar{N}$ for the two cases separately: (1) $f_1(\zeta(1)) > f_2(\zeta(1))$; (2) $f_1(\zeta(1)) < f_2(\zeta(1))$.

(1) Supposing that $f_1(\zeta(1)) > f_2(\zeta(1))$, I will show that there is a uniform bound N_1 to the k's which satisfy

$$f_1(u(\zeta(n), 1)) > f_2(u(\zeta(n), 1)) \qquad \text{for all } n = 1, 2, \ldots, k. \tag{A-8}$$

(A-8) implies that $b_1(n) = 1$ and therefore

$$\frac{f_2(u(\zeta(n), 1))}{f_1(u(\zeta(n), 1))} = \frac{a_1}{1 - a_1} \frac{(1 + \lambda)^{(n+1)h}\zeta_1(n + 1)}{\zeta_2(0) + (1 - b_1(0))(1 - a_2)^{a_1}\zeta_1(0)^{1 - a_1}h} \tag{A-9}$$

for all $n = 1, 2, \ldots, k$.

For each $n = 1, 2, \ldots$, each $z \in (0, \bar{x}_1]$, and each $h \in (0, \bar{h}]$, define $Z(n; z, h)$ by

$$Z(n; z, h) = \frac{a_1(1 + \lambda)^{nh}\psi(n; z, h)}{a_1 z + (1 - a_2)^{a_1}z^{1 - a_1}h}$$

where

$$\psi(n; z, h) = \begin{cases} \dfrac{z}{(1 + \lambda)^h} & \text{for } n = 1 \\[4mm] \psi(n - 1; z, h) + \dfrac{(1 - a_2)^{a_1}\psi(n - 1; z, h)^{1 - a_1}h}{(1 + \lambda)^h} & \text{for } n = 2, 3, \ldots. \end{cases}$$

Since

$$\psi(n; \zeta_1(0), h) \leq \zeta_1(n)$$

for all $n \geq 1$ as long as $b_1(n - 1) = 1$, and since (A-6) for the present case implies that

$$(1 - a_1)\zeta_2(0) \leq a_1\zeta_1(0) + a_1(1 - a_2)^{a_1}\zeta_1(0)^{1 - a_1}h,$$

it follows from (A-9) that

$$Z(n + 1; \zeta_1(0), h) \leq \frac{f_2(u(\zeta(n), 1))}{f_1(u(\zeta(n), 1))}.$$

Therefore it suffices to find an N_1 such that

$$Z(N_1 + 1; z, h) \geq 1 \qquad \text{for all } z \in (0, \bar{x}_1] \qquad \text{and all } h \in (0, \bar{h}]. \tag{A-10}$$

In order to find an N_1 satisfying (A-10), we shall use the fact that

$$\left. \frac{\partial Z(n; z, h)}{\partial z} \right|_{Z(n; z, h) = 1} < 0 \qquad \text{for all } n \geq 3 \tag{A-11}$$

and that

$$\lim_{z \to 0} Z(n; z, h) = \infty \qquad \text{for all } n \geq 3. \qquad \text{(A-12)}$$

To see (A-11) and (A-12), first use the definition of $\psi(n; z, h)$ recursively to obtain

$$\psi(n; z, h) = \frac{z}{(1 + \lambda)^{nh}} \prod_{v=1}^{n-1} [1 + (1 - a_2)^{a_1} \psi(v; z, h)^{-a_1} h] \qquad \text{(A-13)}$$

and

$$\frac{\partial \psi(n; z, h)}{\partial z} = \frac{1}{(1 + \lambda)^{nh}} \prod_{v=1}^{n-1} [1 + (1 - a_1)(1 - a_2)^{a_1} \psi(v; z, h)^{-a_1} h] \qquad \text{(A-14)}$$

where $\prod_{v=1}^{0} [\ldots] = 1$. Using (A-13) and (A-14) one can show that, for all $n \geq 2$,

$$\left. \frac{\partial Z(n; z, h)}{\partial z} \right|_{Z(n; z, h) = 1} = \frac{a_1}{z \prod\limits_{v=1}^{n-1} (1 + (1 - a_2)^{a_1} \psi(v)^{-a_1} h)}$$

$$\times \left[\prod_{v=1}^{n-1} (1 + (1 - a_2)^{a_1} \psi(v)^{-a_1} h) - 1 \right.$$

$$- \sum_{v=1}^{n-1} (1 - a_2)^{a_1} \psi(v)^{-a_1} h$$

$$\times \left\{ \prod_{l=1}^{v-1} (1 + (1 - a_1)(1 - a_2)^{a_1} \psi(l)^{-a_1} h) \right\}$$

$$\left. \times \left\{ \prod_{l=v+1}^{n-1} (1 + (1 - a_2)^{a_1} \psi(l)^{-a_1} h) \right\} \right]$$

$$\leq \frac{a_1}{z \prod\limits_{v=1}^{n-1} (1 + (1 - a_2)^{a_1} \psi(v)^{-a_1} h)}$$

$$\times \left[\prod_{v=1}^{n-1} (1 + (1 - a_2)^{a_1} \psi(v)^{-a_1} h) - 1 \right.$$

$$- \sum_{v=1}^{n-1} (1 - a_2)^{a_1} \psi(v)^{-a_1} h$$

$$\left. \times \left\{ \prod_{l=v+1}^{n-1} (1 + (1 - a_2)^{a_1} \psi(l)^{-a_1} h) \right\} \right]$$

where $\Sigma_{v=1}^{0}(\ldots) = 0$ and $\prod_{l=n}^{n-1}(\ldots) = 1$, and where a strict inequality holds for all $n \geq 3$. But it can be shown by induction on n that the extreme right-hand side vanishes. Thus (A-11) follows. (A-12) can be shown by using (A-13) in the definition of $Z(n; z, h)$.

Finally, due to (A-11) and (A-12), N_1 satisfies (A-10) if $N_1 \geq 2$ and if

$$Z(N_1 + 1; \bar{x}_1, h) \geq 1 \qquad \text{for all } h \in (0, \bar{h}].$$

Since $Z(n; z, h)$ can be rewritten

$$Z(n; z, h) = (1 + (1 - a_2)^{a_1} z^{-a_1} h / a_1)^{-1} \prod_{v=1}^{n-1} (1 + (1 - a_2)^{a_1} \psi(v; z, h)^{-a_1} h)$$

and since $\psi(v; \bar{x}_1, h) \leq \bar{x}_1$, N_1 satisfies (A-10) if $N_1 \geq 2$ and if

$$N_1 \geq \sup_{0 < h \leq \bar{h}} \frac{\log(1 + (1 - a_2)^{a_1} \bar{x}_1^{-a_1} h / a_1)}{\log(1 + (1 - a_2)^{a_1} \bar{x}_1^{-a_1} h)},$$

where the right-hand side is well defined because it converges to $1/a_1$ as h goes to zero.

(2) Supposing next that $f_1(\zeta(1)) < f_2(\zeta(1))$, I will show that there is a uniform bound N_2 to the k's which satisfy

$$f_1(u(\zeta(n), 0)) < f_2(u(\zeta(n), 0)) \qquad \text{for all } n = 1, 2, \ldots, k. \qquad \text{(A-15)}$$

If (A-15) holds, then $b_1(n) = 0$ for all $n = 1, \ldots, k$ and it holds that

$$\frac{f_1(u(\zeta(n), 0))}{f_2(u(\zeta(n), 0))} = \frac{1 - a_1}{a_1} \frac{\zeta_2(0) + (1 - b_1(0))(1 - a_2)^{a_1} \zeta_1(0)^{1-a_1} h}{\zeta_1(0) + b_1(0)(1 - a_2)^{a_1} \zeta_1(0)^{1-a_1} h}$$

$$+ \frac{1 - a_1}{a_1} \left[\frac{\zeta_1(0) + b_1(0)(1 - a_2)^{a_1} \zeta_1(0)^{1-a_1} h}{(1 - a_2)(1 + \lambda)^h} \right]^{-a_1} \qquad \text{(A-16)}$$

$$\times \frac{(1 + \lambda)^{h a_1 n} - 1}{(1 + \lambda)^{h a_1} - 1} \times h.$$

For each $n = 1, 2, \ldots$, each $z \in (0, \bar{x}_1]$, and each $h \in (0, \bar{h}]$, define $W(n; z, h)$ by

$$W(n; z, h) = \frac{a_1 z - (1 - a_1)(1 - a_2)^{a_1} z^{1-a_1} h}{a_1(z + (1 - a_2)^{a_1} z^{1-a_1} h)}$$

$$+ \frac{1 - a_1}{a_1} \left[\frac{z + (1 - a_2)^{a_1} z^{1-a_1} h}{(1 - a_2)(1 + \lambda)^h} \right]^{-a_1} \frac{(1 + \lambda)^{h a_1 (n-1)} - 1}{(1 + \lambda)^{h a_1} - 1} \times h.$$

Now, (A-6) for the present case implies that

$$(1 - a_1)\zeta_2(0) \geq a_1 \zeta_1(0) - (1 - a_1)(1 - a_2)^{a_1} \xi_1(0)^{1-a_1} h.$$

Using this, and noting that $0 \leq b_1^0 \leq 1$, one can show that

$$W(n + 1; \zeta_1(0), h) \leq \frac{f_1(u(\zeta(n), 0))}{f_2(u(\zeta(n), 0))}$$

as long as (A-16) holds. Thus it suffices to find an N_2 such that

$$W(N_2 + 1; z, h) \geq 1 \qquad \text{for all } z \in (0, \bar{x}_1] \qquad \text{and all } h \in (0, \bar{h}]. \qquad (A-17)$$

But now it is easy to see that an integral N_2 satisfies (A-17) if

$$N_2 \geq \sup_{0 < h \leq \bar{h}} \frac{\log\left[\dfrac{\{(1 + \lambda)^{ha_1} - 1\}\{1 + (1 - a_2)^{a_1}\bar{x}_1^{-a_1}h\}^{a_1 - 1}}{(1 - a_1) + (1 + \lambda)^{ha_1}}\right]}{h \log(1 + \lambda)^{a_1}} - 1$$

where the right-hand side is well defined beause it can be shown to converge to $a_1(1 - a_1)^{-1}$ as h goes to zero. Proof of Proposition C is now complete.

References

Caton, C. and K. Shell, An exercise in the theory of heterogeneous capital accumulation, *Review of Economic Studies*, Vol. 38, 1971.

Friedman, B., Optimal expectations and the extreme information assumptions of "rational expectations" macromodels, *Journal of Monetary Economics*, Vol. 5, 1979.

Hahn, F. H., Equilibrium dynamics with heterogeneous capital goods, *Quartery Journal of Economics*, Vol. 80, 1966.

Hori, H., Investment allocation and growth in a two-sector economy with nonshiftable capital, in Fujii, T. and R. Sato (eds). *Resource Allocation and Division of Space*, Lecture Notes in Economics and Mathematical Systems, Vol. 147, Berlin: Springer-Verlag, 1977.

Hori, H., Stability of the Neumann ray in a dynamic Leontieff system with finite forecast horizons, *Review of Economic Systems*, Vol. 49, 1982.

Jorgenson, D. W., A dual stability theorem, *Econometrica*, Vol. 28, 1960.

Kuga, K. General saddlepoint property of the steady state of a growth model with heterogeneous capital goods, *International Economic Review*, Vol. 18, 1977.

Nagatani, K., A note on Professor Tobin's "money and economic growth", *Econometrica*, Vol. 38, 1970.

Sargent, T. J. and N. Wallace, The stability of models of money and growth with perfect foresight, *Econometrica*, Vol. 41, 1973.

Shell, K. and J. E. Stiglitz, The allocation of investment in a dynamic economy, *Quarterly Journal of Economics*, Vol. 81, 1967.

Solow, R. M., Competitive valuation in a dynamic input-output system, *Econometrica*, Vol. 27, 1959.

Uzawa, H., On a two-sector model of economic growth, *Review of Economic Studies*, Vol. 29, 1961.

2

Balance of Payments Adjustment under Price Rigidity

MICHIHIRO OHYAMA

Department of Economics
Keio University
Minato-ku, Tokyo
Japan

1. Introduction

The purpose of this paper is to investigate the balance of payments adjustment process of an economy suffering from price rigidity and labor unemployment under the regime of flexible exchange rates. We present a simple dynamic model which explains the determination of exchange rate and output (or employment) in the face of completely rigid prices both in the short run and in the long run. It differs from conventional models of the balance of payments and unemployment such as those of Laursen and Metzler [1950] and Meade [1951] in some important respects.

First, the conventional models are concerned only with the long-run equilibrium where the balance of payments is equilibrated through the adjustment of exchange rates. They disregard the short-run balance of payments disequilibria and fail to pursue the dynamic adjustment of the balance of payments toward the long-run equilibrium. The present model goes beyond them by explicitly considering the process of the balance of payments adjustment in the spirit of the recently developed asset approach to the balance of payments.[1]

[1] For instance, see Kouri [1975]

31

Secondly, it is customary in the conventional models to postulate that each country specializes completely in its exports and that while the domestic price of its exports are fixed, the domestic price of its imports varies flexibly reflecting the exchange rate fluctuations. We follow Negishi [1979a, 1979b] in the present model to assume that all prices are rigid because of the underlying oligopolistic structure of the economy.[2]

We shall demonstrate that given the basic structure of the economy, the supply of domestic money must assume a unique value if the economy is to achieve the long-run equilibrium. If the supply of money falls short of the appropriate level, the economy may experience the early symptom of the paradoxical J-curve effect, e.g., the continuous aggravation of the balance of trade surplus in the face of continuous exchange rate appreciation. On the other hand, if the supply is greater than the appropriate level, the economy will suffer from a chronic balance of payments deficit in the long run irrespective of initial conditions. Thus, the present ultra-Keynesian model of price rigidity and unemployment is ironocally in accord with the monetarist view that money is an important factor in achieving the long-run equilibrium of the economy.

2.   Short-Run Equilibrium and Comparative Statics

In this section we construct the model of a small open economy saddled with rigid commodity prices both at home and abroad under the system of flexible exchange rates. The rate of currency exchange is supposed to be determined in the asset market. With commodity prices given and constant, the economy's output (and employment) is supposed to be determined in the commodity market. The economy is said to be in the short-run equilibrium when both the asset and the commodity markets are cleared.

Let us first specify the asset market. For simplicity, we assume that the stock of financial wealth W consists of domestic money M and foreign money F:

$$W = M + eF,   \tag{1}$$

where e denotes the rate of exchange, i.e., the price of foreign currency in terms of domestic currency. The demand for domestic money is a function of the expected rate of exchange rate depreciation π, the expected rate of output Y^e, and the stock of financial wealth. Foreigners are not supposed to hold

---

[2] This assumption of rigid prices may be justified by the theory of kinked demand curves originally due to Sweezy [1939]. See Negishi [1979a] for an extensive application of this theory to the microeconomic reinterpretation of Keynesian economics. Negishi [1979b] analyzes the short-run effects of devaluation on the same assumption.

domestic money. Thus in the momentary equilibrium of the asset market, the domestic demand for domestic money equals its supply:

$$M^d = L(\pi, Y^e, W) = M, \tag{2}$$

which, in view of the wealth constraint, implies the other equilibrium condition that the demand for foreign money equals its supply:

$$F^d = F(\pi, Y^e, W) = F. \tag{3}$$

Substituting (1) into (2), we obtain

$$L(\pi, Y^e, M + eF) = M. \tag{4}$$

Given the expected rate of depreciation π, the expected rate of output Y^e, the supply of domestic money M, and the stock of foreign money F, this condition of equilibrium in the asset market determines the exchange rate e.

Differentiating (1) and (4), we get

$$L_W F \, de = (1 - L_W) \, dM - eL_W \, dF - L_Y \, dY^e - L_\pi \, d\pi \tag{5}$$

and

$$L_W \, dW = dM - L_Y \, dY^e - L_\pi \, d\pi, \tag{6}$$

where $L_\pi \equiv \partial L/\partial \pi$, $L_Y \equiv \partial L/\partial Y^e$, and $L_W \equiv \partial L/W$. Let us assume that the demand for money satisfies $L_\pi < 0$, $L_Y > 0$, and $0 < L_W < 1$. Table 1 summarizes the comparative statics result of momentary equilibria. Note, for instance, that an increase in the stock of foreign money F results in an equiproportionate decrease in the rate of exchange e with no change in the value of wealth.

Turning to the commodity market, we assume that the economy's exports and imports are carried on by domestic trading firms and that all firms (including trading firms) perceive kinked demand curves everywhere. Under the circumstances, the firms may be taken to stay put with the current prices of their products even in the face of some exchange rate fluctuations. Taking the extreme case for simplicity, let us assume that both the foreign and domestic

TABLE 1.
The Comparative Statics of Momentary Equilibria

Endogenous variables	Exogenous variables			
	M	F	Y^e	π
e	$+$	$-$	$-$	$+$
W	$+$	0	$-$	$+$

money prices of each commodity are given and invariable. In particular, we adjust the units of commodities so that the foreign prices of all commodities are equal to unity.

Abstracting from transport costs, we may regard the income of domestic trading firms as comprising export margin $(e - p_x)X$ and import margin $(p_z - e)Z$ where p_x (resp. p_z) denotes the domestic price of the commodity exported from (resp. imported to) the economy and X (resp. Z) denotes the quantity of export (resp. import). We adjust the unit of domestic money so that the domestic price of the imported commodity is equal to unity, i.e., $p_z \equiv 1$.

The disposable income Y^d of the economy is equal to the value of domestic output Y and trading firm's income $\{(e - p_x)X + (1 - e)Z\}$ less government taxes T:

$$Y^d = Y + (e - p_x)X + (1 - e)Z - T. \tag{7}$$

The expenditure for domestically produced commodities E consists of private consumption C, government expenditure G, and the balance of trade in terms of domestic currency $(p_x X - Z)$:

$$E = C + G + (p_x X - Z). \tag{8}$$

Private consumption C and import demand Z are functionally dependent on disposable income Y^d and the stock of financial wealth W, whereas the quantity of export X is fixed exogenously under the given terms of trade. The commodity market is in equilibrium when

$$E = C(Y^d, W) + G + p_x X - Z(Y^d, W) = Y. \tag{9}$$

Given government expenditure G, the quantity of export X, and the stock of financial wealth W, this condition of equilibrium in the commodity market determines the value of domestic output Y. The balance of trade B in terms of foreign currency, as defined by

$$B = X - Z(Y^d, W), \tag{10}$$

is also determined simultaneously.

The differentiation of (9) and (10) in view of (7) yields the following intermediate results in comparative statics:

$$(1 - C_Y + eZ_Y)dY = E_Y(B\,de - dT)$$
$$+ [1 - (1 - e)Z_Y](dG + p_x\,dX) + E_W\,dW \tag{11}$$

and

$$[1 - (1 - e)Z_Y]dB = [1 - (1 - p_X)Z_Y]dX$$
$$- Z_Y(dY - dT + B\,de) - Z_W\,dW, \tag{12}$$

where $C_Y \equiv \partial C/\partial Y$, $C_W \equiv \partial C/\partial W$, $Z_Y \equiv \partial Z/\partial Y$, $Z_W \equiv \partial Z/\partial W$, $E_Y \equiv \partial E/\partial Y$, and $E_w \equiv \partial E/\partial W$. We may assume that $C_Y > Z_Y > 0$ and $C_W > Z_W > 0$. Since $E_Y \equiv C_Y - Z_Y$ and $E_W \equiv C_W - Z_W$, this implies $E_Y > 0$ and $E_W > 0$. For instance, we get from (11) and (12)

$$\frac{\partial Y}{\partial X} = \frac{Px[1 - (1 - e)Z_Y]}{1 - C_Y + eZ_Y}$$

and

$$\frac{\partial B}{\partial X} = \frac{1}{1 - (1 - e)Z_Y}\left\{1 - (1 - p_X)Z_y - \frac{[1 - (1 - e)Z_Y]Z_Y}{1 - C_Y + eZ_Y}\right\}.$$

Clearly, these reduce to the standard export multipliers when $e = p_Z = p_X = 1$. Substituting (5) and (6) into (11) and (12), we get the ultimate results in the comparative statics of short-run equilibria. In particular, we have

$$\frac{\partial Y}{\partial F} = -\frac{eE_Y B}{(1 - C_Y + eZ_Y)F}$$

and

$$\frac{\partial B}{\partial F} = \frac{eZ_Y B}{(1 - C_Y + eZ_Y)F}.$$

Thus, an increase in the stock of foreign money brings about a decrease (resp. an increase) in domestic output and a balance of trade improvement (resp. deterioration) if the initial balance of trade exhibits a surplus (resp. deficit). This asymmetry is attributable to the fact that the appreciation of exchange rate resulting from an increase in the stock of foreign money affects adversely (resp. favorably) the income of domestic trading firms and hence the disposable income of the economy when the initial balance of trade is in surplus (resp. in deficit). Table 2 shows the qualitative results of comparative statics of short-run equilibria for the special case in which the balance of trade is initially zero.

TABLE 2.
The Comparative Statics of Short-Run Equilibria When $B = 0$

Endogenous variables	Exogenous variables					
	M	F	Y^e	π	$G(=T)$	X
Y	+	0	−	+	+	+
B	−	0	+	−	−	+

3. The Long-Run Equilibrium and the Adjustment Process

To simplify the dynamic adjustment process of the economy, we assume in this section that exchange rate expectations are static ($\pi = 0$). The adjustment process may then be given by

$$\dot{F} = B = X - Z(Y^d, W) \tag{13}$$

and

$$\dot{Y}^e = Y - Y^e. \tag{14}$$

Equation (13) means that the stock of foreign money varies through time at the rate of the balance of payments. Equation (14) postulates that individuals modify their (identical) expectation of output in an adaptive manner when it does not materialize.

The long-run stationary equilibrium of the economy is the state where the stock of financial wealth and its composition are constant and output expectations are self-fulfilling. Given the supply of domestic money M, the size of government balanced budget ($G = T$), and the quantity of export X,

$$B = X - Z(Y^d, W) = 0 \tag{15}$$

and

$$Y - Y^e = 0 \tag{16}$$

are supposed to determine the stock of foreign money F and the value of domestic output Y in the stationary state.

From (5), (6), and (11)–(14), we have[3]

$$\frac{\partial \dot{F}}{\partial F} = \frac{e Z_Y B}{(1 - C_Y + e Z_Y)F}, \tag{17}$$

$$\frac{\partial \dot{Y}^e}{\partial F} = -\frac{(C_Y - Z_Y)eB}{(1 - C_Y + e Z_Y)F}, \tag{18}$$

$$\frac{\partial \dot{F}}{\partial Y^e} = \frac{L_Y(Z_y B/F + Z_W)}{(1 - C_Y + e Z_Y)L_W}, \tag{19}$$

and

$$\frac{\partial \dot{Y}^e}{\partial Y^e} = -\frac{L_Y(E_Y B/F + E_W)}{(1 - C_Y + e Z_Y)L_W} - 1. \tag{20}$$

---

[3] For simplicity, we assume here that $C_W/Z_W = C_Y/Z_Y$. This means that consumption and imports are affected in relation to each other quite similarly either by a change in wealth or by a change in income.

In view of (17) and (18), we find that the stock of foreign money is not uniquely determined in the long-run equilibrium of the economy. In fact, there are an infinite number of values for the stock of foreign money which are compatible with the stationary state.

On the other hand, it can be shown that long-run equilibrium conditions (15) and (16) determine uniquely the stock of domestic money M and the value of domestic output Y. To see this point, we derive from (5), (6), and (11)–(14)

$$\frac{\partial \dot{F}}{\partial M} = \frac{(1 - L_W)Z_Y B/F - Z_W}{(1 - C_Y + eZ_Y)L_W} \tag{21}$$

and

$$\frac{\partial \dot{Y}^e}{\partial M} = \frac{E_Y B + E_W}{(1 - C_Y + eZ_Y)L_W}. \tag{22}$$

When $B = 0$, we get

$$-\frac{\dfrac{\partial \dot{F}}{\partial M}}{\dfrac{\partial \dot{F}}{\partial Y^e}} = \frac{1}{L_Y}$$

and

$$-\frac{\dfrac{\partial \dot{Y}^e}{\partial M}}{\dfrac{\partial \dot{Y}^e}{\partial Y^e}} = \frac{E_W}{L_Y E_W + (1 - E_Y + eZ_Y)L_W}$$

from (19)–(22). Hence, we have

$$-\frac{\dfrac{\partial \dot{F}}{\partial M}}{\dfrac{\partial \dot{F}}{\partial Y^e}} > -\frac{\dfrac{\partial \dot{Y}^e}{\partial M}}{\dfrac{\partial \dot{Y}^e}{\partial Y^e}} > 0 \tag{23}$$

when the balance of trade is zero. In the light of (17) and (23), the set of pairs (Y^e, M) satisfying condition (15) for any value of F may be illustrated by the FF schedule in Figure 1. In a similar fashion, the set of pairs (Y^e, M) satisfying condition (16) for a certain value of F may be shown as the YY schedule in the same figure. Both FF and YY are upward-sloping at the point of intersection E, with the former being steeper than the latter. Furthermore, in view of (18), the YY schedule is not affected by a change in F at the point of intersection E. Thus, we may conclude that FF and YY intersect each other at most once for

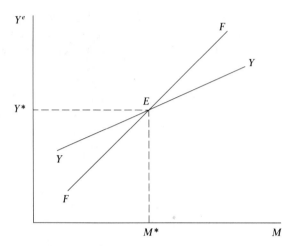

Figure 1. The supply of domestic money and output in the long run.

all values of F. In other words, the values of Y^e and M consistent with the long-run equilibrium of the economy are uniquely determined.

Let us assume that there exists such an intersection as of the given values of other exogenous variables such as $G(=T)$ and X and designate the corresponding values of Y^e and M by Y^* and M^*, respectively. The dynamic adjustment process of the economy defined by (13) and (14) may then be considered separately for three distinct cases, i.e., (a) $M = M^*$, (b) $M < M^*$, and (c) $M > M^*$.

Case a. The supply of money (M) is just appropriate and the dynamic adjustment process is quasi-stable. Some possible paths of adjustment are illustrated by Figure 2(a).

Case b. The supply of money falls short of the quantity compatible with the long-run equilibrium of the economy. Starting from an arbitrary initial condition, the balance of trade will ultimately be in surplus. A possible path of adjustment is shown in Figure 2(b). If the public is possessed of perfect foresight with respect to output movements, the economy moves along the curve $\dot{Y}^e = 0$. In this instance, the balance of payments exhibits a surplus at all times. Furthermore, we will observe the symptom of the paradoxical J-curve phenomenon that the balance of trade surplus grows through time in the face of continuous exchange rate appreciation.[4]

[4] For instance, Japan experienced the J-curve phenomenon during the 1978–1979 period and the 1985–87 period when it failed to cut down its current account surplus despite considerable appreciation of the yen.

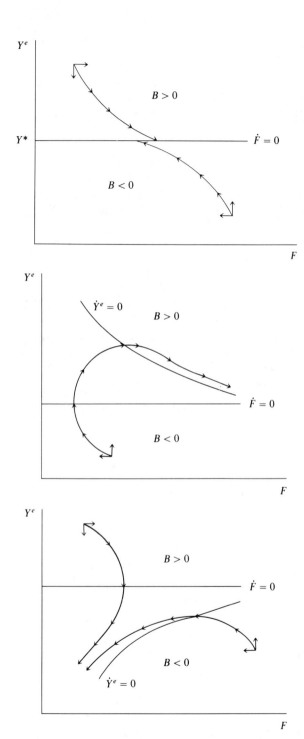

Figure 2. (a) The adjustment process when $M = M^*$. (b) The adjustment process when $M < M^*$. (c) The adjustment process when $M > M^*$.

Case c. The supply of money is overabundant, and the balance of trade is bound to be in deficit in the long run regardless of the initial position. Figure 2(c) illustrates a possible adjustment path.

4. Fiscal Policy and the Supply of Money

In this section we consider the effects of a tax-financed increase in government expenditure if only to exemplify the comparative dynamics of the present model.

From (11) it is immediate that a tax-financed increase in government expenditure gives rise to an equivalent increase in the value of domestic output in the short run (i.e., the short-run balanced budget multiplier is unity). The disposable income is therefore unaffected. Consequently, the YY schedule shifts upward while the FF schedule remain unchanged as illustrated in Figure 3. Before the shift, the economy is at point E_0 with domestic output Y_0 and the supply of money M_0. In the new short-run equilibrium, the economy moves to point E' with domestic output Y' and the supply of money M_0. The new long-run equilibrium is, however, indicated by point E^* where domestic output Y^* is supported by the supply of money M^*. Figure 3 picturizes the

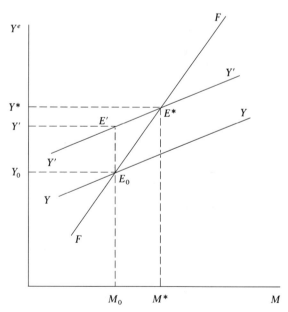

Figure 3. The effects of a tax-financed increase in government expenditure.

possibility that domestic output increases more than government expenditure in the long run (i.e., the long-run balanced budget multiplier exceeds unity). At this point, it is important to note that the supply of money must *increase* if the economy is to move from point E' to the new long-run equilibrium E^*. With commodity prices being rigid everywhere, an increase in output yields an increase in the transactions demand for money, calling for a matching monetary expansion in the long run. If this condition is not fulfilled, the economy goes through a dynamic adjustment process discussed as case (b) in the preceding section. Thus, the initial increase in domestic output is bound to be short-lived. Domestic output will revert to its old level with the balance of trade recording a chronic surplus as time elapses.

This result may be taken to support the monetarist view that fiscal expansion not accompanied by new issue of money does not effectively increase employment in the long run. It is also in agreement with the fundamental proposition of the monetary approach to the balance of payments that the balance of payments disequilibrium is essentially a monetary phenomenon.[5] Money is thus all the more important for the present ultra-Keynesian rigidity of commodity prices.

It is an easy matter to analyze the effects of changes in other exogenous variables such as the value of exports, the propensity to save, and liquidity preference. The importance of money will be confirmed in each case in a similar fashion. It should be remembered, however, that this outcome of a monetarist flavor depends crucially upon the basic assumption of the paper, i.e., the overall rigidity of commodity prices, which is hardly justifiable in practice especially in the long run.

We have assumed that the economy's foreign trade activities are conducted by domestic trading firms. This assumption may be relaxed to account for the possibility that foreign firms may also take part in the economy's exports and imports. Similarly, we can enrich the content of financial wealth by introducing government bonds into the domestic asset market without seriously affecting the analysis of the paper.

References

Frenkel, J. A. and H. G. Johnson, The monetary approach to the balance of payments: Essential concepts and historical origins. In J. A. Frenkel and H. G. Johnson (eds). *The Monetary Approach to the Balance of Payments*, London: Allen & Unwin, 1976.

Kouri, P. J., The exchange rate and the balance of payments in the short run and in the long run, *The Scandinavian Journal of Economics*, Vol. 78, p. 280–304, 1976.

[5] See, for instance, Frenkel and Johnson [1976].

Laursen, S. and L. A. Metzler, Flexible exchange rates and the theory of employment, *Review of Economics & Statistics*, Vol. 32, p. 281–99, 1950.

Meade, J. E., *The Balance of Payments, Mathematical Supplement*, London: Oxford Univ. Press, 1951.

Negishi, T., *Microeconomic Foundations of Keynsian Macroeconomics*. Amsterdam: North Holland Publishing Co., 1979a.

Negishi, T., Foreign exchange gains in a keynesian model of international trade, *Economic Appliqué*, vol. 32, 1979b.

Sweezy, P. M., Demand under conditions of oligopoly, *Journal of Political Economy*, Vol. 47, p. 568–573, 1939.

3

Market Equilibrium and Optimum Social Welfare in a Two-Region Economy

NOBORU SAKASHITA

Institute of Socio-economic Planning
University of Tsukuba
Tsukuba, Ibaraki
Japan

1. Introduction*

In spite of a vast amount of literature on the theoretical model of a multiregion economy, a simple neoclassical model of a two-region economy was, for the first time, worked out very recently by Carlberg [1981].[1] Although he took the equivalence between the social optimum and a free market equilibrium almost for granted in his two-region model,[2] we need some simple but rigorous assumptions to claim that. Boadway and Flatters [1982] dealt with this problem more carefully and discussed the possible inefficiency of a free market (free migration) solution for a two-region economy in the setting of a federal nation as well as policy measures to eliminate this inefficiency. Their inclusion of the third factor of production other than capital and labor (e.g., land, natural resources, etc.) in production functions made their analysis more realistic than cases of linear homogeneous two-factor production functions.

---

*This chapter is an abbreviated version of Sakashita [1984].
[1] However, there was an argument concerning exactly the same model of two-region economy as Carlberg's in Sakashita [1980].
[2] Carlberg [1981] p. 193 194.

43

On the other hand, this made it impossible for them to utilize the convenience of ratio-variable models.

Other cases in which policy intervention is justified were discussed in Borts [1966] very rigorously and in Boadway and Flatters [1981] a little more intuitively.[3] These are cases where there is unemployment in one of the regions owing to several reasons. Existence of migration cost *and* inflexibility of the wage rate in the poor region is one of the possible combinations that causes the underemployment equilibrium. This interesting setting is, however, hardly applicable to a country like Japan where the interregional mobility of labor is extremely high, in other words, migration cost is negligible.

Another case of possible policy intervention dealt with in Sakashita [1983a, 1983b] was that in which social objectives other than national income maximization were established. In these papers, the objective was a fixed ratio allocation of labor force (population) between two regions. Similar to Carlberg's paper, in these papers equalization of *wage rates* between regions was taken for granted as a condition of market equilibrium without additional assumptions, and this could be an unrealistic specification in such an economy, as will be discussed in this paper.

In the present paper, we wish to develop a series of neoclassical models of a two-region economy by which we can examine discrepancy between market equilibrium and the social optimum under alternative specifications of the pattern of migration and to discuss policy measures to fill the discrepancy. This sort of analysis is, we think, quite relevant to an economy like present-day Japan, where the reasons for people's migration among regions are becoming more and more complicated.

In the next section, the simplest model with no public sector goods and no region-specific factors is analyzed. Even in this simplest case, some intervention by the public sector becomes necessary in order to make the market equilibrium equivalent to the social optimum, unless a particular pattern of rental income distribution between the two regions exists. A quantitative appraisal of the inefficiency of market equilibrium is also attempted. In Section 3, uncontrollable region-specific factors are introduced into the utility functions. Then we see the collapse of equivalence among the social optimum, productive efficiency, and market equilibrium. Market equilibrium becomes only the second best social optimum, even with some intervention, in this model. Inefficiency brought by the presence of region-specific factors is also quantitatively appraised. In Section 4, public sector goods are introduced into the model instead of, or in addition to, uncontrollable region-specific factors. Controllability of the supply of own sector goods by the public sector assures

---

[3] See also Sakashita [1970].

the equivalence of the market equilibrium and the social optimum, again, but it cannot overcome the difficulty caused by the presence of uncontrollable region-specific factors. In the final section, the direction of extending the model is briefly discussed.

2.   The Social Optimum for a Two-Region Economy and Its Equivalence to the Market Equilibrium Under Certain Assumptions

Consider an economy consisting of two regions which produce a homogenous output by employing two factors of production, i.e., capital and labor with neoclassical, linear homogeneous, and well-behaved technology. Each region has a production function which characterizes its production technology, and the production function of one region differs from that of another region in such a manner that one function never dominates the other completely. This means that there is at least one common wage-rental ratio under which both production functions are guaranteed to have positive outputs simultaneously. Let us express the per capita production function of region i as $f_i(k_i)$ where k_i is the capital-labor ratio in that region.

We assume that endowments of capital and labor in the nation are fixed as well as the national capital-labor ratio $\bar{k}$. If we denote the relative share of national labor to region i by n_i, we have the following two definitional relations among $k_i, n_i, i = 1, 2$, and $\bar{k}$.

$$n_1 + n_2 = 1 \tag{1}$$

$$n_1 k_1 + n_2 k_2 = \bar{k} \tag{2}$$

Now we can give a definition of the national per capita output x by

$$x = n_1 x_1 + n_2 x_2 \tag{3}$$

in which x_i is the per capita output in region i, i.e., $x_i = f_i(k_i)$ and $i = 1, 2$, and we can formulate the following maximizing problem:

Maximize x

with respect to k_i and n_i, $i = 1, 2,$ (4)

subject to (1) and (2).

Assuming the existence of an interior solution, the optimal conditions for (4) are easily derived as

$$f'_1(k_1) = f'_2(k_2) \tag{5}$$

$$f_1(k_1) - k_1 f'_1(k_1) = f_2(k_2) - k_2 f'_2(k_2) \tag{6}$$

in which $f_i'(k_i) = df_i/dk_i$ and $i = 1, 2$. Equations (5) and (6) are, of course, the well-known marginal productivity conditions.[4] It is also easy to check whether or not an interior solution actually holds in this case. By equations (5) and (6) we can obtain the optimal k_1 and k_2 for the case of an interior solution without consulting equations (1) and (2). If we can obtain the solutions for n_1 and n_2, both of which are positive by equations (1) and (2), for these optimal values of k_1 and k_2, we can say that we have an interior solution to the problem. In other words, $\bar{k}$ must be a convex combination of the optimal k_1 and k_2 for the existence of an interior solution.

A free market equilibrium for this two-region economy produces the same conditions as (5) and (6) provided that the following two assumptions are met. First, the capital moves freely between the regions corresponding to the rental (return) differential. This assumption, which assures (5), can be taken beyond question as an indispensable characteristic of a free market economy. Secondly, the labor also moves freely between regions corresponding to the *wage differential*. This second assumption, which corresponds to (6), can be justified only under certain institutional settings, because the distributive pattern of rental income is not yet specified in our model.

One situation that justifies the second assumption is the case in which each labor unit of the nation receives an equal share of the national rental income and, therefore, equalization of per capita incomes y_i, $i = 1, 2$, of the two regions, distinct from per capita outputs x_i, $i = 1, 2$, becomes equivalent to that of wages. We may call this case the "uniform national dividend scheme."

If there is any regional bias in the distribution of rental income, equation (6) ceases to be a market equilibrium condition. In the strongest case in which there is no interregional flow of rental income, we have the following expression for the regional per capita income:

$$y_i = w_i + rk_i, \qquad i = 1, 2. \tag{7}$$

In equation (7), $r = f_1' = f_2'$ and $w_i = f_i - k_i f_i'$, $i = 1, 2$, which corresponds to the real rental income and the real wage, respectively. It is easily shown that $y_i = x_i = f_i(k_i)$, $i = 1, 2$, in this case so that the corresponding market equilibrium conditions will be as follows.[5]

$$f_1'(k_1) = f_2'(k_2) \tag{8}$$

$$f_1(k_1) = f_2(k_2). \tag{9}$$

---

[4] These conditions already appeared in Sakashita [1980] p. 604, Carlberg [1981] p. 194, and Sakashita [1983a] p. 1176.

[5] It is unlikely for us to have an interior solution to the system of equations (1), (2), (8), and (9) if $\bar{k} > k°$ in which $k°$ is the solution to $f_1(k) = f_2(k)$. See Mathematical Appendix for the detailed discussion.

Assuming that both of the systems expressed by equations (1), (2), (5), and (6), and by equations (1), (2), (8), and (9), (system I and system II) have interior solutions—although we need rather strong conditions for it in the case of system II[6]—we are first interested in the degree of inefficiency involved in system II. In order to evaluate this we start with the following general system (system III) with equations (1) and (2).[7]

$$f'_1(k_1) = f'_2(k_2) = r \tag{10}$$

$$f_1(k_1) - \alpha k_1 f'_1(k_1) = f_2(k_2) - \alpha k_2 f'_2(k_2), \qquad 0 \leq \alpha \leq 1. \tag{11}$$

If $\alpha = 1$ in system III we have system I, and if $\alpha = 0$ system II follows. Actually system III implies a situation in which 100α percent of the regional rental income in each region is poured into the uniform national dividend but $100(1 - \alpha)$ percent is retained within the region.

Applying a comparative static technique to system III, we obtain the following[8]:

$$\frac{dk_1}{d\alpha} = -\frac{1}{A} r(k_2 - k_1) f''_2 \tag{12}$$

$$\frac{dk_2}{d\alpha} = -\frac{1}{A} r(k_2 - k_1) f''_1 \tag{13}$$

in which

$$A = (1 - \alpha)(f'_1 f''_2 - f'_2 f''_1) + \alpha f''_1 f''_2 (k_2 - k_1), \tag{14}$$

and then

$$\frac{dn_1}{d\alpha} = \frac{1}{k_2 - k_1} \left\{ n_1 \frac{dk_1}{d\alpha} + (1 - n_1) \frac{dk_2}{d\alpha} \right\} \tag{15}$$

$$\frac{dx}{d\alpha} = -\frac{1 - \alpha}{A} r^2 (k_2 - k_1) \{ n_1 f''_2 + (1 - n_1) f''_1 \}. \tag{16}$$

Without loss of generality we can assume $k_2 > k_1$ in the relevant range of solution to system III, and under this assumption we may further assume that

$$\left| \frac{f''_1}{f'_1} \right| > \left| \frac{f''_2}{f'_2} \right| \tag{17}$$

again in the relevant range.[9] Under these assumptions, we can show that $A >$

---

[6] See Mathematical Appendix again.

[7] Notice that system III may have an interior solution even if system II fails to do so when α is close to 1.

[8] This technique of using α was suggested by Mr. Jun Nishimura for which the present author wishes to thank him.

[9] See Mathematical Appendix for a related discussion.

0 and therefore

$$\frac{dx}{d\alpha} \geq 0 \qquad \text{for all } \alpha, \qquad 0 \leq \alpha \leq 1. \tag{18}$$

Now we can evaluate the difference between x in system I (x_I) and the same in system II (x_{II}) using a theorem of mean values as follows:

$$x_I - x_{II} = \int_0^1 \left(\frac{dx}{d\alpha}\right) d\alpha \tag{19}$$

$$= \phi(\hat{\alpha}), \qquad \hat{\alpha} = \text{some } \alpha \text{ between } 0 \text{ and } 1,$$

in which $\phi(\alpha)$ is the right-hand side of equation (16). Equation (16) also implies that x attains its maximum when $\alpha = 1$ so that a regional cross transfer of income implied by a more than unity value of α generates an inefficient equilibrium as well as a partially-retained rental income equilibrium with $\alpha < 1$.

Second, we wish to explore a tax-subsidy policy which realizes the same production equilibrium as system I under the setting of system III. Denoting the optimal values of k_1, k_2, and n_1 in system I as k_1^*, k_2^*, and n_1^*, a self-financing tax-subsidy policy of this type will be expressed as follows:

$$(1 + s)\{f_1(k_1^*) - \alpha k_1^* f_1'(k_1^*)\} = (1 - t)\{f_2(k_2^*) - \alpha k_2^* f_2'(k_2^*)\} \tag{20}$$

$$sn_1^*\{f_1(k_1^*) - \alpha k_1^* f_1'(k_1^*)\} = t(1 - n_1^*)\{f_2(k_2^*) - \alpha k_2^* f_2'(k_2^*)\}, \tag{21}$$

in which s is the rate of income subsidy to region 1 and t is the rate of income tax to region 2. (Recall that $k_1^* < k_2^*$ and therefore $f_1(k_1^*) < f_2(k_2^*)$, but $f_1(k_1^*) - k_1^* f_1'(k_1^*) = f_2(k_2^*) - k_2^* f_2'(k_2^*)$.) From equations (20) and (21) we have

$$t = \frac{n_1^*}{f_2^* - \alpha k_2^* f_2'^*}\{(f_2^* - f_1^*) - \alpha r^*(k_2^* - k_1^*)\} \tag{22}$$

$$s = \frac{1 - n_1^*}{f_1^* - \alpha k_1^* f_1'^*}\{(f_2^* - f_1^*) - \alpha r^*(k_2^* - k_1^*)\}, \tag{23}$$

in which $f_i^* = f_i(k_i^*)$ and so on.[10] For system II with $\alpha = 0$ these equations become

$$t(0) = \frac{n_1^*}{f_2^*}(f_2^* - f_1^*) \tag{24}$$

$$s(0) = \frac{1 - n_1^*}{f_1^*}(f_2 - f_1^*) \tag{25}$$

which imply a simple scheme of regional income redistribution.

[10] Both of the values of t and s naturally become zeros when $\alpha = 1$ because $r^* = f_1'^* = f_2'^* = (f_2^* - f_1^*)/(k_2^* - k_1^*)$ in system I.

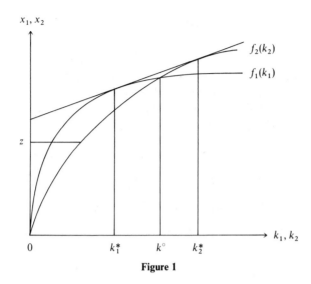

Figure 1

In this section we have examined the degree of inefficiency involved in regional income redistribution schemes other than the uniform national dividend scheme and also have discussed a possible tax-subsidy policy usable to restore the efficient equilibrium.[11] So far the cause of market distortion has been an institutional one, and, therefore, the necessary form of intervention can also be a simple institutional measure of correction. Now, in the next section, we turn to the case in which region-specific factors enter as causes of distortion.

3.   Existence of Region-Specific Factors and Discrepancy Between the Social Optimum and the Market Equilibrium

In the previous section, we have been implicitly assuming that the level of utility of an individual and that of per capita income are practically equivalent to each other in both of the two regions. However, even if the utility functions are basically the same in the two regions, they can be different as functions of per capita incomes between the regions because of the existence of *costless* region-specific factors $\bar{q}_i$, $i = 1, 2$, which affect the level of utility. Such factors could be regional amenities or attractive landscape influences which are common to all residents in a specific region as a sort of *costless* local public goods.

---

[11] A model similar to system II was already discussed in Mera [1975] but from the different viewpoint of trade-off between equity and efficiency.

In such a case, the utility of a resident in a specific region, u_i, is expressed by

$$u_i = u(y_i, \bar{q}_i) = u_i(y_i), \qquad i = 1, 2 \tag{26}$$

in which y_i is the level of per capita income and $\bar{q}_1 \neq \bar{q}_2$.

Firstly we describe the Benthamite social optimum in this setting. The maximizing problem takes the following form.

$$\text{Maximize } \{W = n_1 u(y_1, \bar{q}_1) + n_2 u(y_2, \bar{q}_2,)\} \tag{27}$$

with respect to y_i, k_i, and n_i, $\qquad i = 1, 2,$

and subject to (1), (2), and

$$n_1 y_1 + n_2 y_2 = n_1 f_1(k_1) + n_2 f_2(k_2). \tag{28}$$

Again assuming the existence of an interior solution, we have the following set of optimal conditions:

$$u_1' = u_2' = \mu \tag{29}$$

$$f_1' = f_2' = \frac{\lambda}{\mu} = r \tag{30}$$

$$u_1 + \mu\{(f_1 - k_1 f_1') - y_1\} = u_2 + \mu\{(f_2 - k_2 f_2') - y_2\} \tag{31}$$

$$(1), \quad (2), \quad (28),$$

in which λ and μ are Lagrangian multipliers corresponding to constraints (2) and (28). We call this system of social optimum, system RS-I.

It should be noticed that we have equalization of marginal utilities of income between the two regions (see equation (29)) but not equalization of utilities in this social optimum. As an example, let us assume that the utility function (26) is separable with respect to y and q. Then certainly we will have $y_1 = y_2$ at the optimum by equation (29), but then it is obvious that $u_1 \neq u_2$ because $\bar{q}_1 \neq \bar{q}_2$ by assumption. Inequality of the utilities in this case means a difference between the residents of region 1 and region 2 in their *abilities* to enjoy utility owing to the difference in regional amenities, for instance. In the present case of separable utility, this utility difference is compensated by the opposite difference of marginal productivities of labor between the two regions (see equation (31)). The latter means that there is no equalization of these marginal productivities so that there is no maximization of per capita national output in system RS-I.

Equation (31) in general implies that the net social benefit produced by moving one labor unit (resident) from region 1 to region 2 or vice versa is exactly equal to zero as an intuitively clear condition of the optimum. For the capital which has no ability to enjoy utility by itself, we observe an ordinary condition of equalized marginal productivities between the two regions ((30)). Therefore, we can say that the failure of marginal productivities equalization for the labor comes from its dual character as a factor of production and as a resident of the particular region enjoying utility. This duality also makes the comparison between the social optimum and market equilibrium more complicated for this sort of model.

For the model with region-specific factors in utility functions, market equilibrium under free migration and uniform national dividend assumption takes the following form.

$$u_1(y_1) = u_2(y_2) \tag{32}$$

$$f'_1 = f'_2 = r \tag{33}$$

$$y_i = (f_i - k_i f'_i) + r\bar{k}, \qquad i = 1, 2. \tag{34}$$

$$(1), \quad (2)$$

Constraint (28) can be derived from equations (34) and (2) so that it is not an independent constraint to the model. We call this type of market equilibrium system RS-II.

Apparently the market equilibrium described by system RS-II does not coincide with the social optimum of system RS-I. This situation is generally known as the inefficiency of free migration.[12] Since $\bar{q}_1 \nleqgtr \bar{q}_2$ it is obvious that $y_1 \nleqgtr y_2$ in general, by equation (32), and it follows that the marginal productivities of labor are not equalized between the two regions (see equation (34)) but by a different reason from the case of system RS-I. In addition, it is very important to notice that system RS-I cannot be derived from system RS-II using an ordinary fiscal measure of income transfer because the latter system cannot get rid of equalization of utilities which does not exist, in any case, in the former system.

However, whether or not market equilibrium without intervention is also different from the possible second-best optimum, in the sense of the best situation with an equal utility constraint, is a different question. In order to see this point, we formulate the following sub-maximizing problem with an additional constraint of utility equalization (a Rawlsian problem).

Maximize $\{W = n_1 u_1(y_1) + n_2 u_2(y_2)\}$

with respect to y_i, k_i, and $n_i, \qquad i = 1, 2$, and $\tag{35}$

subject to (1), (2), (28), and

$$u_1(y_1) = u_2(y_2). \tag{36}$$

---

[12] See Boadway and Flatters [1982], particularly p. 620–623. Also see Hartwick [1980], in which region-specific factors appear in the production functions.

The set of optimal conditions will be:

$$\left(\frac{n_1 + v}{n_1}\right)u'_1 = \left(\frac{n_2 - v}{n_2}\right)u'_2 = \mu \tag{37}$$

$$f'_1 = f'_2 = r \tag{38}$$

$$(f_1 - k_1 f'_1) - y_1 = (f_2 - k_2 f'_2) - y_2 \tag{39}$$

$$(1), \quad (2), \quad (28), \quad (36),$$

in which v is a new Lagrangian multiplier corresponding to constraint (36). We may call this set of equations, system RS-III, but it is easily shown that system RS-II with equations (32), (33), (34), (1), and (2) is exactly equivalent to system RS-III with equations (36), (38), (39), (28), (1), and (2).[13] There is, therefore, no really distinct RS-III.

Now it has become clear that market equilibrium with the assumption of uniform national dividend is just equal to the second-best social optimum in system RS's. Even in the case in which the above assumption is not met, we can find some regional income transfer scheme by which market equilibrium is made equivalent to the second-best social optimum, similar to the case in the previous section. We are, however, more interested in the question of by how much will the per capita national output be increased when the two regions tend to have similar amenity conditions, for instance, when $\bar{q}_2$ approaches $\bar{q}_1$. In order to examine this matter, we start with the following summary of market equilibrium.

$$u\{f_1 - f'_1(k_1 - \bar{k}), \bar{q}_1\} = u\{f_2 - f'_2(k_2 - \bar{k}), \beta\bar{q}_1\}, \qquad 0 < \beta \le 1 \tag{40}$$

$$f'_1 = f'_2 = r. \tag{41}$$

For this system we have

$$\frac{dk_1}{d\beta} = \frac{1}{B}u_q\bar{q}_1 f''_2 \tag{42}$$

$$\frac{dk_2}{d\beta} = \frac{1}{B}u_q\bar{q}_1 f''_1 \tag{43}$$

in which

$$B = -f''_1 f''_2 (k_2 - k_1)\{n_1 u_y(y_2, \beta\bar{q}_1) - (1 - n_1)u_y(y_1, \bar{q}_1)\} \tag{44}$$

and $u_y = \partial u/\partial y$ and $u_q = \partial u/\partial q\,(y_2, q_2)$, both of which are being assumed to be positive. Referring to equation (15) (replace α by β), finally we have the

---

[13] Equation (39) is easily derived from equation (34), and the reverse derivation of (34) from (39), etc. can be done as follows:

$$y_i - (f_i - k_i f'_i) = n_1\{y_1 - (f_1 - k_1 f'_1)\} + n_2\{y_2 - (f_2 - k_2 f'_2)\}$$
$$= n_1 y_1 + n_2 y_2 - n_1 f_1 - n_2 f_2 + (n_1 k_1 + n_2 k_2)r = r\bar{k}, \qquad i = 1, 2,$$

following expression:

$$\frac{dx}{d\beta} = \left(r - \frac{f_2 - f_1}{k_2 - k_1} \right) \left(\frac{u_q \bar{q}_1}{B} \right) \{ n_1 f_2'' + (1 - n_1) f_1'' \}. \tag{45}$$

Firstly, let us assume $\beta < 1$, then it must be that $y_2 > y_1$, because both u_y and u_q are positive. This implies $r < (f_2 - f_1)/(k_2 - k_1)$ under the assumption of $k_2 > k_1$, which does not harm generality, so that the first bracket in the right-hand side of (45) is negative. Secondly, since $y_2 > y_1$ it might be the case that $u_y(y_1) > u_y(y_2)$. If production technologies and the national capital-labor ratio $(\bar{k})$ are not so biased in favor of region 1, i.e., n_1 is not much bigger than $(1 - n_1)$, we usually have $n_1 u_y(y_2) - (1 - n_1) u_y(y_1) < 0$, and $B > 0$, subsequently. Under the circumstances described above, we will have $dx/d\beta > 0$ at a particular value of β which is smaller than unity. In addition, it is highly likely that we have the persistence of positive $dx/d\beta$ throughout $0 < \beta \leqq 1$ because $dn_1/d\beta < 0$ when $B > 0$, particularly if $n_1 < 1 - n_1$ when $\beta = 1$.[14] If we have all of these favorable conditions we can say that

$$\frac{dx}{d\beta} > 0 \qquad \text{for } 0 < \beta \leqq 1, \tag{46}$$

and then we can make a similar quantitative evaluation of continuous change in β as was done by equation (19). At least we can say that market equilibrium, welfare maximization, and productive efficiency are mutually compatible with each other only when $\beta = 1$, therefore $y_1 = y_2$ and $dx/d\beta = 0$.

In this section, we have analyzed the difference between the social optimum and market equilibrium in the presence of region-specific factors in the utility functions of residents. It has been shown that there is no way to fill the gap between the two systems by fiscal measures, in this case, and also that both systems have to sacrifice some of their productive efficiency in order to achieve the first-best or the second-best social optimum, respectively.

4. Public Sector Goods as Region-Specific Factors or in Addition to Region-Specific Factors

In system RS-II, the impossibility of bringing market equilibrium to the social optimum came from the uncontrollability of region-specific factors. How will the picture change when these factors are manipulated by the public

---

[14] Actually we can show that

$$\frac{dn_1}{d\beta} = \frac{u_q \bar{q}_1}{B(k_2 - k_1)} \left\{ n_1 f_2'' + (1 - n_1) f_1'' \right\}$$

in this case.

sector? To examine this problem let us replace q_i in the utility function (26) by public sector goods p_i supplied by that sector. Here we confine ourselves to a case in which public sector goods have no externality, i.e., they are pure private goods but are supplied by the public sector. The education voucher may be a good example.

Now, the maximizing problem for the social optimum will take the following form:

$$\text{Maximize } \{W = n_1 u(y_1, p_1) + (1 - n_1)u(y_2, p_2)\} \tag{47}$$

with respect to y_i, p_i, k_i, $i = 1, 2$, and n_i, and subject to

$$\bar{k} - n_1 k_1 - (1 - n_1)k_2 = 0, \text{ (Lagrangian multiplier: } \lambda) \tag{48}$$

$$n_1 f_1 + (1 - n_1)f_2 - n_1 y_1 - (1 - n_1)y_2 - n_1 p_1 - (1 - n_1)p_2 = 0,$$

$$\text{(Lagrangian multiplier: } \mu). \tag{49}$$

Optimal conditions are as follows (system PS-I):

$$f'_1 = f'_2 = \frac{\lambda}{\mu} = r, \tag{50}$$

$$u_y(y_1, p_1) = u_y(y_2, p_2) = u_p(y_1, p_1) = u_p(y_2, p_2) = \mu,$$

$$u_y = \frac{\partial u}{\partial y}, \qquad u_p = \frac{\partial u}{\partial p}, \text{ and} \tag{51}$$

$$u(y_1, p_1) - u(y_2, p_2) + \mu\{r(k_2 - k_1) + (f_1 - f_2) - (y_1 + p_1) + (y_2 + p_2)\} = 0,$$

$$(48), \quad (49) \tag{52}$$

If we assume strict concavity of the utility function, a set of equations in (51) gives a solution of $y_1 = y_2$ and $p_1 = p_2$. Therefore, $u(y_1, p_1) = u(y_2, p_2)$ and equation (52) is reduced to the usual condition of marginal productivities of labor, i.e.,

$$f_1 - k_1 f'_1 = f_2 - k_2 f'_2. \tag{53}$$

Thus there is no contradiction between the social optimum and productive efficiency in this case of controllable region-specific factors and identical individuals. In addition, this social optimum is attainable from a market equilibrium with the uniform national dividend. Let the solution to system PS-I be $y_1^* = y_2^*, p_1^* = p_2^*, k_1^*, k_2^*, n_1^*$, and r^*. Then a common tax rate t^* derived from

$$y_i^* = (1 - t^*)\{(f_i^* - k_i^* f_i'^*) + r^* \bar{k}\}, \qquad i = 1, 2 \tag{54}$$

and a corresponding common value of p_i^* given by

$$t^*\{(f_i^* - k_i^* f_i'^*) + r^* \bar{k}\} = p_i^*, \qquad i = 1, 2 \tag{55}$$

assure the optimum-equivalent market equilibrium because conditions of marginal utilities and marginal productivities are already satisfied by equations (50), (51), and (53) as well as the equal utility requirement, and equation (55) is derived from equations (54) and (49).

Even if we do not have the uniform national dividend assumption, the social optimum can still be achieved by an additional lump-sum income transfer between the regions. Therefore, the region-specific factors do not cause any difficulties regarding the equivalence of the market equilibrium to the social optimum as far as they are controllable by the public sector. If there still are, however, uncontrollable region-specific factors as the third arguments of the utility functions, we encounter the difficulty again. In this new case there are two different utility functions, $u_1(y_1, p_1)$ and $u_2(y_2, p_2)$, practically, and equation (51) is changed into

$$u_{1y}(y_1, p_1) = u_{2y}(y_2, p_2) = u_{1p}(y_1, p_1) = u_{2p}(y_2, p_2) = \mu,$$

$$u_{iy} = \frac{\partial u_i}{\partial y_i}, \, u_{ip} = \frac{\partial u_i}{\partial p_i}, \qquad i = 1, 2, \tag{56}$$

for which we have $y_1 \neq y_2, p_1 \neq p_2$, and $u_1(y_1, p_1) \neq u_2(y_2, p_2)$ in general. We can, therefore, derive neither the condition of productive efficiency nor the market equilibrium condition from the set of optimal conditions in this system with public sector goods and uncontrollable region-specific factors (system PS-II).

In this section, the relation between controllability/uncontrollability of region-specific factors and the equivalence of the market equilibrium and the social optimum has been discussed using a model with an active public sector.

5.   Concluding Remarks

In this paper we have analyzed several cases of correspondence between the social optimum and the market equilibrium in a neoclassical two-region economy. There are three possibilities. The first is the case in which equivalence of the two systems is established without any policy intervention. Secondly, there are cases in which some appropriate policy intervention can bring the equivalence. Finally, in some cases it is impossible to modify market equilibrium to be equivalent to the social optimum with any policy instruments other than a compulsory planning with prohibition of free migration. Differentiation among the cases depends on the presence of uncontrollable region-specific factors and/or the availability of appropriate policy instruments.

The present paper excluded the possibility of a federal nation with different levels of governments by assuming one consolidated public sector.[15] Also, we

[15] See Boadway and Flatters [1982] for a discussion of the federal economy.

excluded the analysis of public goods or quasi-public goods supplied by the public sector and financed by some form of taxation.[16] Finally, heterogeneity of the individuals in the sense of different tastes and/or of different labor productivity was excluded, although it can be introduced without essential difficulty.[17] This sort of exclusion in our models itself suggests possible directions of extending the analysis.

Mathematical Appendix: On the Existence of a Solution to System II

Let us specify an independent variable z at the level of which $f_1(k_1)$ and $f_2(k_2)$ are equalized (see Figure 1), i.e.,

$$z = f_1(k_1) = f_2(k_2). \tag{57}$$

Then let us define a function $\phi(z)$ as

$$\phi(z) = f'_1\{k_1(z)\} - f'_2\{k_2(z)\}, \tag{58}$$

in which $k_1(z)$ and $k_2(z)$ are the solutions to equation (57). By appropriately general specifications of $f_1(k_1)$ and $f_2(k_2)$, we can assume that

$$\lim_{z \to +0} \phi(z) > 0 \tag{59}$$

and

$$\phi\{f_i(k^\circ)\} < 0, \qquad i = 1 \text{ or } 2, \tag{60}$$

in which k° is the solution to $f_1(k^\circ) = f_2(k^\circ)$ (see Figure 1).

Since we can safely assume the continuity of $\phi(z)$, there will certainly be a value of $z(=\hat{z})$ between 0 and $f_1(k^\circ)$ which satisfies

$$\phi(\hat{z}) = f'_1\{k_1(\hat{z})\} - f'_2\{k_2(\hat{z})\} = 0 \tag{61}$$

as well as equation (57). If we can get the national capital-labor ratio k as a convex combination of $k_1(\hat{z})$ and $k_2(\hat{z})$, both of which are smaller than k°, this is the case in which we have an interior solution to system II.

Since

$$\frac{d\phi}{dz} = \frac{f''_1\{k_1(z)\}}{f'_1\{k_1(z)\}} - \frac{f''_2\{k_2(z)\}}{f'_2\{k_2(z)\}}, \tag{62}$$

and it is most likely that $d\phi/dz$ is always negative in the case of (59) and (60), i.e., f_1 may have stronger curvature than f_2 does for the same value of z, there

---

[16] See Hartwick [1980] in this respect.

[17] The former aspect, which has some resemblance to the model in Tiebout [1956], was analyzed in Sakashita [1984].

will be no solution to system II if $\bar{k} > k^\circ$. Even if we have an interior solution to system II, the possibility that we have $k_1^* < \bar{k} < k_2^*$ (k_1^* and k_2^* are solutions to equations (5) and (6)), at the same time is very limited. This point can be seen by an example of Cobb-Douglas functions, such as

$$f_1(k_1) = Ak_1^\alpha, \qquad f_2(k_2) = k_2^\beta, \qquad A > 1, \quad . \quad \beta > \alpha, \tag{63}$$

(see Sakashita [1983a] for a similar example).

For this example, the solutions to equations (5) and (6) will be

$$k_1^* = \left\{ A\left(\frac{\alpha}{\beta}\right)^\beta \left(\frac{1-\alpha}{1-\beta}\right)^{1-\beta} \right\}^{1/(\beta-\alpha)} \tag{64}$$

$$k_2^* = \left\{ A\left(\frac{\alpha}{\beta}\right)^\alpha \left(\frac{1-\alpha}{1-\beta}\right)^{1-\alpha} \right\}^{1/(\beta-\alpha)} \tag{65}$$

and those to equations (57) and (61) will be

$$\hat{k}_1 = \left\{ A\left(\frac{\alpha}{\beta}\right)^\beta \right\}^{1/(\beta-\alpha)} \tag{66}$$

$$\hat{k}_2 = \left\{ A\left(\frac{\alpha}{\beta}\right)^\alpha \right\}^{1/(\beta-\alpha)} \tag{67}$$

A necessary condition for both system I and system II to have interior solutions is $\hat{k}_2 > k_1^*$, and this requires

$$\left(\frac{\beta}{\alpha}\right)^{\beta-\alpha} \left(\frac{1-\beta}{1-\alpha}\right)^{1-\beta} > 1. \tag{68}$$

Relation (68) may be satisfied only when the gap between β and α is rather big; that means great heterogeneity between the two regions' technologies (e.g., $\beta = 0.9$ and $\alpha = 0.1$). Also notice that definitely $\hat{k}_1 < \hat{k}_2 < k^\circ$ ($= A^{1/(\beta-\alpha)}$) in this example.

References

Boadway, R. and F. Flatters, The efficiency basis for regional employment policy, *Canadian Journal of Economics*, Vol. 14, p. 58–77, 1981.

Boadway, R. and F. Flatters, Efficiency and equalization payments in a federal system of government: A synthesis and extension of recent results, *Canadian Journal of Economics*, Vol. 15, p. 613–633, 1982.

Borts, G. H., Criteria for the evaluation of regional development programs, in W. Z. Hirsch (ed), *Regional Accounts for Policy Decisions*, Baltimore: John Hopkins University Press, p. 183–218, 1966.

Carlberg, M. A neoclassical model of interregional economic growth, *Regional Science and Urban Economics*, Vol. 11, p. 191–203, 1981.

Hartwick, J. H., The Henry George rule, optimal population and interregional equity, *Canadian Journal of Economics*, Vol. 13, p. 695–700, 1980.

Mera, K. *Income Distribution and Regional Development*. Tokyo: University of Tokyo Press, 1975.

Sakashita, N. Efficiency evaluation of regional development policy, *Papers and Proceedings of the Eighth Congress of Econometrics at Rokko, Kobe,* Kansai Economic Research Centre, Osaka, p. 363–392, 1970 (in Japanese).

Sakashita, N., Regional Economics, in: *Encyclopedia of Economics*, Vol. 2, Tokyo: Toyokeizai Simpoh-sha, p. 599–609, 1980. (in Japanese).

Sakashita, N., Evaluation of regional development policy—an alternative approach, *Environment and Planning A*, Vol. 15, p. 1175–1184, 1983a.

Sakashita, N., Population dispersion and regional economic policy, in Y. Okano and T. Negishi ed., *Development of Public Economics—in Honor of Professor Yasuhiko Oishi*, Tokyo: Toyokeizai Simpoh-sha, p. 209–225, 1983b (in Japanese).

Sakashita, N., Market equilibrium and social optimum in a two-region economy, Institute of Socio-Economic Planning Discussion Paper No. 242, University of Tsukuba, 1984.

Tiebout, C. M., A pure theory of local expenditures, *Journal of Political Economy*, Vol. 64, p. 416–424, 1956.

4

Economic Expansion, Industrialization, and Dutch Disease Economics in the Context of International Monetary Economics

AKIRA TAKAYAMA

Department of Economics
Southern Illinois University
Carbondale, Illinois

1. Introduction

The purpose of this paper is to obtain some new results and to assemble various threads of thought on certain problems of international monetary economics, discussed by the present author and his former students and developed in Anderson-Takayama [1977], Takayama [1977], Drabicki-Takayama [1983], and others, within a unified simple model. Our emphasis here is on economic development. Although the present paper is theoretical, we shall freely illustrate our results in terms of some real world experiences. The theory is developed in the hope of explaining some experiences in Japan and other countries. In Section 2, we exposit the basic framework and the workings of an international monetary economy under fixed and flexible exchange rates, using the diagrammatical apparatus developed by Drabicki-Takayama [1983]. To ease the exposition and to sharpen our analysis, we (unlike D-T) impose the small country assumption. Section 3 begins with a clarification of the pattern of shifts of the production possibility curve and a discussion of the sources of such shifts. Economic expansion is then classified

*The material here has been used and developed in my lectures at various Universities in the U.S. and Japan over the past decade. I am indebted to John Drabicki and Richard Anderson for many useful and exciting discussions, which produced a number of joint articles.

59

by the relative configuration of the demand and supply parameters of the commodity sectors. Based on such groundwork, Section 3 then seeks the condition for a "successful" industrialization under a flexible exchange rate regime. Conditions for successful industrialization have been discussed heavily in the development literature. Though many of these works have their own merit, there seems to be much confusion in some discussions, and, in any case, few have analyzed this problem explicitly in the context of an open monetary economy. Section 4 introduces nontradeables into the model and discusses how the analysis and results in the previous sections are affected. Finally, Section 5 deals with "Dutch Disease Economics," which has attracted a great deal of attention recently. Typically, the literature on this topic emphasizes the "real" side of the problem, such as shifts of resources due to changes in relative prices, and few individuals have discussed this problem in the context of a monetary economy. This is rather unfortunate since the topic explicitly deals with an open economy, which inevitably involves the problem of the balance of payments and, hence, of money. In Section 5, we shall thus analyze the problem of Dutch Disease Economics by using the simple framework of an open monetary economy (developed in the present paper). We shall not attempt to discuss all aspects of the problem, as it would simply clutter the paper, but rather we shall discuss certain important aspects which, in turn, also illustrate the use of our model. We shall find that certain important conclusions usually accepted in the literature on this topic are, unfortunately, false or at least misleading.

2. Basic Model

We consider an economy ("home country") which is capable of producing two commodities ($i = 1, 2$). Let D_i, X_i, and p_i, respectively, be the demand for, the output of, and the (domestic money) price of the ith commodity. Then we may write the budget condition of this country as,

$$p_1 D_1 + p_2 D_2 + H \equiv p_1 X_1 + p_2 X_2, \qquad (1)$$

where H denotes the hoarding (or dishoarding) of cash balances, which is equal to the money to be carried over to the next period L minus the initial stock of (nominal) money M, i.e., $H \equiv L - M$. If the country is under autarky, we have $H = 0$. Here we assume that all financial assets are consolidated under the name of "money," for the sake of simplicity.

Assume the usual neoclassical, negatively sloped, strictly concave production possibility curve, which we denote by $X_i(p_1, p_2, \alpha)$, where α signifies the shift parameter of the production possibility curve by economic expansion. Denote the national income by Y,

$$Y(p_1, p_2, \alpha) \equiv p_1 X_1(p_1, p_2, \alpha) + p_2 X_2(p_1, p_2, \alpha). \tag{2}$$

Then the demand functions can be written as,

$$D_i = D_i[p_1, p_2, Y(p_1, p_2, \alpha), M], \qquad i = 1, 2, \qquad L = L[p_1, p_2, Y(p_1, p_2, \alpha)].$$

Define E_i by $E_i \equiv D_i - X_i$, $i = 1, 2$. Then we have,

$$E_i = E_i(p_1, p_2, M, \alpha), \qquad H = H(p_1, p_2, M, \alpha), \tag{3}$$

where the function $E_i (i = 1, 2)$ (resp. H) is homogenous of degree zero (resp. homogenous of degree one) in p_1, p_2, and M.

Then the budget condition (1) can be rewritten as,

$$p_1 E_1 + p_2 E_2 + H \equiv 0. \tag{1'}$$

The equilibrium prices (p_1 and p_2) *in the absence of trade* are determined by,

$$E_i(p_1, p_2, M, \alpha) = 0, \qquad i = 1, 2, \qquad H(p_1, p_2, M, \alpha) = 0, \tag{4}$$

for given values of M and α. In view of the budget condition (1), one of the three conditions in (4) is superfluous.

To ease our discussion we assume gross substitutability and positive wealth effects,[1]

$$E_{ij} > 0, \qquad i \neq j, \qquad i = 1, 2, j = 1, 2, 3,$$

$$E_{ij} < 0, \qquad i = 1, 2,$$

$$H_1 > 0, \qquad H_2 > 0, \qquad 0 < -H_3 < 1, \tag{5}$$

where $E_{ij} \equiv \partial E_i / \partial p_j$, $H_j \equiv \partial H / \partial p_i$, $i, j = 1, 2$, $E_{i3} \equiv \partial E_i / \partial M$, $H_3 \equiv \partial H / \partial M$, where not all of conditions in (5) are independent. Then on the (p_1, p_2) plane,

---

[1] For the neoclassical production possibility curve, we may assume

$$\frac{\partial X_i}{\partial p_j} < 0, \qquad i \neq j, \qquad \frac{\partial X_i}{\partial p_i} > 0, \qquad i = 1, 2.$$

For the demand side, we assume gross substitutability and positive wealth effects, which can be specified by,

$$\frac{\partial D_i}{\partial p_j}, \qquad i \neq j, \qquad \frac{\partial D_i}{\partial p_i} < 0, \qquad \frac{\partial D_3}{\partial M} > 0, \qquad i, j = 1, 2,$$

$$\frac{\partial L}{\partial p_j} > 0, \qquad j = 1, 2, \qquad 0 < \frac{\partial L}{\partial M} < 1.$$

From these we obtain the sign specification of the E_{ij}'s and H_j's in the text. Note that not all of these conditions are independent.

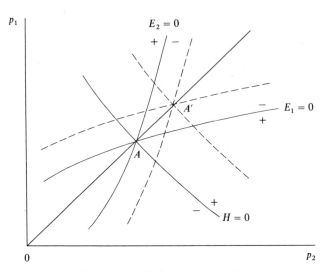

Figure 1. Equilibrium under Autarky.

$E_i = 0$ curve [the locus of (p_1, p_2) pairs for which $E_i(p_1, p_2, M, \alpha) = 0$ for given values of M and α] is upward-sloping for $i = 1, 2$, and the $H = 0$ curve [the locus of (p_1, p_2) pairs for which $H(p_1, p_2, M, \alpha) = 0$ for given values of M and α] is downward-sloping. Also, we have $E_1 < 0$ (resp. $E_1 > 0$) to the left (resp.) right) of the $E_1 = 0$ curve, $E_2 > 0$ (resp. $E_2 < 0$) to the left (resp. right) of the $E_2 = 0$ curve, and $H < 0$ (resp. $H > 0$) to the left (right) of the $H = 0$ curve. Furthermore, it can be shown that the slope of the ray from the origin to any point on the $E_1 = 0$ (resp. of the $E_2 = 0$) curve is greater (resp. less) than the slope of the $E_1 = 0$ (resp. the $E_2 = 0$) curve at that point.[2] (For the proof, see Drabicki-Takayama [1983], p. 4). These results are illustrated in Figure 1, where point A denotes the point of equilibrium in the absence of trade (under "autarky")

---

[2] By the homogeneity of the function E_1 we have

$$E_{11}p_1 + E_{12}p_2 + E_{13}M = 0.$$

From this we may conclude

$$p_1/p_2 = -\frac{E_{12}}{E_{11}} - \frac{E_{13}M}{E_{11}p_2} > -\frac{E_{12}}{E_{11}} = \frac{dp_1}{dp_2}\bigg|_{E_1 = 0}$$

Similarly, by using the homogeneity of E_2, we may show that the slope of the ray from the origin to any point on the $E_2 = 0$ curve is less than the slope of the $E_2 = 0$ curve, i.e., $p_1/p_2 < dp_1/dp_2$ for $E_2 = 0$.

Note that these excess demand curves (the $E_1 = 0$, the $E_2 = 0$, and the $H = 0$ curves) are drawn assuming that the money supply M remains fixed. It can be shown easily from (5) that an increase in M shifts the $E_1 = 0$ curve (resp. the $E_2 = 0$ curve) to the left (resp. right) and the $H = 0$ curve to the right. Such shifts of the excess demand curves are also illustrated by the dashed curves in Figure 1, where at point A', the price of each commodity increases. Similarly, a fall in the money supply causes the shifts of these excess demand curves to the opposite direction, so that the price of each commodity falls at the new equilibrium point under autarky.

A change in M thus moves the equilibrium point under autarky. Note, however, that the equilibrium price ratio p remains fixed by changes in M: for example, point A' lies on the OA ray. This is because under the homogeneity of the function E_i's, the equilibrium under autarky can be described by

$$E_i(p, 1, \bar{M}, \alpha) = 0, \qquad i = 1, 2, \qquad \text{where } p \equiv \frac{p_1}{p_2}, \qquad \bar{M} \equiv \frac{M}{p_2}. \qquad (4')$$

Namely, a change in nominal balances M causes a proportionate change in p_1 and p_2 so as to keep $\bar{M}$ (real cash balances) and p (real price) constant. This corresponds to the classical doctrine of the *neutrality of money* for a closed economy.

We now introduce international trade. Let p_{if} signify the foreign price of commodity $i (i = 1, 2)$, and let e be the exchange rate (the price of the foreign currency in terms of the home currency). Then assuming free trade with no impediments to trade (for the sake of simplicity), the familiar arbitrage condition requires,

$$p_i = e p_{if}, \qquad i = 1, 2. \qquad (6)$$

Define the balance of payments B by,

$$B \equiv -(p_1 E_1 + p_2 E_2), \qquad (7)$$

where we assume that both goods are tradeables. Then, from (1), we obtain,

$$B = H(p_1, p_2, M, \alpha), \qquad (8)$$

which is the fundamental relation in the monetary approach to the balance of payments (cf., Johnson [1958], Mundell [1968], and Komiya [1969]).

For the sake of simplicity, assume that the home country is "small in the sense that the foreign prices, p_{1f} and p_{2f} are imposed on the home country by the rest of the world, so that

$$p_i = e \bar{p}_{if}, \qquad i = 1, 2 \qquad (6')$$

where $\bar{p}_{if}$, $i = 1, 2$, are exogenously given.

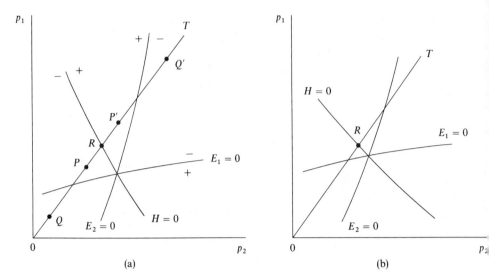

Figure 2. International Equilibrium: (a) Fixed exchange rates, (b) Flexible exchange rates.

We first consider the fixed exchange rate case, in which e is fixed by policy authorities. In panel (a) of Figure 2, we illustrate different international equilibrium points such as Q, P, R, P', and Q', in alternative exchange rates that are fixed, where the slope of the OT ray is equal to $\bar{p}_{1f}/\bar{p}_{2f}$ (the world terms of trade). Note that depending on the value of the exchange rate, we obtain different international equilibrium points [determined by (9)] and different configurations of the sign pattern of E_1, E_2, and $H(=B)$. For example, in panel (a) of Figure 2, we have:

$$E_1 < 0, \quad E_2 > 0, \quad H < 0, \quad \text{at point P}$$

$$E_1 < 0, \quad E_2 > 0, \quad H > 0, \quad \text{at point P}'$$

$$E_1 < 0, \quad E_2 > 0, \quad H = 0, \quad \text{at point R}$$

$$E_1 > 0, \quad E_2 > 0, \quad H < 0, \quad \text{at point Q}$$

$$E_1 < 0, \quad E_2 < 0, \quad H > 0, \quad \text{at point Q}'$$

Thus, at any of the points P, P', and R, the home country exports commodity 1 and imports commodity 2, while the balance of payments shows a deficit at P, a surplus at P', and equilibrium at R. At point Q the home country imports both commodities (in return for its money), and at point Q' the home country exports both commodities. Namely, if the exchange rate is sufficiently undervalued (i.e., e is set sufficiently low), then the country exports all of its (traded) commodities, while if the exchange rate is sufficiently overvalued, then it imports all of its (traded) commodities.[3]

Needless to say, the situation in which the balance of payments shows a disequilibrium cannot last long. As is clear from $H = B$, the balance of payments shows a deficit (resp. a surplus), the home money supply decreases (resp. increases), which in turn causes shifts of the excess demand curves as described earlier. Such a dynamic process, which is obtained for a fixed value of e, is described by,

$$\dot{M} = eH(\bar{p}_{1f}, \bar{p}_{2f}, M/e, \alpha) \equiv \phi(M),$$

by recalling (8) and the homogeneity of $H_3 < 0$. Since $H_3 < 0$, we have $\phi' < 0$, so that the *long-run equilibrium* (LRE) point M^* defined by $\phi(M^*) = 0$ is asymptotically globally stable. Such a dynamic process is at the heart of the classical mechanism of international adjustment. At the LRE, $H = 0$, so that real cash balances M/p_2 remain fixed. Hence any disturbances in nominal balances have no real effect *in the long-run*; i.e., the classical *neutrality of money* holds in the international context. In the diagram, LRE is determined by the intersection of the OT ray and the $H = 0$ *(evaluated at the LRE money stock, M^*).*

Under a flexible exchange rate system, e fluctuates so as to bring about the balance of payments equilibrium. For example, if the initial point is given by P (resp. P′) in Panel a of Figure 2, the balance of payments shows a deficit (resp. a surplus) so that e goes up (resp. down) and the economy reaches point R in which the balance of payments equilibrium is brought about. Note that such an adjustment process takes place *without* accompanying changes in the home money supply and hence *without* any shift of the excess demand curves, since the excess demand curves are defined by the locus of (p_1, p_2) pairs for which

$$E_i(p_1, p_2, M, \alpha) = 0, \qquad i = 1, 2, \qquad \text{and } H(p_1, p_2, M, \alpha) = 0.$$

They stay put as long as M and α stay put. A change in the exchange rate e moves equilibrium points only along the OT ray, so that the international equilibrium point under the flexible exchange rate system is determined by the intersection of the OT ray and the $H = 0$ curve, where the $H = 0$ curve is evaluated at the *initial* money stock. Such a point is illustrated by point R in Panel b of Figure 2, where all the excess demand curves are evaluated at the

---

[3] For example, Japan, right after the Meiji restoration of 1868, did not have many goods to export. The resulting balance of payments deficit could be paid only by outflows of species. Another example is the United States right after the World War II "dollar shortage." After World War II, Japan kept the fixed exchange rate system (i.e., 1 U.S. dollar = 360 yen) for many years (from 1949 until 1971). Though this rate was an overvaluation of the yen initially, it turned into an undervaluation of the yen in the 1960s. This in turn caused Japan to export many commodities, the so-called "sobanateki" (overall) increase in exports.

initial money stock M. Under flexible exchange rates, it is thus *impossible* to obtain the trade patterns in which a country exports or imports both commodities.

3. Economic Expansion and Conditions for Industrialization

To analyze the effects of economic expansion, we first define the following symbols:

$$c_i \equiv \frac{\partial D_i}{\partial Y}, \qquad i = 1, 2, \qquad c_M \equiv \partial L/\partial Y,$$

$$\alpha_i \equiv \frac{\dfrac{\partial X_i}{\partial \alpha_i}}{\dfrac{\partial Y}{\partial \alpha}}, \qquad i = 1, 2,$$

where $c_i (i = 1, 2)$ signify the marginal propensity to spend on the ith commodity out of current income Y. Partial differentiation of (1) with respect to Y yields,

$$p_1 c_1 + p_2 c_2 + c_M = 1, \tag{9a}$$

where we may assume $c_1, c_2, c_M > 0$. By "economic expansion," we mean an outward expansion of the production possibility curve. Since this increases Y for given values of p_1 and p_2, economic expansion means $Y_\alpha \equiv \partial Y/\partial \alpha > 0$. The magnitude of α_i signifies the ith industry's share of economic expansion. Note that α_i can be positive or negative, although partial differentiation of (1) with respect to α yields:

$$p_1 \alpha_1 + p_2 \alpha_2 = 1. \tag{9b}$$

From (9b), we may conclude that if $\alpha_1 < 0$, for example, then $\alpha_2 > 0$. Also, from (9a) and (9b), we have

$$p_1(c_1 - \alpha_1) + p_2(c_2 - \alpha_2) + c_M = 0. \tag{10}$$

Hence it is *not* possible to have $c_1 > \alpha_1$ and $c_2 > \alpha_2$ simultaneously, while it is possible to have $c_1 < \alpha_1$ *and* $c_2 < \alpha_2$. In Figure 3, we illustrate the following three patterns of shifts of the production possibility curve by growth:

(a) $\alpha_1 > 0, \alpha_2 > 0$;   (b) $\alpha_1 > 0, \alpha_2 < 0$;   (c) $\alpha_1 < 0, \alpha_2 > 0$.

Note that by virtue of (9b), we may conclude that $\alpha_2 < 0$ implies $\alpha_1 > 0$, and that $\alpha_1 < 0$ implies $\alpha_2 > 0$. Borrowing the terms developed after the famous

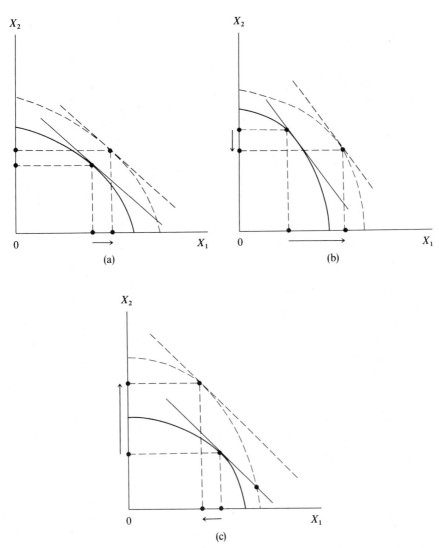

Figure 3. Patterns of Shifts of the Production Possibility Curve: (a) $\alpha_1 > 0, \alpha_2 > 0$, (b) $\alpha_1 > 0$, $\alpha_2 < 0$, (c) $\alpha_1 < 0, \alpha_2 > 0$.

discussion following Hicks' inaugural lecture [1953] (cf., Johnson [1959] and Takayama [1964]), we may say that economic growth is:

"ultra-commodity 1-biased" (or "ultra-biased towards 1"), if $\alpha_2 < 0$;

"ultra-commodity 2-biased" (or "ultra-biased towards 2"), if $\alpha_1 < 0$.

Utilizing the Heckscher-Ohlin type of model in which both commodities employ the same two factors that are free between the two industries, the well-known Rybczynski Theorem [1955] asserts that an increase in the endowment of one factor raises the output of the industry which uses that factor relatively more intensively and reduces the output of the industry, if the commodity prices are fixed. Namely, the Rybczynski Theorem provides a sufficient condition for ultra-biased growth. If labor is relatively more intensively used in agriculture compared to the manufacturing goods sector and if labor is growing rapidly (as is the case in many LDC's today), then such a growth would be ultra-biased towards agriculture.

One may question, however, the validity of the assumption that both sectors use the same two factors (say, labor and capital). An alternative important model is the one with specific factors, which has become well-known through the works of Samuelson [1971], Jones [1971], and others (cf., Takayama [1982] for a survey). To apply such a model to the present two-commodity framework, assume that agriculture uses land and labor and the manufacturing goods sector uses capital and labor, and assume further that land is specific to agriculture and capital is specific to the manufacturing goods sector. Then we may conclude that if capital increases with the other factors remaining constant, the expansion is ultra-biased towards the manufacturing goods sector (i.e., $\alpha_1 < 0$ and $\alpha_2 > 0$). The land under cultivation for agriculture may not grow as rapidly as other factors in many cases (with notable exceptions such as the U.S. in the 19th century, and Thailand and Burma in the late 19th century). If labor grows with the other factors remaining constant, then the expansion is no longer ultra-biased, as it increases the output of each sector when the commodity prices remain fixed ($\alpha_1 > 0$, $\alpha_2 > 0$). In short, if an upward shift of the production possibility curve is caused by a (rapid) accumulation of capital in the manufacturing goods sector, then such an expansion is ultra-biased towards that sector ($\alpha_1 < 0, \alpha_2 > 0$). If such a shift is caused by both capital accumulation and labor growth, then we have $\alpha_1 > 0$ and $\alpha_2 > 0$. On the other hand, if the land for agriculture grows rapidly with the other factors remaining fairly constant compared to the land, then the expansion of the production possibility curve is ultra-biased towards agriculture ($\alpha_1 > 0, \alpha_2 < 0$).

Another important factor which causes a shift in the production possibility curve is technological progress. In the past, at least, important technological progress in the manufacturing goods sector tended to bring about ultra-biased growth towards the manufacturing goods sector.

A note of caution may be in order here. Agriculture is, contrary to the customary belief, no longer a section in which technological progress is slow, as exemplified in U.S. agriculture. For example, the production of corn in the

U.S. tripled between 1932 and 1979, while the land for the production of corn was reduced by 33 million acres, as pointed out by Theodore Schultz in his 1979 Nobel lecture. Namely, agriculture is now becoming an industry in which rapid technological progress can take place. Thus, agriculture may become a high technology industry suitable for advanced countries in the future.

To proceed with our analysis, let $E_{i\alpha} \equiv \partial E_i / \partial \alpha$, $i = 1, 2$, and $H_\alpha \equiv \partial H / \partial \alpha$. Thus we can easily compute:

$$E_{i\alpha} = (c_i - \alpha_i) Y_\alpha, \qquad i = 1, 2, \qquad H_\alpha = c_M Y_\alpha. \tag{11}$$

Under fixed exchange rates, the balance of payments shows a deficit or a surplus in the short run. Since we can easily observe $H_\alpha > 0$ from (11), we may at once conclude that economic expansion always improves the balance of payments regardless of the pattern of growth (as long as M and e are fixed), assuming that the country in question is "small." This corresponds to the well-known Komiya-Mundell Theorem (cf., Komiya [1969], Mundell [1968]) which sheds an important light on the problem addressed in Hicks' inaugural lecture.

From (11), we may also observe that $E_{i\alpha}$ can be positive or negative. More specifically, we have:

$$E_{i\alpha} \gtrless 0 \text{ according to whether } c_i \gtrless \alpha_i.$$

There are three possible patterns of economic expansion:

(a) $c_1 > \alpha_1$;   (b) $c_2 > \alpha_2$;   (c) $c_1 < \alpha_1$ and $c_2 < \alpha_2$,

where we exclude the knife-edge cases in which equalities hold. From (10), we may note that $c_1 > \alpha_1$ implies $c_2 < \alpha_2$, and that $c_2 > \alpha_2$ implies $c_1 < \alpha_1$, while (as mentioned earlier) it is not possible to have $c_1 > \alpha_1$ and $c_2 > \alpha_2$ simultaneously. Hence, the above three cases, respectively, correspond to:

(a) $E_{1\alpha} > 0, E_{2\alpha} < 0$;   (b) $E_{1\alpha} < 0, E_{2\alpha} > 0$;   (c) $E_{1\alpha} < 0, E_{2\alpha} < 0$.

That $c_1 > \alpha_1$, for example, means that for fixed prices an increase in the demand for commodity 1 (by economic expansion) is greater than the increase in the output of commodity 1. If economic expansion is ultra-biased towards community 2 (i.e., if $\alpha_1 < 0$) then we always have $c_1 > \alpha_1$ so that we have $E_{1\alpha} > 0$ and $E_{2\alpha} < 0$. Similarly, if economic expansion is ultra-biased towards commodity 1 (i.e., if $\alpha_2 < 0$), then we always have $E_{1\alpha} < 0$ and $E_{2\alpha} > 0$, i.e., case b of the above classification.

We now seek the possibility of "industrialization," i.e., the possibility that the country changes from an agricultural goods (commodity 1) exporting country to a manufacturing goods (commodity 2) exporting country. Here we focus our attention on the *flexible exchange rate case*. Recalling that the

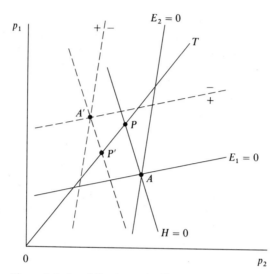

Figure 4. Industrialization under Flexible Exchange Rates.

international equilibrium point in this case is determined by the intersection of the OT ray and the $H = 0$ curve, international equilibrium *before* economic expansion is illustrated by point P in Figure 4. Note that at point P, $E_1 < 0$, $E_2 > 0$, so that the country exports commodity 1 and imports commodity 2. The excess demand curves depicted in Figure 4 must shift by economic expansion. To obtain the direction of the shifts of these curves, we may compute:

$$\left.\frac{\partial p_2}{\partial \alpha}\right|_{E_1 = 0} = -\frac{E_{1\alpha}}{E_{12}}, \qquad \left.\frac{\partial p_2}{\partial \alpha}\right|_{E_2 = 0} = -\frac{E_{2\alpha}}{E_{22}}, \tag{12a}$$

$$\left.\frac{\partial p_2}{\partial \alpha}\right|_{H = 0} = -\frac{H_\alpha}{H_2} > 0. \tag{12b}$$

From (12b) we may assert that the $H = 0$ curve always shifts to the left by economic expansion. To determine the direction of the shifts of the $E_i = 0$ curve ($i = 1, 2$), we conclude the above three cases in turn.

Case a. $(c_1 > \alpha_1)$ In this case, we have $E_{1\alpha} > 0$ and $E_{2\alpha} < 0$. Hence from (12a), we have $\partial p_2/\partial \alpha < 0$ for both $E_1 = 0$ and $E_2 = 0$. Thus we may conclude that $E_1 = 0$ and $E_2 = 0$ both shift to the left by economic expansion. This shift of the excess demand curves for case a is illustrated by the dotted curves in Figure 4. Since the money stock remains fixed under flexible exchange rates, the new international equilibrium point is determined by the intersection of

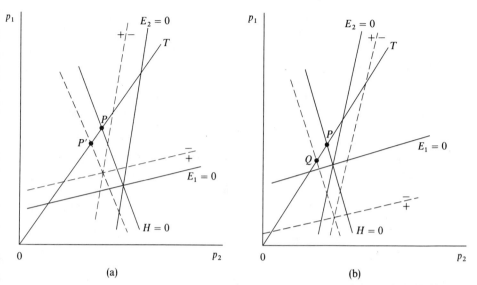

Figure 5. Cases of No Industrialization under Alternative Patterns of Expansion: (a) No industrialization with $c_1 < \alpha_1$, (b) The case of $c_2 > \alpha_2$.

the OT ray and the $H = 0$ after growth, which is illustrated by point P' in Figure 4.[4]

Note that at point P', E_1 becomes positive and E_2 becomes negative, so that the country now exports manufacturing goods and imports agricultural goods. Thus the home country *successfully industrializes* by economic expansion, as actually happened in many western countries and Japan. Note, however, that whether or not the country is successful in industrialization depends on the relative magnitude of the shift of excess demand functions. It is perfectly possible that the country continues to be an agricultural goods exporting country in case a, or even when expansion is ultra-biased towards manufacturing activity ($\alpha_1 < 0$). This is illustrated in panel a of Figure 5.

Case b. ($c_2 > \alpha_2$) In this case we have $E_{2\alpha} > 0$ and $E_{1\alpha} < 0$. Then by using (12a), we may conclude that the $E_1 = 0$ and the $E_2 = 0$ curves both shift to the

---

[4] Note that the equilibrium under autarky moves to the left (i.e., from point A to point A' where the OA' ray is steeper than OA ray), if $E_{1\alpha} > 0$ and $E_{2\alpha} < 0$. The economic interpretation of this is as follows. If $E_{1\alpha} > 0$, then $c_1 > \alpha_1$, i.e., an increase in the demand for 1 by economic expansion exceeds an increase in its output for given prices. This tends to increase the autarkic price of 1 *vis à vis* 2. Similarly, if $E_{2\alpha} < 0$, then $c_2 < \alpha_2$, i.e., an increase in the demand for 2 by economic expansion falls short of an increase in its output. This tends to lower the autarkic price of 2 *vis à vis* 1. Thus, in both ways, the autarkic equilibrium price ratio p_1/p_2 rises.

right, while the $H = 0$ curve again shifts to the left. Such shifts of excess demand curves are illustrated by panel b of Figure 5, where point Q denotes the international equilibrium point after growth. In this case, the signs of E_1 and E_2 would remain unchanged. In fact, it can be seen easily from panel b of Figure 5 that under such a pattern of expansion (i.e., if $c_2 > \alpha_2$) the trade pattern remains unchanged. The home country continues to be an exporter of agricultural goods and an importer of manufacturing goods. A sufficient condition for this to happen is, as mentioned earlier, that the expansion is ultra-biased towards agriculture (i.e., $\alpha_1 < 0$). Thailand and Burma during the period of 1870–1910 may, in a sense, offer examples of case b, where their production and exports of rice grew very rapidly (about 10 to 13 times during the period). Such an expansion (which was instigated by the opening of the Suez Canal, etc.) was made possible by the cultivation of vast lands in the delta areas for the production of rice in these countries. Thus, such an expansion may be ultra-biased towards agriculture ($\alpha_1 > 0$ and $\alpha_2 < 0$), which in turn implies $c_2 > \alpha_2$.

Case c. ($c_1 < \alpha_1, c_2 < \alpha_2$). In this case we have $E_{1\alpha} < 0$ and $E_{2\alpha} < 0$. Hence again using (12a), we may conclude that the $E_1 = 0$ curve shifts to the right and the $E_2 = 0$ curve shifts to the left. The analysis for this case is left to the interested reader. In this case, "industrialization" may or may not take place, depending on the relative magnitude of shifts of the $E_1 = 0$ and $E_2 = 0$ curves.

From the above condition, it is clear that in case b, industrialization will never take place, so that a sufficient condition for industrialization to *fail* is given by $c_2 > \alpha_2$ (which implies $c_1 < \alpha_1$). Hence a necessary condition for successful industrialization is given by $c_2 \leqq \alpha_2$, i.e., the growth contribution of the manufacturing goods sector does not fall short of the marginal propensity to spend on such goods.

From the above analysis, we may conclude that successful industrialization requires proper combinations of the demand and supply parameters of the commodity sectors, and it cannot, in general, be realized by manipulating only *some* of such parameters. For example, successful industrialization cannot be achieved by making an effort only to improve the productivity of the manufacturing goods sector α_2. This is because if the marginal propensity to spend on the manufacturing goods c_2 is large enough, then we may still have $c_2 > \alpha_2$ even after such an effort, and the effort of industrialization is bound to fail.

That successful industrialization depends on proper combinations of the demand and supply parameters may sound obvious. However, such a consideration is very often glossed over in the literature that seeks the means to accomplish successful industrialization.

Note that in all three cases, the home currency always appreciates (i.e., e falls), since the $H = 0$ curve always shifts to the left. That the home currency always appreciates by economic expansion regardless of its patterns can also be seen by observing that the balance of payments equilibrium ($H = 0$) can be written as

$$H(\bar{p}_{1f}, \bar{p}_{2f}, M/e, \alpha) = 0,$$

where we may recall (9') and the homogeneity of H. A simple differentiation of this equation yields,

$$H_3 \, d(M/e) + H_\alpha \, d\alpha = 0.$$

Recalling $H_3 < 0$ and $H_\alpha > 0$, we can at once conclude that economic expansion (an increase in α) must always lower e (for a fixed value of M). This conclusion is really the mirror image of the Komiya–Mundell Theorem that the balance of payments always improves by growth under fixed exchange rates. Also, from the above equation it is clear that a change in M only causes a proportional change in e so as to keep M/e constant for a given value of α. Namely, a change in nominal balances does not affect whether or not a country industrializes.

The above analysis for successful industrialization is done assuming a flexible exchange rate regime. The analysis for the fixed exchange rate case is analogous to the above analysis and is left to the interested reader. The analysis for such a case is slightly more complicated than the flexible exchange rate case. Namely, even if we start from the LRE position, the shifts of excess demand curves due to economic expansion create a balance of payments surplus, which in turn causes further shifts of excess demand curves due to changes in nominal balances.

4.   The Introduction of Nontradeables

In the previous discussion, we assumed away nontraded goods. However, it is well-known that nontradeables (such goods as services, the construction of buildings, highways, railways, dirt roads, medicare, education, etc.) play a large role in the national economy and often play an important role in the working of an open economy.

To consider the effect of nontradeables, we introduce a third commodity, which represents nontradeables. Let D_3 and X_3, respectively, signify the demand for and the output of commodity 3 (nontradeables). Then the budget condition (1) should be rewritten as,

$$p_1 D_1 + p_2 D_2 + p_3 D_3 + (L - M) \equiv p_1 X_1 + p_2 X_2 + p_3 X_3, \qquad (13)$$

where

$$D_i = D_i[p_1, p_2, p_3, Y(p_1, p_2, p_3, \alpha), M],$$

$$L = L[p_1, p_2, p_3, Y(p_1, p_2, p_3, \alpha), M]$$

$$X_i = X_i(p_1, p_2, p_3, \alpha), \quad Y(p_1, p_2, p_3, \alpha) \equiv \sum_{i=1}^{3} p_i X_i(p_1, p_2, p_3, \alpha).$$

Again defining $E_i \equiv D_i - X_i$, $i = 1, 2, 3$ and $H \equiv L - M$, we obtain

$$E_i = E_i(p_1, p_2, p_3, M, \alpha), \qquad i = 1, 2, 3, \qquad H = H(p_1, p_2, p_3, \alpha). \quad (3')$$

The function E_i, $i = 1, 2, 3$ (resp. H) is homogeneous of degree zero (resp. one) in p_1, p_2, p_3, and M. In terms of the E_i's and H, the budget condition (13) can be rewritten as,

$$p_1 E_1 + p_2 E_2 + p_3 E_3 + H \equiv 0. \quad (13')$$

Again assume the neoclassical, "bowed-out" production possibility surface and also assume gross substitutability with positive wealth effects for the demand side. Then we have, for $i, j = 1, 2, 3$,

$$\frac{\partial E_i}{\partial p_j} > 0, \qquad i \neq j, \qquad \frac{\partial E_i}{\partial p_i} < 0,$$

$$\frac{\partial E_i}{\partial M} > 0, \qquad \frac{\partial H}{\partial p_j} > 0, \quad (14)$$

$$0 < -\frac{\partial H}{\partial M} < 1,$$

where not all of the conditions in (14) are independent. We again use the notations such as $E_{ij} \equiv \partial E_i / \partial p_j$, $H_j \equiv \partial H / \partial p_j$, etc. Again denoting $c_i \equiv \partial D_i / \partial Y$, $i = 1, 2, 3$, $c_M \equiv \partial L / \partial Y$, $\alpha_i \equiv (\partial X_i / \partial \alpha) / Y_\alpha$, $i = 1, 2, 3$, and $Y_\alpha \equiv \partial Y / \partial \alpha$, we have from (13),

$$p_1 c_1 + p_2 c_2 + p_3 c_3 + c_M = 1, \qquad p_1 \alpha_1 + p_2 \alpha_2 + p_3 \alpha_3 = 1. \quad (9')$$

where we may assume $c_1, c_2, c_3, c_M > 0$, and where α_i's can be positive or negative. From (9'), we may easily obtain,

$$p_1(c_1 - \alpha_1) + p_2(c_2 - \alpha_2) + p_3(c_3 - \alpha_3) + c_M = 0. \quad (10')$$

Hence, unlike the two-commodity case, $c_1 > \alpha_1$ does *not* necessarily imply $c_2 < \alpha_2$. Similarly $c_2 > \alpha_2$ does not necessarily imply $c_1 < \alpha_1$.

Since the market for nontradeables must be cleared within the country, we must have

$$E_3(p_1, p_2, p_3, M, \alpha) = 0$$

in equilibrium. Solving this for p_3, we obtain,

$$p_3 = p_3(p_1, p_2, M, \alpha), \tag{15}$$

where it can be shown that the function p_3 is homogeneous of degree one in p_1, p_2, M, $p_{3j} \equiv \partial p_3/\partial p_j > 0$, $j = 1, 2$, $p_{3M} \equiv \partial p_3/\partial M > 0$ and that

$$\frac{\partial p_3}{\partial \alpha} = -\frac{(c_3 - \alpha_3)Y_\alpha}{E_{33}}, \tag{16}$$

so that

$$\frac{\partial p_3}{\partial \alpha} \gtreqless 0 \text{ according to whether } c_3 \gtreqless \alpha_3. \tag{17}$$

The possibility that $\partial p_3/\partial \alpha > 0$ is emphasized in the so-called "Scandinavian theory of inflation."

Substituting (15) into (3'), we may define the functions E_i^* and H^* by

$$E_i^*(p_1, p_2, M, \alpha) \equiv E_i[p_1, p_2, p_3(p_1, p_2, M, \alpha), M, \alpha], \qquad i = 1, 2, \tag{18a}$$

$$H^*(p_1, p_2, M, \alpha) \equiv H[p_1, p_2, p_3(p_1, p_2, M, \alpha)] \tag{18b}$$

where E_i^*, $i = 1, 2$, (resp. H^*) is homogeneous of degree zero (resp. one) in p_1, p_2, and M. Using the homogeneity of E_i^* and assuming $(-H^*) < 1$, we again obtain,

$$E_{ij}^* > 0, \qquad i \neq j,$$
$$E_{ii}^* < 0, \qquad H_j^* > 0, \qquad i, j = 1, 2, \tag{19}$$
$$0 < -H_3^* < 1,$$

where $E_{ij}^* \equiv \partial E_i^*/\partial p_j$, $i, j = 1, 2$, $H_j^* = \partial H^*/\partial p_j$, $H_3^* \equiv \partial H^*/\partial M$. Also, letting $p_{3\alpha} \equiv \partial p_3/\partial \alpha$, we may compute:

$$E_{i\alpha}^* \equiv \frac{\partial E_i^*}{\partial \alpha} = (c_i - \alpha_i)Y_\alpha + E_{i3}p_{3\alpha}, \qquad i = 1, 2, \tag{20a}$$

$$H_\alpha^* \equiv \frac{\partial H^*}{\partial \alpha} = c_M Y_\alpha + E_{i3}p_{3\alpha}. \tag{20b}$$

The equilibrium prices p_1 and p_2 under autarky can be determined by any two of the following three equations:

$$E_i^*(p_1, p_2, M, \alpha) = 0, \qquad i = 1, 2, \qquad H^*(p_1, p_2, M, \alpha) = 0.$$

The equilibrium value of p_3 under autarky can then be determined by using (16).

Let the $E_i^* = 0$ curve be the locus of (p_1, p_2) pairs for which

$$E_i^*(p_1, p_2, M, \alpha) = 0$$

for given values of M and $\alpha(i = 1, 2)$, and let the $H^* = 0$ curve be the locus of (p_1, p_2) pairs for which $H^*(p_1, p_2, M, \alpha) = 0$ for given values of M and α. Then it can be shown by using (19) that the $E_i^* = 0$ and the $E_2^* = 0$ curves are both upward-sloping, while the $H^* = 0$ curve is downward-sloping. Since E_i^* is homogenous of degree one in p_1, p_2, and M, the relative configuration of the $E_1^* = 0$ and the $E_2^* = 0$ curves are the same as the one described in Figure 1, in which E_1, E_2, and H are, respectively, replaced by E_1^*, E_2^*, and H^*.

We now introduce international trade and define the balance of payments again by (6). Then using the budget condition (13′), we have

$$B = H^*(p_1, p_2, M, \alpha), \tag{8′}$$

in which the market for nontradeables is cleared (i.e., when $E_3 = 0$ holds). Equation (8′) corresponds to (8), the fundamental equation of the monetary approach to the balance of payments. Imposing the small country assumption, we again obtain the international arbitrage condition (9′). Using the homogeneity of the function H^* and (9′), we can rewrite (8′) as,

$$B = eH^*(\bar{p}_{1f}, \bar{p}_{2f}, M/e, \alpha).$$

First consider the fixed exchange rate case in which e is fixed. Then $B \neq 0$, in general, in the short-run situation in which M is fixed. Partial differentiation of H^* with respect to α yields

$$\frac{\partial H^*}{\partial \alpha} = c_M Y_\alpha + \frac{\partial p_3}{\partial \alpha}, \qquad \text{where } \frac{\partial p_3}{\partial \alpha} = -\frac{(c_3 - \alpha_3) Y_\alpha}{E_{33}},$$

as obtained in (20b). If nontradeables are assumed away, then $c_3 \equiv \alpha_3 \equiv 0$, so that $\partial H^*/\partial \alpha = c_M Y_\alpha > 0$, i.e., economic expansion always improves the balance of payments, which corresponds to the Komiya-Mundell Theorem mentioned earlier. However, with the presence of nontradeables, such a theorem does not hold in general. It can be seen easily from the above that the sign of $\partial H^*/\partial \alpha$ is indeterminate, depending on the sign of $\partial p_2/\partial \alpha$, the effect of expansion on the price of nontradeables. More specifically,

$$\frac{\partial H^*}{\partial \alpha} > 0, \qquad \text{if } \frac{\partial p_3}{\partial \alpha} > 0 \quad (\text{if } c_3 > \alpha_3),$$

$$\frac{\partial H^*}{\partial \alpha} \gtreqless 0, \qquad \text{if } \frac{\partial p_3}{\partial \alpha} < 0 \quad (\text{if } c_3 < \alpha_3).$$

Thus, economic expansion *can* deteriorate the balance of payments if $\partial p_3/\partial \alpha < 0$. This means that if economic expansion lowers the price of nontradeables, then due to the "expenditure switching effect" from money into nontradeables (or from tradeables into nontradeables), the balance of payments can deteriorate. This result is obtained by Takayama [1977]. Thus, if economic expansion is such that it pushes α_3 sufficiently high, it will give an adverse effect on the balance of payments. Thus the Komiya-Mundell Theorem need *not* hold in general.[5]

In many LDCs the import substitution policy that protects the domestic production of certain final products is often pursued. Such a policy turns the industries thus protected into *de facto* nontraded sectors. Also under such a policy, we would expect to have a situation in which $c_3 < \alpha_3$; it may then not be surprising that import substitution policies adopted in many LDCs after World War II resulted in the deterioration of their balance of payments.[6]

We now turn to the flexible exchange rate case and analyze the possibility for industrialization. The directions of the shift of excess demand curves are now indicated by (20). Note that such directions now depend also on $p_{3\alpha} \equiv \partial p_3/\partial\alpha$ as well as the relative magnitude of the c_i's and α_i's. Observe again

$$\left.\frac{\partial p_2}{\partial\alpha}\right|_{E_1^* = 0} = -\frac{E_{1\alpha}^*}{E_{12}^*}, \qquad \left.\frac{\partial p_2}{\partial\alpha}\right|_{E_2^* = 0} = -\frac{E_{2\alpha}^*}{E_{22}}, \qquad (12'a)$$

$$\left.\frac{\partial p_2}{\partial\alpha}\right|_{H^* = 0} = -\frac{H_\alpha^*}{H_2^*}. \qquad (12'b)$$

Recalling (5'), we may conclude from (12'):

(a) The $E_1^* = 0$ curve moves to the left (resp. right), if $E_{1\alpha}^* > 0$ (resp. < 0)
(b) The $E_2^* = 0$ curve moves to the left (resp. right), if $E_{2\alpha}^* < 0$ (resp. > 0)
(c) The $H^* = 0$ curve moves to the left (resp. right), if $H_\alpha^* > 0$ (resp. < 0)

Assume initially $E_1^* < 0$ and $E_2^* > 0$ so that the home country exports commodity 1 and imports commodity 2, while $H^* = 0$ by the assumption of

---

[5] This may explain the background of a large-scale devaluation of Mexican pesos in 1976, for example. Prior to the devaluation, Mexico engaged in a massive investment in nontradeables such as education, medicare, the construction of highways, dirt roads, etc., while the Mexican rate of growth was kept quite high (say, compared to that of the U.S.). Such a pattern of expansion pushed α_3 up [possibly making $(p_1\alpha_1 + p_2\alpha_2)$ negative, i.e., ultra-nontraded goods-biased growth], which in turn had an adverse effect on the balance of payments. In the meantime, the Mexican government increased the money supply to finance such a massive investment on nontradeables, which also had an adverse effect on the balance of payments. These two adverse effects caused a balance of payments crises *in spite of* Mexico's rapid growth, resulting in the devaluation of pesos in 1976.

[6] This point was raised by Motoyoshi Suzuki, a graduate student at Kobe University of Commerce in the course of my lectures in the spring of 1985.

flexible exchange rates. Then we may conclude:

(a) If $E^*_{1\alpha} > 0$ and $E^*_{2\alpha} < 0$, then the $E^*_1 = 0$ and the $E^*_2 = 0$ both shift to the left so that industrialization may or may not take place.

(b) If $E^*_{1\alpha} < 0$ and $E^*_{2\alpha} > 0$, then the $E^*_1 = 0$ and the $E^*_2 = 0$ curves both shift to the right so that industrialization cannot take place.

(c) If $E^*_{1\alpha} < 0$ and $E^*_{2\alpha} < 0$, then the $E^*_1 = 0$ curve shifts to the right and the $E^*_2 = 0$ curve shifts to the left so that industrialization may or may not take place.

(d) If $E^*_{1\alpha} > 0$ and $E^*_{2\alpha} > 0$, then the $E^*_1 = 0$ curve shifts to the left and the $E^*_2 = 0$ curve shifts to the right, so that industrialization may or may not take place.

Note that cases a, b, and c in the above, respectively, correspond to cases a, b, and c in Section 3. Although case d is impossible in Section 3, it is possible here with the presence of nontradeables. In case a in which $E^*_{1\alpha} > 0$ and $E^*_{2\alpha} < 0$, industrialization can take place. However, unlike the case of Section 3, it is not possible to obtain a simple condition to warrant case a. The neccessary and suffcient condition for industrialization for this case can be written as,

$$(c_1 - \alpha_1)Y_\alpha + p_{3\alpha} > 0 \quad \text{and} \quad (c_2 - \alpha_2)Y_\alpha + p_{3\alpha} < 0,$$

where $p_{3\alpha} \equiv \partial p_3/\partial \alpha = -E_{13}(c_3 - \alpha_3)Y_\alpha/E_{33}$. If nontradeables are assumed away, then $p_{3\alpha} \equiv 0$ and the above condition reduces to the simple condition, $c_1 - \alpha_1 > 0$ and $c_2 - \alpha_2 < 0$, as obtained in Section 3. With the presence of nontradeables, the sign of $p_{3\alpha}$ is indeterminate depending on the relative magnitudes of c_3 and α_3. Hence the above condition cannot be warranted even if $c_1 - \alpha_1 > 0$ and $c_2 - \alpha_2 < 0$.

In short, the conditions for industrialization and nonindustrialization become more complicated with the introduction of nontradeables. Yet the main conclusion still remains. Namely, successful industrialization depends on proper combinations of the demand and supply parameters involved.

5. Dutch Disease Economics

Recently, there has been a considerable interest in the so-called "Dutch Disease Economics" (DDE) (cf., Gregory [1976], Snape [1979], Corden-Neary [1982], Corden [1982]). This is concerned with the general equilibrium effects of a sectoral boom in the traded goods producing part of the economy. The booming sector can be North Sea oil for Britain in the 1970s, Schlochteren natural gas in the 1960s for the Netherlands, manufacturing goods in the 1960s for Japan, and gold in the 1850s for Australia, as described by Corden [1982]. As he pointed out, there can be many examples to which DDE may be applied.[7]

Typically, DDE is concerned with the three-sector economy, the "booming sector" (sector 1), the "lagging sector" (sector 2), and the nontradeable goods sector (sector 3), where the commodities in the first two sectors are traded internationally. In the case of Japan in the 1960s (to 1970s), for example, a rapid growth during the period is achieved by a remarkable expansion of the manufacturing goods sector (heavy and chemical industries such as steel and automobiles) accompanied by a sharp decrease in the domestic production of agricultural goods (such as wheat and corn).

The heart of DDE is not hard to understand. There is a boom in sector 1 having the initial effect of increasing income of the factors employed in that sector. The domestic prices of tradeables are fixed under the assumptions of a small country and fixed exchange rates. The extra income due to the boom would lower the relative price of tradeables *vis à vis* nontradeables (p_2/p_3), where the relative price of tradeables (p_1/p_2) is fixed under the small country assumption. In the pioneering study by Gregory [1976], it is assumed that the volume of imports is a decreasing function of p_2/p_3 and that the volume of exports is an increasing function of p_2/p_3. From this it follows at once that an increase in p_2/p_3 lowers the volume of imports and increases the volume of exports.

The analysis by Snape [1977], Corden-Neary [1982], and Corden [1982] is more sophisticated. Assume that each sector uses labor and the factor specific to the sector, where labor is assumed to be mobile among the sectors. A rise in the booming sector (1) pushes the real wage rate up, which causes the movement of labor away from sectors 2 and 3 into sector 1. Identifying sectors 1 and 2 as the mineral sector and the industrial sector, a fall in the output of sector 2 as a result of such an outflow of labor is called *direct de-industrialization*. As in Gregory, it is assumed that a rise in the booming sector increases the relative price of nontradeables *vis à vis* tradeables. This then causes outflow of labor from the traded goods sectors into the nontraded goods sector. Thus, the labor employed in and the output of sector 2 decreases further. This is called *indirect de-industrialization*. With these two effects, the output of sector 2 reduces sharply, making sector 2 the "lagging sector." Direct de-industrialization is distinguished from indirect de-industrialization in the sense that the relative price of nontradeables *vis à vis*

---

[7] Corden [1982, p. 2] remarked, "The term Dutch Disease was coined around 1975 when the problems that North Sea oil might create for Britain were widely discussed." The first printed reference that he can trace is the article "The Dutch Disease" in the *Economist*, November 26, 1977, p. 82–83. Calling the British problem the Dutch *disease* sounds outlandish. At least, the term "disease" may give the wrong focus, as Corden [1982] remarked. However, the term Dutch Discease Economics has gained much popularity, and, perhaps, few people pay much attention to the term "disease." Hence, following much of the literature, we call it DDE.

tradeables (which is often called the *real exchange rate*) is fixed in the former. In any case, the crux of the problem in DDE is simply the shift of resources due to changes in relative prices (which, in turn, is initiated by a "boom" in one sector).

The purpose of this section is to analyze DDE using the framework developed in the present paper. In spite of the fact that the problem of DDE involves international trade and balance of payments, few have analyzed the problem in such a context explicitly.[8] The first problem is how to define the "booming sector." Since there can be many causes of booms there are many facets involved in analyzing the problem, and we can naturally obtain different conclusions depending upon the causes of "booms." To avoid clutter and also to discuss the problem within the framework of the present paper, we simply say that sector 1 is the booming sector when α_1 is large. For given prices, economic expansion is heavily biased towards sector 1.

To consider DDE under the present framework, we define $p_T \equiv p_1/p_2$ (the relative price of tradeables) and $p_N \equiv p_3/p_2$ (the relative price of non-tradeables *vis à vis* tradeables). Imposing the small country assumption, we have $p_1 = p_2 = e$, where we set $\bar{p}_{1f} = \bar{p}_{cf} = 1$ by the choice of the unit of measurement. Then $p_T = 1$ and $p_N = p_3/e$. As mentioned earlier, a focal point of DDE is the effect of a "boom" on the relative price of nontradeables (p_N); it is argued that the boom increases p_N. We now examine the validity of this assertion. Under fixed exchange rates (which is typically assumed in DDE, e is fixed so that we may set $e = 1$ by the choice of the unit of measurement. Then we have $p_N = p_3$. Then simply recalling (17), we may assert that $\partial p_N/\partial \alpha > 0$ if and only if $c_3 > \alpha_3$. On the other hand, if $c_3 < \alpha_3$, i.e., if an increase in the demand for nontradeables due to an increase in income falls short of the increase in the output of the nontraded sector (for fixed prices), we have $\partial p_N/\partial x < 0$. This means that the relative price of nontradeables can decrease contrary to the DDE contention. It is possible that in the case of mineral booms such as North Sea oil and Schlochteren natural gas, we have $\alpha_3 < 0$, so that $c_3 > \alpha_3$ and $\partial p_N/\partial \alpha > 0$ (as contended by DDE). However, such an assumption may be questionable in other circumstances. At the least, we need to provide an explanation to link the assumption of $c_3 > \alpha_3$ with the type of "booms."

DDE also asserts that the volume of imports of the lagging sector increases (i.e., E_2 increases), and that the volume of exports of the booming sector also increase (i.e., $-E_1$ increases), where we assume $E_1 < 0$ and $E_2 > 0$. (See Gregory [1976], for example). To examine the validity of such assertions, we may recall (18a). Under fixed exchange rates, we have $p_1 = p_2 = e = 1$, and in

---

[8] This is often justified on the ground that the model focuses on the *real* aspect. However, as is well known, the balance of payments is intrinsically a monetary phenomenon, and we cannot discuss the real aspect of the problem separately from the monetary aspect.

the short-run situation M is fixed. Then recalling (20a), i.e.,

$$\frac{\partial E_i^*}{\partial \alpha} \equiv (c_i - \alpha_i)Y_\alpha + E_{i3}p_{3\alpha} \qquad i = 1, 2, \tag{21}$$

where $p_{3\alpha} = -(c_3 - \alpha_3)Y_\alpha/E_{33}$, and where $E_{i3} > 0$, $i = 1, 2$, and $E_{33} < 0$, we may assert that

$$-\frac{\partial E_1^*}{\partial \alpha} > 0 \qquad \text{if and only if } (c_1 - \alpha_1)Y_\alpha - \frac{E_{13}(c_3 - \alpha_3)Y_\alpha}{E_{33}} < 0,$$

$$\frac{\partial E_2^*}{\partial \alpha} > 0 \qquad \text{if and only if } (c_2 - \alpha_2)Y_\alpha - \frac{E_{23}(c_3 - \alpha_3)Y_\alpha}{E_{33}} > 0.$$

Thus, we cannot in general assert $-\partial E_1^*/\partial \alpha > 0$ and $\partial E_2^*/\partial \alpha > 0$ (as contended by DDE) even if $c_1 < \alpha_1$ and $c_2 > \alpha_2$. This is because the signs of these partial derivatives depend on the sign of $(c_3 - \alpha_3)$. If $c_3 - \alpha_3 > 0$ and $c_1 - \alpha_1 > 0$, then $-\partial E_1^*/\partial \alpha > 0$ as contended by DDE. However, if $c_3 - \alpha_3 < 0$, this may make the sign of $\partial E_2^*/\partial \alpha$ negative, contrary to DDE.

To examine the effect of a boom on the output of each commodity, we may observe:

$$X_i(p_1, p_2, p_3, \alpha) \equiv X_i[1, 1, p_3(1, 1, M, \alpha), \alpha] \equiv X_i^*(\alpha), \qquad i = 1, 2, 3,$$

where we may recall $p_1 = p_2 = e = 1$ in the present context. From this we may compute:

$$\frac{dX_i^*}{d\alpha} = X_{i3}\left(\frac{\partial p_3}{\partial \alpha}\right) + X_{i\alpha} = \left[-\frac{X_{i3}(c_3 - \alpha_3)}{E_{33}} + \alpha_i\right]Y_\alpha, \qquad i = 1, 2, 3, \tag{22}$$

where $X_{i3} \equiv \partial X_i/\partial p_3$. DDE asserts $dX_2^*/d\alpha < 0$, i.e., the output of the lagging sector should decrease by "direct and indirect de-industrialization." It should be easy to see from (22) that such a conclusion may not hold. The necessary and sufficient condition for $dX_2^*/d\alpha < 0$ can easily be obtained from (22) as

$$\alpha_2 - \frac{X_{23}(c_3 - \alpha_3)}{E_{33}} < 0, \qquad \text{or } \alpha_2 + X_{23}\frac{\partial p_3}{\partial \alpha} < 0, \tag{23}$$

where $X_{23} < 0$ and $E_{33} < 0$. If $\alpha_2 < 0$, then condition (23) is satisfied provided that $\partial p_3/\partial \alpha < 0$, i.e., the price of nontradeables falls as a result of the boom (which corresponds to the DDE contention).

DDE is concerned with some remarkable experiences such as North Sea oil, Schlochteren natural gas, Japanese industrialization in the 1960s, and the Australian gold rush in the 1850s. Its explanation is quite lucid. However, the above discussion indicates that the lucid exposition can be misleading. It appears that DDE requires a more careful analysis.

In the above, we assumed fixed exchange rates following much of the literature on this topic. The flexible exchange rate case can be analyzed analogously by using the framework developed in the previous section. We leave such a task to the interested reader. Also, the analysis of DDE when the boom is due to an exogenous rise in the foreign price of exportables (such as oil for Indonesia) can be analyzed analogously by considering an exogenous increase in $\bar{p}_{1f}$.

References

Anderson, R. K. and A. Takayama, Devaluation, the specie flow mechanism and the steady state, *Review of Economic Studies*, Vol. 44, p. 347–361, 1977.

Corden, W. M., Booming sector and Dutch disease economics: A survey, New York Meeting of the American Economic Association, Dec. 1982.

Corden, W. M. and J. P. Neary, Booming sector and de-industrialization in a small open economy, *Economic Journal*, Vol. 92, p. 825–848, 1982.

Drabicki, J. Z. and A. Takayama, The theory of comparative advantage in a monetary world, *Southern Economic Journal*, Vol. 50, p. 1–17, 1983.

Gregory, R. G., Some implications of the growth of the mineral sector, *Australian Journal of Agricultural Economics*, Vol. 20, p. 71–91, 1976.

Hicks, J. R., An inaugural lecture, *Oxford Economic Papers*, Vol. 5, p. 117–135, 1953.

Johnson, H. G., Toward a general theory of the balance of payments, in: H. G. Johnson, *International Trade and Economic Growth* Cambridge: Harvard University Press, Chapter 6, p. 153–168, 1958.

Johnson H. G., Economic development and international trade, *National ϕkonomisk Tidsskrift*, Vol. 97, p. 253–272, 1959. (Reprinted in his *Money, Trade, and Economic Growth* London: George Allen & Unwin, 1962).

Johnson, H. G., The monetary approach to the balance of payments, *Journal of International Economics*, Vol. 7, p. 251–262, 1977.

Jones, R. W., A three-factor model in theory, trade and history, in: *Trade, Balance of Payments and Growth* (J. N. Bhagwati, R. W. Jones, R. A. Mundell, and J. Vanek (eds). Amsterdam: North-Holland, 1971.

Komiya, R., Economic growth and the balance of payments: A monetary approach, *Journal of Political Economy*, Vol. 77, p. 33–45, 1969.

Mundell, R. A., *International Economics*. New York: Macmillan, 1968.

Rybczynski, T. M., Factor endowments and relative commodity prices, *Economica*, Vol. 22, p. 336–341, 1955.

Samuelson, P. A., Ohlin was right, *Swedish Journal of Economics*, Vol. 73, p. 365–384, 1971.

Snape, R. H., Effects of mineral development on the economy, *Australian Journal of Agricultural Economics*, Vol. 21, p. 147–156, 1977.

Takayama, A., Economic growth and international trade, *Review of Economic Studies*, Vol. 31, p. 206–220, 1964.

Takayama, A., *International Trade: An Approach to Theory*. New York: Holt, Rinehart, and Winston, 1972.

Takayama, A., Economic growth and the balance of payments: A further analysis, *Journal of Economics and Business*, Vol. 30, p. 1–7, 1977.

Takayama, A., On theorems of general competitive equilibrium of production and trade—a survey of some recent developments in the theory of international trade, *Keio Economic Studies*, Vol. 19, p. 1–37, 1982.

Part II

THEORY AND APPLICATIONS

5

Expenditure Patterns and International Trade in Quesnay's Tableau Economique

TAKASHI NEGISHI

Department of Economics
The University of Tokyo
Hongo Bunkyo-ku, Tokyo
Japan

1.

The traditional interpretation of the simplified form or the final version of Quesnay's tableau economique was based on suppositions that landowners spend half their rent income on agricultural and half on manufactured products, while workers both in agriculture and manufacturing spend their whole wage income on food (agricultural products), and that the fixed capital (the original advance) of agriculture (the productive sector) consists entirely of the products of manufacture (the unproductive sector).[1] This interpretation suffers from some weaknesses. Firstly, the supposition of different expenditure patterns between landowners and workers is not consistent with Quesnay's assumption of the identical expenditure pattern of all the classes in his original tableau with zigzags. Secondly, it is more natural to consider that the fixed capital of agriculture consists entirely of the agricultural products, since it mainly consists of horses and other animals.[2]

---

[1] Blaug [1978], p. 27; Eagly [1974], p. 23. See also Engels [1878], p. 234.

[2] Apart from the problem of what Quesnay really meant, the traditional supposition in this respect may be defended purely logically, since in the tableau agriculture is defined not as agriculture in general but as a sector which can yield rent, represented by grain farming with the most efficient horse-drawn plough technique, and all other activities, which may include cattle breeding, are called manufacturing.

Meek [1962], Barna [1975, 1976], and Eltis [1975a, 1975b] insist, however, that all the problems and apparent inconsistencies in the interpretations of Quesnay's tableau economique are solved when Quesnay's published works including *L'Ami des hommes* and *Philosophie rurale* are read as a whole. According to this new interpretation, the fixed capital of agriculture consists entirely of the agricultural products and international trade, i.e., export of food and import of manufactured products is emphasized so as to make an identical expenditure pattern between landowners and workers possible. It is, however, one thing to accept the new interpretation as superior to the traditional one, and it is quite another to follow uncritically all the conclusions derived by Quesnay by using the tableau economique. The introduction of international trade, particularly, makes the following argument of Quesnay entirely untenable.

It can be seen from the distribution delineated in the tableau that if a nation's expenditure went more to the sterile expenditure side than to the productive expenditure side, revenue would fall proportionally, and this fall would increase in the same progression from year to year successively. It follows that a high level of expenditure on luxury in the way of ornamentation and conspicuous consumption is ruinous. If, on the other hand, a nation's expenditure goes to the productive expenditure side, revenue will rise, and this rise will in the same way increase successively from year to year. Thus, it is not true that the type of expenditure is a matter of indifference.[3]

The type of expenditure is actually a matter of indifference, however, since any change in it can always be adjusted by a corresponding change in international trade so that there are no changes in the production and the revenue (rent) of the nation.[4] We shall demonstrate this by using the final version of the tableau in Section 2 and by using the original version of the tableau after a critical review of Eltis' [1975b] arguments to support Quesnay in Section 3. It should be emphasized that not merely changes in the expenditure pattern but changes in capital accumulation, if any, induced by it are relevant for economic growth or decline. While changes in expenditure pattern are entirely absorbed in changes in trade, and no changes in accumulation are induced under the new interpretation of the tableau, the expenditure pattern does matter for capital accumulation, somewhat ironically, under the traditional interpretation which assumes autarky, as will be shown in Section 4.

---

[3] Kuczynski-Meek [1972], p. 12 and Eltis [1975b].

[4] Samuelson [1982] is also against Quesnay in this respect but argued that expenditure patterns have effects on the level of output of different sectors, without paying attention to international trade.

2.

Consider Table 1, the final version of the tableau economique, though somewhat modified.[5] Each year agriculture advances £1 billion, i.e., 500 million in agricultural products and 500 million in manufactured products, for workers and produces £2.5 billion in agricultural products; while manufacturing advances £1 billion, i.e., 500 in agricultural products for raw materials and 250 million in agricultural products and 250 million in manufactured products for workers, and produces £1 billion in manufactured products. Landowners spend their rent income of £1 billion, half on agricultural products and half on manufactured products, so that the first 500 million in agricultural products and the first 500 million in manufactured products are sold out. Manufacturing buys the second 500 million in agricultural products using the £500 million received from landowners, and agriculture buys the second 500 million in manufactured products in return. Finally, manufacturing buys the third 500 million in agricultural products with the £500 million received from agriculture for the second 500 in manufactured products. Now £1 billion in money, 500 million in manufactured products, and 1 billion in agricultural products are in the hands of agriculture. Agriculture pays £1 billion rent to landowners, replaces annual advances of 500 million in agricultural products and 500 million in manufactured products, and covers the depreciation of the fixed capital, the so-called "interest" cost of agriculture (to replace

TABLE 1.

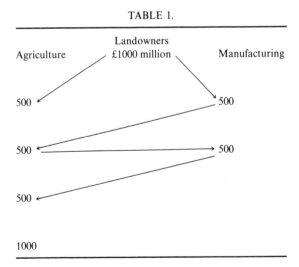

[5] Bauer [1895] and Eagly [1969].

TABLE 2.

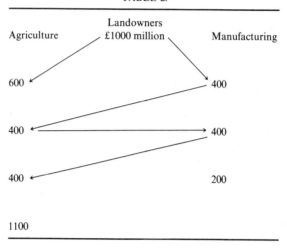

horses, etc.) by the remaining 500 million in agricultural products. Manufacturing, having 1 billion in agricultural products, exports 250 million in agricultural products and imports 250 million in manufactured products, so that annual advances of 750 million in agricultural products and 250 million in manufactured products are replaced. The economy can continue, therefore, to produce 2.5 billion in agricultural products and 1 billion in manufactured products.

Suppose the propensity to consume agricultural products changes from 0.5 to 0.6 not only for landowners but also for workers in agriculture and manufacturing. The tableau shifts from Table 1 to Table 2, though identical outputs, 2.5 billion in agricultural products and 1 billion in manufactured products, are already produced from the annual advances made before the propensity to consume has changed. Now landowners spend £600 million on agricultural products and £400 million on manufactured products, so that the first 600 in agricultural products and the first 400 in manufactured products are sold out. Manufacturing then buys 400 in agricultural products with the £400 million received from landowners, and agriculture in return buys the second 400 in manufactured products. Finally, manufacturing buys a further 400 in agricultural products with the £400 million received from agriculture. Now, 1 billion livres in money, 400 million in manufactured products, and 1.1 billion in agricultural products are in the hands of agriculture, so that it can pay £1 billion to landowners as rent, advance 600 million in agricultural products and 400 million in manufactured products to workers, and cover the interest cost with the remaining 500 million in agricultural products.

Having now 800 million in agricultural products and 200 in unsold manufactured products, manufacturing can replace advances for raw materials (500 in agricultural products) and advance 300 in agricultural products and 200 in manufactured products for workers. Changes in propensity to consume are entirely absorbed in changes in international trade, and the economy can continue to produce the unchanged outputs (2.5 billion in agricultural products and 1 billion in manufactured products), under the changed patterns of expenditure.

Similarly, Table 3 shows the case where the propensity to consume agricultural products changes from 0.5 to 0.4. Landowners spend £400 million on agricultural products and £600 million on manufactured products, so that the first 400 in agricultural products and the first 600 in manufactured products are sold out. Manufacturing then buys 600 in agricultural products with the £600 million received from landowners, and agriculture buys 400 in manufactured products with the £400 million received from landowners. The next step for manufacturing is to export 500 in agricultural products to be able to import 500 in manufactured products, which implies that manufacturing can supply 1.5 billion in manufactured products in all, i.e., 1 billion produced and already sold and 500 million imported and circled in Table 3. Agriculture then buys 200 million in imported manufactured products from manufacturing with £200 million, i.e., a part of the money already received from manufacturing when 600 in agricultural products are sold. Finally, manufacturing uses this £200 million and £400 million already

TABLE 3.

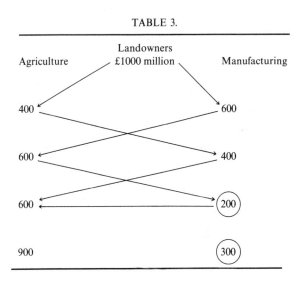

received when 400 in manufactured products are sold to agriculture to buy a further 600 in agricultural products. Since £400 million are left unused, out of £600 million received from manufacturing when the first 600 of agricultural products are sold, agriculture now has £1 billion to pay rent. Also 600 million in manufactured products and 900 million in agricultural products are in the hands of agriculture, so as to advance 400 in agricultural products and 600 in manufactured products for workers and to cover interest with the remaining 500 in agricultural products. Having bought 1.2 billion in agricultural products and exported 500 million, manufacturing has 700 million in agricultural products and 300 in unsold manufactured products, just enough to replace the advanced raw materials (500 in agricultural products) and to advance 200 in agricultural products and 300 in manufactured products for workers. The economy can continue, therefore, to produce 2.5 billion in agricultural products and 1 billion in manufactured products under the new patterns of expenditure.

Changing expenditure patterns make neither growth nor decline in output possible. There must be something wrong in Quesnay's reasoning which led him to the conclusion cited in Section 1.

3.

According to Eltis [1975b], accounts of the effect of the propensity to consume agricultural products on the rate of growth are found in *Philosophie rurale* and *L'Ami des hommes*, written by Quesnay and Mirabeau, and can best be analyzed by using the original Tableau with zigzags and by focusing attention on the financial receipts of the agricultural producers.[6]

The original Tableau economique with zigzags is given in Table 4 when the propensity to consume agricultural products is q and rent or revenue is R.[7] Landowners spend qR on agricultural products and $(1 - q)R$ on manufactured products. Agriculture then spends $(1 - q)qR$ on manufactured products out of qR received from landowners, while manufacturing spends $q(1 - q)R$ on agricultural products out of $(1 - q)R$ received from landowners. Agriculture further spends $(1 - q)q(1 - q)R$ on manufactured products out of $q(1 - q)R$ just received from manufacturing, while manufacturing spends $q(1 - q)qR$ on agricultural products out of $(1 - q)qR$ just received from agriculture. In this way, agriculture ends up with the total receipt of money

---

[6] We cannot, however, understand Eltis' explanation of why the final tableau cannot be used to consider the effect of variable expenditure patterns. As we shall see, the original version is rather inconvenient for this purpose.

[7] Table 4 is originally due to Hishiyama [1960] and reproduced in Eltis [1975a].

TABLE 4.

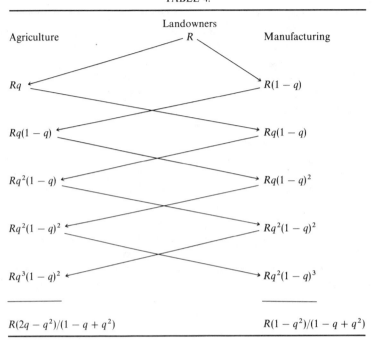

Agriculture   Landowners   Manufacturing
                                     R

Rq $R(1-q)$

$Rq(1-q)$ $Rq(1-q)$

$Rq^2(1-q)$ $Rq(1-q)^2$

$Rq^2(1-q)^2$ $Rq^2(1-q)^2$

$Rq^3(1-q)^2$ $Rq^2(1-q)^3$

$R(2q-q^2)/(1-q+q^2)$ $R(1-q^2)/(1-q+q^2)$

$R(2q - q^2)/(1 - q + q^2)$, while manufacturing ends up with the total receipt of $R(1 - q^2)/(1 - q + q^2)$.

Suppose agriculture advances annually £1 billion and pays rent of £1 billion, and the propensity to consume agricultural products is 0.5. In the Tableau's zigzags, both agriculture and manufacturing receive £1 billion and spend £500 million on the products of the other sector, while manufacturing uses the other £500 million as advances for raw materials which are bought from agriculture at the end of the year. Thus, the economy's whole stock of money, £1 billion, will reach agriculture by the end of the year. Since agriculture is assumed to produce £2 billion in products from £1 billion in annual advances, it is left with £1 billion in money, £500 million in manufactured products, and £500 million in agricultural products, so that it can pay again £1 billion in rent and advance again £1 billion in agricultural and manufactured products for workers. Manufacturing is left with £500 million in raw materials and £500 million in other agricultural products, half of which are assumed to be exported in order to be able to import manufactured products. The economy can continue, therefore, to produce £2 billion in agricultural products and £1 billion in manufactured products.

Eltis [1975b] insists, however, that things will be quite different when q is not equal to 0.5, say when $q = 0.4$. The Tableau's zigzags bring £842 million (obtained by substituting $q = 0.4$ into $1000(2q - q^2)/(1 - q + q^2)$) instead of £1 billion to agriculture and £1.105 billion (obtained from $1000(1 - q^2)/(1 - q + q^2)$) instead of £1 billion to manufacturing. Agriculture receives a further £552.5 million from manufacturing for sales of raw materials at the end of the year, since half of the £1.105 billion that manufacturing receives is assumed to be put aside by manufacturing for its advances. However, agriculture spends six-tenths of £842 million it receives from the zigzags (or £505 million) on manufactured products and has to pay £1 billion on rent. Agriculture therefore has a financial deficit of £110.5 million (i.e., 842 + 552.5 − 505 − 1000). Following Quesnay and Mirabeau, Eltis assumes that half the deficiency is met by landowners who accept lower rents than those previously agreed. Then half of £110.5 million has to be met by a fall in the annual advance in agriculture from £1 billion to £945 million, since Eltis considers that agriculture must sell its advance for the next year to get enough money to pay rent. The economy has to start next year with £945 million in agricultural advances and the same amount of rent, which implies that agricultural products are only £1.89 billion. It can be shown, in this way, that the economy eventually declines at a rate of 5.5 percent per annum.

Naturally, questions may arise with regard to the above arguments of Eltis concerning Quesnay's theory of economic growth and decline. When $q = 0.4$, the Tableau's zigzags bring £1.105 billion to manufacturing and manufacturing spends four-tenths of it or £442 million on agricultural products in zigzags, so that at the end of the year manufacturing has £663 million in money. Why does manufacturing not spend the whole £663 million instead of only £552.5 million on agricultural products at the end of the year? Since manufacturing need not pay rent to landowners, it is of no use for it to keep money unutilized.[8] Eltis insists that a part of the annual advances in agriculture has to be sold, i.e., capital must be expended in agriculture when agriculture has a financial deficit. Since a financial deficit means that agriculture has unsold products which were originally intended to be sold, however, it implies the accumulation of an unintended stock of products, and not necessarily the decline in capital to be advanced. To get enough money to pay rent, therefore, it is enough to sell those products originally intended to be sold, and it is not necessary to sell products which were intended to be advanced.

As a matter of fact, agriculture receives $R(2q - q^2)/(1 - q + q^2)$ from the Tableau's zigzags and manufacturing receives, similarly, $R(1 - q^2)/$

---

[8] Hoarding is not the problem here. Eltis himself must admit that manufacturing is willing to buy more than £552.5 million in agricultural products at the end of the year, since he argued. as we just saw, that agriculture must sell its advances for the next year to get enough money to pay rent, which of course can be bought only by manufacturing.

$(1 - q + q^2)$, i.e., 842 and 1105 respectively if $R = 1000$ and $q = 0.4$. If manufacturing spends on agricultural products all the money that it does not spend in zigzags, i.e., $(1 - q)R(1 - q^2)/(1 - q + q^2)$ or 663, agriculture can pay rent R or 1000 after it spends $(1 - q)R(2q - q^2)/(1 - q + q^2)$ or 505 on manufactured products in zigzags, since we have generally

$$R(2q - q^2)/(1 - q + q^2) + R(1 - q)(1 - q^2)/(1 - q + q^2)$$
$$- R(1 - q)(2q - q^2)/(1 - q + q^2) = R,$$

or $842 + 663 - 505 = 1000$. A propensity to consume agricultural products that is lower than 0.5 does not cause any financial deficit for agriculture, and the economy can continue to produce unchanged amounts of agricultural and manufactured products. Incidentally, manufacturing has to sell £1105 million in manufactured products in zigzags, while it produces only £1000 million in manufactured products if $R = 1,000$ and $q = 0.4$. In the course of zigzags, therefore, manufacturing has to export some of the agricultural products it bought so as to be able to import the additional manufactured products necessary to carry on the zigzags. This was already pointed out in our consideration of Table 3 in Section 2.

Similarly, we cannot accept Eltis' argument that agriculture has a financial surplus and the economy grows eventually at 4.2 per cent when $q = 0.6$. Eltis considered that agriculture receives £1.105 billion in the Tableau's zigzags, spends there £442 million on manufactured products, and receives £421 million from manufacturing at the end of the year. In the course of zigzags, manufacturing receives merely £842 million and spends there £505 million, however. How can manufacturing spend £421 million at the end of the year? If manufacturing spends all the money it has, i.e., £337 million (obtained by 842×0.4), on agricultural products at the end of the year, agriculture has neither surplus nor deficit, since $1105 + 337 - 442 = 1000$. Manufacturing need not buy more than £337 million agriculture at the end of the year, since it has already bought enough agricultural products in the course of zigzags so as to advance raw materials (500) and feed workers (300), since $500 + 300 < 505 + 337$. Actually, we have to understand that manufacturing sold back £42 million in agricultural products to buy back £42 million in manufactured products in the course of the Tableau's zigzags. Similarly, agriculture has to sell £42 million in manufactured products to buy back £42 million in agricultural products in zigzags, since otherwise it sold £1.442 billion $(1105 + 337)$ in agricultural products and the remaining £558 million $(2000 - 1442)$ in agricultural products are not enough to advance £600 million in agricultural products to workers. We have to say that the original Tableau with zigzags is in this respect clumsy, inconvenient, and likely to confuse even such an eminent scholar as Eltis.

We have to conclude that Quesnay's theory of economic growth is not a successful one so far as it is related to the effects of expenditure patterns on economic growth. As Eltis [1975b] pointed out, many developing countries today face precisely the same conditions which Quesnay used to analyze the problems involved in achieving economic growth. However, we cannot blame these countries for adopting policies of favoring manufacturing at the expense of agriculture on the basis of Quesnay's theory of economic growth.

4.

It may be interesting to see that different expenditure patterns may induce economic growth or decline in the traditional interpretation of the final version of the tableau economique. Table 1 is interpreted such that each year agriculture advances £1 billion in agricultural products for workers while manufacturing advances £500 million in agricultural products for raw materials and £500 million in agricultural products for workers, the fixed capital of agriculture consists entirely of manufactured products, and there is no possibility for international trade. Landowners spend their £1 billion half on agricultural and half on manufactured products. Agriculture buys 500 in manufactured products to cover the depreciation of the fixed capital, and manufacturing buys 500 in agricultural products to replace the advances for raw materials and another 500 in agricultural products to replace advances to workers. Agriculture ends up with £1 billion in money to pay rent and £1 billion in unsold agricultural products to replace advances to workers. The economy can continue, therefore, to produce 2.5 billion in agricultural products and 1 billion in manufactured products.

If the expenditure pattern of landowners is changed and they spend £600 million on agricultural and £400 million on manufactured products, manufacturing ends up, as before, with 1 billion in agricultural products, just enough to replace advances, while agriculture has £1 billion in money to pay rent, £600 million in manufactured products as gross investment to the fixed capital or £100 million in manufactured products as net investment to the fixed capital, and £900 million in agricultural products, which means a £100 million decline in annual advances to workers, as is shown in Table 5. Since manufacturing can continue to produce £1 billion in manufactured products, therefore, agricultural products grow or decline depending on the relative marginal productivity of the fixed and circulating capitals. Table 6 shows similarly the case where landowners spend £400 million on agricultural products and £600 million on manufactured products. The fixed capital declines by £100 million and circulating capital increases by £100 million. The economy grows, in the case of Table 6, if it declines in the case of Table 5, and vice versa.

TABLE 5.

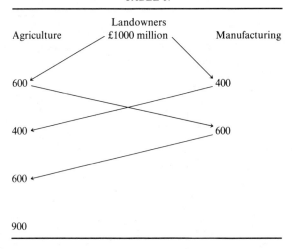

900

TABLE 6.

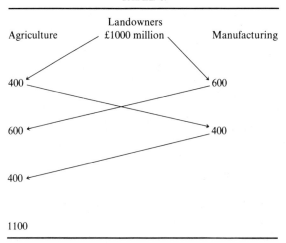

1100

The point is that changes in expenditure patterns are relevant for economic growth or decline only if they induce changes in the composition of capital such that productivity changes. Higher propensity towards consuming agricultural products leads to economic growth only if manufactured products which are saved are more productive as capital than as agricultural products which are dissaved. This seems to have more relevance for developing countries than the physiocratic dogma that agriculture itself has something to do with economic growth. Larger consumption of agricultural products itself has nothing to do with economic growth, even if agriculture is more productive than manufacturing in the sense that agriculture alone can yield rent. We can admit that "the rate of growth can be a function of what is consumed rather than the rate of investment to consumption," in a way different from Eltis' [1975b] argument.

5.

On the occasion of the publishing of our comments on Eltis' studies of Quesnay in a volume entitled *Recent Developments in Japanese Economics*, it is our pleasant duty to acknowledge my indebtedness to the Japanese tradition of studies in the history of political economy. As an importer of economic sciences in the past, intensive studies have been made in Japan on mercantilism, physiocrasy, classical economics, and Marxian economics. Results of such studies were, unfortunately, published chiefly in Japanese and consequently were not well known internationally. The case of Hishiyama [1960], which was published in English, is a rare exception. It should be emphasized, however, that what Japan can export is not limited to the area of mathematical and quantitative economics.

In as early as 1956, K. Shibata, a famous economic theorist known for the so-called "Shibata-Okishio theorem" on the falling rate of profit, argued that expenditure pattern of landowners and workers in manufacturing is a matter of indifference (see p. 86) for the original tableau economique with zigzags, if it is rationally interpreted as a model of reproduction. T. Watanabe, an historian of early economic thought, supported the conclusion of Shibata's study, though his reason was somewhat different from Shibata's. According to Watanabe [1961], the original tableau economique is a model designed to express Quesnay's view on the importance of the expenditure pattern of landowners, which was influenced by Cantillon and is incomplete as a model of reproduction so that it cannot be interpreted rationally.[9] These studies were made, however, before the publication of Meek [1962] and therefore international trade was not taken into consideration. Our conclusion in this article is that expenditure patterns are a matter of indifference even if international trade is introduced following Meek [1962] in the interpretation of the tableau economique.

---

[9] See Shibata [1946] and Watanabe [1961, p. 341–398]. The latter also contains a useful survey of Japanese literature on Quesnay. For the Shibata-Okishio theorem, which denies Marx's law of falling rate of profit, see Shibata [1934] and Okishio [1961].

References

Barna, T., Quesnay's tableau in modern guise, *Economic Journal*, Vol. 85, p. 485–496, 1975.

Barna, T., Quesnay's model of economic development, *European Economic Review*, Vol. 8, p. 315–338, 1976.

Bauer, S., Tableau economique, *Economic Journal*, Vol. 5, p. 1–21, 1895.

Blaug, M., *Economic Theory in Retrospect* (3rd ed.). Cambridge: Cambridge University Press, 1978.

Eagly, R. V., A physiocratic model of dynamic equilibrium, *Journal of Political Economy*, Vol. 77, p. 66–84, 1969.

Eagly, R. V., *The Structure of Classical Economic Theory*, Oxford: Oxford University Press, 1974.

Eltis, W. A., Francois Quesnay: A reinterpretation 1. The tableau economique, *Oxford Economic Papers*, Vol. 27, p. 167–200, 1975a.

Eltis, W. A., Francois Quesnay: A reinterpretation 2. The theory of economic growth, *Oxford Economic Papers*, Vol. 27, p. 327–351, 1975b.

Engels, F., Herrn Eugen Dührings Umwälzung der Wissenschaft, 1878, in: *Karl Marx Friedrich Engels Werke*, 20, Berlin: Dietz Verlag, pp. 1–303, 1962.

Hishiyama, I., The tableu economique of Quesnay, *Kyoto University Economic Review*, Vol. 30(1), p. 1–45, 1960.

Kuczynski, M., and R. L. Meek. (ed.), *Quesnay's Tableau Economique*. London: Macmillan, 1972.

Meek, R. L., *The Economics of Physiocracy*. London: Allen and Unwin, 1962.

Okishio, N., Technical changes and rate of profit, *Kobe University Economic Review*, Vol. 7, p. 85–99, 1961.

Samuelson, P. A., Quesnay's tableau economique as a theorist would formulate it today, in: I. Brandley and M. Howard (eds). *Classical and Marxian Political Economy*, London: Macmillan p. 45–78, 1982.

Shibata, K., Quesnay no keizaihyo no nazo nitsuite (On the mystery of Quesnay's Tableau Economique), *Yamaguchi Journal of Economics*, Vol. 7 (5, 6), p. 1–10, 1956.

Shibata, K., On the law of decline in the rate of profit, *Kyoto University Economic Review*, Vol. 9(1), p. 61–75, 1934.

Watanable, T., *Sosetsusha no Keizaigaku (Economics of Founders)*. Tokyo: Miraisha, 1961.

6

Progress of Japanese National Accounts in an International Perspective of the SNA Review*

YOSHIMASA KURABAYASHI

HIROSHI MATSUURA

The Institute of Economic Research
Hitotsubashi University
Kunitachi, Tokyo
Japan

Faculty of Arts and Science
Tokyo Kasei Gakuin College
Machida-shi, Tokyo
Japan

1. Introduction

The publication of the new national accounts series by the Economic Planning Agency of the Japanese Government in August 1978 marked an epoch in the progress of Japanese National Accounts. In essence, the new national accounts followed the guidelines set forth with the most scrupulous attention by Kokumin Keizai Keisan Chosa Iinkai (the Council for National Accounts Studies), which were established by the Japanese Government for the review and revision of Japanese national accounts. During the course of deliberations at the council, it was strongly recommended that the new Japanese system of national accounts should adapt itself to the United Nations system of national accounts, usually called SNA in as much detail as possible. Why did the council recommend SNA for the model system? First, SNA was considered as the most comprehensive and integrated system of national accounts ever designed for practical implementation, and economic data could be collected and processed in a consistent way so that they might adequately meet any analytical demands of highly technical levels. Second, the

---

*The views expressed in this paper are those of the authors and do not represent those of the institutions with which they are affiliated.

DEVELOPMENTS IN
JAPANESE ECONOMICS

99

council considered that a full adaptation of Japanese national accounts to international standards would enhance the international comparability of national accounts data. As one of the French experts on national accounts once wrote (Bérnard [1972] p. 636), SNA could be regarded as one of the standard languages for collection, processing, and dissemination of economic data in both syntactic and morphological aspects. The new Japanese system of national accounts used to be called in Japanese *Shin SNA* (a new SNA) by Japanese economists and national accounts statisticians, implying that the system itself was brand-new and was also adapted to the United Nations revised system of national accounts.

With the introduction of the new system of national accounts, Japan has become one of a few countries in the world whose system of national accounts can provide all kinds of necessary information that can be extracted from the SNA. The special merit of the Japanese system has been internationally appreciated by national accounts statisticians and has often been referred to in their works. Having learned from the accumulation of adequate knowledge and experiences of data collection and processing since the introduction of the new Japanese system, now Japanese national accounts statisticians have sufficient reasons to believe that they will be able to actively participate in international discussions for further development of the SNA. Emerging from the necessary outcome of the progress of the events, it happens that the SNA is undergoing the review for the revision, 1990 being the target year of the revision. In what follows in this paper, the authors intend to review the major issues of Japanese national accounts in the light of recent developments of the SNA review for the revision and to present a simplified and integrated system of national accounts for the revision of the SNA. In doing this, experiences of compiling a Japanese system of national accounts that have been accumulated in the past decade will be duly reflected upon and incorporated in the design of the simplified and integrated system.

2. Towards the Revision of the 1968 SNA

First, recent developments of the SNA review work with which the United Nations Statistical Office, with the joint efforts and cooperation of other international organizations, has been concerned will be discussed. It was in March 1982 that a group of experts convened at the headquarters of the United Nations to consider a number of major issues on the SNA for clarification and updating which were incorporated in a paper prepared by Professor Richard Ruggles in his capacity as a consultant to the United Nations Statistical Office. At the meeting, the expert group concluded to recommend that a long-term review of the SNA should be undertaken and that its revision should be finalized and take effect by 1990. Moreover, the expert group set forth priorities for implementing the revisions and recommended that the review should be extended in close cooperation with the statistical offices of interested international organizations. Based on, to a great extent, the recommendations by the expert group, the United Nations Statistical Office proposed a long-term work program for the revision of the SNA for consideration at the twenty-second session of the Statistical Commission, which, in turn, endorsed the work program.

Subsequently, the Inter-Secretariat Working Group on National Accounts was established with the participation of the secretariat from the United Nations Statistical Office and the statistical offices of the Organization for Economic Cooperation and Development (OECD) and the European Communities (EUROSTAT); that group was later expanded to include the secretariats from the International Monetary Fund (IMF) and the World Bank. The Working Group has convened for several meetings since its establishment in 1982 with the intention of planning and coordinating the implementation of the SNA review work. The outline of the work program and the strategy to achieve the revision of the SNA by 1990 was drawn up by the Working Group. It recommended that the implementation of the SNA review should proceed along the following lines: In the first phase, topics that need to be reviewed should be identified and reflected upon in the work program. In the next phase, the topics should be considered in a series of expert group meetings, each of which would take up an appropriate group of subjects along the lines of the topics identified in the first phase. Finally, in the third phase, one or a few expert groups should be organized to integrate the solutions of the separate expert group meetings into a revised SNA. The approximate time schedule for the SNA review would be 1983–1985 for the preparation and execution of the first phase, 1986–1988 for expert group meetings on groups of topics concerning the SNA review of the second phase, and, finally, 1989–1990 for the concluding reviews by an expert meeting (or meetings) of the third phase so that the solution proposed by the expert group meetings could be integrated into a revised version of the SNA.

It should be also noted that a full-day SNA review session was organized at the Nineteenth General Conference of the International Association for Research in Income and Wealth which took place in August 1985 at Noordwijkerhout, the Netherlands, highlighting on such issues as SNA structure and sectoring and reconciliation with other statistical standards relating to the SNA [United Nations, 1986a]. Other sessions of the General Conference also included those topics of income distribution statistics, flow-of-funds and financial statistics, regional accounts, treatment of interest and financial intermediaries, integration of economic and social statistics, and measurement of services which are quite relevant to the SNA review work.

It would be quite unfair to conclude this section without referring to the most recent expert meeting which was organized by the United Nations Statistical Office and held in July 1986 at Palais des Nation, Geneva, in which issues of concern to developing countries regarding the SNA review and the structure of the revised SNA were discussed. The major issues taken up at the first expert meeting were: 1) SNA review organization, 2) uses of SNA information, and 3) the SNA conceptual framework. It is true that a wide range of topics was covered at the meeting, but it is particularly pertinent here that selected issues concerning the SNA conceptual framework that were discussed at the meeting be mentioned. They are: the structure of the revised SNA, the reconciliation of the SNA with related statistical systems, micro-macro links, input-output tables, treatment of the household sector, public sector accounts, and national accounting in constant prices. The second expert meeting was specifically focused on the conceptual framework of the revised SNA, its transactors and transactions and valuation, some conceptual issues concerning the entries of the revised SNA, and the links between the SNA and related statistical systems. Having in mind the points discussed at the expert meeting on the SNA structure, the next section will be directed to specific issues for designing the basic structure of the revised SNA.

3.   Structure and Sectoring of National Accounts

As has been noted before, the major focus of this paper is to present a simplified and integrated system of national accounts for the revised SNA. However, the system cannot be designed without touching on some of the basic issues of the structure and sectoring of national accounts which several academic and expert meetings have addressed in the past years. Two issues are specifically relevant to the discussions that follow. They are: 1) core accounts versus the building blocks approach and 2) the dual sectoring principle and its implications.

a.   Core Accounts and the Building Blocks Approach

At the 1983 meeting of national accounts experts at the OECD, R. van Eck, G. N. Gorter, and H. K. van Tuinen argued in their paper [van Eck, Gorter, and van Tuinen, 1983] that the SNA could be made more flexible by restructuring it in the form of a central system of core accounts to which building blocks would be added to meet particular analytic needs. The building blocks could employ modified definitions of the aggregates contained in the core accounts, nonstandard classifications, and alternative valuation schemes. The authors also argued that the core should be simplified in some respect by adhering more strictly to the so-called transactor/transaction principle. This would imply omitting some conventional elements of imputation such as the income ascribed to owner-occupation of dwelling or to owner-consumption of farm produce and avoiding attributions such as the inclusion of employers' contribution to private pension schemes in the compensation of employees.

The Netherlands paper was used subsequently as the basis for discussing the future structure of the SNA at several informal expert group meetings. No final conclusions were reached on the coverage of the "core" accounts, which could be defined in terms of the present accounting structure of the SNA contained in the "blue book" (*A System of National Accounts*), could be restricted to a simplified set of accounts, or could be further extended beyond the present scope of the blue book. Further discussion will be needed, in this connection, on the exact nature of the supplementary guidelines in terms of satellite accounts and/or building blocks and their relation to the guidelines contained in the blue book. Again, the idea of the core accounts was further elaborated by van Tuinen and van Bochove [van Tuinen and van Bochove, 1986] in a paper presented to the Nineteenth General Conference of the International Association for Research in Income and Wealth:

> The core describes the most restricted part of the economy for which it is still possible to establish all interrelations specified in advanced systems of social accounting; thus it is a canonical accounting system. Its concepts are, due to the parsimony principle ["remain close to the perceptions of the economic agents"], as close as possible to those of the economic agents themselves and hence, too, to those of the respondents to the surveys on which its accounts and tables are based. As a consequence, the core is the system with the *maximum institutional content*. It is, in this sense, merely the logical next step in the evolution of the SNA, since conceptually a major difference between the 1968 SNA and the 1953 SNA was the institutional content. [van Bochove and van Tuinen, 1986, p. 150]

The core accounts, according to van Bochove and van Tuinen, are supplemented by a set of modules which are distinguished from the core accounts:

> The *core*, as outlined in section 5, is the economic statistician's exercise in restraint. Wherever possible, the conceptions and perceptions of transactor have been accepted as they are and the transactions described as they appear; the temptations of superimposing the economic statistician's own views have been resisted. The *modules*, in contrast, are the analysts' backyard. Here alternative economic theories, national accountants' own views, and purposes of special analysis may be drawn upon to obtain analytic descriptions of the economy or parts of it. Thus, whereas the core has maximum *institutional* content, modules transform the core data to *functional* systems. [van Bochove and van Tuinen, 1986, pp. 150–151]

It is clear from these remarks that van Bochove and van Tuinen's idea of the "core" has a strong predilection for the institutional approach. This is particularly the case for their institutional definitions of transactors and transactions. The institutional approach to the design of national accounts is sharply contrasted with the functional approach, as they state:

> The functional approach, in contrast, is analytic: it starts out with an analysis of the function of transactions. It looks behind their formal appearance to determine their "true" nature. In fact, it frequently concentrates on "processes," "products" and similar categories rather than on transactions. Consequently, transactions that are quite different in formal appearance may be lumped together and vice versa. Transactors are, in the functional approach, defined (if at all) in an indirect way, *viz.* as the performers of functions. They do not have to correspond to directly observable persons or institutions. Clearly, functional definitions and classifications reflect the view and judgements of the designer of the statistical system rather than those of the economic agents. [van Bochove and van Tuinen, 1986, p. 129]

Another way to introduce additional flexibility into the present SNA was suggested by Andre Vanoli in a paper [Vanoli, 1986] which was also presented at the Nineteenth General Conference of the International Association for Research in Income and Wealth. His approach to the flexibility of SNA is more orthodox than that of the Dutch authors in that flexibility would be introduced into the central framework but the present SNA should be retained by adding two subsystems that supplement the central framework. They are: 1) the intermediate system of accounts which are closely related to micro data and 2) the satellite accounts which are particularly useful for dealing with specific areas of socio-economic concerns to the system. A sharp contrast between the Dutch approach and the one by Vanoli becomes immediately clear if a few sentences are quoted from Vanoli's paper:

> Si l'on retient comme agrégat principal de production du système le Produit intérieur brut défini comme il l'est actuellement dans le SCN, il s'ensuit que certaines imputations (production pour compte propre, production imputée de services bancaires) font intégralement partie du système central et que les discussions générales sur l'élimination des imputations sont oiseuses....
>
> De meme si l'on voulait mettre à la base du système central le critère de l'entregistrement des transactions effectives, avec élimination de toute imputation ou ré-orientation de flux, il faudrait définir en conséquence de nouveau concepts et agrégats de production, consummation, revenue, etc....
>
> Le SCN actuel, complété par les comptes partimoine qui ne figuraient que pour mémoire dans le livre bleu de la révision 3, correspond à une des nombreuses variantes de Système central concevables. Comme il résulte d'une longue évolution et de nombreux compromis, il est sage de ne travailler qu'à la marge par rapport à lui. [Vanoli, 1986, pp. 159–161]

b.   Dual Sectoring of the SNA and Its Implications

At a paper presented to the Working Party on National Accounts and Balances of the Conference of European Statisticians which took place in March 1986, the statistical offices of the United Nations, OECD, EEC, in cooperation with the IMF and the World Bank jointly proposed a set of simplified core accounts structured on monolithic institutional sectoring and on the design of a fully articulated system so that the flexibility of the system could be attained by laying building blocks upon the core set of accounts. Contrary to the proposal made by Vanoli for maintaining the present structure of SNA intact so that it may be made flexible by linking the central system with other data sets, it is observed from the set of accounts that the proposed core set of accounts by the joint paper diverges from the fundamental structure of the 1968 SNA in two aspects. First, the proposed core set of accounts entirely ignores the dual sectoring principle on which the 1968 SNA is structured. Here, the dual sectoring principle means that the accounting design of national accounts should be subject to the duality of classifying transactors and transactions which stems from the real-financial dichotomy of the economy. It follows from the dual sectoring principle that in 1968 SNA transactors relating to production and capital formation are classified and recorded according to a kind-of-activity type of sectors, on the one hand, and those relating to income and outlay and capital financing are sorted out and recorded according to an institutional type of sectors, on the other.

Second, it should be stressed that the amount of statistical information that might be incorporated in the 1968 SNA could be magnified owing to the introduction of the so-called market (or screen) accounts in the structure. The market accounts are an ingenious device for introducing the *ex post* statistical information concerning the demand (uses) for and the supply (sources) of goods and services or the financial claim into the accounting framework of national accounts in which transaction flow is often distinguished and recorded according to different groups of transactors. As a result, the demand for and the supply of a commodity, for example, is explicitly recorded in the accounting framework by introducing a commodity account as indicated below:

Commodity Account	
Sources	Uses

Then the conventional recording of a transaction flow of the commodity between the producer and the consumer would be intervened by a commodity account (a market account) [Kurabayashi and Sakuma, 1980]:

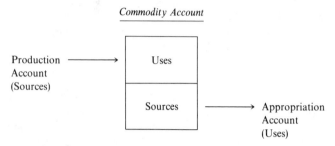

Commodity Account

A wide range of analytical dimensions could be added if market accounts are introduced in case of analytical needs. The monolithic structure of the proposed accounting framework in the joint paper precludes information from being put into the transactions flow of goods and services, of financial claims, or of different kinds of transfers together so that it may provide a coherent set of data. Still, one might argue that there is a so-called transactor/transaction principle at the heart of the 1968 SNA such that every transaction is to be recorded in the accounts of the individual who performs it and in the way he or she perceives it. However, the transactor/transaction principle should be immediately discredited if we recall the important roles played by a variety of market accounts in the 1968 SNA.

Brief comments on paragraph 31 of the United Nations document on the progress in the revision of SNA which were presented to the twenty-fourth session of the Statistical Commission held 23 February–4 March 1987 at the headquarters are pertinent to the point in question. The document states:

> One modification was to include value added in addition to operating surplus, as a balancing item in the accounts, by subdividing the present SNA production accounts into two parts. That would make explicit in the accounts an important concept—value added—which was now only implicitly available through alternative table presentations. Accepted also was the suggestion to subdivide the income and outlay account further between compensation of employees, operating surplus, entrepreneurial income, net indirect taxes and property income, on the one hand, and current transfers, on the other, so that an intermediate income concept would be made explicit, which would be the sectoral equivalent of national income for the economy as a whole. The latter concept might be useful for analysing the rentability of the enterprise sector, which does not generate income only through investments in its own production process, but also through financial investments in other production processes and elsewhere. [United Nations, 1986b, p. 16]

As shall be seen in the following section, the explicit presentation of the concept of value added in both the production account and in income and outlay in the class of Accounts I [SNA, 1968, para. 8.11, p. 139] would present additional and great complexity in the revised SNA, which is absolutely adverse to the cause of simplifying the revised SNA. Indeed, the concept is not only redundant for a simplified system of national accounts, but it also has less analytical uses. By placing undue importance on rentability of the enterprise, it appears that for the author of the United Nations document the enterprise should be looked on not as if it might be an institution seeking an efficient combination of factors of production, but as if it is a reckless going concern which is madly engaged in the money game of rentability, as many Japanese enterprises currently conduct on a worldwide scale without regarding their own social function.

Looking at the problems from all perspectives, we have to conclude that the dual sectoring structure of the 1968 SNA is not only necessary for the pillar of the revised structure of SNA but also sufficient to add the flexibility of the structure. We cannot help sharing the view expressed in a paper by the Central Bureau of Statistics of the Netherlands which criticizes the monistic nature of the accounting system proposed by the United Nations Statistical Office for consideration of 1985 OECD Meeting on National Accounts. The Dutch paper points out that the accounting system "should be considered a great impoverishment with respect to the current SNA, as the production process and the formation of value added are not described adequately and consequently the interdependence between that process and the financial one cannot be charted". Moreover, the paper continues by stating:

> "the strongest method for estimating national income cannot be used for the construction of the core of the system. This proposal would mean a step backwards in the development of the SNA". [A1, 1985, p. 17]

4.   A Simplified and Integrated System of National Accounts and Its Application to the Japanese Economy

Having commented on the conceptual issues arising out of discussions at the SNA review meetings, we have now reached the point at which a grand design for a simplified and integrated system of national accounts can be presented. Broadly speaking, a grand design for the system is constituted of three sets of accounts:

(a) an integrated system of national accounts
(b) a summary statement focusing on the interactions between the national and international transactions
(c) a simplified system of flow of funds accounts

In what follows, the component accounts will be discussed one after the other. After the design of an account is presented, the actual figures taken from the Japanese system of national accounts for the year of 1984 are filled in so that the system might be feasibly implemented. Then comments on the features of the Japanese economy will follow from the figures.

a.   An Integrated System of National Accounts

The structure of the system consists of four types of accounts. They are:

(a) sector production accounts, which give summary statements on the balance between the aggregate demand and supply of goods and services

(b) income formation accounts by sector, which describe the distribution of GDP and the formation of incomes that result from the distribution

(c) income appropriation accounts by sector, which report the sources and uses of incomes by sector

(d) capital formation and financing accounts by sector

Two additional comments are needed regarding the design of an integrated system of national accounts. First, it is true that there exist three alternative presentations for a fully articulated system of national accounts. They are: (1) a set of equations, (2) the accounting form of the profit and loss statement, which are often called "T-accounts", and (3) a matrix presentation. Though one of the authors of this paper feels it easy to represent a fully articulated system into a matrix presentation as the structure of SNA is illustrated in Table 2.1 in SNA, here the integrated system will be supplemented with another alternative, complying with the suggestions made by some of the experts at the United Nations Expert Group Meeting on the SNA Structure [United Nations, 1986, para. 25, p. 14]. Second, the idea of the dual sectoring principle, which has been referred to in the earlier section will be faithfully followed. Accordingly, the following groupings of sectors are applied to the sets of accounts of (a) and (b):

(1) industries, which are further subdivided into
    (i) non-financial activities,
    (ii) financial activities, including insurances
(2) producers of government services
(3) producers of private non-profit services serving households

It is particularly important to retain the producers of private non-profit services as an independent sector, because the contribution of the sector to the GDP is growing as the service economy grows, definitely with no exception in the Japanese economy. It is greatly feared from the recent discussions of the expert group on the SNA structure that a large and important amount of information will be lost if the sector is merged into private households without discerning unique activities of private non-profit institutions. In contrast, institutional sectoring is applied to the sets of accounts (c) and (d), which are given below:

(1) non-financial corporate enterprises
(2) households
(3) financial institutions
(4) general government
(5) private non-profit institutions serving households

The rest of the world is added to both types of sectoring as an independent segment which is in contradistinction to the domestic economy as a mirror image. Then it is easy to illustrate in Table 1 the integrated system of national accounts that we propose as an alternative framework for the revised SNA.

Panel a of the production and income formation part of Table 1 illustrates the sector production accounts in terms of gross transactions in the sense that those related to intermediate inputs are incorporated in the accounts. The aggregate supply in an entry in the accounts is equated, by definition, with the aggregate demand and is derived from the balancing relationship of the accounts as an internal bookkeeping item. It is self-explanatory that the upper part of panel a stands for the receipt side of the production of output gross of intermediate inputs, whereas the lower part of panel a represents the expenditure side of the production of output. In contrast, panel b of the production and income formation part of the table is concerned with the formation of the GDP as the source of the primary distribution of the GDP to the factors of production. While the GDP is defined as the residual of output subtracting from intermediate input, operating surplus is incorporated in the income formation account as an internal bookkeeping item. It is also clear from the balancing relationship for the income formation account that the following relationship is established:

$$\text{gross domestic product} = \text{gross domestic expenditure}$$
$$+ \text{ statistical discrepancy}$$

The item of "statistical discrepancy" has to be introduced in the relation, because it is quite a normal procedure for national accounts statisticians that the expenditure approach is used for the measurement of GDE and the production approach is used for the measurement of GDP. This also explains that a slight valuation difference arises between intermediate consumption and intermediate inputs in the table. Again, note that entries in the production and income formation part of Table 1 are expressed by domestic concepts.

TABLE 1.

An Integrated System of National Accounts (for 1984 calendar year; unit: 1,000 million yen)

I. Production and Income Formation

NO.			industries (1)		producers of government services (2)	producers of private non-profit services (3)	total	rest of the world
			non-financial activities (1.i)	financial activities (1.ii)				
1		output	588,204.1	21,950.4	34,735.9	9,318.4	654,208.8	—
2		imports	37,008.4	439.8	—	—	37,448.2	35,721.7
3		aggregate supply	625,212.5	22,390.2	34,735.9	9,318.4	691,657.0	—
4	a	intermediate consumption	338,258.3	17,360.4	885.0	130.7	356,634.4	—
5		final consumption	156,952.5	4,691.4	33,850.9	9,187.7	204,682.5	—
6		capital formation	84,317.4	—	—	—	84,317.4	—
7		exports	45,684.3	338.4	—	—	46,022.7	−44,806.0

8	output	588,138.0	22,016.4	34,735.9	9,318.4	654,208.7	—
9	intermediate inputs	338,493.9	5,878.2	9,584.2	3,605.8	357,562.1	—
10	gross domestic product	249,644.1	16,138.2	25,151.7	5,712.6	296,646.6	—
11 b	capital consumption	37,515.2	761.3	2,024.1	444.0	40,744.6	—
12	indirect taxes (net)	18,772.6	268.7	35.7	49.9	19,126.9	—
13	compensation of employees	127,045.0	9,900.2	23,091.9	5,218.7	165,255.8	—
14	operating surplus	66,311.3	5,208.0	—	—	71,519.3	—
15	statistical discrepancy	—	—	—	—	1,437.6	—
16	gross domestic expenditure	—	—	—	—	298,084.2	—

(continued)

111

TABLE 1 (Continued)

II. Income Outlay and Capital Financing

NO.		non-financial corporate enterprises (1)	households (2)	financial institutions (3)	general government (4)	private non-profit institutions (5)	total	rest of the world
1	compensation of employees	—	165,162.2	—	—	—	165,162.2	93.6
2	operating surplus	43,759.9	35,397.7	−7,638.3	—	—	71,519.3	—
3	indirect taxes (net)	—	—	—	19,126.9	—	19,126.9	—
4	property incomes	−24,403.7	19,227.4	11,560.8	−6,147.6	361.9	598.8	−598.8
5 c	casualty insurance	4.1	2.2	−1.1	−0.9	−4.3	—	—
4	direct taxes	−11,726.4	−20,340.0	−3,225.0	35,291.4	—	—	—
5	social security	—	10,124.4	—	−8,611.8	−1,512.6	—	—
6	current transfers	−737.7	−2,359.0	−384.1	−738.7	3,980.8	−238.7	238.7
7	disposable income	6,896.2	207,214.9	312.3	38,919.3	2,825.8	256,168.5	—
8 c	consumption expenditure	—	173,774.7 (16.1)	—	29,424.6 (24.4)	2,367.0 (16.2)	205,566.3 (19.8)	883.8
9	saving	6,896.2	33,440.2	312.3	9,494.7	458.8	50,602.2	—

112

#		Col1	Col2	Col3	Col4	Col5	Col6	Col7
10	saving	6,896.2	33,440.2	312.3	9,494.7	458.8	50,602.2	—
11	capital consumption	24,682.9	12,832.3	761.3	2,024.1	444.0	40,744.6	—
12	capital transfers	1,009.0	-1,631.6	—	-119.1	625.2	-116.5	116.5
13	capital formation	46,469.0	20,709.9	855.8	15,147.9	1,134.8	84,317.4	—
14	land	254.8	-3,062.8	104.8	2,682.9	20.3	—	—
15	net lending	-14,135.7	26,993.8	113.0	-6,431.1	372.9	6,912.9	-8,350.5
16	statistical discrepancy	-1,826.8	-1,004.4	4,022.2	161.3	85.3	1,437.6	—
17	net lending adjusted	-15,962.5	25,989.4	4,135.2	-6,269.8	458.2	8,350.5	-8,350.5
18	sources of funds	42,893.2	13,272.6	69,891.2	16,069.5	1,112.6	143,239.1	16,190.9
19	in which (domestic)	41,363.7	13,272.6	64,229.5	15,420.3	1,112.6	135,398.7	—
20	(rest of the world)	1,529.5	—	5,661.7	649.2	—	7,840.4	16,190.9
21	uses of funds	26,930.7	39,262.0	74,026.4	9,799.7	1,570.8	151,589.6	7,840.4
22	in which (domestic)	21,548.8	39,057.3	64,418.2	8,839.8	1,534.6	185,398.7	—
23	(rest of the world)	5,381.9	204.7	9,608.2	959.9	36.2	16,180.9	7,840.4

Turning our attention to the income outlay and capital formation and financing part of the table, we can immediately observe that both panels c and d are further subdivided into two subsets. The first subset of panel c illustrates the primary and secondary distribution of incomes resulting in the derivation of disposable income by institutional sectors, the secondary distribution of incomes serving to account for in-and-out flows concerning transfer incomes. The second subset of panel c explains how the disposable income is allocated into consumption expenditure and saving, the latter being an internal bookkeeping item in the outlay of disposable income. It is easy to see from the subsets of panel c that their entries, particularly of disposable income, are changed into the national concept when we discover that primary and transfer incomes are transmitted to the rest of the world.

While the first subset of panel d represents the capital formation account, including land sales, so that we can derive net lending by institutional sectors as an internal bookkeeping item from the balancing relationship of the capital formation account, the second subset of panel d illustrates the capital financing account by institutional sectors. In order to close the account so that an entire system of accounts in the table may constitute a fully articulated system, the item of net lending appearing in the first subset of panel d has to be adjusted to a new concept that takes into account the amount of statistical discrepancy that emerges from the production and income formation part of the table. After the necessary adjustments, uses and sources of funds come to balance via the adjusted item of net lending.

b. A Summary Statement Focusing on the Interactions Between the National and International Transactions

The interactions between national and international transactions are highlighted in the summary statement given in Table 2. With the exception of a few entries in Table 2 which can be derived from other entries, almost all entries in the table are transcribed from Table 1. Indeed, some entries are defined and derived from others, as is indicated in the notes of the table. We can also see that the summary statement of the table is expressed in the form of so-called T-account. It can be immediately seen from the table that the upper panel represents transactions which are related to the production of goods and services gross of intermediate inputs. The item of current surplus debited in gross transactions of goods and services of the domestic economy is counter-recorded in the credit side for the rest of the world. Against this, the lower panel of the table refers to those transactions which are related to the income and outlay, on the one hand, and financial transactions, on the other. First, with adjustments for transfers, capital consumption, and statistical discrepancy, the disposable income is allocated for current (consumption expenditure) and future (capital formation) uses. It is also interesting to see that the balance of financial transactions is established by way of the item of net surplus between real and financial transactions which turns out to be a mirror image of the item of current surplus that appears in the upper panel of the table. Then, it can be understood that there exists an exact and parallel treatment between the two items. In fact, net surplus between real and financial transactions, which appears in the financial transactions of the domestic economy, is counterbalanced by the corresponding entry that is located in the financial transactions of the rest of the world.

It is of particular interest that the following identities are implicit behind the summary statement of Table 2. Indeed, with recapitulation of some relations, which are illustrated in the notes of the table, one has:

(i) The production account in GDP terms is derived from

$$U + X + DC + GDCF = V + M + e \quad \text{(gross transactions of goods and services),}$$

and

$$V - U = DDY + G \quad \text{(definition of GDP).}$$

It can be immediately seen that

$$DC + GDCF + X - M = GDP + e$$

(ii) the rest of the world account follows from

$$DC + RC + GDCF + RCT + \Delta A = DDY + ROY + G + e + \Delta L$$

(a flow of funds statement represented in the lower panel of Table 2),

noting that the production account in GDP terms also holds. Then

$$X^* + (\Delta L - \Delta A) = M^* + RCT,$$

recalling that both exports and imports are expressed in the national concept after the adjustments of RC and RDY, both of which are evaluated at net values between the domestic economy and the rest of the world. X^* and M^* stands for exports and imports which are transformed into the national concept.

c.   A Simplified System of the Flow of Funds by Institutional Sectors

The financial transactions by sectors which are illustrated in the subset panel d in Table 1 are further broken down in Table 3, which features a simplified system of the flow of funds accounts and provides the sector

TABLE 2.

A Summary Statement Focusing on the Interactions between National and International Transactions (for 1984 calendar year; unit: 1,000 million yen)

expenditure/uses of funds

				national economy	
				domestic economy	rest of the world
gross transactions of goods and services	intermediate inputs	(U)	357,562.1	357,562.1	—
	exports	(X)	44,806.0	—	44,806.0
	domestic demand		288,999.9	288,999.9	—
	total		691,368.0	646,562.0	44,806.0
	current surplus			9,084.3	—
GDP and its expenditure	gross domestic expenditure	(GDE)		298,084.2	—

receipt/sources of funds

				national economy	
				domestic economy	rest of the world
	output	(V)	654,208.7	654,208.7	—
	imports	(M)	35,721.7	—	35,721.7
	statistical discrepancy	(e)	1,437.6	1,437.6	—
	total		691,368.0	655,646.3	35,721.7
	current surplus			—	9,084.3
	gross domestic product	(GDP)		296,646.6	—
	statistical discrepancy	(e)		1,437.6	—

income and outlay					disposable income			
consumption expenditure	(DC)	205,566.3	204,682.5	883.8	disposable income	256,168.5	255,902.0	266.5
domestic economy		—	204,682.5	—	domestic economy (DDY)	—	255,902.0	—
rest of the world	(RC)	—	—	883.8	rest of the world (RDY)	—	—	266.5
capital formation	(GDCF)	84,317.4	84,317.4	—	capital consumption (G)	40,744.6	40,744.6	—
capital transfer to the RW	(RCT)	116.5	—	116.5	statistical discrepancy (e)	1,437.6	1,437.6	—
financial transactions								
use of funds	(ΔA)	151,589.6	135,398.7	16,190.9	sources of funds (ΔL)	143,239.1	135,398.7	7,840.4
domestic economy	(ΔDA)	—	135,398.7	—	domestic economy (ΔDL)	—	135,398.7	—
rest of the world	(ΔRA)	—	—	16,190.9	rest of the world (ΔRL)	—	—	7,840.4
total		441,589.8	424,398.6	17,191.2	total	441,589.8	433,482.9	8,106.9
net surplus between real and financial transactions		—	9,084.3	—	net surplus between real and financial transactions	—	—	9,084.3

Notes: domestic demand = DC + GDCF

GDE = DC + GDCF + X − M; GDP = V − U = DDY + G; GDE = GDP + e

117

TABLE 3.
A Simplified System of the Flow of Funds by Institutional Sectors (for the Fiscal Year 1984; unit: 1,000 million yen)

		non-financial corporate enterprises		financial institutions		general government			private non-profit institutions	households	total	rest of the world
		private enterprises	public enterprises	private institutions	public institutions	central government	local goernment	social security funds				
flow	saving	8,292.3	−1,798.8	941.5	−701.1	−5,130.4	6,682.7	8,519.5	400.4	33,550.0	50,756.1	—
	(saving ratio)						(23.1)	(95.0)	(14.1)	(16.0)	(19.6)	—
	net lending	−8,969.4	−6,438.0	788.8	−725.9	−12,322.2	−1,712.2	8,176.4	336.4	27,068.8	6,202.7	—
	statistical discrepancy	−2,241.7	1,756.8	2,158.2	1,613.7	76.8	−1,463.1	−879.2	141.6	1,651.5	2,814.6	−9,017.3
	net lending adjusted	−11,211.1	−4,681.2	2,947.0	887.8	−12,245.4	−3,175.3	7,297.2	478.0	28,720.3	9,017.3	−9,017.3
	domestic economy	−14,243.3	−4,596.9	−1,418.3	159.6	−12,930.9	−3,156.2	7,267.0	439.9	28,479.1	—	−9,017.3
	rest of the world	3,032.2	−84.3	4,365.3	728.2	685.5	−19.1	30.2	38.1	241.2	9,017.3	−9,017.3
stocks	net claims to the rest of the world	781.8	338.3	9,657.6	6,208.7	168.3	−138.4	114.4	95.0	624.8	17,173.9	−17,173.9
	direct investment	6,864.9	—	865.1	—	—	—	—	—	—	7,730.0	−7,730.0
	trade credits extended	5,266.8	—	—	—	274.7	—	—	—	—	5,541.5	−5,541.5
	long-term loans	1,572.5	−23.7	8,020.4	5,127.9	22.9	—	—	—	—	14,720.0	−14,720.0
	bonds and securities	−11,649.8	−314.6	13,134.5	112.3	−6,340.5	−138.4	114.4	95.0	624.8	−4,362.3	4,362.3
	foreign reserves	—	—	—	1,681.4	4,396.9	—	—	—	—	6,078.3	−6,078.3
	net position in banks	—	—	−12,135.8	—	—	—	—	—	—	−12,135.8	12,135.8

Note: Flow figures in the table refer to fiscal year 1984 (April 1984 – March 1985). Hence, those in this table are not comparable with those in Tables 1 and 2.

118

breakdowns of net outstanding claims of assets to the rest of the world so that the current development of the Japanese economy mirrored in financial flows and stocks may be featured in a concise accounting framework. The statistical information incorporated in Table 3 is especially amplified by the breakdown of institutional sectors within which private institutions are distinguished from public institutions or the central government is differentiated from local government. Specifically, (1) nonfinancial corporate enterprises are broken down into private enterprises and public enterprises. Similarly, (2) financial institutions are subdivided into private institutions and public institutions. It is illuminating for us that the financial activities of the general government becomes more clarified if it is broken down into central government, local government, and social security funds, respectively. Thus, Table 3 indicates that no further breakdowns in the remaining institutional sectors are attempted.

The upper panel of Table 3 refers to the flow of financial transactions, starting with saving by sectors and ending with the derivation of net lending by sectors, which in turn is subdivided into those transactions related to the domestic economy and those related to the rest of the world. The lower panel of the table indicates the sector breakdowns of net outstanding claims of financial assets to the rest of the world at the end of a period, i.e., at the end of the 1984 fiscal year for the table. The lower panel was produced with the intention of linking the flow concepts that appear in the upper panel with stock concepts and highlighting the structure of the accumulation of the stocks of financial claims to the rest of the world in the recent trend of emerging trade surpluses that have been earned by the Japanese economy. It would be also possible to link the flow concepts in the upper panel with stock figures for both real and financial assets so that a full-fledged system of sector balance sheets may be produced. However, the primary concern of this paper is to indicate that a sufficient amount of good information concerning both real and financial transactions of the aggregate economy could be squeezed out of a simplified system of national accounts with a moderate level of integration of their component segments. Thus, the scope of Table 3 is limited to the extent that entries of a simplified flow of funds accounts are partially linked with selected stock concepts.

The net outstanding claims of financial assets in the lower panel is further classified according to the items of financial assets. The classification of financial assets given here is not exactly in harmony with their classification in the SNA or with that which is given by the United Nations in the *Provisional International Guidelines on the National and Sectoral Balance-Sheet and Reconciliation Accounts of the System of National Accounts*. The following points aid in understanding our classification in terms of the system given by the United Nations in its guidelines.

(a) The item of "direct investment" follows the definition given by the IMF in its *Balance of Payments Manual,* Fourth Edition. Thus, the concept covers "all transactions between direct investment enterprises and the direct investors themselves or any of those investors' other direct investment enterprises." [IMF, 1977, para. II 193]. Hence, the item is interpreted as the component of long-term loans, n.e.c. in the U.N. guidelines.

(b) It should be noted that the item of "trade credit extended" is classified by the flow of funds accounts in Japan under the category of the long-term assets.

(c) For the remaining items in the classification of net outstanding claims of financial assets to the rest of the world, the definition and classification seems to be self-explanatory.

It should be noted, in addition, that the figures in Table 3 refer to the 1984 fiscal year and are not directly comparable with those appearing in Tables 1 and 2, in which the reference period is not the 1984 fiscal year but the 1984 calendar year. It is unfortunate that the figures in Table 3 are not comparable with those in Tables 1 and 2. This is caused by the fact that the detailed breakdown of institutional sectors indicated in Table 3 is only feasible for the figures concerning fiscal years. The complete harmonization of statistical data between three sets of tables has to be left to future exercises after statistical information becomes available.

d. Looking at the Japanese Economy Through an Integrated and Simplified System of National Accounts

Having designed the accounting framework of an integrated and simplified system of national accounts that is proposed for consideration in the revision of SNA, the recent performance of the Japanese economy will now be analyzed using the simplified and integrated system of national accounts that has just been presented.

The characteristics of the production activities of the Japanese economy are featured in the production and income formation segment of Table 1 (rows 1-16) as specified below:

(a) While 84.2% of the GDP consists of the contribution of those industries which are engaged in non-financial activities, the industries of financial activities accounts for 5.4% of the GDP. 8.5% of the GDP is attributed to the producers of government services, whereas the contribution of the producers of nonprofit private services to the GDP amounts approximately to 2%.

(b) The expenditure of the GDP (GDE) is largely explained by final consumption, consisting of private and government final consumption, which amounts to 68.9% of the GDP. Gross domestic capital formation accounts for 28.4% of the GDP.

(c) 55.7% of the GDP is distributed to primary factors of production as compensation of employees, with 24.1% being left for operating surplus. The distribution of compensation of employees to different groupings of producers is 75.6% for non-financial industries, 6.0% for financial industries, 14.0% for producers of government services, and 3.1% for producers of private nonprofit services. It is also noted that 6.4% of the GDP is explained by net indirect taxes.

The features of primary and secondary distribution as well as the outlay of disposable income by institutional sectors are portrayed in panel c of Table 1. They are specified as follows:

(a) It is interesting to see the structure of tax revenues by the general government focusing on the relationship between direct and indirect taxes. It is calculated from the figures in Table 1 that the D/I ratio amounts to 1.85, D and I being direct and indirect taxes, respectively. The long-term estimates of the D/I ratio were made by Nosse, the estimates being 1.89 for 1965, 3.13 for 1970, and 3.44 for 1975 [Nosse, 1982, p. 148]. However, the estimates are not directly comparable to our computation, because the scope of both direct and indirect taxes in Nosse's estimates is only limited to those for the central government. The share of direct taxes in the total of direct and indirect taxes $(D/D + I)$ amounts to 64.9%. If the scope of direct and indirect taxes is limited to those for the central government, the ratio for 1984 becomes 71.4%, suggesting that the derivation of the D/I ratio from Table 1 seems quite reasonable. Drastic changes in tax structures should be invited if the D/I ratio could be substantially lowered [Nosse, 1982, p. 166 et.seq.].

(b) Turning our attention to the second subset of panel c, the figures in parenthesis above the saving row (row 9) stand for the saving ratio to disposable income by institutional sectors. While the saving ratio of households, i.e., 16.1%, is significantly lower than that for the aggregate economy, which amounts to 19.8%, the lower saving ratio for households is counterbalanced by a significantly higher saving ratio by the general government, i.e., 24.4%. In passing, it should be noted that the higher saving ratio by the general government has gradually declined in recent years owing to growing deficits caused by the central government.

(c) It is seen from the figures in row 17 of the second subset of panel d that net lending of the aggregate economy, which amounts to 8350.0 billion yen, is counterbalanced by net borrowing of the same amount by the rest of the world. The amount of net lending by the aggregate economy results from the difference between the uses and sources of funds. Among the uses of funds totaling 151,589.6 billion yen, 135,939.7 billion yen are for domestic uses, implying that the remaining 16,190.9 billion yen go to the uses of the rest of the world. Similarly, sources of funds amounting to 143,239.1 billion yen call for the domestic economy in the amount of 135,398.7 billion yen and for the rest of the world in the amount of 7,840.4 billion yen. Note that the difference between 16,190.9 billion yen and 7840.4 billion yen exactly matches the net borrowing of the rest of the world.

The interactions of both real and financial transactions between the domestic economy and the rest of the world are further summarized in a concise form in Table 2. It is particularly interesting to see from the table that the current surplus arising out of the gross transactions of goods and services by the domestic economy is counterbalanced by that for the rest of the world. In addition, it should be noted that the current surplus caused by the production of gross ouput is reflected in net surplus between real and financial transactions in the same amount that is recorded in the bottom row of the table. We can notice that a net surplus of the same size is again recorded in the rest of the world so that the summary statement can be represented as a fully articulated system. Thus, we might argue that the current surplus arising out of the gross transactions of goods and services, which amounts to 9084.3 billion yen, could be utilized for the expansion of domestic demand so as to avoid criticism from abroad that Japan ought to be restrained in keeping its exports within a permissible size.

Although the figures in Table 3 are not directly comparable with those in earlier tables, a few words deserve to be noted here. The lower panel of Table 3 indicates the sectors in which the net outstanding stocks of claims to the rest of the world emerged and the items of financial assets in which they accumulated at the end of the 1984 fiscal year. Thus, the table indicates that a substantial portion of net claims to the rest of the world was accumulated in financial institutions, both private and public. As for the distribution of finanical assets which constitute net claims to the rest of the world, the following features can be immediately ascertained from the figures:

(a) An overwhelming portion of direct investment and loans extended were borne by private enterprises, whereas the burden of long-term loans was shared by private and public financial institutions.

(b) It is interesting to see that private enterprises owed to the rest of the world in the form of bonds and securities, whose substantial portion flowed from financial centers in Europe, and that no small amounts of government bonds were owned by foreign investors. It should be noted that at the end of the 1984 fiscal year Japan was a net borrower of bonds and securities from the rest of the world. However, the situation was completely reversed at the end of the 1985 fiscal year, Japan then being a net lender of bonds and securities to the rest of the world.

In conclusion, if we compare the time-series estimates of the table, Table 3 illuminates the recent financial development of the Japanese economy in a summarized form.

References

Al, P. G., Dual sectoring in national accounts, Working Party on National Accounts and Balances, March 1986; Conference of European Statisticians, December 1985.

Benard, J., *Comptabilité Nationale et Modèles de Politique Économique*. Paris: Presses Universitaires de France, 1972.

van Bochove, C. A., and H. K. van Tuinen, Flexibility in the next SNA: The case for an institutional core, *Review of Income and Wealth*, June 1986.

van Eck, R., C. N. Gorter, and H. K. van Tuinen, *Flexibility in the system of national accounts*, Voorburg, Netherlands: Central Bureau of Statistics, 1983.

International Monetary Fund, *Balance of Payments Manual*, Fourth Edition. Washington D.C., 1977.

Ruggles, R., *The System of National Accounts. Review of Major Issues and Proposals for Future and Short-term Changes*. United Nations, ESA/STAT/AC. 15/1, February 1982.

United Nations, *A System of National Accounts*. Studies in Methods Series F No. 2 Rev. 3, New York, 1968.

United Nations, *Provisional International Guidelines on the National and Sectoral Balance-sheet and Reconcilliation Accounts of the System of National Accounts*. Statistical Papers, Series M, No. 60, New York, 1977.

United Nations, Special issue on the review of the United Nations System of National Accounts, *Review of Income and Wealth*, June 1986a.

United Nations, *Progress in the Revision of the System of National Accounts (SNA)*. E/CN.3/1987/5, December 1986b.

Vanoli, A., Sur la structure général du SCN, à partir de l'expérience du système élargi de comptabilité national français, *Review of Income and Wealth*, June 1986.

Kurabayashi, Y. and I. Sakuma, *Kokumin Keizai Keisan* (National Accounting). Tokyo: Toyo Keizai Shinpo Sha, 1980, in Japanese.

Nosse, T., *Zaisei no Keiryo Bunseki* (An econometric analysis of public finance). Tokyo: Sobun Sha, 1982, in Japanese.

7

Revaluation of Durable Capital Stock in Japanese Manufacturing and Its Application for the Measurement of Potential Growth Rate During the OPEC Decade

SHUNSUKE MORI

Department of Science and Technology
Science University of Tokyo
Noda-shi, Chiba
Japan

TAKAMITSU SAWA

Kyoto Institute of Economic Research
Kyoto University
Sakyo-ku, Kyoto
Japan

1. Introduction

It is widely believed that when energy prices increase suddenly and unexpectedly, as was the case in the periods 1973–1974 and 1979–1980, a portion of the durable capital stock becomes economically less valuable. In order to make studies of production functions more reasonable and more meaningful, it would be indispensable to revaluate obsolete capital stock so that it can be plausibly summed up with newly invested capital.

Berndt and Wood proposed a very attractive procedure to revaluate the durable capital stock in response to the changes in energy prices relative to capital services price. Following their pioneering work, we aim at revaluating the durable capital stock accumulated by Japanese manufacturing. Also, we propose an alternative revaluation procedure for comparison with that of Berndt and Wood.

In Section 2 Berndt and Wood's procedure is briefly reviewed. In Section 3, some problems intrinsic to their procedure are pointed out and an alternative procedure, whose characteristics are examined in detail, is proposed.

DEVELOPMENTS IN
JAPANESE ECONOMICS

125

In Section 4 the data base necessitated to revaluate capital stock owned by Japanese manufacturings is presented. In Section 5 the durable capital stock of Japanese manufacturings is revaluated by the two procedures.

In Section 6, utilizing time-series of the revaluated capital stock, the potential production capacity of Japanese manufacturing is evaluated in order to compare it with realized output. This throws light on the controversy on how to enumerate the demand-supply gap.

2. Outline of Berndt and Wood's Method

When firms undertake an investment decision in new equipment, the following assumptions would be quite reasonable: In the first place, they decide the amount of funds that should be allocated to capital services, including the operating cost. The decision is based on the expected growth of demand as well as the relative factor prices. Thereafter, they decide how to allocate the funds on capital services and energy that is indispensable to operate the capital stock where the decision is based on the expected prices of capital services and energy.

Berndt and Wood assumed constant *ex ante* elasticity of substitution between capital services and energy, while the *ex post* elasticity of substitution was assumed to be zero. Let $P_{E,t}$ and $P_{K,t}$ be energy and capital services prices at the time period t, respectively; let $P_{E,t}^*$ be the relative energy price, namely, $P_{E,t}/P_{K,t}$. Following the conventional neoclassical theory of firms, they suppose as follows: At time $t - s$, given the current relative energy price $P_{E,t-s}^*$ a firm decides to install the cost-minimizing capital equipment with fixed energy-capital ratio, which is I_{t-s} in money terms. In the future, say at time t, however, the relative energy price may change so that the equipment installed at time $t - s$ may no longer be optimal. In this situation the following problem naturally occurs: The firm has to decide whether or not it is reasonable to conventionally aggregate existing capital equipment with a different energy-capital ratio reflecting the relative energy price prevailing at each vintage. For instance, if the relative energy price has suddenly increased, capital equipment installed earlier should be recognized to be economically less valuable as compared with newly installed equipment whose energy-capital ratio is optimal under the higher energy piece. The above problem may be answered by introducing some formula to discount each price of existing capital equipment in such a way that its energy efficiency is somehow reflected. Berndt and Wood proposed the following procedure to revaluate the capital equipment I_{t-s} of vintage $t - s$:

Let $I_{t,t-s}^*$ be the revaluated value of the capital equipment I_{t-s} at time t. According to Berndt and Wood, the revaluation coefficient $\lambda_{t,t-s} = I_{t,t-s}^*/I_{t-s}$

is given by

$$\lambda_{t,t-s} = \left(\frac{P^*_{E,t-s}}{P^*_{E,t}}\right)^{\sigma}, \tag{1}$$

where σ is the *ex ante* elasticity of substitution between energy and capital services. The existing capital equipment are aggregated after being multiplied by the revaluation coefficient, in addition to the physical deterioration rate

$$K_t = \sum_{s=0}^{T} \lambda_{t,t-s} I_{t-s} (1-\delta)^s, \tag{2}$$

where δ is a constant rate of physical deterioration and T is a fixed physical lifetime common to all capital equipment.

The assumption of the *ex ante* constant elasticity of substitution (CES) between capital services and energy is explicitly formulated as

$$Q_t^{-\beta} = aE_t^{-\beta} + bI_t^{-\beta}, \tag{3}$$

where Q_t is the output produced by operating the capital equipment I_t with energy input E_t. The equilibrium condition is given by

$$\ln R_t = \ln\left(\frac{E_t}{I_t}\right) = C - \sigma \ln\left(\frac{P_{E,t}}{P_{K,t}}\right), \tag{4}$$

where

$$R_t = \frac{E_t}{I_t}, \tag{5}$$

and

$$\sigma = \frac{1}{(1+\beta)}. \tag{6}$$

From (4) it follows that

$$\lambda_{t,t-s} = \frac{R_t}{R_{t-s}}$$

$$= \left(\frac{P^*_{E,t-s}}{P^*_{E,t}}\right)^{\sigma}. \tag{7}$$

This expression leads to the following interpretation of Berndt and Wood's capital revaluation procedure. Suppose that at time $t - s$ the optimal energy-capital ratio is R_{t-s}. If the relative energy price goes up at time t, the optimal energy capital ratio necessarily shifts to R_t. Since the higher energy price motivates firms to invest more energy-efficient equipment, R_t is definitely smaller than R_{t-s}. Now suppose that the less energy-efficient equipment of amount I_{t-s} is operated with energy input $R_t I_{t-s}$ which is required to fully operate the optimal and hence newly installed equipment of amount I_{t-s}. Obviously, the operation rate of the less energy-efficient equipment I_{t-s} with vintage $t - s$ turns out to be less than one and equals R_t/R_{t-s}.

The above consideration justifies the idea of revaluating I_{t-s} by multiplying R_t/R_{t-s}. In short, Berndt and Wood's revaluation procedure may be interpreted as focusing upon the difference of energy efficiency among the existing capital equipment. The revaluated value of capital stock is necessarily less than the conventionally aggregated capital stock in cases when the present relative energy price exceeds that in the past periods. Hereafter this revaluation coefficient $\lambda_{t,t-s}$ is denoted as $\lambda^A_{t,t-s}$ to distinguish it from another revaluation coefficient proposed later.

Capital stock usually includes not only equipment but also structures and other instruments. The energy efficiency is really crucial to equipment but almost irrelevant to structures and instruments. Therefore, Berndt and Wood confined the revaluation only to equipment. The total capital stock K^*_t is obtained as the Divisia-type aggregation of equipment and other items (mostly structures)

$$K^*_t = A K^{*\,\alpha}_{E,t} K_{S,t}^{(1-\alpha)}, \tag{8}$$

where $K^*_{E,t}$ is the stock of capital equipment revaluated by the above procedure (2) and $K_{S,t}$ is the stock of structures and other items conventionally aggregated, taking into account only the physical deterioration; α is the parameter that must be determined before aggregation.

3.   An Alternative Method of Revaluation

A serious problem must be pointed out with regard to Berndt and Wood's revaluation procedure. From the definition of $\lambda^A_{t,t-s}$ the following may be easily deduced: If the relative energy price goes down after equipment is installed, the revaluation coefficient $\lambda^A_{t,t-s}$ exceeds unity; namely, the revaluated capital stock is greater than the conventionally aggregated capital stock. According to Berndt and Wood, the existing capital equipment is recognized as "too effective" under the present lower energy price. However, this monotonicity of the revaluation coefficient is more or less counterintuitive because any equipment installed earlier is not "optimal" under the present relative energy price unless the exact same relative energy price was prevailing when it was installed.

To overcome this counterintuitive property of Berndt and Wood's revaluation coefficient, we are motivated to propose an alternative procedure that is based on another reasoning.

Rewrite equation (3) as follows

$$q_t = \left(\frac{Q_t}{I_t}\right) = F\left(1, \frac{E_t}{I_t}\right) = f(R_t). \tag{9}$$

In period t, the return to unit capital equipment is

$$y_{t,t} = f(R_t) - P_{E,t}R_t \tag{10}$$

for the equipment newly installed at period t and

$$y_{t,t-s} = f(R_{t-s}) - P_{E,t}R_{t-s} \tag{11}$$

for the equipment installed at period $t - s$. The latter may be interpreted as the present rental price of the capital equipment installed at $t - s$. An alternative revaluation coefficient is their ratio

$$\lambda^B_{t,t-s} = \frac{f(R_{t-s}) - P_{E,t}R_{t-s}}{f(R_t) - P_{E,t}R_t}. \tag{12}$$

Note that $\lambda^B_{t,t-s}$ is less than unity as long as R_t differs from R_{t-s}.

In order to rewrite $\lambda^B_{t,t-s}$ as a function of relative energy price $P^*_{E,t}$, the equilibrium conditions

$$P_{E,t} = \frac{dq_t}{dR_t}, \qquad P_{K,t} = q_t - R_t\left(\frac{dq_t}{dR_t}\right) \tag{13}$$

of the CES production function are inserted in (4). After rearranging terms, we obtain

$$\lambda^B_{t,t-s} = \frac{\{1 + A^\sigma(P^*_{E,t-s})^{1-\sigma}\}^{-\sigma/(1-\sigma)}}{\{1 + A^\sigma(P^*_{E,t})^{1-\sigma}\}^{-1/(1-\sigma)}} \tag{14}$$

$$- A^\sigma(P^*_{E,t-s})^{-\sigma}P^{*-\sigma}_{E,t},$$

where

$$A = \frac{b}{a}. \tag{15}$$

The right-hand side of (14) involves two parameters (A and σ) and one variable (relative energy price).

The behavior of $\lambda^B_{t,t-s}$ is visualized in Figure 1, where the horizontal axis measures $\ln(P^*_{E,t}/P^*_{E,t-s})$. Each curve corresponds to $A = 1$, $\sigma = 0.1$, $0.2, \ldots, 0.9$. This figure shows that even when the relative energy price goes

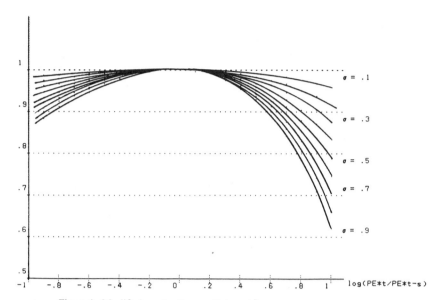

Figure 1. Modified revaluation coefficient: λ^B
$\sigma =$ *ex ante* elasticity of substitution between energy and capital services

down, $\lambda^B_{t,t-s}$ falls below unity, but not as steeply as in the case of a price hike. This asymmetry of the curve is intuitively quite plausible.

Next, let us introduce technical progress in the *ex ante* production function to see how it affects λ^B. Here assume Solow-neutral technical progress. In this case, the return, say v_t, to unit capital equipment newly installed at period t is given by

$$v_t = F(e^{at}I_t, E_t) - P_{E,t}E_t$$
$$= e^{at}I_t\{f(e^{-at}R_t) - e^{-at}P_{E,t}R_t\}, \tag{16}$$

where use is made of linear homogeneity of F and $f(x) = F(1, x)$. It should be noted that the capital equipment I_t with vintage t is augmented by multiplying e^{at} as follows

$$I_t^S = e^{at}I_t. \tag{17}$$

Accordingly, the energy-capital ratio is modified as

$$R_t^S = e^{-at}R_t. \tag{18}$$

Equation (16) may be rewritten in terms of I_t^S and R_t^S as

$$v_t = I_t^S\{f(R_t^S) - P_{E,t}R_t^S\}. \tag{19}$$

The total return, say V_t, to the whole existing capital equipment at period t is

$$V_t = \sum_{s=0}^{T} [F(e^{a(t-s)}(1-\delta)^s I_{t-s}, E_{t-s}) - P_{E,t} E_{t-s}]$$

$$= \sum_{s=0}^{T} \{e^{a(t-s)}(1-\delta)^s I_{t-s}[f(R_{t-s}^S) - P_{E,t} R_{t-s}^S]\} \tag{20}$$

$$= e^{at} \sum_{s=0}^{T} I_{t-s}(1-\delta)^s \frac{e^{-as}[f(R_{t-s}^S) - P_{E,t} R_{t-s}^S]}{f(R_t^S) - P_{E,t} R_t^S} [f(R_t^S) - P_{E,t} R_t^S].$$

To simplify the expression let us introduce a new symbol

$$\lambda_{t,t-s}^S = \frac{e^{-as}\{f(R_{t-s}^S) - P_{E,t} R_{t-s}^S\}}{f(R_t^S) - P_{E,t} R_t^S}, \tag{21}$$

the right-hand side of which is no more than the product of $\lambda_{t,t-s}^B$, with R_{t-s}^S in place of R_{t-s} and the term e^{-as} indicating the deterioration caused by technical progress that occurred during the last s periods. Now the total return V_t is written as

$$V_t = e^{at} K_t^S [f(R_t^S) - P_{E,t} R_t^S], \tag{22}$$

where

$$K_t^S = \sum_{s=0}^{T} \lambda_{t,t-s}^S I_{t-s}(1-\delta)^s. \tag{23}$$

It should be noted that the right-hand side of (22) is the product of the augmented revaluation capital stock in terms of $\lambda_{t,t-s}^S$ and the return to unit capital equipment newly installed at t. Therefore, in the case of Solow-neutral technical progress, the revaluation may be reasonably done by using the series of the revaluation coefficients $\lambda_{t,t-s}^S$.

In practice, however, it is hard to enumerate $\lambda_{t,t-s}^B$, because it involves the two parameters A and σ, which are hard to estimate econometrically.

4.   Data Base for Revaluation of the Capital Stock of Japanese Manufacturing

In order to revaluate the capital stock of Japanese manufacturing, the following data base will be needed; 1) capital formation of equipment $I_{E,t}$ and structures and other items $I_{S,t}$, 2) energy inputs and aggregated energy price index $P_{E,t}$, and 3) price of capital services $P_{K,t}$.

We want to carry out capital revaluation for the period 1955-1981. Let us denote the physical lifetime and deterioration rate of equipment (structures and others) as T_E (T_S) and δ_E (δ_S), respectively. The conventionally aggregated gross capital stock $K_{E,t}$ of equipment and its revaluated value $K^*_{S,t}$ are as follows

$$K_{E,t} = \sum_{s=0}^{T_E} I_{E,t-s}(1 - \delta_E)^s \tag{24}$$

and

$$K^*_{E,t} = \sum_{s=0}^{T_E} I^*_{E,t-s}(1 - \delta_E)^s = \sum_{s=0}^{T_E} I_{E,t-s}\lambda_{t,t-s}(1 - \delta_E)^s, \tag{25}$$

respectively. The gross capital stock of structures and other items is conventionally aggregated and given by

$$K_{S,t} = \sum_{s=0}^{T_S} I_{S,t-s}(1 - \delta_S)^s. \tag{26}$$

a. Capital Formation of Structures and Other Items

The consecutive time-series of capital formation of producers' durable equipment is not available. In particular, no data source exists for the period during World War II. Thus, the three data sources were combined as consistently as possible.

For the period 1903-1940, a series of the gross capital formation of producers' durable equipment (non-primary industries) is given by *Estimates of Long-Term Economic Statistics of Japan since 1868* (Institute of Economic Research, Hitotsubashi University). The time-series jumps up suddenly for the last three years, presumably due to the sharp increase in investment by military industries.

On the other hand, a series of the gross capital formation of non-residential structures given by the *Long-Term Economic Statistics* behaves quite smoothly during the war period. Therefore, the figures for $I_{E,t}$ during the period 1938–40 are replaced by regressing $I_{E,t}$ on $I_{S,t}$ for the period 1929–1937 and extrapolating for the former period. Since there exists no data source at all for the war period 1941–1945, the values of $I_{E,t}$ and $I_{S,t}$ in the year 1940 are sustained for this period. For the post-war period 1946–1954, $I_{E,t}$ and $I_{S,t}$ are both extracted directly from the *Census of Manufactures* (Ministry of International Trade and Industry). The *Annual Report on National Accounts* (Economic Planning Agency) provides a time-series of the total gross capital formation by manufacturing, i.e., ($I_{E,t} + I_{S,t}$), after the year 1955, which does not necessarily coincide with the series given by the *Census of Manufactures*.

The discrepancy between the two series is simply due to the fact that the *Census of Manufactures* does not cover small manufactures with less than, for instance, 20 employees in 1970. Finally, the gross capital formation given by the *Annual Report on National Accounts* is divided into $I_{E,t}$ and $I_{S,t}$ proportionally to those given by the *Census of Manufactures*. The time-series of these capital formations data are shown in Table 1.

b. Energy Inputs and the Divisia Price Index of Energy Including Feedstocks

In order to evaluate the Divisia price index of energy, data is needed on inputs as well as price indexes for each fuel. Data on energy inputs were obtained from the following sources.

For the period 1929–1948 the amount of petroleum consumed by manufacturing is given by the *Census of Manufactures*. For the period after 1949, the amounts of A-heavy oil, B-heavy oil, C-heavy oil, kerosene, and

TABLE 1(a).
Capital Formation of Japanese Manufacturing: 1903–45

YEAR	IEQUIP	ISTRUC	YEAR	IEQUIP	ISTRUC
1903	21146	10766	1925	176634	16574
1904	39431	13032	1926	193673	28946
1905	61844	13411	1927	228020	51612
1906	51692	13411	1928	240680	52178
1907	58167	17236	1929	260342	57373
1908	56926	10247	1930	213670	46320
1909	42801	15677	1931	182052	35983
1910	56886	29418	1932	186332	44720
1911	79881	5356	1933	257072	66440
1912	97857	4580	1934	372693	117776
1913	96759	3872	1935	435990	122081
1914	79177	13222	1936	494163	102003
1915	88430	10294	1937	482140	140646
1916	148734	26207	1938	509053	146900
1917	221393	32629	1939	533601	156252
1918	283069	46937	1940	425439	116118
1919	362935	44859	1941	425439	116118
1920	369521	46323	1942	425439	116118
1921	230862	36642	1943	425439	116118
1922	244209	33715	1944	425439	116118
1923	139495	10530	1945	425439	116118
1924	161731	20919			

IEQUIP = Investment of capital equipment
ISTRUC = Investment of structures and other items

TABLE 1(b).
Capital Formation of Japanese Manufacturing: 1946–81

YEAR	IEQUIP	ISTRUC	YEAR	IEQUIP	ISTRUC
1946	90865	78324	1964	1968470	2089640
1947	135854	113210	1965	1880790	1853420
1948	223987	178966	1966	2091430	1832290
1949	216210	173267	1967	2813770	2489020
1950	185800	150806	1968	4032800	3147550
1951	224549	179377	1969	5139650	3815550
1952	244796	194137	1970	6376320	4420980
1953	293389	229158	1971	5782310	4207010
1954	317342	245131	1972	5924070	3969870
1955	260964	259594	1973	6489220	3709070
1956	314782	322257	1974	6434140	3765260
1957	548844	531836	1975	5684930	3514010
1958	580353	592248	1976	6246440	3071150
1959	749054	717196	1977	6247070	3154790
1960	1156140	1290920	1978	5317100	3034260
1961	1504690	1519210	1979	6468350	3224640
1962	1743240	1859490	1980	7931130	3496380
1963	1839390	1908900	1981	8052560	4402140

IEQUIP = Investment of capital equipment
ISTRUC = Investment of structures and other items

gasoline consumption are available from the Year Book of Oil Statistics (MITI).

For the period 1929–1948, the amounts of gas, coal, coke, and charcoal consumption may be extracted from the Census of Manufactures. For the period after 1949 they may be available from the Census of Manufactures (MITI).

Electricity consumption is given by the Census of Manufactures for the period up until 1948, and by the Year Book of Coal, Petroleum and Coke Statistics (MITI).

Prince indices for each fuel are extracted from the Price Index Annual (Bank of Japan) for the period 1929–1981.

The Divisia price index may be calculated from these data sources. The final results are shown in Table 2.

c. Price of Capital Services

The rental price of capital stock is of the Hall-Jorgenson form, with effective tax rates incorporated. Kuroda [1982] estimated the effective tax rates data for the period 1960–1978. Following his procedure, the effective tax rate of

TABLE 2.
Price Indexes of Energy, Capital Equipment, and Structures

YEAR	PE	PEQUIP	PSTRUC	YEAR	PE	PEQUIP	PSTRUC
1929	1.6304D−03	2.5757D−03	1.2696D−03	1956	3.2874D−01	6.5346D−01	4.6073D−01
1930	1.4789D−03	2.2530D−03	1.0763D−03	1957	3.4316D−01	7.0659D−01	4.9008D−01
1931	1.4136D−03	2.0129D−03	1.0755D−03	1958	3.3142D−01	6.8907D−01	4.5175D−01
1932	1.2898D−03	2.2126D−03	1.1113D−03	1959	3.1844D−01	6.8281D−01	4.6689D−01
1933	1.3480D−03	2.3690D−03	1.0468D−03	1960	3.1471D−01	6.8360D−01	4.7854D−01
1934	1.3774D−03	2.2453D−03	9.2972D−04	1961	3.0920D−01	6.6091D−01	4.9017D−01
1935	1.3389D−03	2.1257D−03	9.6206D−04	1962	3.0842D−01	6.4146D−01	4.7356D−01
1936	1.3964D−03	2.1294D−03	9.6853D−04	1963	3.0714D−01	6.1217D−01	4.5830D−01
1937	1.5104D−03	3.1834D−03	1.0714D−03	1964	3.0229D−01	6.1961D−01	4.6786D−01
1938	1.7301D−03	3.1757D−03	1.2663D−03	1965	3.0079D−01	6.0198D−01	4.5907D−01
1939	1.7727D−03	3.0804D−03	1.5084D−03	1966	2.9735D−01	5.7831D−01	4.6990D−01
1940	1.8542D−03	3.0729D−03	2.0489D−03	1967	2.9271D−01	5.9016D−01	5.0097D−01
1941	1.9101D−03	3.0270D−03	2.0593D−03	1968	2.9301D−01	5.7735D−01	4.8902D−01
1942	2.0845D−03	3.1530D−03	2.1323D−03	1969	2.8591D−01	6.0576D−01	5.2200D−01
1943	2.0040D−03	3.4216D−03	2.2418D−03	1970	2.8439D−01	6.2529D−01	5.7023D−01
1944	2.0100D−03	3.6110D−03	2.6067D−03	1971	3.1271D−01	6.2573D−01	5.4510D−01
1945	3.1270D−03	4.7857D−03	3.7710D−03	1972	3.1374D−01	5.9566D−01	5.3462D−01
1946	1.1738D−02	3.1084D−02	1.9806D−02	1973	3.3727D−01	6.7065D−01	7.1705D−01
1947	4.2447D−02	8.9938D−02	8.5038D−02	1974	8.2892D−01	9.8064D−01	1.0844D+00
1948	1.1495D−01	2.1571D−01	1.9994D−01	1975	1.0000D+00	1.0000D+00	1.0000D+00
1949	1.7766D−01	2.9619D−01	2.6105D−01	1976	1.0853D+00	9.9910D−01	1.0346D+00
1950	2.0483D−01	4.0091D−01	2.9997D−01	1977	1.1067D+00	9.8454D−01	1.0113D+00
1951	2.3962D−01	6.2631D−01	4.4267D−01	1978	9.6221D−01	1.1844D+00	1.1879D+00
1952	3.1107D−01	6.6989D−01	4.4895D−01	1979	1.1706D+00	1.2510D+00	1.4286D+00
1953	3.1046D−01	6.6376D−01	4.8063D−01	1980	1.9761D+00	1.3887D+00	1.7523D+00
1954	2.9138D−01	6.5946D−01	4.8707D−01	1981	2.2143D+00	1.3817D+00	1.6257D+00
1955	3.1031D−01	6.4898D−01	4.5263D−01				

PE = Price index of energy; PEQUIP = Price index of capital equipments;
PSTRUC = Price index of structures

135

legal persons for the period 1929–1981 (TAXRTE) was estimated from the *Annual Report of Tax Office* and *Annual Report of Local Finance*. The interest rate used here is the *ex ante* industrial bonds yield (RBOND). These are shown in Table 3. This is obtained from the *Annual Report on Economic Statistics*. The physical deterioration rates are derived in the following manner.

According to the *National Wealth Survey of Japan* (Bureau of Statistics, Prime Minister's Office) the physical lifetimes of producers' durable equipment and nonresidential structures are supposed to be twice as long as the legal lifetimes, which are 11.1 and 26.6. years for equipment and structure, respectively. Accordingly, we can safely suppose that the physical lifetimes are 22 and 53 years for equipment and structure, respectively.

Following Berndt and Wood, moreover, suppose that the asset is geometrically deteriorating and the asset completely disappears when 95% of the assets have deteriorated. Based on these assumptions, the rates of physical deterioration are calculated as 0.133 for equipment and 0.056 for structures.

Kuroda and Yoshioka [1984] estimated the rates of deterioration by applying the both-sided benchmark year method to the data of the *National Wealth Survey*, which is conducted every ten years. Kuroda's estimate for equipment is 0.082, the physical lifetime implied by this is 35 years. It would be fair to say that Kuroda and Yoshioka's estimate is not necessarily reliable enough, because their solution turned out to be infeasible for approximately one-fourth of itemized assets. Moreover, it seems that the implied lifetime is rather long. Therefore, we gave up making use of Kuroda and Yoshioka's estimate.

The price indices of producers' durable equipment, and non-residential structures, say P_{EQUIP} and P_{STRUC}, are obtained from *Estimates of Long Term Economic Statistics of Japan since 1868* for the period 1929–1951 and from the *Price Indexes Annual* for the period 1952–1981. These price indices are shown in Table 2.

From the above data base the rental price of capital services $P_{K,t}$ and the relative energy price P_{Et}^{*} can be estimated. The results are shown in Table 3.

5. Revaluation of Durable Capital Stock: Empirical Results

The data base needed for capital revaluation has been obtained. Berndt and Wood employed the extended translog cost function involving K, L, E, and M on the right-hand side, whose parameters were estimated simultaneously with the *ex ante* substitution elasticity σ. Since our efforts were mostly devoted to developing a plausible data base and solving some theoretical issues, our work is still in its preliminary stage. We are now ready to compute series of $\lambda_{t,t-s}^{A}$ and $\lambda_{t,t-s}^{B}$ for three different values of the *ex ante* substitution elasticity σ, that is, $\sigma = 0.333, 0.667; 1.0$ for λ^{A} and $\sigma = 0.333, 0.667$, and 0.9; and $A = 0.5, 1.0,$

TABLE 3.
Relative Energy Price and Price Index of Capital Services

YEAR	PEK	RBOND	TAXRTE	PK	YEAR	PEK	RBOND	TAXRTE	PK
1929	1.27214	6.420	5.50	5.82168D-04	1956	0.46646	7.679	56.40	3.20122D-01
1930	1.30947	6.494	6.20	5.13019D-04	1957	0.46684	7.641	54.80	3.33898D-01
1931	1.41314	6.345	5.38	4.54376D-04	1958	0.46438	7.889	54.60	3.24182D-01
1932	1.16976	6.743	5.64	5.00841D-04	1959	0.45625	7.904	54.00	3.17046D-01
1933	1.13108	5.544	6.53	5.41349D-04	1960	0.44352	7.907	54.70	3.22318D-01
1934	1.21137	4.692	7.15	5.16507D-04	1961	0.45543	7.657	53.30	3.08387D-01
1935	1.21521	4.498	9.28	5.00471D-04	1962	0.47500	7.478	51.80	2.94944D-01
1936	1.25991	4.377	9.66	5.03464D-04	1963	0.48560	7.485	51.50	2.87304D-01
1937	0.86473	4.356	14.30	7.93408D-04	1964	0.47706	7.483	51.50	2.87834D-01
1938	0.92690	4.321	20.00	8.47878D-04	1965	0.49662	7.481	49.40	2.75122D-01
1939	0.89341	4.319	27.00	9.01297D-04	1966	0.50729	7.488	47.40	2.66252D-01
1940	0.86875	4.310	32.30	9.69487D-04	1967	0.49848	7.487	47.10	2.66734D-01
1941	0.87363	4.320	34.90	9.93162D-04	1968	0.50070	7.559	46.50	2.65826D-01
1942	0.83376	4.316	40.70	1.13568D-03	1969	0.46913	7.675	47.00	2.76830D-01
1943	0.70998	4.296	43.00	1.28216D-03	1970	0.45049	7.976	48.10	2.86755D-01
1944	0.58124	4.290	50.90	1.57085D-03	1971	0.49762	7.941	47.80	2.85451D-01
1945	0.66284	4.286	52.30	2.14295D-03	1972	0.51585	7.192	47.70	2.76270D-01
1946	0.26261	6.563	67.30	2.03034D-02	1973	0.49343	7.504	48.40	3.10488D-01
1947	0.37640	9.855	62.50	5.12263D-02	1974	0.83312	9.265	51.60	4.51953D-01
1948	0.47370	10.425	58.20	1.10225D-01	1975	1.00000	9.458	49.90	4.54252D-01
1949	0.57531	9.206	54.90	1.40276D-01	1976	1.06388	8.857	51.80	4.63366D-01
1950	0.41507	8.982	61.80	2.24162D-01	1977	1.08691	7.804	53.00	4.62492D-01
1951	0.30919	9.007	62.00	3.52040D-01	1978	1.00957	6.375	52.60	4.32933D-01
1952	0.38218	9.001	61.30	3.69724D-01	1979	1.17019	7.225	52.30	4.54390D-01
1953	0.39291	9.002	60.50	3.58921D-01	1980	1.53331	8.492	58.90	5.85415D-01
1954	0.35143	9.026	62.60	3.76617D-01	1981	1.58824	8.017	62.20	6.33307D-01
1955	0.41692	8.907	59.00	3.38088D-01					

PEK = Relative energy price; PBOND = Bond rate (%); TAXRTE = Rate of cooperate tax (%);

PK = Price index of capital services

TABLE 4.
Life-Cycle Forecast of Relative Energy Price

YEAR	PEK*	PEKLF1	PEKLF2
1950	0.415066	0.344303	0.343661
1951	0.309189	0.237288	0.259472
1952	0.382181	0.267607	0.267507
1953	0.392908	0.297906	0.276022
1954	0.351432	0.274025	0.272085
1955	0.416923	0.313396	0.304775
1956	0.466463	0.369734	0.343494
1957	0.466838	0.384260	0.370760
1958	0.464383	0.385190	0.380230
1959	0.456245	0.380944	0.377340
1960	0.443515	0.371810	0.369793
1961	0.455434	0.380542	0.376152
1962	0.474999	0.400371	0.391380
1963	0.485603	0.414896	0.406176
1964	0.477057	0.412294	0.407610
1965	0.496622	0.427700	0.422292
1966	0.507291	0.442046	0.433793
1967	0.498484	0.438873	0.434577
1968	0.500702	0.440376	0.437528
1969	0.469134	0.417090	0.416993
1970	0.450492	0.397442	0.400314
1971	0.497624	0.431807	0.424932
1972	0.515847	0.457839	0.444831
1973	0.493430	0.444730	0.441586
1974	0.833123	0.703789	0.659333
1975	0.999999	0.950298	0.862931
1976	1.063880	1.039173	1.015748
1977	1.086910	1.071124	1.062424
1978	1.009570	1.000678	1.002935
1979	1.170190	1.141208	1.134595
1980	1.533310	1.521491	1.467334
1981	1.588240	1.631324	1.589624

PEK* = Myopic forecast; PEKLF1 = Forecast based on ARIMA(1, 1, 0);
PEKLF2 = Forecast based on ARIMA(2, 1, 0)

and 2.0 for λ^B. Specify α in equation (8) as the share of return to capital equipment relative to structures and other items.

As was pointed out by Berndt and Wood, the relative energy price $P^*_{E,t}$ on which firms base their choice of new equipment should be some characteristic value of an expected life cycle relative price function. Given the series $P^*_{E,t}$ of forecasts of the relative energy price up to T periods ahead, firms base their decision on the weighted average $P^{**}_{E,t}$ of the forecasted series of the relative energy price, where the weights are linked to the real discount rate r and the annual deterioration rate δ in the following manner

$$
P_{E,t}^{**} = \frac{\left[\sum_{k=0}^{T} P_{E,t+k}^{*} \dfrac{(1-\delta)^{k}}{(1+r)^{k+1}} \right]}{S} \tag{27}
$$

where

$$
S = \sum_{k=0}^{T} \frac{(1-\delta)^{k}}{(1+r)^{k+1}} \tag{28}
$$

Suppose that firms make forecasts of future time-series of $P_{E,t}^{*}$ based on their own past series, namely, they predict $P_{E,t+s}^{*}$ by making use of conventional ARIMA models. The series of forecasts is updated year to year. There remains the problem of how to identify the orders of the ARIMA model. We estimated ARIMA models with various orders and carried out some diagnosis checking to compare their performances. It turns out that the moving average part of the model may not be estimable because the maximum likelihood is infeasible within the region in which invertability conditions are fulfilled. We have chosen the two models ARIMA (1, 1, 0) and ARIMA (2, 1, 0) that behave almost similarly (see Table 4.).

The time-series of the revaluated gross capital stock is given in Figure 2. The time-series of the ratio of the revaluated capital stock to the conventional gross capital stock is exhibited in Figure 3.

The result clearly shows the remarkable drop of the revaluated capital stock that occurred after the oil shock.

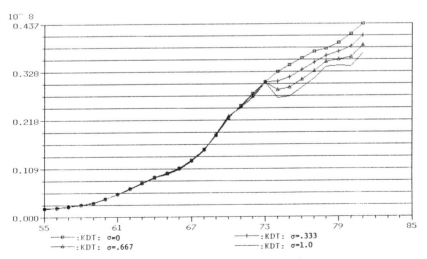

Figure 2(a). Revaluated capital stock: $K^{A}t$

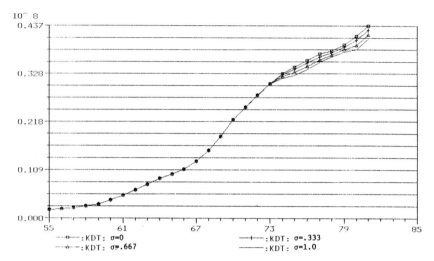

Figure 2(b). Revaluated capital stock: $K^B t$

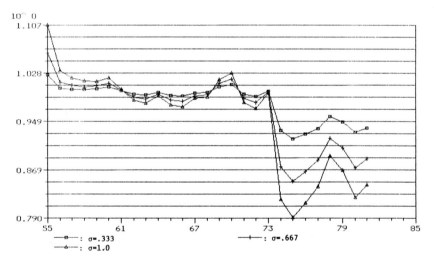

Figure 3(a). Revaluated coefficient: $\lambda^A t = \dfrac{K^A t}{Kt}$

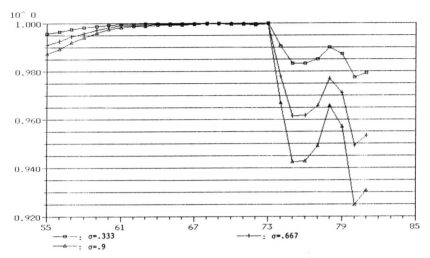

Figure 3(b). Revaluated coefficient: $\lambda^B t = \dfrac{K^B t}{K t}$

6. Measuring the Gap between Actual Production and Potential Production Capacity

The Ministry of International Trade and Industry periodically publicizes the indicator of the so-called demand-supply gap. The indicator is often utilized to measure the discrepancy between the realized production and the potential production capacity, the latter being measured on the basis of a sample survey. The indicator may be interpreted as follows in the context of the production function.

Let K_t be the conventional capital stock, L_t be the number of employees, Qt be the value added, ρ_t be the utilization rate of capital, and η_t be that of labor force. The production function is formulated as follows:

$$Q_t = f(\rho_t K_t, \eta_t L_t). \tag{29}$$

The potential production capacity $\hat{Q}_t$ is hypothetically defined as

$$\hat{Q}_t = f(K_t, L_t). \tag{30}$$

The indicator of the demand-supply gap is the ratio:

$$\zeta_t = \frac{Q_t}{\hat{Q}_t}. \tag{31}$$

From the time-series data of Q_t and ζ_t, we can estimate $\hat{Q}_t$ by the relationship (31). Assuming Cobb-Douglas function for (30), we can estimate the production function by regressing $\ln \hat{Q}_t$ on $\ln K_t$ and $\ln L_t$

$$\ln \hat{Q}_t = .589 \ln K_t + .411 \ln L_t + .0337t + .354 \qquad (32)$$

or

$$\hat{Q} = 1.4243 \cdot K_t^{.589} L_t^{.411} e^{.0337t}. \qquad (33)$$

So far our discussion has been based on the conventional capital stock, which does not necessarily reflect the energy efficiency of capital equipment of different vintages. In order to take into account the energy efficiency more explicitly, it would be more appropriate to evaluate the potential production capacity in terms of the revaluated capital stock K_t^* instead of the conventional capital stock K_t.

Since the rate of distribution between labor and capital is invariant with respect to the measurement of capital, we can estimate the potential production capacity $\hat{Q}_t^*$ in terms of the revaluated capital stock K_t^* by inserting K_t^* in place of K_t in (33). The modified demand-supply gap is finally computed as the ratio of the actual production over the modified production capacity

$$\zeta_t^* = \frac{Q_t}{\hat{Q}_t^*}. \qquad (34)$$

There has been controversy among economists on the issue of whether or not the effective demand fell short of the supply capacity of the Japanese economy during the OPEC decade, the consequence of which stretches to either the acceptance or rejection of the Keynesian policy that aims at stimulating the effective demand. Indeed, some economists who participated in the controversy utilized the production function in order to justify their arguments, but they have never taken into account the dispersion of energy efficiency among capital equipment of different vintages.

The comparison of the growth rate of the potential production capacity with that of actual production is interesting. If they coincide with each other, then the demand and supply are well harmonized. If the former exceeds the latter significantly, the shortage of effective demand is suggested.

Table 5 shows the actual growth rates and potential growth rates for some chosen periods. As is expected, the growth rate of Q that is simply based on MITIs demand-supply gap indicator is far above that of modified production capacity Q after the oil crisis in 1973.

It is quite likely that the potential production capacity has been cut back by oil shocks through the economical deterioration of the energy inefficient capital stock installed before the oil shock in 1973. This reduction of potential production capacity is concealed if we use the traditionally aggregated capital stock instead of the revaluated one.

TABLE 5.
Actual and Potential Growth Rates

Growth Rates

Year	Actual	$\hat{Q}_t$ $\sigma = 0$	$\hat{Q}_t^A$ $\sigma = .33$	$\hat{Q}_t^A$ $\sigma = .66$	$\hat{Q}_t^A$ $\sigma = 1.0$	$\hat{Q}_t^B$ $\sigma = .66$ $A = 0.5$	$\hat{Q}_t^B$ $\sigma = .66$ $A = 1.0$	$\hat{Q}_t^B$ $\sigma = .66$ $A = 2.0$	$\hat{Q}_t^B$ $\sigma = .33$ $A = 1.0$	$\hat{Q}_t^B$ $\sigma = .90$ $A = 1.0$
1955–1965	15.5%	16.8%	16.4%	15.8%	15.2%	16.9%	16.9%	15.8%	16.9%	17.0%
1965–1973	14.7	13.3	13.5	13.4	13.4	13.4	13.4	13.3	13.3	13.4
1973–1977	2.67	5.48	4.34	3.34	2.48	4.49	4.72	4.92	5.16	4.31
1973–1981	5.58	5.54	5.01	4.57	2.93	4.88	5.03	5.17	5.32	4.76

$\hat{Q}$ = Growth rate of production capacity based on MITI's indicator; $\hat{Q}^A$ = Growth rate of production capacity based on revaluated capital stock K^A; $\hat{Q}^B$ = Growth rate of production capacity based on K^B.

143

If our revaluation is recognized to be plausible, then the demand-supply gap after the oil shock has not been as spread as was suggested by the conventional production function approach.

References

Berndt, E. R. and D. O. Wood, Energy prices and induced revaluation of durable capital in U.S. manufacturing during the OPEC decade, *Studies in Energy and the American Economy*, MIT, 1984.
Kuroda, M., Measurement of capital services input, *Mita-Shougaku-Kenkyu*, Vol. 25, No. 4, 1982.
Ookawa, K., Long-Term Economic Statistics of Japan, Toyo-Keizai Co., 1966.

8

Why Is Japan's Private Saving Rate So High?*

CHARLES YUJI HORIOKA

Institute of Social and Economic Research
Osaka University
Ibaraki, Osaka-fu
Japan

A massive current account surplus is perhaps the most serious problem facing Japan today and is generating considerable discontent and protectionist sentiment abroad. There are many factors behind this current account surplus, but Japan's saving rate, which is one of the highest in the world, has been suggested as a major cause. The reasoning is as follows: In recent years, domestic investment and government deficits have been insufficient to absorb the high level of private saving, and as a result, much of this saving has been invested abroad, leading to capital account deficits that must be offset by current account surpluses. Of course, Japan's capital outflows also have a positive side inasmuch as they are helping to meet capital shortages abroad and contributing toward the expansion of investment opportunities available to Japanese savers. In any case, no one can deny the importance of the role being played by Japanese saving both at home and abroad. It is thus important to have a better understanding of Japanese saving behavior and the causes of Japan's high saving rate. Considerable research has been conducted on these topics, but our understanding is still far from complete.

The aim of the present paper is to help fill this gap in our knowledge. In particular, the determinants of intercountry differences in private saving rates

*An earlier version of this paper (Horioka [1985b]) was prepared while the author was a consultant in the Asian Department of the International Monetary Fund during the summer of 1985. The author wishes to thank the staff of the International Monetary Fund (especially Dr. Ching-yuan Lin, Mr. Hiroshi Shibuya, and Dr. Shinji Takagi) for their valuable advice and assistance and participants in seminars at the Institute of Fiscal and Monetary Policy of the Japanese Ministry of Finance and the Economic Research Institute of the Japanese Economic Planning Agency and several anonymous referees for their valuable comments. The views expressed herein are those of the author and should not be attributed to any institution or organization. Moreover, any errors that remain are the responsibility of the author alone.

145

are analyzed, and, based on this analysis, the relative importance of the various factors that have been suggested as possible causes of Japan's high private saving rate is assessed and future trends in Japan's private saving rate are projected.

The organization of the paper is as follows: Section 1 presents data on household and private saving rates for the member countries of the Organization for Economic Cooperation and Development (OECD). Section 2 discusses the specification of the econometric model, and Section 3 presents the estimation results. Based on these results, Section 4 analyzes the factors responsible for Japan's high private saving rate and Section 5 speculates about future trends. There is a brief concluding section and a data appendix.

1.   An International Comparison of Saving Rates

Tables 1 and 2 present data on the household saving rate and the private saving rate, respectively, for the OECD member countries for which data are available. The household saving rate is defined as the ratio of household saving (including the saving of households, private unincorporated enterprises, and private nonprofit institutions serving households) to household disposable income, while the private saving rate is defined as the ratio of private saving (the sum of household saving and corporate saving) to private national income (calculated as the sum of household disposable income and corporate saving). A net concept of saving is used throughout, meaning that depreciation (the consumption of fixed capital) is excluded. (Refer to the data appendix for a more detailed description.) Both tables give figures for each year between 1975 and 1984 as well as averages for the 1975–1979, 1980–1984, and 1975–1984 periods.

As the tables show, there is considerable variation in both the household saving rate and the private saving rate. For example, the former ranges from 3.2% in Sweden to 21.4% in Italy for the 1975–1984 period as a whole, while the latter ranges from 4.1% in Iceland to 30.0% in Luxembourg for the same period. Moreover, intercountry differences in both saving rates are remarkably stable over time. For example, with respect to the private saving rate, Luxembourg occupies the top position in every year for which data are available for that country (except that it is tied with Ireland in 1975), and Japan and Italy are also always in the top four (except for Italy in 1983), with private saving rates of close to or above 20%. At the opposite extreme, Iceland is virtually always in last place with a private saving rate of less than 10%, and Norway, Sweden, Finland, and the United States are also near the bottom with private saving rates of at most 12%–13%. Furthermore, generally the same countries occupy the two extremes with respect to the household saving

An International Comparison of Household Saving Rates

Country	SNA	1975	1976	1977	1978	1979	1980	1981	1982	1983	1984	1975–79	1980–84	1975–84
Australia	Present	16.8	16.4	16.1	16.0	14.5	14.8	14.7	13.8	14.9	14.1	15.97	14.47	15.22
Austria	Present	9.9	10.4	7.8	11.3	11.2	10.4	8.1	10.1	8.9	9.8	10.16	9.47	9.82
Belgium	Former	17.1	18.7	16.6	16.6	15.1	16.2	15.9	14.2	15.8	15.0	16.84	15.41	16.12
Canada	Present	11.1	9.5	9.3	11.2	11.8	12.9	14.5	15.7	13.5	13.6	10.59	14.02	12.31
Denmark	Present	na	na	na	na	na	na	na	na	na	na	na	na	na
Finland	Present	6.1	4.5	3.9	5.0	4.7	5.3	4.3	5.1	5.6	5.1	4.82	5.10	4.96
France	Present	15.4	13.0	13.3	14.2	12.8	11.5	12.4	12.4	11.0	10.3	13.75	11.51	12.63
Germany (Fed. Rep.)	Present	15.1	13.3	12.2	12.0	12.6	12.8	13.4	12.8	11.2	11.6	13.04	12.36	12.70
Greece	Former	na	na	na	na	na	na	na	na	na	na	na	na	na
Iceland	Present	na	na	na	na	na	na	na	na	na	na	na	na	na
Ireland	Present	na	na	na	na	na	na	na	na	na	na	na	na	na
Italy	Present	22.7	22.3	22.0	23.3	22.5	20.4	20.5	20.1	18.9	na	22.56	19.97[1]	21.41[2]
Japan	Present	22.9	23.3	21.8	21.0	18.3	18.0	18.4	16.6	16.3	16.1	21.44	17.09	19.27
Luxembourg	Present	na	na	na	na	na	na	na	na	na	na	na	na	na
Netherlands	Present	14.6	13.9	12.7	12.7	12.2	11.6	13.0	15.6	14.1	14.7	13.22	13.79	13.50
New Zealand	Present	na	na	na	na	na	na	na	na	na	na	na	na	na
Norway	Present	4.2	6.1	4.7	8.4	4.6	3.4	4.5	3.8	4.9	5.3	5.58	4.39	4.99
Portugal	Present	na	na	na	na	na	na	na	na	na	na	na	na	na
Spain	Present	11.3	9.9	8.7	9.8	9.0	7.4	7.8˙	na	na	na	9.75	7.60[3]	9.14[4]
Sweden	Present	5.0	2.7	4.3	4.8	3.2	5.2	4.0	0.8	1.4	0.7	4.00	2.40	3.20
Switzerland	Former	13.8	11.7	10.1	10.8	10.0	9.9	11.3	12.7	12.5	12.4	11.27	11.76	11.51
Turkey	Present	na	na	na	na	na	na	na	na	na	na	na	na	na
United Kingdom	Present	8.5	7.8	7.4	8.8	9.4	10.9	9.0	8.6	7.1	7.6	8.39	8.63	8.51
United States	Present	10.4	8.8	7.9	7.9	7.7	8.0	8.6	8.2	7.0	na	8.53	7.93[1]	8.27[2]
Yugoslavia	Former	na	na	na	na	na	na	na	na	na	na	na	na	na

Notes: Refer to the main text (Section 1) and to the data appendix for the definition and data source.
All figures represent percentages.
na: not available.
[1] 1980–1983
[2] 1975–1983
[3] 1980–1981
[4] 1975–1981

TABLE 2.
An International Comparison of Private Saving Rates

Country	SNA	1975	1976	1977	1978	1979	1980	1981	1982	1983	1984	1975–79	1980–84	1975–84
Australia	Present	20.4	20.4	19.1	20.5	19.3	18.6	16.4	14.7	18.2	17.0	19.93	17.00	18.46
Austria	Present	14.9	16.8	14.2	16.3	17.0	15.9	13.0	15.0	14.0	14.7	15.83	14.52	15.18
Belgium	Former	17.4	19.3	17.1	17.5	16.0	16.9	16.2	15.1	17.0	16.4	17.46	16.30	16.88
Canada	Present	17.1	16.1	15.5	17.6	20.0	20.7	19.0	15.6	17.4	18.0	17.25	18.14	17.69
Denmark	Present	13.3	11.5	11.8	11.3	10.0	9.5	10.6	14.2	15.1	13.8	11.58	12.65	12.11
Finland	Present	9.3	2.9	3.1	6.9	12.2	12.2	10.2	10.4	12.3	12.1	6.88	11.44	9.16
France	Present	15.1	11.9	13.7	15.3	14.1	11.6	10.4	9.4	9.3	10.5	14.01	10.23	12.12
Germany (Fed. Rep.)	Present	15.2	15.2	12.9	14.2	14.3	12.6	11.5	11.2	11.9	12.2	14.36	11.92	13.14
Greece	Former	18.7	18.7	19.7	22.0	23.6	24.6	25.6	17.4	15.4	17.1	20.55	20.00	20.29
Iceland	Former	2.4	4.0	8.6	9.3	5.4	5.2	na	na	na	na	5.92	na	na
	Present	na	na	na	na	na	8.0	3.2	−2.5	0.3	−6.3	7.67[1]	0.54	4.10[1]
Ireland	Present	23.1	18.4	20.2	20.6	18.4	13.5	12.2	16.9	18.6	na	20.15	15.32[2]	18.00[3]
Italy	Present	20.7	21.5	21.1	22.6	23.3	21.2	20.4	20.0	17.3	20.1	21.84	19.80	20.82
Japan	Present	22.2	24.0	23.1	24.4	22.1	21.1	20.3	19.4	18.7	18.9	23.16	19.68	21.42
Luxembourg	Present	23.1	29.9	26.7	28.6	30.9	32.1	32.8	36.2	na	na	27.84	33.69[4]	30.03[5]
Netherlands	Present	17.0	18.1	16.5	16.0	15.3	13.5	15.2	17.6	17.1	19.3	16.58	16.54	16.56
New Zealand	Present	na	na	na	na	na	na	na	na	na	na	na	na	na
Norway	Present	8.2	4.9	6.9	4.3	8.4	10.6	12.7	9.4	12.4	13.3	5.28	11.67	8.48
Portugal	Present	na	na	na	na	na	na	na	na	na	na	na	na	na

148

Spain	Present	14.5	12.8	11.8	14.4	13.3	11.1	10.3	10.6	na	na	13.38	10.63[4]	12.35[5]
Sweden	Present	13.0	6.1	2.7	5.3	9.0	11.3	9.3	8.3	10.0	10.5	7.24	9.90	8.57
Switzerland	Former	18.1	16.7	16.1	16.7	16.8	16.6	18.0	18.9	18.9	19.5	16.87	18.39	17.63
Turkey	Present	na	na	na	na	na	na	na	na	na	na	na	na	na
United Kingdom	Present	7.2	9.1	12.8	14.5	13.7	12.0	9.9	10.8	11.4	13.3	11.45	11.48	11.47
United States	Present	12.4	11.3	11.3	11.4	10.5	9.2	10.1	9.1	9.6	na	11.39	9.53[2]	10.56[3]
Yugoslavia	Former	na	na	na	na	na	na	na	na	na	na	na	na	na

Notes: Refer to the main text (Section 1) and to the data appendix for the definition and data source.
All figures represent percentages.
na: not available.
[1] Figures based on the present SNA are not available for 1975–1979 but were estimated as follows: Complete data based on both the former and present SNAs are available for 1980 only; for each year between 1975 and 1979 and for each component needed to compute the private saving rate, the figure based on the present SNA was estimated from the figure based on the former SNA on the assumption that the ratio between the two was the same in each year as it was in 1980.

[2] 1980–1983
[3] 1975–1983
[4] 1980–1982
[5] 1975–1982

149

rate as well. Data on the household saving rate are not available for Luxembourg and Iceland, but as in the case of the private saving rate, Italy and Japan are at the top of the rankings, with household saving rates of 16%–23%, and Sweden, Finland, Norway, and the United States are at the bottom (together with the United Kingdom and Spain) with household saving rates of less than 10% in virtually every case.

Thus, Japan's saving rate is not the highest among the OECD countries nor is that of the United States the lowest, but Japan is near the top and the United States is near the bottom with respect to both measures of saving. The household and private saving rates for the 1975–1984 period as a whole were, respectively, 19.3% and 21.4% in the case of Japan and 8.3% and 10.6% in the case of the United States. Thus, the U.S. figure was less than half of the corresponding figure for Japan with respect to both measures. One objective of this paper is to determine the reasons for this sizable gap between the U.S. and Japanese saving rates.[1]

2. The Specification of the Model

In this section, a brief description of the specification of the model is provided. This specification is based largely on the life-cycle hypothesis and is similar to the specifications used in previous econometric analyses of international differences in saving rates [see, for example, Barro and MacDonald, 1979; Feldstein, 1977, 1980; Kopits and Gotur, 1980; Koskela and Viren, 1983; Leff, 1969; Modigliani, 1970; Modigliani and Sterling, 1983; and Ram, 1982]. More detailed descriptions of all of the variables (including definitions, calculation methods, time period, and data sources) are given in the data appendix.

Following Feldstein [1977, 1980], Modigliani [1970], and Modigliani and Sterling [1983], SPVT, the private saving rate, has been used as the dependent variable. As discussed earlier, the private saving rate differs from the household saving rate by the inclusion of corporate saving (undistributed corporate profits) in both the numerator and the denominator, and its use requires the assumption that household saving and corporate saving are perfect substitutes. Although the empirical evidence on this point is mixed, theoretical considerations favor the use of the private saving rate "... because any wealth-oriented theory of saving will suggest that increments of asset value, wherever they are located, will be of approximately equal relevance to the saver [Solow,

---

[1] Boskin and Roberts [1986] and Hayashi [1986] show that much (though not all) of the U.S.–Japan gap in saving rates is due to differences in the measurement of saving and income. Such differences are undoubtedly important, not only for the United States and Japan but also for other countries, but a detailed analysis thereof is beyond the scope of this paper.

1982, p. 163]." In any case, the two saving ratios appear to be highly correlated with one another, as can be seen from Tables 1 and 2.[2]

We now turn to a description of the explanatory variables. According to the life-cycle hypothesis of Modigliani et al., the primary motive for saving is to provide for one's retirement; thus, individuals save during their working years and dissave during their retirement years. In a stationary economy, the saving of the young will be exactly offset by the dissaving of the old, leading to aggregate household saving of zero, but in the presence of either population growth and/or productivity growth, a positive amount of household saving will result because the saving of the young will exceed the dissaving of the old. Moreover, the higher the rate of population or productivity growth is, the higher will be the household saving rate. Thus, the life-cycle hypothesis predicts that population growth and productivity growth will be important determinants of the level of household saving [see, for example, Modigliani, 1966, and Modigliani and Brumberg, 1980].

Thus, the rate of population growth and the rate of productivity growth are logical candidates for inclusion as explanatory variables in the saving function. However, as Modigliani [1970, pp. 210–213] has argued, it is not population growth per se but the ratio of retired households to working households that would be expected to influence the saving rate, and, moreover, if population growth were not balanced, the rate of population growth would not necessarily bear a stable relationship to this ratio. Since population growth has been far from balanced in our sample, it appears preferable to use the ratio of the aged population to the working-age population rather than the population growth rate. Moreover, since the population that has not yet reached working age contributes to consumption without contributing to income, their ratio to the working-age population may also exert a negative impact on the saving rate [Modigliani, 1970, p. 213]. The variable AGE has therefore been defined as the ratio of the population aged 65 and over to the population aged 20 to 64 and DEP as the ratio of the population aged 19 and under to the population aged 20 to 64.

With respect to productivity growth, the appropriate variable is the rate of growth of output per worker, but because data on employment are not available on an annual basis for all countries, population has been used as a proxy for employment. Thus, the variable used was GYPC (the growth rate of real per capita private national income).

Another influence on the saving rate that is identified by the life-cycle hypothesis is the ratio of the retirement span to lifespan [Modigliani and

---

[2] As Modigliani [1970, p. 203] and others have noted, saving in the form of net additions to the stock of durable goods should be included in saving, but, as done in previous studies, this component has been omitted due to the unavailability of data.

Brumberg, 1980, pp. 130–136]. The higher this ratio is, the higher will be the percent of income that must be saved during one's working years in order to ensure that adequate resources are available to finance life during retirement. Moreover, the earlier the retirement age is and the longer life expectancy is at retirement, the longer will be the retirement span. Thus, the retirement age would be expected to exert a negative impact on the saving rate, while life expectancy at retirement would be expected to exert a positive impact thereon. With these considerations in mind, the following variables have been defined: RETAGE (the retirement age, proxied by the qualifying age for public old-age pensions); LE65 (the life expectancy of males at age 65); LERET (the life expectancy of males at the standard retirement age RETAGE); and LPAGED (the labor force participation rate of males aged 65 and over).[3] In addition, the methodology of Modigliani and Sterling [1983, pp. 32–33] has been followed to construct a rough measure of the average retirement span. Note that the retirement span of those retiring at the standard retirement age RETAGE is equal to LERET, while the retirement span of those not retiring is obviously zero. Thus, if we assume that LPAGED is a measure of the proportion of males who choose not to retire, the average retirement span, RETSPAN, can be calculated as follows

$$RETSPAN = LERET * (1 - LPAGED) + 0 * LPAGED$$
$$= LERET * (1 - LPAGED). \tag{1}$$

Alternatively, since RETAGE may not be an accurate measure of the actual retirement age, the average retirement span can be defined on the assumption that the retirement age is 65 for all countries

$$RETSPAN' = LE65 * (1 - LPAGED) + 0 * LPAGED$$
$$= LE65 * (1 - LPAGED). \tag{2}$$

RETSPAN' is essentially the measure used by Modigliani and Sterling, but RETSPAN is the preferred measure because it incorporates intercountry differences in the standard retirement age.

The final set of variables identified by the life-cycle hypothesis are those relating to social security. As shown by Feldstein [1974] using his extended life-cycle model, public old-age pensions represent an alternative source of funds for financing life during retirement and hence will tend to reduce private saving (the wealth replacement effect), but to the extent that they induce

---

[3] Modigliani and Sterling [1983] essentially adjust LPAGED for differences among countries in the labor force participation rate of working-age males, but this practice has not been adopted here inasmuch as such variations are minimal (the labor force participation rate of males aged 25 to 44 varies within the relatively narrow range of 93% to 98%).

workers to retire earlier, thereby necessitating more saving for retirement, they will tend to increase private saving (the induced retirement effect). Since the two effects operate in opposite directions, the net impact of public old-age pensions on private saving cannot be determined *a priori.*

The appropriate measure of public old-age pensions is the amount of benefits that current workers can expect to receive when they retire, but in the absence of such data, data on current benefit expenditures for public pensions have been used. Following Barro and MacDonald [1979], Feldstein [1977], Kopits and Gotur [1980], and Koskela and Viren [1983], SSPENY is used and is defined as the ratio of public pension benefits per person over 65 to per capita private national income. Feldstein [1977, 1980] also uses a measure of social security that equals benefits per *retired* person in countries with a retirement test and benefits per *aged* person in countries with no retirement test, but since the detailed provisions of retirement tests (for example, the extent to which pensions are reduced or eliminated if the individual does not retire completely) vary greatly from country to country, it did not appear to be fruitful to make this distinction. Moreover, in some of his variants, Feldstein [1977] breaks up the social security variable into two components—benefits per recipient and the coverage ratio (the number of recipients as a ratio of the aged population or of the retired population), but the data needed to perform this calculation (in particular, data on the number of pension recipients) were not available. Modigliani and Sterling [1983] use data on benefits per retired individual, but this procedure is conceptually flawed because, in many countries, retirement is not a precondition for receiving benefits. Finally, Feldstein [1980] and Modigliani and Sterling [1983] use Haanes-Olsen's [1978] data on the "effective replacement rate" for a newly retiring standardized worker in the manufacturing sector. These data come closest to the theoretically appropriate concept, but they are not available for recent years and are available for only 12 countries. It thus appears that the variable used is the best that can be done given the available data.

An alternative measure, SSPENYT (the ratio of public pension benefits to aggregate private national income), was also tried, but SSPENY is the preferred measure because it controls for differences in the age structure of the population.

Two related variables pertain to a broader concept of social security that encompasses not only pensions but also other forms of social insurance (sickness/maternity, employment injuries, and unemployment) as well as family allowances, public assistance, etc. The first of these variables is SSTY (the ratio of benefit expenditures for social security broadly defined to private national income), while the second is SSOY (the ratio of benefit expenditures for social security programs other than public pensions to private national income). (Kopits and Gotur [1980] use a measure essentially identical to

SSOY.) Although the life-cycle hypothesis does not incorporate a role for social security programs other than old-age pensions, it is possible that other forms of social security will reduce the need for precautionary saving and thereby exert a negative impact on private saving.

Another variable that was tried is INVYPC (the reciprocal of per capita private national income in United States dollars). Following Kopits and Gotur [1980], the conversion from national currencies to United States dollars was done using purchasing power parities; this represents an improvement over earlier studies, which use official exchange rates.

Three variables relating to the real rate of return were also tried: INT (the nominal yield on long-term government bonds), INFL (the rate of consumer price inflation), and RINT (the real interest rate). No account was taken of differences across countries in marginal tax rates on property income due to the unavailability of data. Assuming a positive interest elasticity of saving, INT and RINT should have a positive impact on saving and INFL a negative impact.

Finally, HRS (the average number of hours worked per week in the manufacturing sector) was also tried on the basis of the argument advanced by Makin [1986]: If consumption and leisure are complementary goods, a greater number of hours worked (less leisure) should lead to less consumption (more saving).

Other variables tried by previous authors, such as the corporate saving rate [Feldstein, 1977; Kopits and Gotur, 1980; Modigliani, 1970; and Modigliani and Sterling, 1983], some measure of the size distribution of income [Kopits and Gotur, 1980] or of the functional distribution of income [Modigliani, 1970], etc., could not be included because the data needed to construct them were available for only a subset of the countries and because their coefficients were generally found to be insignificant in previous studies. It would have been desirable to include variables relating to household wealth holdings, bonus income as a percent of total worker compensation, the tax treatment of property income, the availability of consumer credit, and other factors that have been suggested as possible causes of Japan's high saving rate,[4] but, unfortunately, the unavailability of data precluded their inclusion in the analysis.

The present study represents an improvement over past studies in the following respects: First, it makes use of more recent data, as discussed in more detail in the next section. Second, it includes variables that have never been tried before in similar cross-section analyses, such as the number of hours

[4] Refer to Horioka [1985a] for a comprehensive survey of the factors that have been suggested as possible causes of Japan's high household saving rate.

worked, the retirement age, and life expectancy at retirement (computed using a country-specific retirement age). Third, it is one of the few studies (together with Kopits and Gotur [1980] and Koskela and Viren [1983]) that include variables relating to the rate of return on saving and the inflation rate. Fourth, it is the only study other than Modigliani and Sterling [1983] that makes use of a measure of the average retirement span, and, moreover, one of our measures represents an improvement over their measure. Fifth, it is the only study other than Kopits and Gotur [1980] that converts income to United States dollars using purchasing power parities.[5] Sixth, it is the only study other than Kopits and Gotur [1980] that includes a measure of social security benefits other than pensions.

3. Estimation Results

The saving model discussed in the previous section was estimated using cross-section data for the 21 OECD countries for which data on net private saving are available. The countries included are (in alphabetical order) Australia, Austria, Belgium, Canada, Denmark, Finland, France, Germany (Federal Republic), Greece, Iceland, Ireland, Italy, Japan, Luxembourg, the Netherlands, Norway, Spain, Sweden, Switzerland, the United Kingdom, and the United States. Four OECD countries (New Zealand, Portugal, Turkey, and Yugoslavia) had to be omitted because of the unavailability of data on net private saving. In addition, variants that include variables relating to social security benefits also exclude Iceland from the sample because such data are not available for that country.

The sample was restricted to the OECD countries for three reasons: First, the OECD compiles national income data for member countries that have been standardized to conform to the United Nations' System of National Accounts (SNA) [see Blades and Sturm, 1982]. Second, it was felt that it would be better to restrict the sample to countries with more highly developed statistical frameworks, particularly because saving is typically calculated as a residual and hence is especially sensitive to measurement error. Third, and most important, it appeared to be desirable to compare countries that are at a similar stage of economic development and to which the life-cycle model would be expected to apply. As noted by Modigliani [1970, p. 215], it is not desirable to lump together countries differing radically in terms of socio-economic structure and stage of economic development for the

---

[5] Modigliani and Sterling [1983] also follow this procedure but do not introduce the income variable into the saving equation.

following reason:

> ... the life cycle model does not purport to represent a universal theory of
> individual and aggregate saving formation and wealth holding, but is instead
> basically designed to apply to private capitalistic economies in which at least the
> bulk of income, consumption, and accumulation transactions occur through
> markets. Furthermore, even for economies satisfying this requirement, signifi-
> cant differences in economic structure might be associated with differences in
> such factors as tastes, life cycle profiles of earnings, and family structure, which,
> in turn, affect the parameters of the long run saving function.

Following previous studies, the dependent variable, SPVT, was averaged over a number of years (1975–84 for most countries in the case of the present study) in order to smooth out cyclical fluctuations. This is the most recent period for which data were available at the time this study was undertaken, and it has the added advantage of avoiding the abnormal period following the first oil crisis of 1973. It should be noted that no other similar study makes use of data more recent than 1977, and most previous studies use data from the 1950s and 1960s. It will be interesting to see whether the relationships that were found by other authors using data from the 1950s, 1960s, and early 1970s still hold in the late 1970s and early 1980s.

The explanatory variables relating to income growth, interest rates, and inflation pertain to the same 10-year period to which the saving rate data pertain, while the demographic and social security-related variables, which are generally more stable over time than the economic variables, pertain to a single year (usually 1980 or the closest year to 1980 for which data are available).

Feldstein [1977] and Modigliani [1970] have been followed in weighting each observation by WT, the country's population times the number of years used to calculate its saving rate. (For several countries, the necessary data were not available for one or two years of the standard ten-year period.) Estimating the basic variants without weighting the observations was also tried for purposes of comparison.

Preliminary results (not reported) showed that the coefficients of HRS and INT were always insignificant and that INFL performed better than RINT. Thus, HRS, INT, and RINT were not included in the final variants.

Before presenting the estimation results of the present study, the results of a similar study based on data for the 1976–1982 period, a shorter period than that used in the present study, will be briefly discussed for purposes of comparison. [Refer to Horioka, 1985b, for a more detailed discussion of the 1976–1982 results.] Table 3 shows the parameter estimates of the basic variants (with and without the inflation rate INFL) for the full sample of 21 countries, and, as the table shows, the overall fit is exceptionally good and all

TABLE 3.
Parameter Estimates based on Data for the 1976–1982 Period

Constant	GYPC	AGE	DEP	LPAGED	INVYPC	INFL	R^2 Adj. R^2
1. 1.0349	4.2267	−2.8242	−0.8834	−0.6105	1782.1		0.9935
0.1729	1.1618	0.3571	0.2129	0.1093	163.2		0.9914
5.984	3.638	−7.909	−4.150	−5.583	10.918		
2. 1.1079	3.6310	−2.5511	−1.1462	−0.4663	1392.1	0.4435	0.9954
0.1539	1.0433	0.3317	0.2157	0.1128	216.4	0.1854	0.9934
7.200	3.480	−7.692	−5.314	−4.134	6.432	2.392	

Notes: The dependent variable is SPVT, the private saving rate.
The sample size is 21—the 21 OECD countries for which data are available.
The observations were weighted by WT (each country's population times the number of years of data used to calculate SPVT).
Refer to the main text (Sections 1 and 2) and to the data appendix for variable definitions and data sources.
The top figure is the estimated coefficient, the middle figure is the standard error, and the bottom figure is the *t*-statistic.

of the coefficients are highly significant. Moreover, all of the coefficients of the life cycle-related variables have the expected signs. The only problem is that the coefficients of the life-cycle-related variables are far larger than in the case of previous studies [Barro and MacDonald, 1979; Feldstein, 1977, 1980; Kopits and Gotur, 1980; Koskela and Viren, 1983; Leff, 1969; Modigliani, 1970; Modigliani and Sterling, 1983; and Ram, 1982][6] and also far larger than Modigliani and Sterling's [1983] *a priori* estimates.

Turning to the coefficients of the other variables, the life cycle/permanent income hypothesis predicts that the coefficient of INVYPC will be zero, and the Keynesian absolute income hypothesis predicts that it will be negative, but, somewhat surprisingly, the coefficient of INVYPC is found to be *positive* and significant. It is not clear why this result is obtained, but dropping INVYPC from the regression equation does not alter the other parameter estimates significantly.

As for INFL, its coefficient is positive and significant, implying that inflation has a positive impact on the private saving rate. The impact of inflation on saving is theoretically ambiguous because of a number of mutually offsetting effects, but our results suggest that the positive effects more than outweigh the

[6] Only Feldstein [1980], Leff (1969), and Ram [1982] (in certain variants) obtain comparable or higher estimates of the coefficient of DEP, and only Feldstein [1980] obtains comparable or higher estimates of the coefficients of GYPC and LPAGED. No study of which I am aware obtains comparable or higher estimates of the coefficient of AGE.

negative ones. It could be, for example, that the income effect dominates the substitution effect, leading to a negative interest elasticity of saving, or that households save more in times of inflation in order to maintain the real value of their (financial) assets and/or because high inflation increases the amount of uncertainty about the future.

Lines 1 and 2 of Table 4 show the parameter estimates for the same variants based on data for the longer 1975–1984 period. A comparison of Tables 3 and 4 reveals that the estimation results for the two time periods are strikingly different despite the fact that they overlap.[7] In particular, the fit of the variants based on data for the 1975–1984 period is far worse (but still respectable, especially if one considers the cross-sectional nature of the data), and the coefficients are, without exception, far smaller and far less significant than in the case of the variants based on data for the 1976–1982 period. For example, the coefficients of GYPC, LPAGED, and INFL are now insignificant, and the coefficient of DEP is only marginally significant in the variant without INFL. This suggests that the estimation results are highly sensitive to the choice of time period.

It should be noted, however, that all of the coefficients of the life cycle-related variables still have the expected signs and that the coefficients of AGE and DEP are at least marginally significant. Moreover, the coefficients of AGE and DEP are now broadly consistent with both the results of previous studies as well as with Modigliani and Sterling's [1983] a priori estimates. In some ways, therefore, the 1975–1984 results provide stronger support for the life cycle hypothesis than the 1976–1982 results.

The lower significance levels of the coefficients of GYPC, LPAGED, and (to a lesser extent) AGE and DEP in the results based on data for the 1975–1984 period are somewhat troubling, but a preliminary investigation showed that the primary culprit was multicollinearity. For example, there is a high degree of correlation between GYPC and DEP, GYPC and INFL, LPAGED and AGE, LPAGED and INFL, and DEP and INFL. Moreover, another problem may be the lack of variation in GYPC and LPAGED (both exhibit considerably less variation than they did in earlier periods).[8]

As for the other variables, the constant term is still positive and significant, the coefficient of INVYPC is positive and at least marginally significant, and the coefficient of INFL is still positive but no longer significant.

---

[7] It should be noted that the difference in time period is not the only difference. The OECD's National Accounts data for all of the countries in the sample were revised between the time the earlier study was conducted and the time the present study was conducted, with the revisions being fairly major ones in some cases.

[8] Interestingly enough, the coefficient of GYPC is positive and significant, as expected, in the unweighted regressions, but the other coefficients become far less significant.

TABLE 4.
Parameter Estimates based on Data for the 1975–1984 Period

	Constant	GYPC	AGE	DEP	LPAGED	INVYPC	INFL	RETAGE	LERET	RETSPAN	R^2 Adj. R^2
1.	0.4647	0.7858	−1.0947	−0.4350	−0.1522	1140.1					0.5519
	0.2074	1.6455	0.4606	0.2516	0.1515	399.7					0.4025
	2.240	0.478	−2.377	−1.729	−1.004	2.853					
2.	0.5360	0.6836	−1.0339	−0.5875	−0.0827	805.8	0.3709				0.5892
	0.2151	1.6333	0.4597	0.2836	0.1623	494.8	0.3290				0.4131
	2.492	0.419	−2.249	−2.071	−0.509	1.629	1.127				
3.	1.0243	−0.1155	−0.8912	−0.2634	−0.1321	753.6		−0.0099			0.7351
	0.2441	1.3412	0.3724	0.2077	0.1208	341.5		0.0032			0.6216
	4.196	−0.086	−2.393	−1.268	−1.094	2.207		−3.112			
	0.2155	0.2091	−0.8972	−0.3129	−0.1889	967.3			0.0123		0.6959
	0.2016	1.4208	0.4002	0.2197	0.1300	347.3			0.0048		0.5656
	1.069	0.147	−2.242	−1.424	−1.453	2.785			2.575		
5.	0.2642	0.4402	−1.0951	−0.4084		1114.2				0.0140	0.6865
	0.1347	1.3042	0.2261	0.1943		275.4				0.0050	0.5820
	1.961	0.338	−4.843	−2.102		4.046				2.807	

Notes: See Table 3.

159

Turning now to the results of variants 3 through 5 in Table 4, which include the retirement-related variables, it can be seen that the fit is reasonably good in all cases. Moreover, the coefficients of AGE, DEP, and INVYPC are relatively stable, although the coefficient of DEP is sometimes not significant. As before, the coefficients of GYPC and LPAGED exhibit the correct signs (with one exception) but are not significant, while the constant term remains positive but is insignificant in one case.

Looking next at the performance of the retirement-related variables themselves, line 3 of Table 4 presents the results of the variant that includes RETAGE, a variable unique to the present study. As the table shows, the coefficient of RETAGE is negative and significant, which is as expected because, according to the life-cycle hypothesis, a later retirement age should reduce the need to save by shortening the retirement span (refer to the discussion in the previous section).

As for the variables pertaining to the life expectancy of the elderly, LE65 and LERET, the coefficient of LE65 was found to be insignificant, and thus the results of the variants that include it are not shown. Line 4 of Table 4 presents the results of the variant that includes LERET, a measure of the retirement span of those retiring at the standard retirement age, and shows that the coefficient of LERET is, as expected, positive and significant. LERET is the preferred measure because it takes account of intercountry differences in the retirement age, and hence it is reassuring that it performs far better than LE65.

The final retirement-related variables, RETSPAN and RETSPAN', represent rough measures of the average retirement span and were computed from LPAGED and LERET/LE65, as explained in the previous section. Thus, both LPAGED and LERET/LE65 were dropped from the regression equation in variants that include RETSPAN or RETSPAN'. The coefficient of RETSPAN' was found to be insignificant, and thus the results of the variants that include it are not shown. Line 5 of Table 4 presents the results of the variant that includes RETSPAN and shows that the coefficient of RETSPAN is, as expected, positive and significant. RETSPAN, a variable unique to the present study, is the preferred measure because it takes account of intercountry differences in the retirement age, and hence it is reassuring that it performs far better than RETSPAN'.[9]

Thus, all three of the retirement-related variables that were ultimately retained perform as expected, and their coefficients are significant. This lends

---

[9] Introducing two or more of the retirement-related variables into the regression equation together caused one or more of their coefficients to become insignificant, which is not surprising since the variables are closely related: RETSPAN was computed from LPAGED and LERET, as already noted, and LERET was computed using RETAGE.

further support to the validity of the life cycle hypothesis. Moreover, all three of the variables are unique to the present study, and thus their strong performance is especially noteworthy.

Turning finally to the social security-related variables, the estimation results are not shown, but the coefficients of the variables relating to social security benefits (SSPENY, SSPENYT, SSTY, and SSOY) were all totally insignificant, suggesting that the total effect of social security on saving is negligible. Moreover, the coefficient of SSPENY remained insignificant even when two-stage least squares was used and LPAGED was made endogenous following Feldstein [1977, 1980] and Koskela and Viren [1983]. This suggests that the wealth replacement effect is also negligible. The coefficient of SSPENY was found to be negative and significant, as expected, in the LPAGED equation, but because the impact of LPAGED on the private saving rate was found to be insignificant, the implied increase in saving due to the induced retirement effect is negligible. Thus, the results suggest that the total effect of social security on saving is negligible, not because the wealth replacement effect and the induced retirement effect roughly offset one another, but because both effects are negligible.

However, the insignificance of the social security-related variables may be due to data problems rather than to the absence of a relationship between social security benefits and saving. One problem is multicollinearity between SSPENY and the other explanatory variables, especially AGE (0.65). It appears that countries with a high ratio of the aged tend to be the countries with generous public pension benefits, perhaps because a larger aged population increases the political pressure for improvements in benefit levels. As a result of this problem of multicollinearity, it is difficult to estimate the independent impact of SSPENY on the private saving rate.[10]

An additional problem is the crude nature of the benefit variable used. The evidence from previous international cross-section studies is mixed, but it is noteworthy that Feldstein [1980] obtains a negative and significant coefficient on the benefit variable when Haanes-Olsen's [1978] data on replacement rates (the most careful estimates to date) are used, and Modigliani and Sterling [1983] also obtain a negative and significant coefficient on the Haanes-Olsen variable in some of their variants. It is unfortunate that the Haanes-Olsen data are available for only 12 countries and that more recent data are not available. A definitive verdict on the impact of social security on saving will have to await the availability of better data.

To summarize, the estimation results show that much of the intercountry variation in private saving rates is capable of being explained. Moreover, they provide qualified support for the life cycle hypothesis: the coefficients relating

[10] The simple correlation between SSPENY and the private saving rate is negative (-0.29).

to the age structure of the population and those relating to the length of the retirement span all exhibit the correct signs and are at least marginally significant. The insignificant coefficients on the variables relating to income growth, the labor force participation rate of the aged, and social security are somewhat disturbing but appear to be due at least partly to multicollinearity, the lack of variation in these variables, and (in the case of the social security-related variables) measurement error.

4. An Analysis of the Factors Responsible for
Japan's High Private Saving Rate

Recall from Section 2 that the private saving rate averaged 21.42 percent in Japan during the 1975–84 period, which is a full 10.86 percentage points higher than the U.S. figure of 10.56 percent and 6.80 percentage points higher than the OECD-wide mean of 14.62 percent (refer to Tables 2 and 5). In this section, I will employ the parameter estimates presented in the previous section in order to determine why Japan's private saving rate is so much higher than those of the United States and the OECD countries as a whole.[11]

First, however, it is necessary to know how the values of the explanatory variables differ between Japan and other countries. Table 5 presents data on the mean, the minimum, the maximum, and the values for Japan and the United States for each of the variables used in the analysis, and as the table shows, Japan has the lowest value for AGE of any of the 21 OECD countries included in the sample, and the highest value for LPAGED. Moreover, GYPC is higher in Japan than both the U.S. value and the OECD-wide mean, while DEP and YPC80 are lower. There is usually an inverse relationship between the ratio of the young to the working-age population and the corresponding ratio for the aged, so it is somewhat odd that both ratios are relatively low in the case of Japan. The reasons for this are the following: First, the postwar baby boom has temporarily swelled the ranks of the working-age population. Second, wartime casualties reduced the number of older persons. Third, the low birth rate since the postwar baby boom has led to a decline in the number of young persons. In sum, Japan can be characterized as a country with relatively few young people as well as old people relative to the working-age population, a higher labor force participation rate of the aged, faster productivity growth, and a lower level of per capita income.

[11] There are those who argue that the life cycle hypothesis does not apply in the case of Japan and that the elderly in Japan show little or no tendency to dissave. If this were true, the analyses presented in this section and the next, both of which are based on the life cycle hypothesis, would produce misleading results. However, Horioka [1984] argues that the life cycle hypothesis *does* apply in the case of Japan if appropriately modified and that the failure of household budget survey data to show dissaving by the elderly may be due in large part to defects in those data.

TABLE 5.
Means and Selected Values of the Variables used in the Analysis

Variable	Mean	Minimum	Maximum	Japan	U.S.
SPVT	0.1462	0.0410 (Iceland)	0.3003 (Luxembourg)	0.2142	0.1056
GYPC	0.0171	−0.0016 (Iceland)	0.0500 (Luxembourg)	0.0230	0.0173
AGE	0.2130	0.1499 (Japan)	0.2844 (Sweden)	0.1499	0.1997
DEP	0.5317	0.4486 (Luxembourg)	0.8118 (Ireland)	0.5070	0.5447
LPAGED	0.2465	0.0660 (Belgium)	0.5020 (Japan)	0.5020	0.2430
YPC80	6887	4204 (Greece)	9555 (Luxembourg)	6234	8185
INVYPC	0.149E-3	0.105E-3 (Luxembourg)	0.238E-3 (Greece)	0.160E-3	0.122E-3
INFL	0.0844	0.0340 (Switzerland)	0.4590 (Iceland)	0.0720	0.0700
RETAGE	63.115	60 (5 cos. incl. Japan)	67 (3 cos.)	60	65
LE65	13.873	12.00 (Luxembourg)	15.80 (Iceland)	14.50	14.30
LERET	15.198	11.80 (Ireland)	18.27 (Japan)	18.27	14.30
RETSPAN	11.314	7.068 (Ireland)	15.079 (Austria)	9.099	10.825
RETSPAN'	10.404	7.221 (Japan)	12.110 (Netherlands)	7.221	10.825
HRS	40.413	32.60 (Denmark)	49.12 (Iceland)	43.60	39.70
SSPENY	0.5690	0.3121 (Japan)	1.3804 (Netherlands)	0.3121	0.4734

Notes: Refer to the main text (Sections 1 and 2) and to the data appendix for variable definitions, time period, and data sources.

YPC80 is in United States dollars; INVYPC is in 1/(U.S. dollars); RETAGE, LE65, LERET, RETSPAN, and RETSPAN' are in years; HRS is in hours; and the remaining variables are in ratio form.

All figures pertain to the full sample of 21 OECD countries except for SSPENY, which pertains to the full sample minus Iceland.

The means were computed by weighting each observation by WT (each country's population times the number of years of data used to compute SPVT).

The relative importance of each of these factors as an explanation of Japan's high private saving rate was estimated based on variant 1 of Table 4, and the results are shown in Table 6. As the table shows, Japan's relatively low ratio of the aged to the working-age population is by far the most important factor. Because this variable exerts a negative influence on the private saving rate, the fact that it is the lowest in Japan can explain a full 5.5 percentage points of the excess of Japan's private saving rate over that of the United States and 6.9 percentage points of the excess over the OECD-wide mean. Moreover, Japan's lower ratio of the young to the working-age population explains an additional 1.6 percentage points of the excess of Japan's private saving rate over that of the U.S. and 1.1 percentage points of the excess over the OECD-wide mean. In addition, Japan's lower level of per capita income is estimated to have raised Japan's private saving rate by 4.4 and 1.3 percentage points, respectively, relative to the U.S. and OECD-wide levels because we

TABLE 6.

The Contribution of Each Factor to the High Level of Japan's Private Saving Rate

Factor	Sign of the Coefficient	Contribution of each factor to the excess of Japan's private saving rate over:	
		U.S. Rate	OECD-wide mean
Higher GYPC (growth rate of real per capita income)	+	+0.45	+0.47
Lower AGE (ratio of the aged to the working-age population)	−	+5.45	+6.90
Lower DEP (ratio of the young to the working-age population)	−	+1.64	+1.07
Higher LPAGED (labor force participation rate of the aged)	−	−3.94	−3.89
Lower YPC80 (per capita income)	−[1]	+4.36	+1.29
Subtotal		+7.96	+5.85
Unexplained residual		+2.90	+0.95
Total difference in SPVT (the private saving rate)		+10.86	+6.80

Notes: The calculations shown in this table are based on the estimated coefficients of variant 1 of Table 4.

All figures are expressed in terms of percentage points of the private saving rate.

[1] The coefficient of the reciprocal of per capita income was found to be positive, meaning that per capita income has a negative impact on the private saving rate.

obtained the perverse result that per capita income exerts a negative influence on the private saving rate.

The estimated impact of the other factors are not reliable because they are based on insignificant coefficients, but the results suggest that Japan's higher growth rate of real per capita income may also have contributed to its higher private saving rate, while its higher labor force participation rate of the aged may have worked in the opposite direction.

In sum, Japan's higher private saving rate is attributable to its lower ratio of the aged and, to a lesser extent, its lower ratio of the young, its lower per capita income, and perhaps also to its more rapid growth rate of real per capita income, while its higher labor-force participation rate of the aged may have acted as a negative influence.[12]

It can be seen from Table 6 that the aforementioned factors can explain all but 1.0 percentage points of the difference between Japan's private saving rate and the OECD-wide mean and most of the Japan-U.S. difference as well. This suggests that omitted variables such as culture, tax incentives, the availability of consumer credit, the ratio of bonus income to total worker compensation, the distribution of income, household wealth holdings, etc., explain little of the difference between Japan's private saving rate and that of other countries, but this is not necessarily the case. It may be that the effects of these omitted variables are mutually offsetting or that they are correlated with one or more of the included variables, in which case the coefficients of the included variables will be biased. If possible, it would be desirable to estimate the impact of these omitted variables directly, perhaps by means of an analysis of time-series data for Japan.[13]

Modigliani and Sterling [1983, pp. 44–45] also conduct an analysis of the difference between Japan's private saving rate and the OECD-wide mean and find that the factor making the largest contribution is the growth rate of per

[12] The results of similar calculations based on the other variants in Table 4 are not shown, but the parameter estimates of these variants imply that Japan's earlier retirement age, its longer life expectancy at the standard retirement age, and its longer average retirement span can each explain three or more percentage points of the excess of Japan's private saving rate over both the United States and OECD-wide levels. However, the estimated impact of the other factors declines. Note, moreover, that the three factors are closely interrelated and, therefore, that their contributions cannot simply be added (refer to footnote 9). A final point concerns the apparent inconsistency between the relatively early retirement age and the relatively high labor force participation rate of the aged in Japan. The explanation is that formal retirement from "permanent employee" status occurs relatively early in Japan but that a relatively high proportion of the aged continue working even after formal retirement (either in the same firm, a subsidiary of that firm, an unrelated firm, or on a self-employed basis).

[13] Several such studies have already been conducted. For example, Ishikawa and Ueda [1984] conducted a time-series analysis and found that the bonus system explains up to three percentage points of Japan's household saving rate.

capita income. It was not possible to obtain a precise estimate of the contribution of this factor because its coefficient was not significant, but, even if it had been available, its estimated contribution would have been far less than that obtained by Modigliani and Sterling because the data used pertain to the 1975–1984 period (during which Japan's growth rate of per capita income was only slightly higher than average), while Modigliani and Sterling use data for the 1960–1970 period (during which Japan's growth rate was far higher than average). Another difference is that Modigliani and Sterling find that Japan's high labor force participation rate of the aged made a large negative contribution, whereas I was not able to obtain a precise estimate of this factor because its coefficient was not significant. Two points on which the two studies agree are, first, that the low ratio of the aged made a large positive contribution toward both the Japan-U.S. difference as well as the Japan-OECD difference and, second, that the low ratio of the young made a positive contribution toward the Japan-U.S. difference.[14]

Thus, some factors behind Japan's high private saving rate (such as the low ratio of the aged and of the young) have remained important throughout, while in the case of other factors, as one (such as the high growth rate) declined, others increased in importance, as a result of which the private saving rate remained high. Will such serendipity continue in the future as well? It is to this question that we now turn.

5.   Future Trends in Japan's Private Saving Rate

In this section, projections concerning future trends in Japan's private saving rate will be made using information on future values of the determinants of the private saving rate in conjunction with the estimated coefficients of those variables in the saving equations discussed in Section 3. We will begin by analyzing the impact of changes in the age structure of the population because this factor was found to be by far the most important determinant of intercountry differences in private saving rates.

As we saw in Table 5, Japan's ratio of the aged to the working-age population is the lowest among the OECD countries included in the sample (0.150 versus 0.200 in the United States, 0.284 in Sweden, and 0.213 in the OECD countries as a whole), but Japan's population is aging faster than in any

---

[14] The low ratio of the young was found to have made a positive contribution toward the Japan-OECD difference in the case of the present study but a negligible negative contribution in the case of the Modigliani-Sterling study. As for the impact of social security, Modigliani and Sterling find that its total effect is negligible because the wealth replacement effect is roughly offset by the induced retirement effect.

other country to date due to the sharp decline in the birth rate and the continued increases in life expectancy (Japan now has the longest life expectancy in the world). In fact, the Institute of Population Problems of the Japanese Ministry of Health and Welfare projects that Japan's ratio of the aged will increase rapidly until at least 2020, exceeding 0.20 by 1991, 0.25 by 1998, 0.30 by 2004, 0.35 by 2009, and 0.40 by 2014 (see column 2 of Table 7) and that Japan's population will become the most aged in the world by 2010 (see Table 3–11, p. 132, of Japanese Ministry of Health and Welfare [1987].

Since the ratio of the aged was found to have a negative impact on the private saving rate, this rapid aging of the population would be expected to exert downward pressure on Japan's private saving rate, and column 3 of Table 7 shows that this is indeed the case. These calculations suggest that the increase in the ratio of the aged will cause Japan's private saving rate to decline by 2.2 percentage points by 1985, 4.9 points by 1990, 8.7 points by 1995, 13.2 points by 2000, 17.7 points by 2005, 22.8 points by 2010, and a full 28 to 35 points thereafter.

It must be borne in mind, however, that the increase in the ratio of the aged will be accompanied by a decline in the ratio of the young, at least until 1997 (from 0.51 in 1980 to less than 0.39 in 1997) (see column 4 of Table 7). This decline will occur because of the low birth rate and because the second postwar baby boom generation (born during the years 1967–1974) will reach adulthood beginning in 1987.

Since the ratio of the young was found to have a negative impact on the private saving rate, the decline in this ratio will exert upward pressure on Japan's private saving rate, as shown in column 5 of Table 7. As the table shows, the decline in the ratio of the young will cause the private saving rate to increase by 1.3 percentage points by 1985, 3.1 points by 1990, and 5.0 points by 1995. The ratio of the young is projected to fluctuate after 1997, but because it will remain below the 1980 level, it will continue to exert upward pressure on Japan's private saving rate even after 1997, with the magnitude of its impact falling in the two to five percentage point range.

Column 6 of Table 7 shows the combined impact of changes in the ratio of the aged and in the ratio of the young on future trends in Japan's private saving rate, and, as the table shows, the downward pressure on the saving rate arising from the increase in the ratio of the aged will more than offset the upward pressure on the saving rate arising from the decline in the ratio of the young in every year shown (1985–2085). Moreover, the amount by which the former exceeds the latter will increase steadily until at least 2018, from less than one percentage point in 1985 to 1.7 points in 1990, 3.7 points in 1995, 8.3 points in 2000, 13.7 points in 2005, 19.8 points in 2010, 27.1 points in 2015, and a full 25 to 33 points thereafter. Thus, the combined effect of the two factors will be to lower Japan's private saving rate by progressively larger amounts. This is

TABLE 7.
Future Trends in Japan's Private Saving Rate

(1) Year	(2) Value of AGE	(3) Change in SPVT due to change in AGE	(4) Value of DEP	(5) Change in SPVT due to change in DEP	(6) Total change in SPVT (3)+(5)	(7) Projected value of SPVT
1975–84	.150[1]	—	.507[1]	—	—	21.4
1985	.170	−2.2	.476	1.3	−0.8	20.6
1986	.174	−2.7	.474	1.5	−1.2	20.2
1987	.178	−3.1	.463	1.9	−1.2	20.2
1988	.183	−3.6	.454	2.3	−1.3	20.1
1989	.188	−4.2	.444	2.7	−1.4	20.0
1990	.194	−4.9	.435	3.1	−1.7	19.7
1991	.201	−5.6	.426	3.5	−2.1	19.3
1992	.208	−6.4	.416	4.0	−2.4	19.0
1993	.215	−7.1	.407	4.4	−2.7	18.7
1994	.222	−7.9	.399	4.7	−3.1	18.3
1995	.229	−8.7	.393	5.0	−3.7	17.7
1996	.237	−9.5	.390	5.1	−4.4	17.0
1997	.245	−10.4	.389	5.1	−5.3	16.1
1998	.254	−11.4	.389	5.1	−6.2	15.2
1999	.262	−12.3	.391	5.1	−7.2	14.2
2000	.271	−13.2	.394	4.9	−8.3	13.1
2001	.280	−14.3	.398	4.7	−9.5	11.9
2002	.289	−15.2	.402	4.6	−10.7	10.8
2003	.297	−16.1	.406	4.4	−11.7	9.7
2004	.302	−16.7	.410	4.2	−12.5	9.0
2005	.311	−17.7	.415	4.0	−13.7	7.8
2006	.322	−18.9	.421	3.7	−15.1	6.3
2007	.333	−20.1	.427	3.5	−16.6	4.8
2008	.343	−21.2	.432	3.3	−17.9	3.5
2009	.354	−22.3	.436	3.1	−19.2	2.2
2010	.358	−22.8	.437	3.0	−19.8	1.6
2011	.360	−23.0	.437	3.0	−20.0	1.4
2012	.376	−24.7	.441	2.9	−21.8	−0.4
2013	.392	−26.5	.444	2.7	−23.8	−2.4
2014	.409	−28.3	.446	2.6	−25.7	−4.3
2015	.421	−29.7	.447	2.6	−27.1	−5.6
2016	.430	−30.6	.445	2.7	−27.9	−6.5
2017	.436	−31.3	.442	2.8	−28.5	−7.0
2018	.439	−31.7	.438	3.0	−28.7	−7.3
2019	.440	−31.8	.434	3.2	−28.6	−7.1

TABLE 7. (*continued*)

(1) Year	(2) Value of AGE	(3) Change in SPVT due to change in AGE	(4) Value of DEP	(5) Change in SPVT due to change in DEP	(6) Total change in SPVT (3)+(5)	(7) Projected value of SPVT
2020	.440	−31.8	.429	3.4	−28.4	−7.0
2021	.439	−31.7	.424	3.6	−28.0	−6.6
2022	.436	−31.4	.419	3.8	−27.5	−6.1
2023	.434	−31.1	.415	4.0	−27.1	−5.7
2024	.432	−30.9	.412	4.1	−26.8	−5.4
2025	.430	−30.7	.410	4.2	−26.4	−5.0
2030	.426	−30.2	.415	4.0	−26.2	−4.7
2035	.435	−31.2	.437	3.1	−28.2	−6.7
2040	.464	−34.4	.460	2.1	−32.3	−10.9
2045	.464	−34.4	.457	2.2	−32.2	−10.8
2050	.443	−32.1	.439	2.9	−29.1	−7.7
2055	.418	−29.3	.427	3.5	−25.8	−4.4
2060	.408	−28.2	.433	3.2	−25.0	−3.6
2065	.418	−29.3	.451	2.4	−26.9	−5.5
2070	.434	−31.0	.464	1.9	−29.2	−7.8
2075	.435	−31.3	.461	2.0	−29.2	−7.8
2080	.422	−29.8	.449	2.5	−27.3	−5.8
2085	.407	−28.2	.443	2.8	−25.4	−4.0

Notes: Data on future values of AGE and DEP were computed from data on the medium estimates (*chūi suikei*) of population by age group presented in Tables 2-1, 2-2, and 2-3 (pp. 46–51) of Japanese Ministry of Health and Welfare [1987].

The estimated change in SPVT that is due to the change in AGE was calculated by multiplying the projected change in AGE relative to the initial level by the estimated coefficient of AGE in variant 1 of Table 4 (−1.0947). Similarly, the estimated change in SPVT that is due to the change in DEP was calculated by multiplying the projected change in DEP relative to the initial level by the estimated coefficient of DEP in the same variant (−0.5070). The total change in SPVT was computed as the sum of the change due to the change in AGE and the change due to the change in DEP. The projected value of SPVT was calculated by subtracting the total change therein from the initial level.

Figures may not add due to rounding error.

Only the data for every fifth year are shown for the period after 2025 because of space limitations. The yearly figures are available from the author upon request.

[1] The value for 1980

confirmed by column 7 of Table 7, which shows projections concerning future trends in Japan's private saving rate when only changes in the age structure of the population are taken into account. As the table shows, the private saving rate will decline until at least 2018, but the rate of decline will be only moderate until 1989, with the private saving rate falling only slightly from the 1975–1984 level of 21.4% to 20.0% in 1989. After 1989, however, the rate of decline will accelerate, with the private saving rate dropping to 17.7% by 1995, 13.1% by 2000, 7.8% by 2005, 1.6% by 2010, and becoming negative by 2012. That the private saving rate becomes negative is not surprising because Japan's rate of population growth (the rate of natural increase) is projected to become negative by 2014 [see Table 2–5, pp. 54–55, of Japanese Health and Welfare Ministry, 1987], and the life cycle hypothesis predicts that the saving rate will be negative in an economy with a declining population. The rate of population growth is projected to remain negative until at least 2085, and the private saving rate is also predicted to remain negative until then, fluctuating between −11.3% and −3.5% after 2014.[15]

The problem with the analysis thus far is that it has been implicitly assumed that all influences on the private saving rate other than the age structure of the population will remain constant at their present levels. It is necessary to analyze the impact of these other factors in order to obtain an accurate estimate of future trends in Japan's private saving rate, but, unfortunately, such an analysis is difficult in the case of many of the factors, either because their future values are difficult to predict (as in the case of the growth rate of per capita income) or because perverse coefficients were obtained thereon in the saving equation (as in the case of the reciprocal of per capita income). In what follows, those factors whose impact can be predicted at least qualitatively will be discussed.

The labor force participation rate of the aged. The labor force participation rate of the aged can be expected to continue to decline, due in part to improvements in social security benefits, and thus if its impact on the private saving rate were negative (something which we were not able to confirm), its decline will exert upward pressure on Japan's private saving rate.

The retirement age. The retirement age has been increased from 55 to 60 and may eventually be increased further to 65, pursuant to the increase in the

---

[15] According to the simulation analysis presented in Japanese Economic Planning Agency [1985, pp. 309–315], the household saving rate in Japan will decline from 21% in 1983 to about 7%–13% in 2020 and then begin increasing anew. Thus, the two studies agree with respect to the direction of change but differ with respect to the magnitude of the change.

eligibility age for public old-age pensions from 60 to 65. Since the retirement age was found to exert a negative impact on the private saving rate, the further increase therein will (if and when it comes to pass) exert downward pressure on Japan's private saving rate.[16]

Life expectancy at retirement. Life expectancies in Japan are already the highest in the world but are projected to increase even further, though not significantly (from 15.5 years in 1985 to 17.7 years in 2025 in the case of males aged 65) [see Japanese Ministry of Health and Welfare, 1987, pp. 10–12]. Thus, since life expectancy at retirement was found to exert a positive impact on the private saving rate, the further increase therein will exert some degree of upward pressure on Japan's private saving rate.

Social security. It was not possible to obtain a precise estimate of the impact of social security, but even if this had been possible, it would still not be clear how social security will affect future trends in Japan's private saving rate. On the one hand, it is possible that, as individuals become accustomed to the higher level of social security benefits, they will save less, but, on the other hand, it is also possible that individuals will save *more* out of a fear that the rapid aging of the population will necessitate a reduction in social security benefits.

To summarize, the decline in the labor force participation rate of the aged and the increase in life expectancy at retirement may exert upward pressure on Japan's private saving rate, while any increase in the retirement age can be expected to exert downward pressure thereon, and the impact of social security is ambiguous. The various effects were found to be mutually offsetting, uncertain, and/or small in magnitude, and thus their joint impact is likely to be negligible, meaning that the earlier analysis, which focused exclusively on the impact of changes in the age structure of the population, will not be seriously misleading.

---

[16] There is an apparent inconsistency between the projected changes in the labor force participation rate of the aged and in the retirement age because a lower labor force participation rate of the aged suggests that workers are retiring earlier, not later. The explanation is that, as noted in footnote 12, the retirement age refers not to the age of complete withdrawal from the labor force but to retirement from "permanent employee" status, whereas the labor force participation rate of the aged pertains to males aged 65 and over, most of whom have already retired from "permanent employee" status. A higher retirement age combined with a lower labor force participation rate of the aged means that workers are retiring later from "permanent employee" status but are less likely to continue working thereafter.

6. Summary

An analysis of the determinants of intercountry differences in private saving rates has been conducted using data for the 1975–1984 period for 21 OECD countries and qualified support for the life cycle hypothesis has been found, with the variables relating to the age structure of the population and to the length of the retirement span (some of which are unique to the present study) having the hypothesized effects.

The parameter estimates were found to imply that Japan's exceptionally high private saving rate is due primarily to the peculiarities of the age structure of its population—namely, the much lower ratio of the aged and the somewhat lower ratio of the young. Moreover, the age structure of the population was found to be the primary determinant of future trends in Japan's private saving rate as well, with the rapid aging of the population causing the private saving rate to decline despite upward pressure thereon caused by the decline in the ratio of the young. In particular, the private saving rate was predicted to decline moderately until 1989 and much more sharply thereafter, becoming negative by about 2012. Thus, measures to lower Japan's saving rate appear to be unnecessary (unless a more immediate decline is desired), and, in fact, measures to boost saving may become necessary by the turn of the century.

Data Appendix

In this data appendix, a detailed description of each variable is provided, along with the way in which it was constructed, the time period to which the data refer, and the source of the data.

SHH = the household saving rate, defined as the ratio of net household saving to household disposable income. Net household saving was defined as the sum of the net saving of households, private unincorporated enterprises, and private nonprofit institutions serving households, while household disposable income was calculated as the sum of net household saving and the final consumption expenditure of households and private nonprofit institutions serving households (or, equivalently, total private final consumption expenditure). Averages for the 1975–1984 period were used for most countries, but shorter periods were used for some countries due to the unavailability of data. The data for most of the countries in the sample are based on the present System of National Accounts (SNA), but the data for Belgium, Greece, Iceland (until 1980), and Switzerland are based on the former SNA. The data were taken from Tables 8 and (where applicable) 9 of the accounts for each country, as presented in Organization for Economic Cooperation and Development [1985 and 1986b].

SPVT = the private saving rate, defined as the ratio of net private saving to private national income. Net private saving was calculated as the sum of net household saving (as defined above in the description of SHH), and net corporate saving (defined as the sum of the net saving of nonfinancial and financial corporations and quasicorporate enterprises), except that in cases in which the accounts of the household and corporate sectors were not available but the accounts of the general government were, net private saving was calculated as total net saving minus the net saving of the general government. Private national income was calculated as the sum of household disposable income (as defined above in the description of SHH) and net corporate saving or, equivalently, as the sum of total private final consumption expenditure and net private saving. The time period and the data source are the same as those for SHH, except that Tables 7 and (in some cases) Tables 1 and 6 of the same data source were also used.

GYPC = the growth rate of real per capita private national income. The average annual rate of growth during the 1975–1984 period was used for most countries, but shorter periods were used for some countries due to the unavailability of data. (The same time period to which the private saving rate data pertain was used.) Real per capita private national income for both the starting and ending years was computed by dividing (nominal) private national income by the midyear estimate of population and then deflating by the price index for private final consumption expenditure (1980 = 100). Refer to the description of SPVT above for the definition of private national income and the data source used. The population data were taken from Table 37 (p. 116) of Organization for Economic Cooperation and Development [1986a], while the price index data were taken from Table 32 (p. 114) of the same source.

YPC80 = per capita private national income in 1980 in United States dollars. Refer to the descriptions of SPVT and GYPC above for the data sources used for private national income and population. The conversion from national currencies to United States dollars was done using purchasing power parities (PPPs) for private consumption, estimates of which are given in Tables 2 (p. 117) and A (p. 124) of Organization for Economic Cooperation and Development [1986a].

INVYPC = the reciprocal of 1980 per capita private national income in United States dollars. Calculated as $1/\text{YPC80}$.

INFL = the rate of consumer price inflation. The average annual rate of change of the implicit price deflator for private final consumption expenditure was used. The same time period to which the private saving rate data pertain was used (1975–1984 for most countries). The data were taken from Part 3 (pp. 74–100) of Organization for Economic Cooperation and Development [1986a].

DEP = the ratio of the population aged 19 and under to the population aged 20 to 64. These data were computed from the data on population by age group presented in United Nations [1985, Table 7, pp. 188–253] and earlier editions of the same. Data for 1980 or the closest year to 1980 for which data were available (generally either 1979 or 1981) were used.

AGE = the ratio of the population aged 65 and over to the population aged 20 to 64. Refer to the description of DEP above for the data source and time period.

WT (the weighting variable in the weighted regressions) = the number of years of data used to calculate SPVT (10 for most countries but 8 or 9 for some countries due to the unavailability of data) times each country's midyear population in 1980. Refer to the description of GYPC for the source of the population data.

LPAGED = the labor force participation rate of males aged 65 and over. These data pertain to midyear 1975 and were taken from International Labour Office [1978, Special Table, pp. 15–47]. More recent data are available for many countries in later editions of the same source, but the data used represent the most recent tabulation of age-specific labor force participation rates for which 1) the coverage is comprehensive, 2) the data pertain to the same year, and 3) the data for each country are adjusted for definitional differences.

HRS = the average number of hours worked per week by both sexes in the manufacturing sector in 1980. These data were taken from International Labour Office [1985b, Table 12, pp. 578–583]. The figures refer to the number of hours paid for rather than to the number of hours worked in some countries and hence are not strictly comparable across countries. In the case of Iceland, data for the manufacturing sector were not available, so the figure for the nonagricultural sector was used [Table 11, pp. 573–577, of the same source]. In cases in which data from two sources were available, the average of the two was used. In cases in which no figure was given for both sexes combined, the weighted average of the figures for males and females was computed using the proportion of male and female workers as weights.

INT = the nominal interest rate. The average yield on long-term government bonds or (when not available) the closest available alternative was used. The same time period to which the private saving rate data pertain was used (1975–84 for most countries). The data were taken from various issues of *International Financial Statistics*.

RINT = the real interest rate. This variable was calculated as INT−INFL. Refer to the descriptions of INFL and INT above.

LE65 = the life expectancy of males at age 65 (in years). Data for 1980 or the closest year to 1980 for which data were available (usually 1979 or 1981) were used, but older data had to be used for a number of countries for which recent data were not available. The data were taken from United Nations [1985, Table 22, pp. 470–497; 1986, Table 22, pp. 450–478] and the corresponding table of earlier editions of the same source.

LERET = the life expectancy of males at the age of retirement RETAGE (q.v.). The time period and data source are the same as those for LE65. Since data are available at five-year age intervals only, interpolations were done when necessary.

RETSPAN = the average retirement span of male workers. This variable was calculated as LERET * (1 − LPAGED). Refer to the main text (Section 2) for a justification of this formula and the descriptions of LERET and LPAGED for information on data sources and time periods.

RETSPAN' = the average retirement span of male workers (alternative measure). This variable was calculated as LE65 * (1 − LPAGED); thus, it assumes a retirement age of 65 for all countries. Refer to the main text (Section 2) for a justification of this formula and the descriptions of LE65 and LPAGED for information on data sources and time periods.

RETAGE = the standard retirement age, proxied by the qualifying age for public old-age pensions. More specifically, the age at which a male who has contributed for 40 years becomes eligible for a full pension has been used. The data were taken from United States Department of Health and Human Services [1984].

SSPENY = public pension benefits per person over 65 as a ratio of per capita private national income. Refer to the description of SPVT for the calculation method and data source used for private national income, the description of GYPC for the source of data on the total population of each country, and the description of DEP for the source of data on population by age group. The total amount of benefit expenditures for public pensions was calculated from data presented in International Labour Office [1985a, Table 8, pp. 92–105]. More specifically, it was obtained by multiplying the figure for the total amount of benefit expenditures for social insurance and family allowances by the figure for the percent of this amount that goes toward pensions. Data for 1980 were used.

SSTY = benefit expenditures for social security broadly defined as a ratio of private national income. Refer to the description of SPVT for the calculation method and data source used for private national income. Data on benefit expenditures for social security were obtained from International Labour Office [1985a, Table 5, pp. 68–75] and include benefits for social insurance (sickness/maternity, employment injuries, and unemployment), family allowances, public assistance, etc. Data for 1980 were used.

SSPENYT = benefit expenditures for public pensions as a ratio of private national income. Refer to the description of SPVT for the calculation method and data source used for private national income and the description of SSPENY for the calculation method and data source used for benefit expenditures for pensions. Data for 1980 were used.

SSOY = benefit expenditures for social security programs other than public pensions as a ratio of private national income. This variable was calculated as SSTY–SSPENYT (q.v.).

References

Articles and Books

Barro, R. J., and G. M. MacDonald, Social security and consumer spending in an international cross section, *Journal of Public Economics*, Vol. 11, No. 3, pp. 275–289, 1979.

Blades, D. W., and P. H. Sturm, The concept and measurement of savings: The United States and other industrialized countries. In: Federal Reserve Bank of Boston, *Saving and Government Policy* (Conference Series No. 25) (Proceedings of a Conference held at Melvin Village, N. H., October 1982). Boston: Federal Reserve Bank of Boston, pp. 1–30, 1982.

Boskin, M. J., and J. M. Roberts, *A Closer Look At Saving Rates in the United States and Japan*, unpublished, Stanford University, 1986.

Feldstein, M. S., Social security, induced retirement, and aggregate capital accumulation, *Journal of Political Economy*, Vol. 82, No. 5, pp. 905–926, 1974.

Feldstein, M. S., Social security and private savings: International evidence in an extended life-cycle model. In: Martin S. Feldstein and Robert Inman, eds., *The Economics of Public Services* (An International Economics Association Conference Volume). London: The Macmillan Press Ltd., pp. 174–205, 1977.

Feldstein, M. S., International differences in social security and saving, *Journal of Public Economics*, Vol. 14, No. 2, pp. 225–244, 1980.

Haanes-Olsen, L., Earnings replacement rate of old age benefits, 1965–1975, selected countries, *Social Security Bulletin*, Vol. 41, No. 1, pp. 3–14, 1978.

Hayashi, F., Why is Japan's saving rate so apparently high? In: Stanley Fischer, ed., *NBER Macroeconomics Annual 1986*. Cambridge, Massachusetts: MIT Press, pp. 147–210, 1986.

Horioka, C. Y., The applicability of the life-cycle hypothesis to Japan, *The Kyoto University Economic Review*, Vol. 54, No. 2, pp. 31–56, 1984.

Horioka, C. Y., A survey of the literature on household saving in Japan: Why is the household saving rate so high in Japan, unpublished, Osaka University, 1985a.

Horioka, C. Y., Why is Japan's private saving rate so high, unpublished, Osaka University, 1985b.

Houthakker, H. S., An international comparison of personal saving, *Bulletin of the International Statistical Institute*, Vol. 38, pp. 56–59, 1961.

Houthakker, H. S., On some determinants of saving in developed and underdeveloped countries. In: E. A. G. Robinson, ed., *Problems in Economic Development*. London: The Macmillan Press Ltd., Chapter 10, pp. 212–224, 1965.

Ishikawa, T., and K. Ueda, The bonus payment system and Japanese personal savings. In: Masahiko Aoki, ed., *The Economic Analysis of the Japanese Firm* (Contributions to Economic Analysis, no. 151). Amsterdam: North-Holland, pp. 133–192, 1984.

Japanese Economic Planning Agency (Keizai Kikaku-chō), *Keizai Hakusho* (Economic White Paper), 1985 edition. Tokyo: Ōkura-shō Insatsu-kyoku (Ministry of Finance Printing Bureau), 1985.

Kopits, G., and P. Gotur, The influence of social security on household saving: A cross-country investigation, *International Monetary Fund Staff Papers*, Vol. 27, No. 1, pp. 161–190, 1980.

Koskela, E., and M. Viren, Social security and household saving in an international cross section, *American Economic Review*, Vol. 73, No. 1, pp. 212–217, 1983.

Leff, N., Dependency rates and savings rates, *American Economic Review*, Vol. 59, No. 4, pp. 886–896, 1969.

Makin, J. H., Savings rates in Japan and the United States: The roles of tax policy and other factors. In: F. G. Adams and S. M. Wachter, eds., *Savings and Capital Formation: The Policy Options*. Lexington, Massachusetts: Lexington Books/D. C. Heath and Company, pp. 91–126, 1986.

Modigliani, F., The life cycle hypothesis of saving, the demand for wealth and the supply of capital, *Social Research*, Vol. 33, No. 2, pp. 160–217, 1966.

Modigliani, F., The life cycle hypothesis of saving and intercountry differences in the saving ratio. In: W. A. Eltis, M. F. Scott, and J. N. Wolfe, eds., *Induction, Growth and Trade: Essays in Honor of Sir Roy Harrod*. London: Clarendon Press/Oxford, pp. 197–225, 1970.

Modigliani, F., and R. Brumberg, Utility analysis and aggregate consumption functions: An attempt at integration. In: F. Modigliani, *The Collected Papers of Franco Modigliani* (Andrew Abel, ed.). Cambridge, Mass.: MIT Press, pp. 128–197, 1980.

Modigliani, F., and A. Sterling, Determinants of private saving with special reference to the role of social security—cross-country tests. In: F. Modigliani and R. Hemming, eds., *The Determinants of National Saving and Wealth* (Proceedings of a Conference held by the International Economic Association at Bergamo, Italy). London: The Macmillan Press Ltd., pp. 24–55, 1983.

Ram, R., Dependency rates and aggregate savings: A new international cross-section study, *American Economic Review*, Vol. 72, No. 3, pp. 537–544, 1982.

Solow, R. M., Reflections on saving behavior. In: Federal Reserve Bank of Boston, ed., *Saving and Government Policy* (Conference Series No. 25) (Proceedings of a Conference held at Melvin Village, N. H., October 1982). Boston: Federal Reserve Bank of Boston, pp. 162–174, 1982.

Data Sources

International Labour Office, *Year Book of Labour Statistics*, 1978 edition (38th issue). Geneva: International Labour Office, 1978.

International Labour Office, *The Cost of Social Security: Eleventh International Inquiry, 1978–80*. Geneva: International Labour Office, 1985a.

International Labour Office, *Year Book of Labour Statistics*, 1985 edition (45th issue). Geneva: International Labour Office, 1985b.

International Monetary Fund, *International Financial Statistics*, various issues.

Japanese Ministry of Health and Welfare, Institute of Population Problems (Kōseishō, Jinkō Mondai Kenkyūsho), ed., *Nihon no Shōrai Suitei Jinkō, Shōwa 60–100 nen (Shōwa 101–160 nen Sankō Suikei)* (Population Projections for Japan: 1985–2085). Tokyo: Zaidan Hōjin Kōsei Tōkei Kyōkai (Health and Welfare Statistics Association), 1987.

Organization for Economic Cooperation and Development, Department of Economics and Statistics, *National Accounts, 1960–1984, Volume I: Main Aggregates*. Paris: Organization for Economic Cooperation and Development, 1986a.

Organization for Economic Cooperation and Development, Department of Economics and Statistics, *National Accounts, 1972–1984, Volume II: Detailed Tables*. Paris: Organization for Economic Cooperation and Development, 1986b. Also earlier editions of the same.

United Nations, Department of International Economic and Social Affairs, Statistical Office, *Demographic Yearbook*, 1983 edition (35th issue). New York: United Nations, 1985. Also earlier editions of the same.

United Nations, Department of International Economic and Social Affairs, Statistical Office, *Demographic Yearbook*, 1984 edition (36th issue). New York: United Nations, 1986.

United States Department of Health and Human Services, Social Security Administration, Office of Policy, Office of Research, Statistics, and International Policy, *Social Security Programs Throughout the World—1983* (Research Report No. 59). Washington, D.C.: United States Government Printing Office, 1984.

Part III
___

COMPARATIVE ANALYSIS

9

Labor Market Segmentation, Human Resource Utilization, and Economic Development: The Case of Japan in Historical Perspective*

KOJI TAIRA

Department of Economics
University of Illinois
Urbana-Champaign, Illinois

1. Introduction

In recent years, United States labor scholars have been rewriting U.S. labor market history with special reference to the rise and wane of dominant institutional characteristics associated with changes in economic variables amenable to more standard economic analysis (economic growth, productivity, wages, employment, etc.). "Institutional" and "economic" analyses are thus fused to generate a more comprehensive view of labor market behavior and industrial relations than what has been afforded by conventional labor economics. The institutional approach which inspires this paper is the stage theory of labor market characteristics offered by Gordon, Edwards, and Reich [1982]. According to this work, labor in the United States is "proletarianized," "homogenized," and "segmented" in sequence. The timing and duration of the segmentation phase are practically identical in the U.S. and Japan: 1920s to the present, subdivided into "exploration" (1920s to World War II),

*This is a revised version of a paper presented at the annual meeting of the Allied Social Sciences Association in December 1985. The author is grateful to the panelists, discussants, and other readers of an earlier draft for comments and suggestions which have led to the revision. These are Dr. Mark Leiserson and Professors Bernard E. Anderson, M. Bronfenbrenner, Subbiah Kannappan, S. B. Levine, Michael Piore, T. Paul Schultz, and James G. Scoville. The author is indebted to Professor M. Morishima for the concept of an idiosyncratic national ethos as a useful framework for the organization and presentation of historical information. Of course, the author alone is responsible for the remaining inadequacies and weaknesses of the paper.

181

"consolidation" (World War II to the 1970s), and "decay" (1970s to the present). In the United States, the proletarianization and homogenization phases stretch over a century from the 1820s to the 1920s. In Japan, they are telescoped into a period half as long as in the U.S.: 1870s to the 1920s. It is therefore hypothesized that the deficient proletarianization and homogenization of Japanese labor before World War I resulted in a much more pronounced labor market segmentation in later years in Japan than in the United States. This paper explores this hypothesis and its implications with the help of relevant information on Japan's cultural and social changes.

For a point of departure, we briefly note what is meant by a more pronounced labor market segmentation of labor for Japan than for the United States. Then we discuss premodern values and institutions as constraints on the development of the Japanese labor market in earlier days, how clashes of traditional and modern (imported, imitated, and adapted) values produced the initial exploration of segmentation as a compromise, how segmentation itself was subsequently consolidated and modernized, and how it is likely to change in the future. In conclusion, we suggest that orthodox economic analysis be broadened to cover firms' labor cost minimization strategy involving diverse cost elements, partly substitutable for and partly complementary of one another, in the changing social context of ethos, values, and preferences over time.

In Japan, segmentation largely refers to two sets of firms, large and small, rather than to two sets of jobs, primary and secondary, as in the United State. The size of the firm in Japan is an unusually powerful factor that makes firms and employees behave differently. These differences are observable in all aspects of management, technology, and human resource utilization. Large firms are characterized by elaborate rules, procedures, and processes of "internal labor markets." They can therefore be considered constituting an "ILM sector." The ILM syndrome is entrenched in firms large enough to employ 1000 or more workers. The syndrome may begin to appear in firms with 500 or so employees.[1] The maximum size of the workforce that an owner manager or a general manager can personally manage is about five or six hundred workers. Three distinct features of employment in the Japanese ILM-sector practices are already well known: (1) lifetime employment, (2) seniority wages, and (3) enterprise-based and enterprise-confined labor

---

[1] The dichotomy of "large" and "small" firms should be considered a rhetorical device for sharpening the differences in the characteristics of firms according to size. These differences are actually incremental over the whole continuum of different sizes. The ideal-typical "large" and "small" firms are analytically convenient because they represent two sets of characteristics with a sufficient distance between them on this continuum to be distinct and nonoverlapping. This approach in no way denies the existence or importance of firms of middling sizes with hybrid characteristics of large and small firms.

unions [OECD, 1973; Dore, 1973; Rohlen, 1974; Clark, 1979; Shirai, 1984]. Quantitatively, the Japanese ILM-sector firms show a higher degree of employment security and a more powerful role of the length of service as a wage determining factor than their U.S. counterpart (Shimada 1981; Hashimoto and Raisian, 1985). The prominence of the Japanese ILM sector relative to the rest of the economy may be seen from more pronounced productivity and wage differentials by size of firm in Japan than in the United States (manufacturing census figures). These defining characteristics of labor market segmentation are not free of controversy as to their extent, importance, and implications, but a comparison of the literature on this subject would leave far less doubt for Japan than for the United States about the plausibility of labor market segmentation as a real phenomenon [Cain, 1976; Yasuba, 1976; Odaka, 1984]. We now examine how such segmentation has come about and how it is likely to change.

2.   Incomplete Proletarianization and Homogenization (1870s to the 1920s)

Although the Meiji Restoration of 1868 quickly dismantled the feudal state system and social structure, and affirmed freedom of private enterprise on the part of anyone, regardless of social origin or current status, centuries-old feudal principles, beliefs, values, and habits did not easily disappear. Behavior based on feudal class origin actually persisted for a long time despite drastic changes in socioeconomic structure and economic opportunities. There were four important types of feudal social relationships: lord-vassal relationship with a premium on loyalty in the ruling *samurai* class, extended-family networks of the merchant houses, real or simulated family (*oyakata-kokata*) relationships in the craft households, including masters, journeymen and apprentices, and solidaristic social relationships in peasant villages [Sumiya and Taira, 1979]. Among the *samurai*, the lord was sovereign and the vassal owed him absolute loyalty. In other classes, social relationships were more horizontal and reciprocal, with emphasis on mutual obligations for giving and receiving favors under moral imperatives such as *giri, ninjō*, and *on* (untranslatables all, but approximated by "duty," "humanity," and "debt"). Underwriting all these social relations and behaviors between individuals or between families was the basic family ethic, with an accent on filial piety toward parents. Confucianism is the generic term for the ethical system which defined and enforced these and many more relational imperatives. Basically, Confucianism provided a complete code of individual and interpersonal behavior for a well governed and well ordered society with no market economy. It offered no advice about the meaning of the market or the nature of interpersonal relationships accompanying market transactions. Therefore, there arose a conundrum: Should people reject the market in favor of a well ordered nonmarket Confucian society, or should they adapt the Confucian code of behavior to market transactions? In search for an answer to these questions, it is generally believed that China and Korea chose Confucianism without the market, while Japan chose the market with Confucianism [Morishima, 1982]. In China and Korea, market behavior (profit maximization, for example) remained a moral aberration, while it acquired a moral legitimacy fairly early in Japan. Confucianist-constrained market behavior was bound to differ from Western Protestant-driven market behavior and to result in differences in capital accumulation, technological progress, and economic growth between Japan and the West [Pepper, Janow, and Wheeler, 1985].

Within Japan, interpersonal differences in the kind and quality of moral fiber entailed certain allocative consequences for human resources. Former *samurai* and their descendants, with their strong belief in loyalty, were suited for employment in large scale undertakings in modern industry, banking, railroads, utilities, international trade, and government services. These new large-scale activities based on lumpy investment required committed managers and workers. They generated "markets for loyalty" [Morishima, 1982]. Complementing the loyal core of the workforce, mobile labor markets arose in response to the fluctuating demand for labor as enterprises rose or fell, expanded or contracted. (Morishima calls participants in these labor markets "mercenaries" in contrast to participants in markets for "loyalty.") Thus the nascent labor market of modernizing Japan was already dualized as if to replicate the dual feudal classes of *samurai* and commoners.

However, the bulk of Japan's human resources was in family farms and family enterprises with no hired labor or, if any, with only a few employees. Self employment was considered more desirable or respectable than working for wages as a way of earning a living so that wage labor was seen as only a brief interlude in one's life before settling down with one's own enterprise. The labor market was, and has always been, viewed as the least legitimate form of market. Labor migration from farm households to nonagricultural enterprises was often mediated by family and kinship ties [Vogel, 1967]. The migrants worked for wages for a while, but sooner or later set themselves up as owner-operators of business. In this kind of economic system which encouraged petty entrepreneurship, wage labor was hardly a class concept. In 1872, paid employment was but 9% of total employment. About 50 years later, in 1920, it was still only 29%. Nevertheless, by 1920 economic development of considerable proportions had already taken place in Japan. With victories in the Sino-Japanese (1894–1895) and the Russo-Japanese (1904–1905) wars and the choice of the winning side in the First World War, Japan in 1920 was one of the five leading powers of the world. Although Japanese development was largely based on markets, there was considerable state guidance and participation. It was not yet full-fledged "capitalist" development: The tardy growth of the labor market limited the growth of a proletariat much needed for exploitation by the capitalists.

Japan's difficulty in generating an extensive proletariat appropriate to a capitalist economy was due in large part to a peculiar nature of Japan's absolutist state under the imperial constitution (1889–1947). The state was essentially a family system "meaning a system of legal and political organization whereby the family is the major unit of social organization, is a legal personality in which property rights and duties are vested, and is represented externally by a family head who exercises wide powers of control over family members" [Dore, 1958, p. 94]. In addition, "in Japan, the habit of modeling the structure of social groups outside the family—occupational, educational, recreational, political, artistic, criminal—on the pattern of the family, has been developed with a consistency rare in other societies" [Dore, 1958, p. 94]. Kinship terminology is used liberally to designate positions and relations in an organization, for instance, *oyabun* (parent role) for the boss, *kobun* (child role) for subordinates. This unique serviceability of the family metaphor as an organizational principle made "one big family of an enterprise or a factory."

The transaction cost approach to the family [Pollak, 1985] helps one see the cost-minimizing advantages of an organization successfully modeled after the family. The development of a highly dynamic market economy, as in prewar Japan, under a family system may well be considered *sui generis* as a type of economic development. The role of family farms and non-farm family enterprises as preferred economic organizations in Japanese development stands in sharp contrast to the role of the capitalist sector and wage labor as leading forces in a developing economy in W. Arthur Lewis' model of development. Before the Second World War, many large Japanese firms were family-owned or controlled. Their organizational form was *zaibatsu*, a conglomerate of diversified enterprises held by interlocking directorates under a family-controlled holding company (or its equivalent) [Hirschmeier and Yui, 1975]. The four largest *zaibatsu* were household words throughout the world: Mitsui, Mitsubishi, Sumitomo, and Yasuda. Matsushita and Toyota are good examples of how families generate and continue to control giant firms even today [Taira, 1974].

3. Modern Segmentation: Exploration (1920s to World War II)

The catalyst that transformed the Meiji Era's feudalistic socioeconomic segmentation into a modern labor market segmentation was the labor movement inspired by intellectual, religious, and ideological imports (Western humanism, Christianity, socialism, communism, and many variations in them). With reference to the ethos and values of the times, the labor movement was an anomaly, something foreign, undesirable, and dangerous. Earlier experiments with it in the closing years of the nineteenth century led by Christian socialists and awakened labor leaders who returned from the United States with experience of involvement with the American Federation of Labor were easily nipped in the bud by a repressive legislation, the Public Peace Police Act of 1900. The labor movement was revived in 1912 by a Christian leader and experienced nearly a 30-year saga of growth, glory (1920s), decline (1930s), and death (1940). Its history is filled with internal ideological struggles between Christian moderates and newly risen Communists, resulting in many organizational splits.

Nevertheless, the labor movement forced Japanese employers to look for ways to stabilize employment relations under changing circumstances and to ensure their control on their terms based on the traditional ethos and values that they preferred. Their first reaction was to learn how the American and European employers were coping with labor problems. Study teams were dispatched to America and Europe [Taira, 1973]. As a consequence, the Japanese employers adopted and adapted the "American Plan" and the European works council idea: enlightened self-interest of management coupled with some concessions for worker participation in workplace affairs [Totten, 1967]. Friendly overtures were also made to the labor movement for participation in a national level harmonization movement (kyōchōkai). The outcome of these employer efforts was the newly articulated ideology, strategy, and practices of some enlightened form of employer paternalism (onjōshugi, keiei-kazokushugi), which over the years evolved into the afore-mentioned Japanese Employment System [Tokuda, 1985]. After a series of clashes with labor over the shape of new relations, major enterprises succeeded in subduing or expunging trade unions by the early 1930s [Totten, 1974; Fruin, 1983]. Quantitative indicators also show that a distinct labor market dualism arose during the interwar period [Ohkawa and Rosovsky, 1973; Yasuba, 1976; Odaka, 1985].

Employer paternalism, together with improved rules and procedures of internal labor markets, stabilized industrial relations during the 1930s. However, the ethos of the family metaphor on which paternalism was based was exploitative, because the prewar Japanese family system gave the family head wide powers of control over the family members.[2] There was no pretense

---

[2] It should be noted that an enterprise run like "one big family" does not always practice "good" employer-employee relations. All too often in the literature on Japanese employment, "family" is undefined but used as a concept that implies good interpersonal relations. The family metaphor of a firm must specify what kind of family is at the base.

to democracy in the family or the workplace. Because of the authoritarian bias of the family in prewar Japan, there was always a danger of paternalism degenerating into tyranny. One potential check against employer tyranny was the possibility of spontaneous worker uprising. Many prewar labor disputes were such worker rebellions with little help from labor unions. The workforce of an enterprise was rigidly hierarchical and compartmentalized by age, sex, education, social origin, and function. Executives were the owners, or their relatives, friends, or trusted vassals; managerial employees were college graduates, nepotistically recruited; blue-collar workers were men and women of lesser educations and haphazardly hired. Compensation varied widely among these groups and by age and sex among workers. Men were encouraged to put in long service, but women were not. Promotions were primarily by loyalty and merit (meaning employer discretion in practice), and secondarily by age and length of service. In the personnel pyramid of a firm, better jobs became scarcer as one moved up. For a given age cohort, promotions meant dismissals for some or outplacements for others, because the traditional values dictated against placing a worker under the command of a younger man. Blue collar workers with no college education could become foremen but could rise to no higher positions. This structure of social relations within the enterprise was essentially humiliating to manual workers who desired "modern" (egalitarian, democratic, friendly) social relations. They accepted authoritarian paternalism because there was at least a semblance of promotions and because wages were higher than elsewhere. These socioeconomic inequalities within the enterprise were bulldozed over by wartime controls under the impact of labor shortage, as millions of the most desirable young workers were conscripted and sent to the front.

The family metaphor enjoyed its last irrational application during the second world war, where the State was perceived as One Family with One Voice in One Mind under the Divine Father—Emperor. The implicit tyranny of the family system produced an explicit state tyranny. Industries and enterprises were extensively reorganized under a command system. Each enterprise was made a state instrument to generate resources for war and national survival. All personnel of an enterprise were organized into an association to serve the state (*sang yō hōkoku kai, sanpō*, for short). Intense spiritualism ("mind over matter") conquered hardships and smothered personal complaints. The rationing of daily necessities and the wage and price controls levelled the standard of living down to bare subsistence for all. The solidarity and equality imposed on everyone at the enterprise level during the war were strengthened after the war by the enterprise labor union which everyone joined [Taira, 1980; Moore, 1984]. A social democratic revolution took place at the enterprise level, i.e., a state instrument imposed on workers from above was turned into a workers' instrument to defined worker interest.

Huge business conglomerates (*zaibatsu*) were smashed by the Supreme Commander (General Douglas McArthur) for the allied powers and a whole new corps of professional managers took over new enterprises as many wartime owners and executives were forced out of active life for their "criminal" support of the war. Blue collar workers demanded and obtained full equity with white collar workers in status, pay, and opportunities for promotion. At the national level, the imperial constitution was abolished and the new democratic constitution adopted in 1947. The absolutist monarchy changed into a symbolic monarchy. Along with these and many other drastic reforms, the prewar family system was destroyed by new family law. The family was now based on the free union of a male and a female. Primogeniture was abolished, and all siblings had an equal share in the household resources. The family head with commanding authority over family members disappeared. The family metaphor took on a different connotation and was no longer serviceable as a structural model for the personnel management of a large enterprise. In fact, the postwar industrial relations system was stabilized as an equilibrium of adversarial forces, i.e., efficiency-minded management and security-minded labor union. Industrial peace thus attained and maintained eventually softened the battle-hardened hearts of both sides. With the refinement of rules and procedures of collective bargaining and joint labor-management consultation, the Japanese Employment System had taken hold by the mid-1950s [Levine, 1958].

4.   Segmentation: Consolidation (World War II to the 1970s)

With the transaction-cost minimizing advantages of the family metaphor weakened, management could no longer count upon worker incentives and discipline resulting from the shared image of the company as a family. Furthermore, the postwar family was no model for any large organization that required authority and responsibility for getting work done. Postwar Japanese management again turned to American practices and voraciously absorbed and adapted American management techniques, often misunderstanding them and inventing their own instead. (One of the happiest misunderstandings was the American concept of statistical quality control, which in the Japanese hands turned into a small group activity called "quality circle" to explore all kinds of improvements in the workplace [Cole, 1979].)

In the Japanese company today, the transaction costs broadly interpreted to be those necessary for obtaining desired commitment and performance from employees are considerable. A major difference between American and Japanese practices is that the transaction costs in America are contractual, explicit or implicit, individual or collective, while in the Japanese company these costs are diffuse, taking diverse forms such as elaborate personnel practices, detailed work rules, constant negotiations and consultations over rule making and enforcement, careful recruitment and career planning (even for the blue collar workers), generous donations of time and care after hours by both management and employees for the maintenance of good employer-employee relations. In America, grievances arise out of disagreements about the contractual terms and are resolved through legal or quasilegal procedures. In Japan, grievances are prevented from surfacing because of the diffuse personnel practices. The employment contract in Japan is reduced to one sentence, to the effect: "We are happy to have you as this company's employee." The Japanese transaction costs can be seen as costs of employee acculturation in the company culture so that they will not shirk but will dedicate their all to the prosperity of the company. In view of the strong international competitiveness in recent years, transactions of Japanese companies with employees must be considered highly cost-effective. However, this is not the same thing as saying, as some are apt to say, that Japanese companies can effortlessly obtain a high level of employee commitment and performance. Japanese companies do invest in transactions and are apparently successful in obtaining good returns on the investment.

The Japanese Employment System that emerged from the consolidation of labor market segmentation may well be called "management by an enterprise culture." A company-specific culture now takes the place of erstwhile employer paternalism. It is well known that well run Japanese companies make constant efforts for shaping and maintaining a corporate identity distinct and unique enough to motivate employee identification with it [Matsuura, 1983]. The culture-conscious Japanese companies devote enormous attention to the recruitment of compatible employees of homogeneous qualities [Bronfenbrenner, 1985]. The general practice is to recruit employees once a year in the spring fresh out of schools or colleges, according to careful long-run manpower plans. These companies regularly hire from the nation's best universities and maintain a stable mix of employees by university origin [Azumi, 1969; Matsuura, 1978]. Blue collar recruitment also runs by school or regional origin. Informal groups formed by college, school, or regional ties mesh with formal work groups. The old boys (OB) network is automatically stratified by year of graduation and can be used as an instrument for orderly acculturation and training of employees through senior-junior (*senpai-kōhai*) relationships. Several OB groups in a company also generate intramural competition for performance among them. Each OB group probably desires to maximize its share in good positions and promotions. So long as personnel procedures and evaluations are objective and unbiased, competition among OB groups may be channeled into higher aggregate performance (although it might also degenerate into dysfunctional office politics). The role of a company culture is to integrate competing groups and individuals into a harmonious whole to ensure the aggregate vitality of the firm. The enterprise labor union also facilitates this cultural integration by taking up all non managerial white collar and blue collar workers, regardless of their educational backgrounds. The union then can be viewed as a crucible of social democracy within the enterprise. Union leaders are regularly promoted into managerial ranks so that a significant proportion of the top management of a company are former union leaders. The union and management are thus united in the interest of promoting company prosperity. Externally, managers and organized employees of the ILM sector as a whole constitute an elite of the labor force *vis-à-vis* the rest of the working population of the national economy.[3]

What happens in the other part of the dualistic segmentation, the non-ILM sector? The modernization of the family and interpersonal relations within the family since the postwar democratic revolution has proceeded unevenly in different socioeconomic strata. Studies of lower middle-class merchants and artisans indicate a strong survival of the prewar type of family and its application to employment relationships [deVos, 1975]. Generally, small- and medium-sized enterprises constitute a non-ILM sector (the dual of the ILM sector where the Japanese Employment System is obtained), and labor market indicators like labor turnover, length of service, cyclical sensitivity of employment, etc. are those of relatively open, fluid labor markets. These enterprises obviously make up for the lower wages and less attractive working conditions than in the ILM sector by offering a "psychic income" of a family atmosphere familiar to their employees. Furthermore, employees in the non-ILM sector are in a sense residuals, drop-outs or failures *vis-à-vis* their peers picked by the ILM-sector firms. They are likely to be from the social strata which, because of their relative backwardness, have lagged in modernization and still retain relatively greater doses of traditional values and practices. The familiar syndrome of factors that generates "occupational inheritance" is also observed in Japan [Bowman, 1981]. The survival of the prewar type of "familism" in the non-ILM sector long after the abolition of the family system is a modern analogue of the survival of the feudalistic tendencies in social organization in the Meiji Era long after the formal end of feudalism.

From a different point of view, the employers and employees in small- and medium-sized enterprises are the average Japanese, and those in the ILM sector an exception. On the basis of employment statistics by establishment

---

[3] The "culture" model of the Japanese enterprise explored here may be considered an infrastructure for a game-theoretic bargaining model in which management coordinates and adjusts claims of different participants (workers, stockholders, consumers, etc.) in the operation and output of the firm [Aoki, 1984].

size, regular employees in private establishments employing 500 or more regular employees, public enterprises, and civil service amounted to 16% of the Japanese labor force in 1981 [Management and Coordination Agency, 1981]. This is roughly the size of the ILM sector in Japan by sheer head count. The smallness of this sector enables it to skim off the cream of the human resources of Japan. The employees of the ILM sector are conscious of their elitist position. This labor market segmentation does not generate distrust, misgivings, or even antagonism that arise between the classic classes of capital and labor.

The major division of Japanese society is between large bureaucratized firms in the ILM sector and small and middling enterprises, mostly family-run or family-controlled, in the non-ILM sector. Tensions exist and occasionally flare up between large firms and small firms, as in the case of an organized protest by local store owners against a large national distributor planning to open a branch in their midst. Japanese large firms have long since realized the limits of expansion because of resistance by smaller firms. Instead, they have actively organized the smaller ones into networks of close business relationships known as *keiretsu* (lining them up). However, the transaction costs in getting things done through a *keiretsu* involving hundreds of smaller, but independent, firms are apparently lower than the large firm itself expanding in the equivalent scale to interalize the network. Thus, some workable peace is obtained between large and small firms. It is noteworthy that resilience and political sophistication of small firms limit the physical growth of large firms and direct the attention of the latter to "social" leadership rather than economic domination over a multiplicity of lesser firms.[4]

The employees of the ILM sector are organized into enterprise employee unions and largely coopted into the "share economy" of this elite sector through collective bargaining and joint consultation [Levine and Taira, 1985]. Enterprise unions see no community of interest with the unorganized employees of smaller enterprises, as exemplified by an almost total absence of effort on the part of the established unions to organize the unorganized. The basic behavioral determinant is the union's "enterprise consciousness," meaning that for their well-being, employees depend on their employer's prosperity and that the union's role is to ensure a "fair share" in the employer's

---

[4] A *keiretsu* is a hierarchical association of firms of varying sizes dependent on the leadership of a large firm. Several large firms, each with its *keiretsu*, also form an association known as *kigyō shūdan* (enterprise group) with nominal interlocking share ownership with one another. Major enterprise groups have resulted from the regrouping of firms which in early postwar years sprang from the dissolution of *zaibatsu*. The conventional methodology of industrial organization with its emphasis on market power in specific product markets presents a difficulty in coping with the concentration of economic power (or at the least, regulation of competition) in the hands of enterprise groups and *keiretsu*.

prosperity. With no horizontal (class) solidarity among workers, employees in the non-ILM sector perceive themselves as being in the employee status only so long as they learn the skills and accumulate the resources to strike out on their own. This "Japanese dream" does not become a reality for a majority of wage-earners in the non-ILM secttor. However, it does for a substantial number of them, who set and maintain the entrepreneurial propensity born of that dream. For a major capitalist market economy, Japan still has an unusual proportion of its labor force in self-employment (together with family workers, 27% of the labor force in 1981) and an unusual proportion of nonagricultural, private, regular employment in small establishments with fewer than 30 employees (48% in 1981). For more than a half of Japan's economically active population, "employer" and "employee" do not imply sharp status differences, let alone different class identities. Where class consciousness should have arisen, and did for a while after the war, namely in the ILM sector, employees are now the secure members of the nation's elite. Some call them the "labor aristocracy." Labor market segmentation has thus created in Japan a social stratification that the known formulae of class differentiation cannot explain.

5. Segmentation: Decay (1970s to Date)

The Japanese economy suffered exogenous shocks and domestic upheavals in the 1970s. The Nixon shock of August 1971, by ending the Bretton Woods regime of fixed exchange rates and putting wage and price controls on the U.S. economy, considerably disturbed the world economy. The wobbling economies of the world, including Japan, were knocked out temporarily by the OPEC shock of 1973, which quadrupled the crude oil price. The Japanese economy simultaneously suffered an accelerated inflation, an explosion of labor disputes, and negative economic growth in 1974. Employment cutbacks became real despite lifetime employment under the Japanese Employment System. The rate of unemployment doubled between the early and late 1970s. In the 1980s, it further increased toward three times the earlier level. With an increasing threat of unemployment, labor militancy has considerably weakened since 1975. Under low growth and higher risks, employers have been resorting to a more extensive use of part-time, temporary, or seasonal workers. This suspiciously looks like a thrust toward a homogenization of labor.

Legislation also points in the same direction. Private manpower-supplying business, which was banned until recently, is now permitted to operate as a legitimate labor market institution (Employee-Dispatching Business Law, enacted in July 1985 and effective a year later). There is also the equal employment opportunity legislation for women (enacted in May 1985 and effective from April 1986), which is bound to modify male-based company cultures and employment systems. The aging of the labor force has resulted in a law (enacted in April 1986 and effective from October 1986) to counter age discrimination endemic to the Japanese Employment System, which retires employees at 55 or 60 and in effect throws them out into the labor market, where low demand for aged workers results in unemployment or drastically reduces wages. The firms raising the mandatory retirement age from 55 to 60 have increased in number in the last 10 years. However, many of them, at the same time, have devised a variety of selective early retirement systems once employees have turned 40 years of age. Unions, weakened at the enterprise level, are shifting their attention and resources to national-level consolidation and nationwide economic policy. The upshot of all these new developments is the prospect of less segmentation, as the internal labor markets of major firms become more expensive to maintain in the traditional fashion. Firms can no longer neglect women and the aged in order to concentrate managerial attention on standard male regular workers recruited fresh out of schools and colleges with expectations to serve out their term until mandatory retirement.

Firms can no longer give preference to males at the time of recruitment. Nor can they exclude females from career-track training or from considerations for promotions. Given the greater probability of women to withdraw from the labor force for marriage or family duties than men, firms now expect some margin of waste in training investment due to the attrition of trained women employees. If this rise in the cost of training leads to a reduction in training investment for both men and women, firms will suffer from skill shortages within their internal labor markets in coping with the requirements of rapidly changing technology and products. These shortages will then be filled by hiring the qualified workers from external labor markets. There will then be a lack of correlation between the length of service and skill level, which will eventually undermine the economic efficiency of lifetime employment. There may still be long-term employees, but many of them are bypassed for promotions by qualified, experienced workers that firms can hire from outside. This means that there will be market rates of pay for various types of job capabilities, and market segmentation will decrease.

6.   Conclusion

This paper is a semiformal exercise in the use of institutional cycles (in close parallel to economic cycles) for the understanding of changing labor market structure and processes. Much use is made of the role of Japan's national ethos expressed in some observable characteristics of institutions, values, and preferences. These variables affect the pattern of interpersonal relationships; the channel of communication, the perception of authority, responsibility, and performance, and many other factors that operate through the minds and hearts of people to shape the outcomes of labor market processes.

This does not imply that the labor market behavior assumed in this essay is different from that which makes theoretical, neoclassical analysis of labor markets possible. Here, as in orthodox analysis, the individual is assumed to be intelligent and rational within bounds (bounded rationality). The difference is that orthodox analysis, thanks to short-run orientation, can assume that the intelligence and rationality of the individual and the bounds within which he chooses and acts are constant or given. In historical analysis, it is possible that the individual becomes more (or less) intelligent or rational and that the bounds for his choice and action expand (or contract). When a poor caste society changes into a rich market economy over a long period of time, it is clear that the set of "givens" which can be postulated for short-run economic analysis must change. Certainly, the "givens" are different under a caste system from those under a market economy, although the short-run analysis depends in both cases on the same maximization (or minimization) principle under constraints. Without rejecting the usefulness of economic analysis, this paper directs attention to the nature of changes in the institutional, environmental factors which define the opportunity sets to which the individual responds intelligently and rationally.

It is intellectually comforting that these institutional changes are not always random or at the mercy of unpredictable exogenous shocks. These changes have some systematic tendencies over time. The rise and wane of labor market segmentation are among such tendencies and even appear to be predictable outcomes of aggregates of employer and worker responses to initial givens in much the same way as difference equations are solved. The historical period within which the cycle of labor market segmentation has run its course is identical in Japan and the United States. While the principal causes and outcomes of segmentation processes are similar between the two economies, there are subtle differences in the ways in which cost effectiveness is achieved in the use of human resources. No attempt is so far made for a full enumeration of the cost elements so that a least cost mix of these elements can be identified for an international comparison. However, though by implicit comparison only, it appears clear that in Japan, employers have been far more attentive to the needs and preferences of employees than in America. The upshot of this difference is that the "cultural" costs claim a larger weight in management strategy in Japan than in America, bringing about cost saving by the substitution of pecuniary income with psychic income. This paper explores the economic role of an enterprise culture as a managerial variable and holds it responsible, in part, for the Japanese style of labor market segmentation.

References

Aoki, M., ed., *The Economic Analysis of the Japanese Firm*. Amsterdam: North Holland, 1984.

Azumi, K., *Higher Education and Business Recruitment in Japan*. New York: Columbia University Teachers College Press, 1969.

Bowman, M. J., *Educational Choice and Labor Markets in Japan*. Chicago: University of Chicago Press, 1981.

Bronfenbrenner, M., An essay on negative screening. In: *Economic Policy and Development: New Perspectives*, T. Shishido and R. Sato, eds. London and Sydney: Croom Helm, Ltd, 1985.

Cain, G. G., The challenge of segmented labor market theories to orthodox theory: A survey, *Journal of Economic Literature*, Vol. 14, No. 4, 1976.

Clark, R., *The Japanese Company*. New Haven: Yale University Press, 1979.

Cole, R. E., *Work, Mobility and Participation*. Berkeley: University of California Press, 1979.

De Vos, G. A., Apprenticeship and paternalism. In: E. F. Vogel, *Modern Japanese Organization and Decision-Making*. Berkeley: University of California Press, 1975.

Dore, R. P., *City Life in Japan*. Berkeley: University of California Press, 1958.

Dore, R. P., ed., *Aspects of Social Change in Modern Japan*. Princeton: Princeton University Press, 1967.

Dore, R. P., *British Factory/Japanese Factory*. Berkeley: University of California Press, 1973.

Fruin, M. *Kikkoman: Company, Clan, and Community*. Cambridge: Harvard University Press, 1983.

Gordon, D. M., R. Edwards, and M. Reich, *Segmented Work, Divided Workers*. Cambridge: Cambridge University Press, 1982.

Hashimoto, M. and J. Raisian, Employment tenure and earnings profiles in Japan and the United States, *American Economic Review*, Vol. 75, No. 4, 1985.

Hirschmeier, J. and T. Yui, *The Development of Japanese Business 1600–1973*. Cambridge: Harvard University Press, 1975.

Levine, S. B., *Industrial Relations in Postwar Japan*. Urbana: University of Illinois Press, 1958.

Levine, S. B. and H. Kawada, *Human Resources in Japanese Development*. Princeton: Princeton University Press, 1980.

Levine, S. B. and K. Taira, Japanese industrial relations: A social compact emerges. In: *Industrial Relations in a Decade of Economic Change*, ed. by Hervey Juris et al. Madison, Wisconsin: Industrial Relations Research Association, 1985.

Management and Coordination Agency, Japanese Government, *Jigyōsho tōkei chōsa* (Establishment Census). Tokyo, 1981.

Matsuura, T., *Shūshoku* (Finding Employment). Tokyo: Nihon Keizai Shinbunsha, 1978.

Matsuura, T., *Shafū no kenkyū* (Studies in Corporate Identity). Tokyo: PHP Institute, 1983.

Moore, J. *Japanese Workers and the Struggle for Power, 1945–1947*. Madison: University of Wisconsin Press, 1983.

Morishima, M., *Why Has Japan "Succeeded"?* Cambridge: Cambridge University Press, 1982.

Odaka, K. *Rōdō shijō bunseki* (Analyses of Labor Markets). Tokyo: Tokyo University Press, 1985.

OECD, *Manpower Policy in Japan*. Paris, France: OCED, 1973.

Ohkawa, K. and H. Rosovsky, *Japanese Economic Growth*. Stanford: Stanford University Press, 1973.

Okuda, K. *Hito to Keiei Nihon Keiei Kanrishi Kenkyū* (Man and Management: A Study in Japanese Management History). Tokyo: Manējimentosha 1985.

Patrick, H., ed., *Japanese Industrialization and Its Social Consequences*. Berkeley: University of California Press, 1976.

Pepper, T. M. E. Janow, J. W. Wheeler, *The Competition*. New York: Praeger Publishers, 1985.

Pollak, R. A., A transaction cost approach to families and households, *Journal of Economic Literature*, Vol. 23, No. 2, 1985.

Redford, L. H., ed., *The Occupation of Japan: Economic Policy and Reform*. Norfolk, Virginia: The MacArthur Memorial, 1980.

Rohlen, T. P., *For Harmony and Strength*. Berkeley: University of California Press, 1974.

Shimada, H., *Earnings Structure and Human Investment*. Tokyo: Keio Economic Observatory, 1981.

Shirai, T. ed., *Contemporary Industrial Relations in Japan*. Madison: University of Wisconsin Press, 1983.

Silberman, B. and H. D. Harootunian, eds., *Japan in Crisis*. Princeton: Princeton University Press, 1974.

Sturmthal, A. and J. G. Scoville, eds., *The International Labor Movement in Transition*. Urbana: University of Illinois Press, 1973.

Sumiya, M. and K. Taira, *An Outline of Japanese Economic History 1603–1940*. Tokyo: Tokyo University Press, 1979.

Taira, K. *Economic Development and the Labor Market in Japan*. New York: Columbia University Press, 1970.

Taira, K., Labor markets, unions, and employers in inter-war Japan. In: Sturmthal and Scoville, eds. *The International Labor Movement in Transition*. Urbana: University of Illinois Press, 1973.

Taira, K., Entrepreneurship, management and the growth of firms: Cases from Japanese business history. *International Review of the History of Banking*, No. 8, 1974.

Taira, K., Unions, ideologies, and revolutions in Japanese enterprise during the occupation. In: L. H. Redford, ed., *The Occupation of Japan: Economic Policy and Reform*. Norfolk, Virginia: The MacArthur Memorial, 1980.

Totten, G. O., Collective bargaining and works councils as innovations in industrial relations in Japan during the 1920s. In: R. P. Dore, ed., *Aspects of Social Change in Modern Japan*. Princeton: Princeton University Press, 1967.

Totten, G. O. Japanese industrial relations at the crossroads: The great Noda strike of 1927–1928. In: B. Silberman and H. D. Harootunian, eds., *Japan in Crisis*. Princeton: Princeton University Press, 1974.

Vogel, E. F., Kinship structure, migration to the city, and modernization. In: R. P. Dore, ed., *Aspects of Social Change in Modern Japan*. Princeton: Princeton University Press, 1967.

Vogel, E. Z., ed., *Modern Japanese Organization and Decision-Making*. Berkeley: University of California Press, 1975.

Yasuba, Y., The evolution of dualistic wage structure. In: H. Patrick, ed. *Japanese Industrialization and its Social Consequences*. Berkeley: University of California Press, 1976.

10

A Comparative Study on Financial Development*

KEIMEI KAIZUKA

Department of Economics
The University of Tokyo
Hongo Bunkyo-ku, Tokyo
Japan

1. Introduction

This paper is intended to comparatively trace the financial developments of the major industrialized countries, namely, Great Britain, the United States, West Germany, and Japan, from a new perspective on financial structure.

As Gurley and Shaw [1955] originally pointed out, the financial structure of the economy has changed during the process of economic development. They stressed the shift from self-financing to direct financing and the shift from direct financing to indirect financing. They explained these changes in financial structure mainly as the process of better matching opportunities for savings to opportunities for real investments in the economy.

Although these features of financial development focus on an important aspect of structural changes, there is another characterization which typifies financial systems. This characterization of financial structure is based on two types of financial transactions, transactions in open and competitive markets and transactions through bilateral negotiations.

This paper consists of two parts. The first part explains the theoretical meaning of the new typology of financial structure, and the second part tries to apply the new typology to four cases of financial development, namely, that of Great Britain, the United States, West Germany, and Japan. The paper ends with a few concluding remarks.

*This paper is based on research done during the period in which the author has been an Academic Visitor at the London School of Economics and Political Science in 1984–1985, and the author thanks Professor Mervin King for his helpful advice.

197

2.   The Theoretical Implications of the New Typology

Relationships between financial structure and economic development have been explored by several economists, and among them the typology maintained by J. G. Gurley and E. S. Shaw [1955] is the most interesting.[1] They viewed the role of financial institutions as the matching of opportunities for savings to opportunities for real investments, and financial development, in their sense, meant more efficient or a more mature way to mobilize funds from savings to opportunities for real investments. The shift from self-financing to direct financing and the shift from direct financing to indirect financing could be interpreted in this way.

According to Gurley and Shaw, direct financing means the case where the ultimate or final spending unit invests more than its own savings (internal funds) and directly borrows outside funds from the ultimate or final spending unit, which saves more than its real investment. In this case the instrument of borrowing is the primary security which is issued by the ultimate investors or borrowers. Indirect financing is the case where financial intermediaries (e.g., banks, insurance companies, etc.) mediate between the ultimate savers and the ultimate borrowers. In other words, the ultimate savers do not directly lend funds to ultimate borrowers but lend funds to financial intermediaries through the debts (e.g., deposits, insurance securities, etc.) issued by them, and financial intermediaries lend funds to the ultimate borrowers.

Even though the taxonomy used by Gurley and Shaw sheds a light on the interrelationships between financial structure and economic development, there arise at least two questions on their taxonomy. First, there are cases of developed countries, like West Germany and Japan, where direct financing scarcely played an important role in financial development. In other words, the establishment of the channel of direct financing is not a necessary condition for economic development. Secondly, although the taxonomy used by Gurley and Shaw could be applied operationally in statistical data, the formal application sometimes neglects an important aspect of financial structure. For example, even if two economies show the same weight of direct financing in their financial structures, it is quite possible that one economy has well-developed secondary markets for stocks and bonds and the other economy does not have developed markets for securities. The former economy tends to be more competitive than the latter economy in financial structure, because one of the factors which promotes competitiveness in financial markets depends on the extent of development in open secondary markets.

The role of financial intermediaries and secondary markets (and also new issue markets) could be interpreted from another perspective, namely, the

---

[1] We could also cite the work of R. W. Goldsmith and R. I. Mckinnon.

function of institutions which eliminate or mitigate imperfect information in financial markets [Stiglitz and Weiss, 1981; Leyland and Pyle, 1977; Royama, 1982; Ikeo, 1985)].[2]

Suppose that there is an investor of real capital who needs more funds than his retained profit. He has the most relevant information on his investment project even though there is uncertainty on the prospects of its returns, and he also has the most accurate information on his financial positions (the possibility of bankruptcy, liquidity position, etc.). Imperfections in financial markets arise mainly from the fact that information on borrowers is concentrated on their side, and lenders do not usually have sufficient information on investment projects taken by borrowers and the financial positions of borrowers. As is well known in the recent literature on imperfect capital markets, if these asymmetries of information were left as they are, there would arise adverse selection in the financial market, and the sound and promising borrowers would be wiped out of the market. These distortions in the market could be eliminated or mitigated by several institutional devices, and it is in this respect that such financial arrangements and institutions as the creation of issuing markets for securities and financial intermediaries play their roles. The relationship between financial structure and economic development needs to be reconsidered in this perspective.

It is appropriate for us to explain here the functions of these institutional arrangements in detail.

First, the significance of the creation of new issue markets should be indicated. One way to mitigate adverse selection in financial markets is to create a market for the securities whose quality is easily judged even by ultimate savers or investors. These securities must be of a uniform quality. In other words, debt issued by a specific borrower has the same quality of financial risk even though debt is issued many times for years. Lenders or investors do not hesitate to buy debts of uniform quality because its quality can be easily judged by them. In addition to the uniformness of quality, the debt must be safe in its financial risk because most ultimate savers or investors are risk-averse. The typical example of an institution for these purposes is the establishment of the stock exchange. The stock exchange usually screens the quality of stocks and bonds to be quoted in various ways, and an issuer to the stock exchange must satisfy the qualification. On the flotation of bonds, such rating institutions as those in the United States have the same function.

Secondly, the role of financial intermediaries should be emphasized. These financial intermediaries are usually specialists with the ability to screen various offers for borrowing by judging the financial risks of borrowers and

---

[2] Royama's book [1982] and Ikeo's book [1985] were very helpful in writing this paper. Also see the recently developed works of Stiglitz & Weiss [1981] and Leyland & Pyle [1977].

sometimes even the appropriateness of investment projects undertaken by borrowers. Among these financial intermediaries, the banks have the unique advantage of gathering information by servicing potential borrowers through such mediums of transactions as deposits. In other words, they can judge the state of business of potential borrowers by seeing records in their deposit accounts. Financial intermediaries sometimes get their information on investment projects of potential borrowers from the members of the board of the corporation undertaking a new project, because financial intermediaries might be able to establish a close affiliation with the corporation by sending their members to its board (typically in the case of West Germany).

So far we have mainly explained the functions of institutions in financial markets from the point of view of imperfect information. We can also roughly relate these functions to specific types of transactions in financial markets. The role of institutional arrangement in creating securities which have uniform quality is reflected in the activities of new issue markets based on open secondary markets.[3] The role of financial intermediaries is typically performed by loans made by intermediaries. The decision as to whether intermediaries make loans to potential borrowers or not depends on their judgment of the financial soundness and future prospects of the borrowers, and these transactions are made based on bilateral negotiations between lenders and borrowers. Even though intermediaries frequently invest their funds in securities traded in open markets, in this case their function of screening securities is not as important, because financial soundness of securities is not a chief concern in deciding to buy these securities. Therefore, we can say that the two functions explained so far roughly correspond to the distinction between transactions in open and competitive markets and transactions through bilateral negotiations.

The new typology proposed here has several implications in relation to financial development which promotes economic growth. First, both the creation of new issue markets and the establishment of financial intermediaries contribute to economic development, because both institutions help the economy to mobilize funds for opportunities for real investment. Secondly, there does not exist a kind of priority between two types of financial arrangements in the sense that one must be the prerequisite for the other for economic development. Gurley and Shaw indicated that direct financing preceded indirect financing in financial evolution. Even though direct financing does not necessarily correspond to the creation of issue markets and

---

[3] If issue markets are not competitive and secondary markets are not open and competitive, we still have a market in which bankers and other participants could deal. However, in these cases the dealings turn out to be negotiable transactions and in substance are similar to loans by financial intermediaries.

open secondary markets, it is not a prerequisite of economic development that we must have these institutions, because financial intermediaries could sufficiently finance economic development if they could develop a fully branched system or if interbank markets could be established. On the other hand, it is difficult for the economy relying solely on new issue markets to finance economic development, because there must be a limited number of borrowers who can issue securities in these markets. Usually the government and the big corporations can finance their activities by issuing securities, but small businesses typically cannot finance their investment activities in these ways because these debts cannot be standardized into a uniform safe assets for savers and it is difficult to deal their debts in securities markets.[4]

In the following sections we apply our taxonomy to four countries, namely, Great Britain, the United States, West Germany, and Japan and try to explore in detail the relationships between financial structure and economic development which can be induced from these case studies.

3.   The Case of Great Britain

To begin, we trace the development of financial systems in Great Britain. As the "first industrial nation" the development of its financial market started in the early part of the end of the seventeenth century, when the government began to finance its deficit through issuing government securities. During the 76 years from 1739 to 1815, 45 years were years of wars, and wars were becoming steadily larger, better organized, and more expensive. The trends of public borrowing during the time of these wars reflected this tendency, and the dependence of revenues on public borrowing was very high. In those days the activities of banks was rudimentary, so they could not play any substantial role in intermediating funds from savers to ultimate borrowers. The capital market for government securities became fully developed during the first half of the eighteenth century, and by the 1750s investors in London were placing substantial sums in government securities. Without these facilities for investment, far more varied and flexible than land, "the City's complex structure of services could not have been built up by the mid-eighteenth century." The emergence of this long-term capital market is called "financial revolution," and it is claimed that "delay in the emergence of the city as a financial center would have put back England's industrialization and thus changed the course of European history" [Dickson 1967, p. 11–12].

The following description shows concretely the extent of the development of the long-term capital market. The transactions in the stock exchange

---

[4] This is one of the reasons why the so-called Macmillan Gap arises.

required a considerable sophistication in technique. Even though investors could make transactions directly, it was convenient for them to employ brokers. Time bargains had been familiar since the end of the seventeenth century. The market introduced option dealings for forward sales and purchases, and, when these were forbidden, concentrated on margin transactions and introduced quarterly settlement days for all securities trades. At the beginning of the Seven Year War, the London Stock Exchange had already acquired a comparable position with Amsterdam and became technically a perfect market. By the end of the Napoleonic Wars, it was showing many of the basic features of later times. Stock brokering was a specialized profession, and the distinction between the broker and the jobber was clearly recognized.[5]

From these historical developments, it can be concluded that in the financial development of England the open long-term capital market took the initiative. In other words, the market in government securities was firmly established in the very early stage of financial development.

In contrast with the development of the capital market in the 1750s, banking was still in a rudimentary stage. In London, banking was divided into two groups, the bankers in the West End and the bankers in the city. The former had close associations with the aristocracy, gentry, and wealthy gentlemen and did not act very much in commercial discounting of trade-bills for merchants nor become agents of the country banks which appeared in the 1750s in country areas. The latter included only about 30 bankers in 1750, but their main business began as discounting bills of exchange for merchants and industrialists, making short-term loans to stockholders, and lending on "call."

The activities of bankers had gradually grown to play an active role in financial intermediation after 1770. Country bankers had shown early formation about 1750 and began to develop in the late quarter of the eighteenth century. The number of country bankers was about 120 in 1784 and increased to 370 in 1800 and to about 780 in 1810. The country banks were almost all local, so they could not handle interregional transfers. Local banking or unit banking demanded specialized intermediaries when the flow of funds grew. The bill brokers took the role of intermediation after 1800. The banking sector as a whole has played an important role as a mobilizer of funds on short-term in the total economy since the beginning of the nineteenth century. From the agricultural areas of the east, south, and west, after-harvest flows of short-term credit moved into the industrial and commercial districts of the midlands and the northwest with credit requirements greater than the locally available supply. The emergence of the London discount market was

[5] On the early development of the securities market, see E. V. Morgan & W. A. Thomas' book [1962] and also Dickson's book [1967].

the final stage in these developments. In addition to being a group dealing in bills and short-term credit for these bills from the banks, the availability of rudimentary final resource facilities at the Bank of England for brokers when the banks called in their call loans made the establishment of the discount market possible.[6]

Since, as already described, financial development in England started from financing deficits in the public sector, how did the financial system contribute to financing deficits in the private sector? There were primarily two ways to finance deficits through financial systems, through banks and through the securities market. Several arguments were raised concerning the extent to which loans by bankers contributed to easing the financial shortages of firms. It is usually said that loans by English banks have been dominated by short-term credit and that long-term credit has not played any significant role in financial intermediation by banks. However, in the early 1800s, when country banks flourished, country bankers also made long-term loans for business activities, so the conventional view, the dominance of short-term credit, might not necessarily have been maintained in the early stages of development [Mathias, 1973]. During the second half of the nineteenth century, when joint-stock banks became influential in the scene of banking, the principle of commercial banking had been gradually established, and bankers refrained from providing long-term loans to business activities.

With respect to the activities of securities market, it has already been described that the market for new issues and the secondary market for government bonds was established in the middle of the eighteenth century. However, the market of the stock exchange was very slow in beginning to deal with industrial securities. In the second quarter of the nineteenth century, about 70% of the securities listed on the London Stock Exchange were comprised of securities of the national government and about 10% were from foreign governments. The corporate securities issued in England were almost entirely limited to railroads.[7] These tendencies continued until the 1910s. One could say that there was no open capital market for industrial needs, in comparison with that provided for short-term credits by the banking system. Occasionally domestic savers turned their investments into industrial securities, namely, the coal, iron, and steel industries in the 1870s and domestic issues in the 1890s. However, because of the general thinness of industrial securities, a secondary market for them did not become firmly established

---

[6] On the early development of banking see P. Mathias' paper [1973], and on the establishment of the London Discount Market see King's book [1936] and Scammell's book [1968].

[7] M. C. Reed maintains that railway promotion in the 1830s and the 1840s contributed to the development of the formal capital market and the enlargement of the formal capital market which made it possible to handle other company securities on the stock exchange [Reed, 1975].

until banks and insurance companies, as a result of liquidity requirements, had industrial securities for their investment portfolios.[8]

After the First World War, there were two important developments in the British financial system. One was the change in the banking structure, and the other was the establishment of the new issue market for domestic industries.

During the latter part of the nineteenth century, 1900s and 1910s banking structures had been gradually changed, and the big clearing banks almost dominated the banking sector around the First World War. In the early stages of banking, joint-stock banks were legally restricted, especially in London. However, in 1854 joint-stock banks were admitted in London Clearing. Due to several financial panics, there had been mergers since the 1860s, and in 1884 the proportion of deposits supplied by the five largest banks to total deposits was over 25%. Concentration in the market structure continued and finally, as a result of mergers from 1917–1918, the share of total deposits held by the five largest banks increased to 80%. The collusion among banks began in the 1870s but was not so rigid during the period of pre-1914 cartels. After 1920 the cartel in respect to interest deposits, restrictive agreements in the discount market, and restrictive practices in monetary policy became so rigid that financial historians were much impressed by the tendency. For example, R. S. Sayers wrote that the "price competition has been rarely of any great importance in England but there have been times when it has been locally important." [Sayers, 1957].

During the 1960s, the secondary banks had developed and an element of competition had been introduced into the banking system. The monetary authorities which had backed up the restrictive practices of the past years changed their way of thinking in monetary policy and adopted competition and credit control in 1971.

Another development, the establishment of the domestic new issue market for industrial securities, was a new phenomenon in the securities market wherein government and foreign securities had dominated before the First World War. One of the factors which promoted the new developments was the change in the position of the balance of payments in the U.K. Its prewar short-term creditor position had been wiped out by 1918, so that there were few balances seeking international outlets. The other factor was the restrictive measures on issuing foreign securities. An official embargo on foreign issues was imposed during the war and continued afterwards with varying degrees of

---

[8] It is, rather, the conventional view that English investors had a bias towards favoring government and foreign securities during these periods. However, it was plausibly interpreted by M. Edelstein that difficulty in issuing domestic industrial securities lay not in the investors' biases but in the smaller size of issues when compared with government and foreign issues [Edelstein, 1982 and Cottrell, 1980].

severity. By the mid-1930s, over 50% of the new issue market's work was concerned with financing the home industry, and in the postwar period the new issue market had been more or less entirely oriented towards meeting the requirements of domestic borrowers.

So far, we have traced the financial development of Great Britain without going into detail. It is not easy for us to summarize the development, but it is useful to indicate here several features of the financial development from the theoretical perspectives which were explained in Section 2. First, in the case of Great Britain, the establishment of the new issue market and the secondary market of securities took a lead in the financial development prior to the formation of the banking system. Secondly, though the banking system had financed business through both short-term and long-term credit in the early stages of development, since the middle of the nineteenth century it had concentrated its activity on short-term lending. In this respect, the function of banking systems in screening borrowers had not fully developed in the British case. Thirdly, in spite of the fact that the securities market was developed very early, the scope of its activity had been limited to government securities. Since the First World War the issue market for industrial securities had been at last established. The experience of the British case suggests that the establishment of a securities market does not necessarily mean the formation of a fully developed channel of financing for business activity. The so-called Macmillan Gap has persistently existed in the British financial world, especially in the case of long-term credit, because both the securities market and the banking system do not care for small business in this field.

4.   The Case of the United States

Roughly speaking, the financial development of the United States is comparable with the British case primarily because the United States' financial system was developed under the strong influence of British financial institutions. Of course, Great Britain started as the first industrial nation, so the U.S. followed it in financial development. However, during the nineteenth century there existed a certain contrast between them, and the present state of financial performance of the U.S. is different from that of the British case although the basic features of its financial structure is rather comparable in terms of the typology we have already explained in this paper.

The financial system in the United States started at about the beginning of nineteenth century. It is difficult for us to judge whether or not banking had developed earlier than the securities market, because both the securities market and banking had been rudimentary in the first quarter of the nineteenth century. In 1810, the number of commercial banks was 88, and their lending policy was not so conservative that they were also active on long-term credit. However, after the financial panic of 1837, commercial banks tended to shift their activities from a mixed combination of short-term credit and long-term credit to short-term loans, because one of the causes of the panic was believed to be risky long-term loans. In 1817 the New York Exchange started, but its activity was rather limited. In these financial activities, the influence of London had been dominant in terms of the volume of funds (e.g., capital import on a long-term basis and the financing of import) and also in institutional aspects. Anglo-American merchant bankers played an important role in selling American securities to British and continental investers and in facilitating the buying and selling of old issues of securities.

Most economic historians now agree on the assertion that the Civil War was the watershed in American economic development in the sense that the American economy took off as an industrialized economy during the period of 1860–1890. Even though it is rather questionable how far the financial system helped the take-off of the economy, we can observe the following important changes in the financial scene.

Firstly, securities markets had gotten much wider and deeper in their functions, especially in their activities in government securities. During the war the issue and sale of interest-bearing public debt was unprecedented. This form of federal debt rose from 90 million dollars in 1861 to 2,322 million dollars in 1866. Under the stimulus of this massive borrowing, both financial technologies and financial institutions underwent widespread changes that modernized the American capital market. Jay Cook initiated the method of large-scale securities distribution, and numerous individuals and enterprises were introduced to investments in paper wealth, even though the creation of a national banking system helped government securities to become the chief object of its investment outlet. A single national market began to emerge out of the heterogeneous and loosely related markets of earlier decades, and at the center of this capital market was the market for government securities. Therefore, it is possible to say that an open and competitive market for government securities had been firmly established in this period.[9]

During the period from 1860 to 1890, financial intermediaries grew to such an extent that the assets of financial intermediaries increased at twice the rate achieved by the national income. However, the function of the banking sector in this period is not necessarily evaluated so highly because mobilization of funds among regions was hindered by the behavior of the banking sector. As is well known, L. Davis argued that there existed wide differentials in regional interest rates during the period 1870–1914, and the market for bank loans and

[9]On the development of the government bond market, the work by R. Sylla is a valuable source [1975].

other money and capital markets were decidedly imperfect in the post Civil War American economy [Davis, 1965].

There are differences in opinion on the causes of imperfection of the banking sector and money market in the period. R. Sylla maintained that the entry barriers to local banking had been important [Sylla, 1975], and J. A. James showed the importance of entry by state banks [James, 1978]. In any case, these arguments indicate that in spite of its quantitative development, the banking sector functionally contributed to financial development to a lesser degree.

In respect to activities in the bonds market, the role of investment bankers since the 1890s has been important because they could have mobilized funds for expansion of real investments in manufacturing sectors. The open secondary market for corporate bonds has been established since the days before the First World War, and also the money market has been integrated through the formation of commercial paper market since this period.

On the financial developments since the First World War, we add the few following points. Firstly, in 1913 the Federal Reserve System was established and the function of the money market was strengthened. Secondly, the instability of the financial system originating in the Great Crash induced such tighter regulations as the Glass-Stegal Act, Regulation Q, and Deposit Insurance. It is not easy for us to judge how far these regulations have deteriorated the function of the American financial system. However, it is possible to say that Regulation Q had become effective since the mid 1960s, and before that period interest rates in the financial markets had been free because market rates had been below the regulated rate.

To sum up the financial development of the United States, the following characteristics of its development can be mentioned. Although it is not easy for us to judge whether or not the establishment of the banking system as a whole preceded the establishment of open markets for securities, it is certain that in the latter half of nineteenth century open markets for government securities had been firmly established. Even though the banking sector also developed in quantitative terms in this period, its contribution to real economic growth was not great. Roughly speaking, the American system is similar to the system in Great Britain, but regulation under the decentralized federal system and delay in the establishment of the centralized banking system had weakened the allocational function of the banking sector.

5.   The Case of West Germany

Though the economic development of Germany started slightly later than that of America, its course of financial development was distinctly different from that of America.

From the early days in the nineteenth century to the 1880s financial development was concentrated along the Rhine River, especially Frankfurt am Mein, and private banks played a crucial role in this development. They were eager to finance private business by initially making long-term loans to them and funding these loans through issuing stocks and debts for them. This process was usually referred to as consolidation. In consolidation, banks sought holders of these securities among their customers, and if they could not find holders, they held these securities in their own accounts. The stock exchange was established, but the process of consolidation took place outside the stock exchange. Therefore, the role of the stock exchange was narrowly limited. In a sense, banks played the function of investment banking, while, at the same time, they acted as the commercial banks.[10]

In making long-term loans to business, private bankers wanted to know the activities of borrowers accurately, because bankers themselves bore the risks of investment projects undertaken by borrowers. Private bankers owned the stocks of borrowers and sent their staffs to the board of those firms which took out bank loans. In this way bankers influenced managerial decision-making of borrowers. Thus, there emerged the special tie between bankers and borrowers. These early developments of private banks along the Rhine River were based on negotiated transactions of loans and on consolidation, and the role of such secondary open markets as bonds and stocks was narrowly limited. In this sense, the early development of the financial system in Germany almost totally depended on negotiated intermediation by banks.

From the 1880s to the 1930s the Kreditbanken, in incorporated business, occupied a substantial portion of the banking sector. In this period, private banks had been united and incorporated, amalgamation proceeded among Kreditbanken, and the branch system was utilized extensively. Finally, three major banks dominated the banking sector. In other words, the hey days of Grossbanken had arrived.

As is well known, Gershenkron [1962] argued that though in England, where the industrial revolution proceeded in earlier days, capital formation was financed by retained profits within firms, in such latecomers as Germany, capital formation was financed by banks, and entrepreneurship in banks was also utilized by borrowers. This argument corresponds to the activities of the Grossbanken in this period. However, at least two questions on Gershenkron's thesis were raised. Firstly, the take-off in the German economy was earlier than the 1870s and the Grossbanken were not yet flourishing then [Cameron, 1976]. Secondly, the borrowers from the Grossbanken did not necessarily include strategic sectors for economic development, and the active role of the Grossbanken might be questioned [Neuberger & Stokes, 1974]. In

---

[10] On financial development along the Rhine River the work by R. Tilly is very informative [1966].

spite of these questions, it is evident that the relation between banks and firms was much closer than that in England or America. For example, in 1933 and 1934 banks sent directors to 1,581 of a total of 2,656 corporations. Naturally, in this period securities markets were thin, and their role in financial development was negligible.

After the Second World War, in West Germany the Grossbanken had been broken up by postwar reform. However, commercial banks have been gradually reamalgamated and the three big banks reappeared. At the retail level of banking, three groups, commercial banks, public banks chiefly composed of savings banks, and credit banks of cooperative form, have been competitive with each other. These banks handle the securities business along with the banking business, so they are Universal Banks, and their relations with firms are intimate. In these aspects the financial system in West Germany still preserves the main features of the prewar periods.[11]

With regards to money and capital markets, even now there is no established open market. The operations of the central bank (Bundesbank) use the treasury bonds issued by the central bank, and most operations are with repurchase agreements. Treasury bonds are registered bonds and are not easy to buy or sell in the market. The operation of government bonds is not executed because of legal limitations. The weight of nonmarketable bonds among governments bonds is also great. In any case these examples support the fact that an open market for bonds is not yet established in West Germany.

To summarize the financial development of Germany, firstly, in Germany or West Germany there has never existed the established open market for bonds. Secondly, the banking sector has been active in lending long-term loans and in consolidating these loans into stocks and bonds, not through stock exchanges, but through bilateral negotiations between banks and borrowers (firms). These features in the financial development are quite a contrast with such Anglo-Saxon cases as Great Britain and America. The influence of lenders (banks) on the decision-making of borrowers (firms) has been distinct. Even though there exists competitive pressures from public banks, credit banks of cooperative forms, and commercial banks, the three big banks to maintain cooperative oligopoly in the loan market.

6.   The Case of Japan

It is customarily said that economic development in Japan started with the Meiji Restoration in 1867. This is not really accurate as the Japanese economy in the 1860s had already achieved a significant level of economic activity and

---

[11] On the present state of the financial system in West Germany, the works of the Economist Advisory Group [1981], and of H. Francke and M. Hudson [1984] are valuable resources.

was definitely not an underdeveloped economy. However, it is not easy for us to trace economic development before the 1860s, so we confine the scope of our discussion to development after the 1860s.[12]

Roughly speaking, the course of financial development in Japan is comparable with that of West Germany, even though very recently we have observed the establishment of an open bond market, and this has changed the characteristics of the financial system.

In the course of financial developments after the 1860s it is convenient for us to divide them into developments between 1900 and those after 1900, because traditional ways of financing still strongly influenced the financial world before 1900. For example, such traditional instruments as pawnbrokers and personal borrowing had been utilized extensively. Internal financing carried out by rich landowners and merchants who, at the same time, were investors in real assets had also been important. After 1900 the importance of these traditional ways of financing was diminished, and the role of modern financial intermediaries became dominant.

The banking sector was organized by establishing national banks in 1872, which roughly correspond to the system of the National Banking Act in America. Those banks issued bank notes which were convertible into gold coins. However, the national banks did not work well, because bank notes were frequently converted into gold coins. In 1876, the national banks act was revised, and banks were allowed to issue inconvertible bank notes. Since that time the national banks have grown substantially. Along with the national banks, private banks grew rapidly. The number of national banks and private banks in 1876 was only five and one, respectively, and the number in 1892, when the national banking system was abolished, was 133 and 324, respectively. Other financial institutions which were not formally banks also increased rapidly, and the number in 1892 was 680. The postal savings system was established earlier, in 1875, and accepted savings deposits.

The Bank of Japan was established as the central bank in 1882. At that time the national banks issued bank notes, so the Bank of Japan was not the sole institution that could issue currencies. However, it was expected that the national banks would be transformed into ordinary banks, and their banks notes would be converted to the bank notes issued by the Bank of Japan until the end of nineteenth century.

In 1890 private banks and other financial institutions were legally reorganized under the Act of Ordinal Banks and, at the same time, the Act of Savings Banks was enacted. The savings banks were the banks which accepted

---

[12] In writing the Japanese case, the author depended heavily on the excellent work of J. Teranishi [1982].

only savings deposits. Ordinary banks and savings banks grew rapidly, and the number of these banks in 1900 was 1,854 and 435, respectively.

In addition to ordinary banks and savings banks, the special banks were established. The first special bank was Yokohama Specie Bank, which was established in 1880 and specialized in foreign exchange transactions. Other special banks such as Japan Hypothec Banks, the Japan Industrial Banks, and the Agricultural and Manufacturing Banks, were established around 1900. These special banks had the common characteristic of all being long-term financing banks. They could make long-term loans of assets and could absorb funds by issuing long-term bonds.

As regards secondary markets of securities, the government was eager to encourage the formation of this market, and in 1878 the Stock Exchange Act was enacted. However, the market was thin and speculative, so the function of the secondary market has been insignificant since that time. Public debt was issued, especially during the war with China and Russia, but its absorption into the domestic market was not easy because of large volumes and the thinness of the market. Actually, the absorption was helped by the financing of the Bank of Japan and also by issuing in foreign markets. Therefore, the big issues of public debt did not induce the development of secondary markets [Underwriters' Association, 1980].

In the financial development of the Japanese economy, the role of the banking sector has been, on the whole, crucial, as it was in Germany. However, in the earlier stages before 1900, it is difficult to say that bankers played the role of active entrepreneurs to the borrowers, because bankers themselves had been merchants and landowners. In a sense, entrepreneurs had set up banks to mobilize funds for themselves. So financial funds of real investments had been recruited from accumulated holdings of liquid assets of merchants and landowners. In addition to these sources, the government also had contributed substantial portions of funds raised from banking sectors. Bankers as lenders had not always been active, because in underdeveloped areas a sizeable portion of banks' funds had been invested in government bonds. In the case of developed areas, bankers had made such short-term lending by discounting bills.

After 1900 the role of financial intermediaries became autonomous in the sense that they did not rely on government assistance and mainly depended on deposits from various savers. At the same time, borrowers wanted to get long-term credit because they needed to finance real investments in larger volume, Even though there were savings banks, most banks relied on their resources in current deposits and found it difficult to make long-term loans to borrowers. In this respect, the function of money markets was important, because they could mobilize funds widely in the national economy. A call money market had been developed around 1900, and during and after the First World War it

212 Developments in Japanese Economics

grew rapidly. Around the same time, differentiation of deposit rates among different regions beame narrower according to empirical evidence [Teranishi, 1982]. So there was almost a unification of the national market for short-term funds.

The relationship between banks and borrowers from banks was close, but this relationship must be interpreted cautiously because there have been various views on this subject among economic historians. As was already explained, in the early days of development banks had been organized in a sense, to mobilize funds for entrepreneurs. This phenomena was also seen after 1900, especially in small banks. There were close connections between banks and borrowers with regards to managerial decisions.

Generally speaking, borrowers wanted to get long-term credits because they needed to finance fixed investments in large volumes. However, ordinary banks absorbed funds as short-term deposits. Therefore, they had to investigate carefully the quality and soundness of loans before committing their funds in long-term credits, and they wanted to have close connections with managers in firms which borrowed loans from their banks.

Such special banks as the Japan Industrial Banks and the Japan Hypothec Banks are the long-term credit banks which absorbed the funds by issuing long-term bonds. The development of special banks has supplemented the financial gaps between ordinary banks and borrowers. The special banks have been a feature of the Japanese financial system, and we still maintain this feature now.

With regards to securities market, the activities of the secondary market continued to be very low, even though there had been a slight increase in the turnover of bonds around 1910 because of lower interest rates. Ordinary banks and special banks had done the business of underwriting bonds, so in this respect Japanese banks had worked as German Universal Banks.

Since the beginning of the twentieth century, the structure of the banking sector has changed. The number of banks have decreased considerably. The number of ordinary banks and savings banks peaked (2,334) in 1902 and gradually decreased during the 1900s and 1910s. The number of small banks has been diminished mainly because of the looseness of their management and the riskiness of their long-term credits. During the 1920s the number of banks decreased by one-half, and the decrease was mainly due to the chronic depressions and a government policy forcing amalgamation. The government enacted the Banking Act in 1973, which set the minimum for capital, and, at that time, the number of banks under the minimum was 57% of the total. After 1937, the Japanese economy moved into a war economy, and the government tightly regulated the financial system in order to mobilize the production of munitions. The financial system was reorganized in order to be convenient for channelling funds into defense and related industries. Loans to industries was planned to be allocated mainly through big banks, and other banks became the sole institutions absorbing deposits.

Deposit rates had been free until the middle of 1930s. It is said that the cartel for deposit rates was started in the Osaka area in 1901 and also in the Tokyo area in 1902. However, these cartels were a kind of gentlemen's agreement and actually worked as a standard of minimum rates. With respect to the special banks, there were maintained strict regulations on interest rates on loans. During the war economy the government encouraged deposit rates to be uniform by strengthening the cartel. In issuing bonds, especially corporate bonds and bonds of local governments, the Bank of Japan began to screen the rate and time of issue during the war economy and, finally, issue markets were totally controlled and regulated by the government.

Just after the Second World War, the financial system was reorganized under the occupation of the American army. Special banks were abolished and they were forced to become ordinary banks. However, in 1952 the Long-term Credit Banks Act was enacted, and these banks offered long-term credit matched by issuing long-term bonds. Among the private institutions, the banks owned by the government and financed mainly by postal savings were established in various fields. The separation of banking and securities companies was introduced because the same type of regulation as the Glass-Stegal Act was adopted.

In the process of rapid economic growth, the basic features of financing during the war were maintained. The regulation of interest rates, especially deposits and loans by banks, became more explicit due to a new law on interest rates (1947). Credit allocation through controlling the issue of corporate bonds and bonds of local governments was also maintained, while issuing rates were regulated at the same time. Government banks played a leading role in credit allocation by maintaining lower rates on loans. The banks had a strategic position in managerial decision of borrowers because corporations planning a new investment project usually relied heavily on bank loans. Therefore, banks could influence the decisions of corporations borrowing loans.

With respect to the securities market in the 1950s and 1960s, we can see such features as the speculative stock market and the thin bonds markets which were seen during the prewar period. In the money market, there was a very active call market where the final discrepancy of demand and supply for short-term funds was cleared.

Since the first half of the 1970s, several changes in the financial system have emerged. As we already mentioned, the nonexistence of an open market except the stock market had thus far been one of the important features of the Japanese financial system. However, a new open market, namely, the Gensaki market, has developed since the first half of the 1970s. The Gensaki market is functionally a money market which uses bonds as collateral. Gensaki transactions involve the resale or repurchase of bonds at a fixed price within a fixed period. In contrast with the call market, which is essentially an interbank market, the Gensaki market is an open market in which financial institutions, business corporations, and public organizations operate, even though individuals are still not permitted to participate.

As the Gensaki market developed, the banks found it difficult to gather short-term funds invested by business corporations and public organizations, because the Gensaki market was intermediated by securities companies offering more attractive terms than deposits in the banking sector. Therefore, in May 1979, negotiable certificates of deposit (CD) were introduced, although Japanese CDs require complicated procedures in order to transfer them to a third party. Even though we have seen the development of the money market, it is possible to say that the openness of the market has still been restricted because the access to these markets has been limited to the banking sector and large investors, and the Gensaki and CDs are not necessarily very convenient instruments for investors. Treasury bills, as the most suitable instruments for short-term assets, have not been offered openly in the Japanese financial markets.

With regards to the bonds markets, a significant change has been induced by huge government deficits after the first oil shock. Before 1975, the central government had maintained a balanced budget in a strict sense of the word. Since 1975, the central government has begun to issue long-term debts, even though their deficits were comparatively small. The method of issuing public bonds at that time was different from that in America. Usually banks and securities companies formed a syndicate to accept public bonds at the negotiated coupon rate. This rate was not determined in such competitive way as bidding in the U.S. bonds market but was regulated in accordance with other regulated interest rates, namely, deposit rates and prime rates. The financial institutions which bought public debts could not sell them in the market because of a regulation prohibited reselling public bonds. Therefore, there was no open market for public bonds.

The huge deficits since the first oil shock have made regulatory control on public debts difficult, because the Ministry of Finance was forced to issue public bonds extensively and their restrictive practices were thought to be obstacles to debt financing. The prohibition on reselling of public bonds by financial institutions was relaxed in 1977 and almost completely abolished in 1982. Competitive bidding on new issues of medium-term public bonds was introduced in 1978, and the same method was applied to buying operations by the Bank of Japan. It is possible to say that since the late 1970s the open market for public bonds has been established. There were several empirical research studies which demonstrated the validity of the standard term-structure theory on interest rates in the open market of public bonds. Even though most of the interest rates of long-terms are formally regulated, there are frequent changes in regulated rates in accordance with changes in the market rate of the bonds markets. Considering these tendencies, the basic features of the financial system in Japan have been transformed recently. The transformation is evident, at least, in long-term financing, because an open market for bonds has been established and the asset structure of financial institutions has gradually shifted from loans to portfolio investments. In short-term financing the transformation is not complete, because the function of an open market does not dominate the scene, even though we observed the development of the Gensaki and CD markets. In any way, liberalization and deregulation is continuing in domestic financial activities.

6.   Concluding Remarks

Thus far we have reviewed the financial development of four countries. Roughly speaking, the courses of financial development of Great Britain and United States are comparable in the sense that in both countries open money and bond markets were firmly established in the early days, while the banking sector developed simultaneously or later. Also, the course of financial development in West Germany and Japan are roughly comparable, in the sense that in both countries the banking sector played the dominant role and the function of an open securities market was narrowly limited. However, since the 1970s, this feature has been transformed in Japan because of the establishment of an open market for government long-term bonds. There is a close tie between banks and borrowers in West Germany and Japan, while the Anglosaxon financial system has emphasized commercial banking and has had a limited influence on the decision-making on real investments of borrowers. The question of whether or not the differences between these two types of financial development influenced the course of their economic development is a very interesting one. However, this question remains to be investigated in future research.

References

Cameron, R., et al, *Banking in the Early Stages of Industrialization*. London: Oxford University Press, 1976.
Cottrell, P. L., *Industrial Finance, 1830–1914*. London: Methuen, 1980.
Davis, L. E., The investment market, 1870–1914: The evolution of a national market, *Journal of Economic History*, September, 1965.
Dickson, R. G. M., *Financial Revolution in England*. London: Macmillan, 1967.

Edelstein, M., *Overseas Investment in the Age of High Imperialism*. London: Methuen, 1982.

Economists Advisory Group, *The British and German Banking System: A Comparative Study*. Anglo-German Foundation, 1981.

Francke, H. and M. Hudson, *Banking and Finance in West Germany*. London: Groom Helm, 1984.

Gerschenkron, A., *Economic Backwardness in Historical Perspective*. Cambridge: Harvard University Press, 1962.

Griffiths, B., The development of restrictive practice in the U.K. monetary system, *Manchester School of Economics and Social Studies*, Vol. 61(1), 1973.

Gurley J. G. and E. S. Shaw, Financial aspects of economic development, *American Economic Review* Vol. 14, 1955.

Ikeo K., *Financial Markets and Organization in Japan*. Tokyo: Toyokeizai Shimposha, 1985 (in Japanese).

James, J. A., *Money and Capital Markets in Postbellum America*. Princeton: Princeton University Press, 1978.

King, W. T. C., *History of the London Discount Market*. London: Routledge, 1936.

Leyland, H. E. and D. H. Pyle, Information symmetrics, financial structure and financial intermediation, *Journal of Finance* Vol. 32, 1977.

Morgan, E. V. and W. A. Thomas, *The Stock Exchange*. London: Elek Books, 1962.

Neuberger, H. and H. H. Stokes, German banks and German growth, 1883–1913, *Journal of Economic History*, Vol. 34, 1974.

Reed, M. C., *Investment in Railway in Britain: A Study in the Development of Capital Market*, London: Oxford University Press, 1975.

Royama, S., *The Financial System in Japan*. Tokyo: Toyokeizai Shimposha, 1982 (in Japanese).

Sayers, R. S., *Lloyds Bank in the History of English Banking*. London: Oxford University Press, 1957.

Scammell, W. H., *The London Discount Market*. London: Elek Books, 1968.

Stiglitz, J. E. and Weiss, A., Credit rationing in markets with imperfect information, *American Economic Review* Vol. 13, 1981.

Sylla, R., *The American Capital Market, 1846–1914*. New York: Arno, 1975.

Teranishi, J., *Economic Development and the Financial System in Japan*. Tokyo: Iwanami-shoten, 1982 (in Japanese).

Tilly, R., *Financial Institutions and Industrialization in the Rhineland 1815–1870*. Madison: Univ. of Wisconsin Pr., 1966.

Underwriters' Association, *The History of Japanese Bond Markets*. Tokyo: Underwriters' Association, 1980 (in Japanese).

11

Internationalization of Japanese Commercial Banking and the Yen: The Recent Experience of City Banks*

MASAHIRO FUJITA

The Research Institute for Economic and Business Administration
Kobe University
Nada-ku
Japan

1. Introduction Note

In recent years, the Japanese position in the international economic-political society has risen rapidly. In addition, Japan has been strongly requested to gain international responsibility. This issue came to the surface as a practical problem in the form of the much more intense financial friction between Japan and the U.S.A. The difficult negotiations between both government authorities on this matter had been continuing for a long time. Finance Minister Takeshita and Treasury Secretary Regan's agreement on the Yen-Dollar Committee (Report by the Working Group of Joint Japan-U.S. Ad Hoc Group on Yen/Dollar Exchange Rate, Financial and Capital Market

* I would like to express my deep appreciation for Professor Kazuya Mizushima, Professor Ryoichi Mikitani, and Professor Kenichi Ishigaki. These professors are my closest colleagues at Kobe University.
The members of our research group are Professor M. Fujita, *Kobe University*, Professor K. Mizushima, *Kobe University*, Professor R. Mikitani, *Kobe University*, Professor Y. Futatsugi, *Kobe University*, Professor N. Miyata, *Kagawa University*, Professor K. Ishigaki, *Kobe University*, Associate Professor N. Niwa, *Toyama University*, Associate Professor K. Shimomura, *Kobe University*, and Assistant H. Izawa, *Kobe University*. Moreover, all these members belong to the Special Research Committee of International Finance, Kobe University, and Professor Fujita serves as the chief of that committee. We would like to particularly acknowledge the work of Mr. Miyata, Mr. Ishigaki, Mr. Niwa, and Mr. Izawa as members of our most important working group.
The following banks cooperated in our research. City banks: Daiichi Kangyo, Daiwa, Fuji, Hokkaido-Takushoku, Kyowa, Mitsubishi, Mitsui, Sanwa, Sumitomo, Taiyo-Kobe, Tokai, and

(*footnote continued on pg. 218*)

217

Issues) was announced officially on May 29, 1984. The main problem for Japan in the report on the Yen/Dollar is to implement financial liberalization and yen internationalization. Firstly, financial liberalization implies both liberalization of Japanese financial institutions' business affairs beyond the fence on banks and financial intermediaries and reciprocity of the Japanese financial institutions and the foreign banks in Japan. In particular, it mainly aims at liberalization of interest rates and internationalization of the financial institutions. Secondly, yen internationalization means that the Japan-yen complements the function of the U.S. dollar as the international currency, and bears the cost as an international currency, by the wide use of a bill of exchange denominated in yen at the time of export and import, and the need for yen as a reserve currency held by many Asian countries.

The Japanese economy is confronted with severe financial friction from the main worldwide developed countries. Firstly in spite of the many multilateral negotiation between Japan and the U.S. and the G-5 meeting, our economic relations continue to increase the crisis of financial and trade war.

According to recent statistics, the following large differences in economic strength can be found between Japan and the U.S.

Secondly, the Japanese government at many recent important international conferences has often agreed to intensify economic policy coordination in order to promote more balanced global growth and to reduce external imbalances.

Tokyo; Nihon Saiken Shinyo, Japan Export Import Bank, and some regional banks; Hokuriku, Yokohama, and some stock companies; Nomura, Nikko, Yamaichi, Daiwa, and many life insurance companies; Nihon Seimei, Dai-ichi Seimei, Meiji Seimei. We would like to express our appreciation for their kindly cooperation.

Furthermore, we would like to acknowledge the financial support provided by Grants in Aid for Scientific Research, the Ministry of Education, and Nihon-Shoken-Shogaku-Zaidan (Japan Securities Scholarship Foundation).

The subject of this paper is Internationalization of Japanese commercial banking—the recent experience of city banks in Japan. This is a summary of the results of the questionnaire-based research work that we conducted twice, once in 1977–78 and once in 1981–82. We have been working very closely since the questionnaires were drafted in compiling the responses and in discussing the summary of the results and its interpretation. Therefore this project is really a "joint product" of our cooperation, and the computation of each member's contribution to this project is very difficult to assess.

The actual writing of the summary has been done by our working group—Professor Fujita, Professor Mizushima, Professor Mikitani, and especially Mr. Miyata, Mr. Ishigaki, Mr. Niwa, and Mr. Izawa. The other working members were Professor Yusaku Futatsugi, Professor Nobuo Miyata, and Assistant Hideki Izawa. They could not attend our Canberra seminar at Australian National University in October, 1983, but other members (Mr. Fujita, Mr. Migustima, Mr. Mikitani, Mr. Ishigaki, and Mr. Niwa) could attend, and we were very happy to have fruitful academic discussions.

TABLE 1.
Economic scale of Japan and U.S.A. (1986)

	Japan	U.S.A.
Population	120.75 (million)	239.28
GNP	1329.9 ($billion)	3998.1
Per capita income	17515 ($)	16709
Trade balance	92.6 ($billion)	− 169.7
External assets	129.8 ($billion)	− 107.4
Rate of saving	16.2%	5.1%

For instance, at the September 1985 Plaza Accord and G-6 meeting held on February 22 in Paris, the Japanese Finance Minister, Kiichi Miyazawa, and the Governor of Bank of Japan, Mr. Sumita, stated in the communiqué:

The government of Japan will follow monetary and fiscal policies which will help to expand domestic demand and thereby contribute to reducing the external surplus. The comprehensive tax reform, now before the Diet, will give additional stimulus to vitality of the Japanese economy. Every effort will be made to get the 1987 budget approved by the Diet so that its early implementation is ensured. A comprehensive economic program will be prepared after the approval of 1987 budget by the Diet, so as to stimulate domestic demand, with the prevailing economic situation duly taken into account. The Bank of Japan announced that it will reduce its discount rate by 1/2 of 1 per cent on February 23.

However, both our external (trade) surplus and foreign exchange reserves at the end of the 1986 fiscal year increased by 89.7 billion dollars and 58.3 billion dollars, which showed the largest level in the post-war period.

Thirdly, as a result, the exchange rate for the yen has now appreciated to a level of 140 against 1 US. dollar since March 24, 1987.

Our yen exchange rate per U.S. dollar was ¥360 level under the IMF system (August 15, 1971). However the change in the yen exchange rate since the September 1985 Plaza Accord cannot merely be understood as an extraordinary and rapid fluctuation.

Regarding our forecast on the future of the yen per U.S. dollar exchange rate, it is very difficult and a most important problem, as the yen rate may increase to the level of ¥120 per U.S. dollar by the end of 1987.

The geographical distribution of the business activity of Japanese city banks at the end of 1986 were as follows: the number of Japanese commercial banks in U.S. was 28 banks, 71 branches, 29 local banks, and 53 representatives of banks; securities companies had 11 company offices, 14 branches, and 5 representatives; and life insurance companies had representatives of 8 companies in the U.S..

Changes of yen rate	Day changed	Necessary changing days
¥240 → ¥220	1985. 9.24	
	Plaza Agreement	
¥220 → ¥210	1985. 9.30	6
¥210 → ¥200	1985. 11.1	32
	Huge external deficit in U.S.	
¥200 → ¥190	1986. 1.24	84
	Japan official rate reduction	
¥190 → ¥180	1986. 2.3	10
¥180 → ¥170	1986. 2.19	16
	Treasury Secretary Baker opinion	
¥170 → ¥160	1986. 4.22	62
	Tokyo summit	
¥160 → ¥150	1986. 7.7	76
	General election in Japan	
¥150 → ¥140	1987. 3.24	260

In addition, the number of Japanese commercial banks in the U.K., especially in London, totalled 23 banks, 23 branches, 21 local banks, and 16 representatives of banks; securities companies had 22 local company offices and 3 representatives; and life insurance companies had 19 local offices.

However, the number of foreign banks in Japan was 1) U.S.—19 banks, 29 branches, 6 local banks, and 17 representatives of banks; securities companies had 12 company offices, 14 branches, 24 representatives; and life insurance companies had 8 local offices. 2) U.K.—5 banks, 7 branches, 1 local bank, and 12 representatives of banks. U.K. securities companies had 22 local banks (companies) and 19 representatives.

As mentioned above, Japanese banks and other financial intermediaries are now changing and expanding their areas of overseas business more and more.

This tendency depends mainly upon the strong yen in external finance and the domestic recession.

According to the report of the BIS, the volume of overseas financial assets (loans, indirect investments, or bond investments) amounted to 109.4 billion dollars. In other words, the external financial assets of Japanese banks were the greatest in the world, especially in the world of finance and money. Moreover, such rapid growth was accomplished in only two years, doubling the previous rate of growth, and Japan's city banks acquired a 31.6% share of the external assets of western private banks.

The internationalization of the Japanese economy, the development of an interdependent relationship between Japan and the rest of the world, and an increase in the importance of Japan's status in the world economy in the past

TABLE 2.
Distribution of Overseas Branches of Japanese Banks and Branches in Japan and of Foreign
Banks (end of 1985)

	1950–55	56–65	66–75	76–80	Total
Japanese Banks					
Overseas branches	11	34	54	90	191
Representative offices	4	14	125	314	370
Local Banks	3	2	37	118	155
Total	18	50	216	522	716
Foreign Banks					
Branches in Japan	35	4	44	52	114
Representative offices		7	95	98	116
Local Banks				3	3
Total	35	11	139	153	233

20 years have obviously had a great effect upon the activities of various large banks, which have played a major role in the financial activities of Japan. For example, in the past 10 years, the GNP increased 3.3 times, while the amount of foreign exchange transactions of all Japanese banks increased 7.5 times, the foreign assets of banks 12 times, and earnings profit from international banking 8 times. At the end of 1970, there were 58 overseas branches and 7 overseas local banks; however, at the end of 1981, the number increased to 151 overseas branches, 81 local banks, and 196 representative offices.

The international banking business of Japanese banks has been expanding not only quantitatively, but also changing qualitatively. They have been multinationalizing quite rapidly.

In our survey we not only asked the bankers to respond to a questionnaire, but we also interviewed them. Ten of the 12 city banks and one special foreign exchange bank cooperated with us in this survey. They account for about 84% of the foreign exchange asset balance and about 90% of all overseas branches of Japanese banks. Therefore, it seems to be fairly reasonable to say that this survey would provide a considerably accurate picture of internationalization of Japanese banking.

Generally speaking, the internationalization of finance has three aspects. Firstly, it involves the internationalization of domestic currency, that is, a domestic currency also becomes an international vehicle of currency and a reserve currency.

Secondly, it involves the internationalization of banks and other financial institutions that is, they make transactions in both domestic and foreign currencies with non-residents and residents. Thirdly, it involves the internationalization of money and capital markets, that is, both short-term and long-term funds move freely into and out of the markets across the borders of the countries, and interest rates are determined by market forces.

Of course these three aspects are closely interrelated with each other. On one hand, the internationalization of a currency and of the money and capital markets promotes the internationalization of banking business. On the other hand, the development of international banking contributes to the promotion of internationalization of the currency and the money-capital markets. However, one of the features of the internationalization of Japanese banking is that it has developed without significant corresponding developments in the internationalization of the yen and the financial markets in Japan.

2. The Purpose and Motives of Internationalization of Japanese Banking

Among the purposes and motives of internationalization of Japanese banking, earning profit is the most important, although various other shorter-term objectives are included in this profit motive.

Our survey (Figure 1) indicates that the long-term percentage target of profit from international banking which the city banks consider appropriate is between 11% and 30%. The upper-ranking group of city banks give a figure of 26%–30%, the middle ranking group 21%–25%, and the lower ranking group 11%–20%.

In addition to earning profits Japanese banks consider that it is important to accumulate the techniques and 'know-how' in international banking in order to increase the number of customers. Other objectives include collection of overseas information and the maintenance of the banks' prestige among competing banks. It seems to be interesting that the upper ranking group tends to emphasize increasing numbers of customers and accumulation of knowledge, while some middle and lower groups tend to give more weight to maintaining their prestige.

Next, we would like to examine the motives and methods of internationalization of Japanese banking in the past. There are two main courses in internationalization of banking: 1) Banks may internationalize themselves in accordance with internationalization of their domestic business customers or 2) banks may initiate internationalization on their own. According to our survey, more than half of the banks think the former is more significant, three banks consider the latter is more significant, and the rest of them stated that their internationalization had proceeded along with their business customers. Therefore, it seems to us that internationalization in Japanese banking has been primarily motived by, and has proceeded together with, the internationalization of Japanese business customers. We can say that liberalization

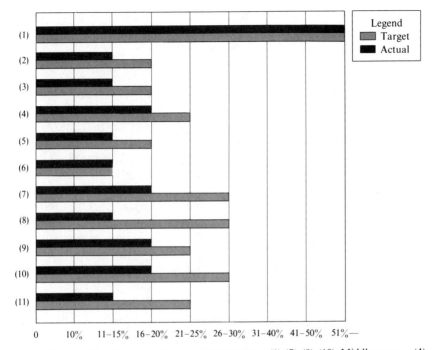

Figure 1. Actual and target profit share. Upper group—(1), (7), (9), (10); Middle group—(4), (6), (8), (11); Lower group—(2), (3), (5).

of trade and capital transactions and an increase in overseas activities of Japanese business companies have resulted in an increase in demand for various foreign exchange dealings and finance in the banks.

However, this is not to say that self-initiated internationalization is an insignificant aspect of the internationalization of banking. For example, the specialized foreign exchange bank proceeded on its own initiative, competing with foreign banks in various aspects of banking business well before the internationalization of Japanese business companies. In the case of other banks, also, there are some examples of this type of internationalization—for instance, some Japanese banks have often helped customers in their inter-nationalization, especially when a customer is of a small- or medium-size and does not have sufficient knowledge of overseas conditions.

In addition, in early 1970s, when the financial market conditions eased due to excessive domestic liquidity and it was thought that the demand for investment funds was going to slacken for a long time to come, banks actively sought new areas of business in the international finance market. Similarly, the easing of regulations on foreign exchange transactions since 1972 by Japanese monetary authorities helped Japanese banks to develop international business.

3. Establishing Branches, Offices, and Local Banks

In order to start international banking business in Japan, banks need to obtain an authorization from the monetary authorities to deal in foreign exchange. Then they have to establish foreign exchange sections within domestic banks and open a correspondence relation with foreign banks overseas. At the end of December 1981, there were 125 authorized foreign exchange banks. However, the establishment of overseas branches, representative offices, and local banks is the main method of international banking. Since the overseas operations of Japanese banks, especially fund-raising and accommodation of funds, are conducted in foreign currency, usually U.S. dollars, the establishing of overseas branches and affiliates is critically important for international banking.

Table 3 shows the geographical distribution of overseas branches, offices, local banks, and Japanese staff. In terms of the geographical distribution of overseas branches, North America has 31.5%, Europe 27.9%, and Asia 31.5%—in total, these three areas cover 90.9% of branches, 39.5% of Japanese staff are located in North America, 34.1% in Europe, and 22.3% in Asia. Representative offices are more scattered, with 19.7% in America, 23.8% in Asia, 18.4% in Central and South America, 15.6% in Europe, 8.8% in Oceania, 10.2% in the Middle and Near East, and 3.4% in Africa. The distribution in terms of staff is similar to the above: 40.3% of local banks are in Europe, 24.2% in Asia, 27.4% in North America, and 8.1% in Central and South America. The distribution of Japanese staff, however, is very different: 58.2% in North America, 22.2% in Europe, and 11.5% in Asia. This indicates that local banks in North America are considerably larger than those in other countries.

In order to know the geographical distribution of overseas branches, offices, and local banks we adopted the total number of Japanese employees as an aggregate measure. Column (4) of Table 1 tells us that North America has 41.4%, Europe has 28.4%, Asia has 19.7%, Central and South America have 6.7%, Oceania has 1.4% and the Middle and Near East have 1.1%. The first three areas together account for about 90% and can thus be considered important areas. Oceania is only 1.4%.

Figure 2 shows the relationship of the geographical distribution of overseas bases of banks (banking), trade, and direct investment overseas. In the case of North America and Europe, the figure for banking is considerably higher than

TABLE 3.

Geographical Distribution of Overseas Branches, Representative Offices, Local Banks and Japanese Staff

	(1) Branches			(2) Representative Offices			(3) Local Banks			(4) Total overseas bases
	I Branches	II Japanese Employees	III Employees of Local Nationality	I Representative Offices	II Japanese Employees	III Employees of Local Nationality	I Local Banks	II Japanese Employees	III Employees of Local Nationality	Total Japanese Employees
(A) North America	31.5	39.5	24.9	19.7	16.7	12.6	27.4	58.2	77.4	41.4
(B) Central and South America	7.2	3.3	7.8	18.4	19.8	18.3	8.1	8.1	10.9	6.7
(C) Europe	27.9	34.1	24.5	15.6	16.3	10.6	40.3	22.2	3.9	28.4
(D) Middle and Near East	0.9	0.6	0.2	10.2	10.8	12.3	0.0	0.0	0.0	1.1
(E) Asia	31.5	22.3	42.6	23.8	24.3	34.6	24.2	11.5	7.9	19.7
(F) Oceania	0.0	0.0	0.0	8.8	10.1	5.3	0.0	0.0	0.0	1.4
(G) Africa	0.0	0.0	0.0	3.4	2.1	6.0	0.0	0.0	0.0	1.2
(H) Others	0.9	0.0	0.0	0.0	0.0	0.0	0.0	0.0	0.0	0.0
Total	100.0	100.0	100.0	100.0	100.0	100.0	100.0	100.0	100.0	100.0
Number of Banks and Employees	111	1,215	6,164	147	287	301	62	554	11,744	

Second survey (1981–82)

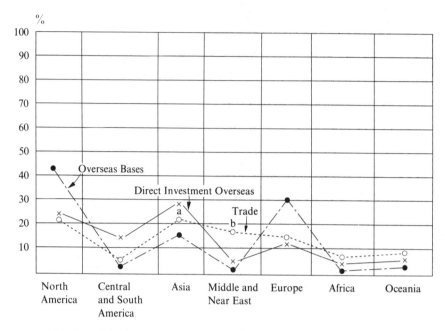

a. Southeast Asia
b. West Asia

Figure 2. Geographical distribution of overseas bases of banks, trade, and direct investment (the first survey 1977–78).

those for trade and direct investment; while in the case of the Middle and Near East and other areas, it is considerably lower. This may mean that even if internationalization of Japanese banks began in response to internationalization of their customers, the banks' internationalization has now taken a different direction from that of their customers. North America and Europe, in particular New York and London, are the two major international financial markets in which almost all fundraising and a lot of loan accommodation are conducted. It is interesting to note that the geographical distribution of representative offices, whose main function is collecting information rather than conducting fundraising and loans accommodation, is similar to figures for trade and direct investment overseas. It should be noted, however, that the present pattern of geographical distribution of banking bases reflects the decisions of banks within the framework of regulations and guidelines issued by authorities in Japan and overseas. It is quite likely that the present distribution may change with the progress of internationalization. The first survey shows that all Japanese banks want to establish new branches in the near future in North America, half of the banks want to establish branches in Europe and Asia, and a few want to establish branches in Central and South America, and the Middle and Near East. It seems, therefore, that North America will continue to be the most important area, with Asia, the Middle and Near East, and Central and South America gaining in importance, and Europe possibly becoming less important in this regard.

However, our second survey shows that in the near future nine city banks want to establish 19 branches in Asia and 10 banks in Australia (Sydney). Half of the banks want to establish branches in Central and South America, Europe, North America, and the Middle and Near East. This would mean that, for the present, city banks compete to establish new branches in the international financial center and turn their eyes to Asia, Oceania, and many principal cities in the world.

These conclusions are based only on predictions of the future distribution of branches of Japanese banks which are already internationalized or in the process of internationalizing. We do not take into account other banks, especially large regional banks and mutual loan and savings banks, which may establish overseas branches in the future. If they want to establish branches in the international financial markets, particularly in New York and London, the future distribution of branches of Japanese banks will not change as much as indicated earlier. Our survey suggests that in recent years, Japanese city banks want to establish new representative offices in socialist countries (China and Soviet Union), but distribution of representative offices will not differ greatly from the present pattern. This would reflect the fact that the function of these offices is not to conduct financial business but to collect local information on the region in which the offices are established.

In the case of the establishment of local banks, Japanese banks must consider the advantages and disadvantages of establishing a local bank as opposed to a branch. Our research indicates that the main advantage of local banks as compared with overseas branches is that they are able to conduct various financial dealings in accordance with local regulations and economic conditions, independent of official Japanese control. The main disadvantage is that local banks cannot benefit directly from economies of scale and the credit power of the parent bank because, legally, local banks must be independent of the parent bank. In fact, however, because of controls imposed on financial activities by both Japanese and overseas authorities, there is often no alternative but to establish a local bank. For example, Japanese banks are not permitted to engage in securities business both domestically and overseas, so it is necessary to establish local banks abroad to carry out this business. Similarly, regulations prevent the establishment of new branches of foreign banks in Australia, so foreign banks are compelled to establish non-bank financial companies (merchant banks, finance companies) instead.

4. The Operation of International Banking

There are several phases in the process of internationalization of banking. Table 4 shows the content of each phase in terms of the internationalization of customer companies, international banking operations, methods of internationalization, and the customers in the international operation.

In the first phase, the initial step is an internationalization of customers themselves. Here the customers are mainly engaged in import and export transactions with foreign companies, therefore the most important aspects of international banking are foreign exchange operations connected with foreign trade. Capital transactions with customers are limited to finance trade that is mainly short-term finance. In this phase, the main method of internationalization is to make correspondence contracts with foreigh banks. In the second phase, as the bank-customers' direct investment to overseas increases, banks increase their loans to Japanese affiliated companies relative to foreign exchange business. Medium- and long-term capital transactions increase correspondingly. Banks aim to internationalize their business by building up a network of overseas branches and representative offices. In the third phase, the multinationalization of big business develops, and foreign as well as Japanese companies become bank customers. International business extends to non-banking activities, such as merchant banking and leasing, through the strengthening of branches and offices, capital participation, business affiliations and the establishing of non-bank business firms. Banks seek the most profitable ways of fund raising and lending. In the fourth phase, retail banking is to be conducted on the worldwide basis and the content of international operations and the methods of internationalization become more advanced and more complex. An aspect of the fourth phase which distinguishes it from the third phase is the declining importance of the exploitation of new businesses and methods for the banks, and more concentration on deepening and strengthening the activities already commenced in the third phase. This may be revealed in terms of an increasing ratio of international transactions to the total transactions of the banks (Table 5).

In Figure 3, our research shows that in 1977–78 four banks were in the fourth phase, five in the third, and two in the second — in other words, on the average, banks have reached the third phase of internationalization. Our second survey shows that in 1981–82 six banks were in the fourth phase and five in the third. Comparing these two surveys, the internationalization of Japanese banking has been steadily advancing. Our survey also confirmed that the internationalization of Japanese banking had progressed rather slowly prior to the 1970s, but it progressed rapidly in the first half of the 1970s before slowing down again in the late seventies.

TABLE 4.

Phases of Internationalization of Banking

Phases	First Phase (National Banking)	Second Phase (International Banking)	Third Phase (in a broader sense)	
			Third Phase (International full-service banking)	Fourth Phase (World full-service banking)
Internationalization of Customer Companies	Export-import	Active direct overseas investment	Multinational corporation	
International Operations in Banking	Mainly foreign exchange operations connected with foreign trade. Capital transactions are mainly short-term ones.	Overseas loans and investments become important and medium- and longer-run capital transactions become important.	Non-banking fringe activities such as merchant-banking, leasing, consulting, and others are conducted.	
			No retail banking	Retail banking is done
Methods of Internationalization	Correspondence contracts with foreign bank	Strengthen own overseas-branches and offices	By strengthening their own branches and offices, capital-participation, affiliation in business, establishing non-bank fringe business firms, the most profitable ways of fund-raising and lending are sought on a global basis	
Customers in International Operations	Mainly domestic customers	Mainly domestic customers	Customers are of various nationalities	

Source: Mitsubishi Bank, *Chosa*, September 1974.

TABLE 5.
Alternation of Treatment by the Type of Transaction

Type of Transaction	Alternation of Treatment	Amounts (in million dollars)		Rate of increase
		During 1980	During 1981	
(1) Impact loans (foreign currency loans to residents)				
Short-term	Individual permission → liberalization	2,174 (1,071)	11,072 (9,455)	5.1 times
Medium and long-term	"	2,245 (2,041)	Δ1,550 (Δ1,293)	8.8 times —
(2) Foreign currency deposits by residents	Limits 3 million yen → "	3,753 (2,314)	4,792 (3,981)	+28% (+72%)
(3) Borrowings between firms				
Short-term	Individual permission → prior notification	3 (—)	573 (518)	
Medium and long-term	(domestic direct investments are examined)	71 (69)	207 (185)	2.9 times (2.7 times)
(4) Loans between firms				
Short-term and medium and long-term (excluding direct investments)	Individual permission → Prior notification (with examination)	19 (—)	824 (809)	
Medium and long-term (direct investments)	Individual permission → (restricted type of industry) "			
	Automatic permission → (general type of industry) "	1,799 (2,081)	3,473 (3,240)	1.9 times (+58%)

230

(5) Issue of foreign bonds in domestic currency	Permission with the payment of issue price → prior notification (with examination)	1,115	2,871	2.6 times
(6) Loans to foreign countries	Permission → (main Japanese banks are generally permitted) → (main Japanese banks need not notify)	in yen 194 billion yen in foreign currency 6,704	464 billion yen 12,688	2.4 times 1.9 times
(7) Issue of foreign bonds (private cooperate bond, government guaranteed bond)	Permission → prior notification (with examination)	3,522 debenture 673 convertible bond 2,413 government guaranteed bond 436	4,697 333 3,901 464	+33%
(8) Domestic security investment (excluding T.B. conditional transaction of bonds)	Approval and permission → prior notification (automatically approved and permitted in principle) → (via designated security company need not notify)	10,318 stock 4,988 bond 5,330	9,294 3,523 5,771	

(continued)

231

TABLE 5. (Continued)

Type of Transaction	Alternation of Treatment		Amounts (in million dollars)		
			During 1980	During 1981	Rate of increase
(9) Foreign security investments (excluding T.B.)	Permission → " (comprehensive permission in principle)		2,912 stock Δ344 bond 3,255	6,048 240 5,808	
(10) Conditional transaction of bonds by nonresidents	Permission → " (automatically permitted in principle)		73	3,224	
(11) Domestic direct investments (stocks and equities)	Approval → prior notification (with examination) (automatically approved in principle)		328 establishing branches 54	389 95	+19% +76%
(12) Foreign direct investments (aquisition of securities, establishment of branches)	Permission → " (restricted type of industry) Notice (general item)		2,211	3,354	+52%

Source: T. Kato, *The Development of International Financial Policy*, 1983.

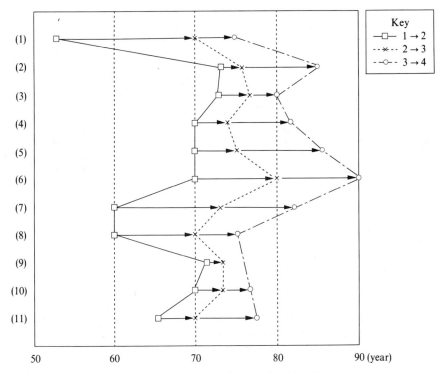

Figure 3. Development of international banking.

What attracted the Japanese banks into international operations? Our survey indicates that the major attractions for them are 1) diversification of banking operations and customers, 2) higher profits, 3) high potential for growth, and 4) access to large, flexible, and free international finance markets. These attractions of international banking have been motivated by both the short-term objectives and the long-term objectives of the banks. It should be noted, however, that risks which are absent in domestic banking, such as the exchange risk, and availability risk, are present in international banking. Moreover, competition is much more keen in the international market, which is a free market by nature. Additionally, there is no lender of last resort in the international sphere.

As previously mentioned, Japanese banks have branches in numerous countries to carry out their international business. We will now examine the relative importance of banking business at the New York, London, and "other" branches (Table 6).

At the New York branch, the order of importance in 1977–78 was that trade finance was the most important, loans to Japanese affiliated companies were in

TABLE 6.
The Order of Business in Each Branch

	The first survey (1977–78)	The second survey (1981–82)
New York Branch	(1) Trade finance	(1) Loans to other companies (non-Japanese)
	(2) Loans to Japanese affiliated companies	(2) Loans to Japanese affiliated companies
	(3) Fund raising	(3) Trade finance
London Branch	(1) Fund raising	(1) Fund raising
	(2) Trade finance	(2) Loans to other companies
	(3) Loans to other companies	(3) Loans to Japanese affiliated companies
Other Branches	(1) Trade finance	(1) Loans to Japanese affiliated companies
	(2) Loans to Japanese affiliated companies	(2) Trade finance
	(3) Fund raising	(3) Loans to other companies

second place, and fund raising was the least important among them. The situation changed greatly in 1981–82. Loans to non-Japanese companies became the most important, and loans to Japanese affiliated companies followed in importance. Trade finance became the least important. At the London branch, on the other hand, fund raising was by far the most important activity, and it is still in 1981–82 the most important business. However, the second importance shifted from trade finance to loans to other companies. This seems to suggest that some Japanese banks have already developed various kinds of international banking operations in the international financial markets. At the other branch locations, the ranking of activities was approximately similar to that of the New York branch.

From the result of this survey we can draw a tentative conclusion that through their networks of overseas branches the banks raise funds at London branches and make use of the funds for trading finance loans to both Japanese affiliated companies and non-Japanese companies through New York and other branches.

Figures 4 and 5 show the geographical distribution of fund raising for overseas operations. Almost all funds for overseas operations are raised by overseas branches, and the funds supplied by head office are surprisingly little. Japanese banks raise about 55% of funds in Europe, 30% in America, 15% in other regions and in the head office. This is consistent with the description of London branch activities given above.

Figure 6 shows the maturity structure of the raised funds. About 80% of all funds are short-term (within 12 months) and 20% are long-term. Generally

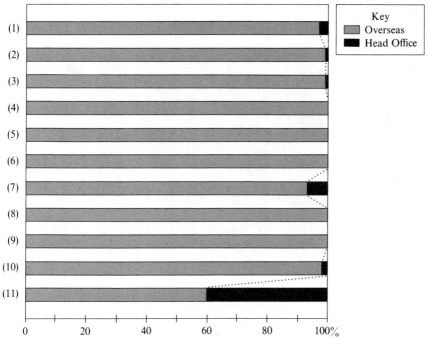

Figure 4. Sources of funds for overseas operation.

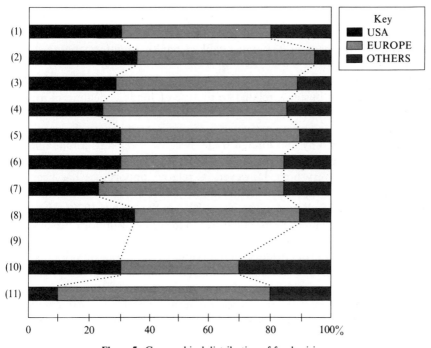

Figure 5. Geographical distribution of fund raising.

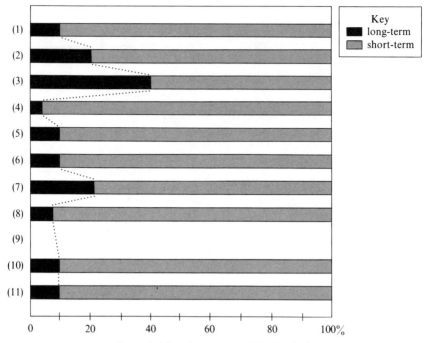

Figure 6. Maturity structure of funds raised.

speaking, in the case of the upper-ranked banks, long-term figure is less than 10%.

Now turning to the use of funds for international business, we note that the main banking business related to the use of funds is dealing in foreign exchange, trade finance, loans to nonresidents, and merchant banking. The first item, dealing in foreign exchange, is growing steadily with the growth of the Japanese economy and foreign trade. Because it remains a fundamental operation of international banking business, the stability and certainty of these dealings is very high. However, its relative importance has been decreasing due to the rapid increase in loan activities. The ratio of the trade bill in foreign assets of all banks was about 80% in September 1970; this fell to about 35% by September 1978. This is due to the growing importance of loans to nonresidents.

Figure 7 shows the distribution of loans among developed, developing, and socialist countries. The developed countries' share is about 60%, that of developing countries is 35%, and of socialist countries 5%. It should be noted that the combined total of loans to developing and socialist countries amounts to 40%. According to our research, 4 out of 10 banks want to increase the

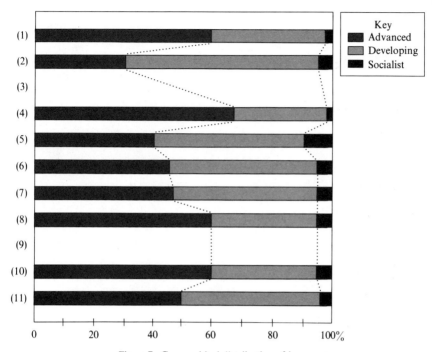

Figure 7. Geographical distribution of loans.

volume and share of loans to developing countries, and three want to increase the volume without changing the share. It can be said, therefore, that Japanese banks generally have an aggressive attitude towards extending loans to developing countries, despite the greater risk that may often be associated with such loans. These risks comprise both individual credit risk and country risk. It is interesting to note that banks which are already lending about 40% of their loan funds to developing countries do not, according to our research, wish to increase the share of developing countries more. This might presumably reflect the rapid increase in the marginal risk of this sort.

Figure 8 shows that the share of loans to Japanese affiliated companies and to non-Japanese companies is about 30% and 70%, respectively. This confirms that the internationalization of Japanese banks has already reached the third of fourth phase. Although almost all Japanese banks place considerable importance on existing relations with Japanese customers when accommodating loans to Japanese affiliated companies overseas, they do not always insist on a past and existing customer relationship in Japan. This means that Japanese banks are trying to acquire new customers through international finance activity.

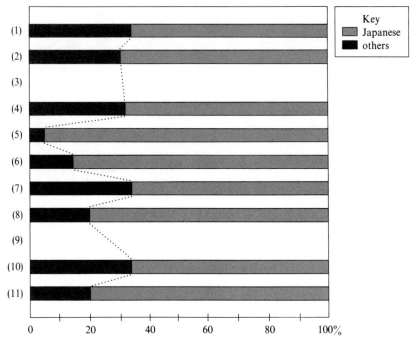

Figure 8. Share of loans to Japanese affiliated companies.

The share of loans to non-Japanese companies increased greatly between our two surveys. This is an evidence of further progress of the internationalization of the Japanese banks.

Figure 9 shows the maturity structure of loans. The percentages of short-term and long-term loans vary among the banks, reflecting the international lending policy of each bank. Roughly speaking, the share of short-term is 45% and the long-term is 55%. Figure 9 indicates that the Japanese banks are conducting a kind of "maturity transformation" by borrowing short and lending long. According to our survey, Japanese banks accept this transformation as one of the functions of banks, but they are also worrying about it.

All banks are interested not only in trade finance and loans to nonresidents but also in other related business, such as merchant banking, securities business, leasing, credit cards, and so on. Among these, securities business and merchant banking are particularly important for them. Almost all banks express their strong interest in securities business.

Recently the syndicate loans and project finance have become very important. Therefore, the knowledge and know-how of merchant banking are very much in need.

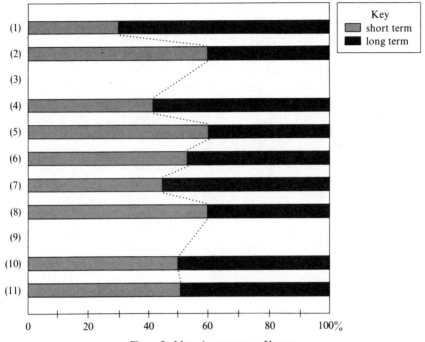

Figure 9. Maturity structure of loans.

5.   The Performance of Internationalization — Phase 1

In this section, we examine the performance of internationalization in Japanese banking. The actual proportion of total bank profits which comes from international business is as follows: Five banks give a figure of 11%–15%, three banks 0%–10%, one bank 16%–20%, and one bank above 51%. On average, the proportion seems to be 10%–15%. This figure is about equal to the proportion of staff in the international section to total bank staff. Comparing this actual figure with the feasible targets for profits shown in Figure 1, the feasible target exceeds the current figure by 5%–10%. The difference between the actual and feasible value of upper rank banks is higher than that for middle and lower rank banks (10% as opposed to 5%). This may suggest that the upper rank banks are more willing to internationalize.

As already discussed, Japanese banks are currently in the third phase of internationalization. We will now compare this with other advanced countries' foreign banks. The proportion of profits from the international section to all the profits of the 10 major American banks was 50.9% in 1979 and 45.7% in 1978. The figures for Citi-corp were 82.2% and 71.8%, respectively. The figures for 1977 for representative British banks (Barclays, National Westminster, and Lloyds) were 38%, 30%, and 22%, respectively. Those for Deutsche, Dresdner, and Commerz in West Germany were 35%, 30%, and 33%, respectively in 1977. It will be noted that, with one exception, the figure for Japanese banks is considerably lower than that for these banks.

Our research shows that almost all Japanese banks are aware of their relatively less developed internationalization. The main ways in which Japanese banks regard themselves as less developed are in the network of overseas bases, the ability to collect information and accumulate 'know-how', and the ability to raise funds, to diversify international business such as securities business, to localize banking business, and to employ a sufficient number of competent staff.

However, too much emphasis should not be given to the less developed nature of internationalization of Japanese banks because, if the degree of development is measured in terms of the number of branches or the volume of loans rather than the ratio of international to total profits, Japanese banks are not much less advanced than other banks, with the exception of the major American banks. Table 7 shows the number of overseas bases that banks from various countries have in New York, London, West Germany and Japan. As a whole, Japanese banks are second only to American banks in number of overseas branches. Table 8 lists the 50 banks which fall into the category of "lead managers," in terms of international syndicate loans and the issue of bonds in the international finance market. Column I of the table shows the syndicate loans, and column II shows syndicate loans together with the issue of bonds. In column I, it can be seen that Japanese banks as a whole rank higher than British and West German banks, and individual Japanese banks are not far inferior to European and Canadian banks, though they are considerably below American ones. In column II, on the other hand, West German banks rank higher, and Japan follows the USA, West Germany, and Canada, with a figure of 10.9%. However, this figure takes into account the activities of Japanese securities companies. If these are excluded, the figure for the six Japanese banks falls to 9.1%, while West Germany's 12.4% is achieved by only four banks. The relative rise of West German and fall of Japanese banks compared with that of foreign banks may be described as follows:

(a) In terms of the degree of internationalization measured by the proportion of total profits obtained from international dealings, Japanese banks are considerably less developed than major American banks and other advanced countries' banks.

(b) Japanese banks are less developed than major American banks, in general and individually, in all the areas described above—number of branches, volume of loans, and proportion of total profits obtained from international profits.

TABLE 7.

Foreign Banks in Major Markets

1. Foreign Banks in Japan

	Banks	Branches	Representative Offices
U.S.A.	22	32	13
U.K.	7	9	10
France	6	7	8
West Germany	5	5	5
Singapore	4	4	0
Korea	3	4	7
Switzerland	3	3	4
Others	11	17	42
Total	61	81	89

2. Foreign Banks in West Germany

	Banks	Branches	Representative Offices	Local Banks
U.S.A.	13	27	14	5
Japan	10	12	8	2
France	4	16	5	0
U.K.	4	11	7	0
Others	21	27	90	2
Total	52	93	124	9

3. Foreign Banks in U.S.A.

	Banks	Branches	Agencies	Representative Offices	Local Banks
Japan	24	16	6	2	4
Italy	14	6	0	8	1
West Germany	11	9	0	2	0
France	11	6	0	4	4
Spain	11	0	8	3	0
U.K.	9	6	2	1	4
Canada	8	0	6	0	5
Others	73	16	30	9	8
Total	161	59	52	29	26

4. Foreign Banks in London

	Banks	Branches	Representative Offices	Local Banks
U.S.A.	65	41	22	14
Japan	23	22	1	1
Italy	18	4	14	0
France	15	6	6	3
Spain	14	6	6	2
Switzerland	11	9	1	1
Australia	11	9	2	0
West Germany	10	8	2	0
Others	101	62	38	3
Total	268	167	92	24

Source: *Kinku Mondai Kenkyu Kai*, op. cit.

TABLE 8.
Achievements of Leading Managers of Banks in Terms of Country with Syndicate Loans and Issue of Securities in 1978

	Order 1—10		Order 11—25		Order 26—50		Order 1—50		Share of Achievements of Leading Managers	
	Iᵃ	IIᵇ	Iᵃ	IIᵇ	Iᵃ	IIᵇ	Iᵃ	IIᵇ	Iᵃ	IIᵇ
U.S.A.	6	5	1	3	4	4	11	12	42.7	38.6
Canada	1	1	4	3	2	3	7	7	14.9	12.4
Japan	1	0	3	4(3)ᶜ	3	4(3)ᶜ	7	8(6)	10.9	11.2(9.1)ᶜ
West Germany	1	2	2	1	2	1	5	4	8.3	12.6
U.K.	1	1	1	1	3	3	5	5	8.7	7.9
France					4	4	4	4	3.5	3.7
Netherlands			1	1	1	1	2	2	2.1	2.5
Switzerland			1	1	1	1	1	2	2.1	3.4
Belgium					1	1	1	1	0.5	0.7
Consortium		1	2	1	5	3	7	5	6.2	6.9
Total	10	10	15	15	25	25	50	50	100	100

ᵃAchievements of leading managers with syndicate loans
ᵇAchievements of leading managers with syndicate loans and issue of securities
ᶜThe figure in the bracket means figure of banks except securities companies
Source: *Kinyu Mondai Kenkyu Kai*, op. cit. Annual Report of Bureau of International Finance, Ministry of Finance, 1983.

(c) In comparison with West German and other advanced banks, Japanese banks, both individually and as a whole, are not as inferior in terms of loans activities and number of branches. However, because Japanese banks cannot conduct securities business, they are not competing with West German banks in this area. This may be a reflection of the less developed degree of internationalization in Japanese banking.

6. The Performance of Internationalization — Phase 2

In this section, we examine the performance of internationalization in Japanese banking.

In accordance with the progress of internationalization of Japanese banks, profits from international activity are increasing steadily and are greatly contributing to total bank profits. In 1982 the total bank profits of 13 city banks increased by 21.0%, while profits from international activity increased by 38.2%. The profits from the commission fees of international business did

TABLE 9.
Profits of International Sector in Japanese City Banks

Banks	Gross business profit (billion yen)	International section Loans and investments	International section Commis- sions	Share of international sector (%)	Amounts of foreign exchange transactions (million dollar)
(1)	159	122	101	22	76.8	201,956
	157	107	83	24	68.1	182,675
(2)	133	15	13	2	11.5	27,155
	117	11	9	2	9.6	20,997
(3)	111	14	12	2	12.6	39,457
	109	12	10	2	10.8	29,161
(4)	203	35	31	5	17.5	106,494
	174	28	23	5	16.1	95,684
(5)	212	23	20	3	10.9	50,114
	185	20	17	3	10.6	42,765
(6)	219	34	28	5	15.4	99,551
	191	26	20	5	13.4	74,950
(7)	301	53	46	8	17.7	139,585
	247	31	32	8	15.9	137,885
(8)	305	43	37	6	14.0	111,507
	261	35	31	4	13.4	88,344
(9)	336	65	57	9	19.4	125,114
	276	50	42	7	18.0	106,286
(10)	342	62	55	7	18.1	157,688
	281	44	37	7	15.5	122,700
(11)	365	43	35	8	11.7	120,877
	321	39	31	8	12.0	106,886
(12)	101	11	10	1	11.3	28,568
	85	8	7	1	8.8	17,029
(13)	122	10	9	1	7.9	34,081
	98	7	6	1	7.6	19,313
Total	2,907	530	452	78	18.2	1,242,147
	2,403	384	346	77	15.9	1,044,675

Note: Upper row 1982; lower row 1981
Source: *Shukan Toyo Keizai*, 1983. Annual Report of Bureau of International Finance, Ministry of Finance, Kinyu-Zaisei-jijyo (Conditions of Money and Finance) Special Series, 1983, 1984.

not change as much, but they had a remarkable increase in profits from loans and investments.

Table 9 shows the profits from the international sector of Japanese city banks, compiled by *Toyo Keizai Shimposha*. The proportion of profits from the international section compared with the total profits of the banks in 1981 and 1982 ranges from about 10% to 15%, except the Bank of Tokyo, which is a special foreign exchange bank. Comparing actual figures with the feasible targets for profits in our survey shown in Figure 1, the feasible target exceeds the actual figure by 5%–10%. The gap between the actual and target values is higher for the upper ranking banks than for the middle and lower ranking banks: 10% as opposed 5%. This may suggest that the upper ranking banks are more willing to internationalize.

7. Difficulties and Limitations in the Internationalization of Japanese Banking

There are two types of limitations in the process of internationalization of banking—internal and external. Internal limitations are basically management problems, while external limitations arise from general economic conditions and various regulations imposed on banks. According to our survey, the main internal limitations as perceived by the banks are, in order of importance, the shortage of competent staff to carry out internationalization, the inability to collect adequate information and know-how, the lack of an adequate system of operations for internationalized banking business, and the cost of establishing foreign bases such as branches, representative offices, and local banks.

The shortage of competent staff is the greatest concern of bankers. As mentioned earlier, as internationalization proceeds, the international banking operation becomes more complicated, moving from mainly foreign exchange and trade finance business to loans to nonresidents and to syndicated loans business. For example, in any project involving the development of resources, finance is extremely important, and banks must play an important role. This extends from the funding of the project through to playing a role in its formation, promotion, and programming, as well as supervising its progress. It is thus necessary for banks to have staff competent in the fields of economics, finance, taxlaw, information collection, research and investigation, and business administration. Many banks feel that to obtain specialists in these areas is a matter of urgency.

As is generally known, a system of "lifetime" employment prevails in Japan. It is thus quite difficult for banks to get competent staff from the "outside." An exception is some senior staff from monetary authorities. Consequently, it is unavoidable for most banks to train their own staff by sponsoring their study at overseas universities, by training them in overseas banks, or by providing in-house training. It takes considerable time and money for a bank to secure personnel who have a high level of expertise in international banking. This is putting Japanese banks at a disadvantage in promoting rapid internationalization. However, it might possibly work to their long-term advantage if the trained staff are to remain in the bank and contribute to its international activities over a span of years. The bank can then harvest the fruit of investment in human capital.

Secondly, information and know-how on international business are extremely important in terms of the development of international banking operations and in assessing and avoiding the associated risks. The lack of such knowledge within their operations is a concern to banks. As mentioned earlier, Japanese banks make use of foreign currency in their international operations. This gives rise to exchange risk and availability risk. In addition, with the increase of non-Japanese firms (including foreign governments) as customers, the big rise in loans to developing countries, and the increase in long-term and large-scale loans for resource development, it has become increasingly necessary for banks to collect authentic information promptly and to analyze it correctly. It is therefore necessary for banks to collect current and comprehensive information on the politics and economy of the foreign countries as well as on the individual customers. To obtain sufficient and current information and to acquire "know-how" on international finance seems to be one of the main present limitations to the future development of internationalization.

The third internal limitation perceived by banks was the lack of an adequate system of operation for international banking business. Japanese banks intend to overcome this problem by localization of the banking operation, that is, by ensuring that the operation conforms with the culture, national character, economic practices, and laws of each country, and by providing clear–cut definitions and assigning broad powers to the local staff in charge.

The fourth limitation is the costs of establishing overseas bases such as overseas branches, representative offices, and local banks. The Japanese banks tend to establish their overseas bases in the same place where rival Japanese banks have their bases. Therefore, Japanese banks, particularly in the lower ranking group, are compelled to establish foreign bases, even if unprofitable, in order to maintain their prestige. They are re-examining these behaviors recently.

There are also three external limitations on the internationalization of banking, according to our research, namely, general world economic conditions, which are reflected in the economic growth rate, price level, exchange rate, interest rate, and so on of individual countries and the international market; the Japanese economic situation, which is reflected in the position of the Japanese economy in the world economy; and the regulations and administrative guidelines from Japanese and overseas authorities on international banking operations.

In the 1970s when the internationalization of Japanese banking was increasing rapidly, the world economic situation was doing as well as it had been in the 1960s. It was characterized by turbulence of the international monetary system, the introduction of the floating exchange rate system, the oil crisis and skyrocketing oil prices, unrest in the financial system due to the bankruptcy of the Herstatt Bank, high interest rates, and the coexistence of high inflation rates and increased unemployment. The general economic situation had effects on both developed and developing countries, especially the latter, with countries like Turkey, Peru, Brazil, Mexico, and Poland having difficulties with debt payment. The prospect for the 1980s is not particularly optimistic, which may be disadvantageous for the internationalization of finance activities, with economic depression making it more difficult to measure a country's risk.

Japan was no exception in experiencing difficulties in the world economy. The oil crisis at the end of 1973 and the failure of economic management caused the Japanese economy to get into difficulties, negative economic growth, and skyrocketing prices. However, the Japanese economy fared reasonably well in the 1970s, compared with other developed countries, with Japanese ranking based on GNP, trade, and capital exports rising. As mentioned earlier, the internationalization of Japanese banking was promoted by the internationalization of the Japanese economy. However, it is not certain whether this pattern can continue in the 1980s. The growth of the Japanese economy in the midst of the stagnation of the world economy, which formed the background for the internationalization of Japanese banking, depended on overseas rather than domestic demand. For this reason, it is said that Japan's pattern of economic growth and the so-called closed market have produced considerable friction between Japan and other developed countries. If the Japanese economy must in the future depend much more on the domestic market and less on overseas markets, the incentive for internationalization of Japanese banking from the economy will weaken. However, it may be that the problem of friction over trading issues will be settled through the increase of overseas investment and that the incentive will continue to work. Even so, it will be necessary for Japanese banks to find ways of diversifying their business with non-Japanese firms in order to develop the internationalization.

Besides the economic conditions surrounding Japanese banks, financial conditions, especially the internationalization of the yen, are very important in considering the internationalization of Japanese banking. One of the features of the internationalization is that Japanese banks have promoted it through making use of foreign currency, without any significant internationalization of the yen. This pattern of internationalization places Japan at a disadvantage compared with American banks, in that the latter can use its domestic currency as international currency, which is not possible for Japan. According to our research, almost all bankers think the internationalization of the yen, and thus the internationalization of the money and capital markets, is extremely important, as it will enable them to enjoy the same advantages (easiness, stability, and efficiency in the use and raising of funds) as the American banks. It should be noted, however, that some banks (for example, the specialized foreign exchange banks) have attained a similar level of internationalization as American banks without the internationalization of the yen, demonstrating that it cannot be regarded as a prerequisite for the internationalization of Japanese banking. In addition, it would be simplistic to discuss the internationalization of the yen solely in terms of the internationalization of Japanese banking, as the former would have widespread effects on the balance of payments, monetary conditions, and the financial market, and the management of monetary policy in Japan. Viewed in this light, it is possible to understand the argument of some banks that the internationalization of the yen is a different problem from the internationalization of banking. However, in general terms, it seems that, for the reasons mentioned above, the former does promote the latter.

The third external limitation on internationalization are the various regulations and guidelines imposed on Japanese banks. Almost all banks think that regulations on foreign exchange operations, the establishing of overseas bases, and other international banking operations constitute a significant limitation. In particular, many banks are greatly concerned about the regulation of the establishing of overseas bases because this is the way they have pursued their internationalization.

According to our research, almost all banks (11 banks) agree that the present licensing policy of the Japanese monetary authorities regarding the establishing of new overseas branches (the so-called one-new-branch-every-two-years license) should be liberalized. One rank regards the present policy as good, while another thinks it should be strengthened because of the undue competition between Japanese banks, which was reflected in the Japan rate in the Eurodollar market in 1974 and the low-interest lending rates in the American market in the late 1970s. It is natural that some banks are concerned about the market disorder brought about by such behavior, and this illustrates one of the features of Japanese banks' behavior—*yokonarabi ishiki*, worrying about comparison with other banks. However, even if such undue competition does exist, it is by no means certain that the cost of competition exceeds the benefit or that strengthening controls on establishing branches would solve the problem. One of the important factors for the development of the international finance market is that it is a "free" market, regulated not by controls, but by rational and prudent management on the part of the banks themselves.

The second aspect of regulation of internationalization is the exchange control. As mentioned previously, in December 1979, the foreign exchange law was revised, leading to "free foreign-exchange dealing in principle." However, in case of an emergency such as an international financial crisis, the regulation of the foreign exchange position and the prohibition of paying interest on the deposits of nonresidents will be put into force by the monetary authorities. In regard to the necessity of the regulation in case of an emergency, our survey indicates that all banks consider it necessary if international financial disorder and the great disturbance in the foreign exchange market should occur. On the regulation of the foreign exchange position of banks, almost all banks except two consider it necessary to maintain the stability of financial market and the soundness of banking. On the prohibition of paying interest on deposits of nonresidents in case of international crisis, all banks consider it unnecessary or doubt its effectiveness.

A further guideline relates to securities. The present laws prohibit bankers from dealings in securities, and this principle is also applied to overseas banking. Japanese banks cannot do the securities business except through local finance companies, even if the monetary authorities in the foreign country are willing to permit it. Due to this guideline, Japanese banks are in a disadvantageous position compared with foreign banks, which can issue both debentures and syndicate loans. The reason for this guideline is the policy of separation between securities dealing and banking. The policy that the maintenance of domestic financial order has been taking precedence over the development of international banking is now one of the concerns of bankers.

8.   Some Conclusions

The main points of this paper can be summarized as follows.

(1) The internationalization of Japanese banking has developed primarily due to the development and internationalization of the Japanese economy itself (although there are some aspects in which the banks have taken the initiative towards internationalization).

(2) A feature of the internationalization of Japanese banking is that it has not been accompanied by internationalization of the yen or the money and capital markets.

(3) By establishing overseas branches, representative offices, and local

banks, Japanese banks raise funds in foreign currencies through the international market, especially via branches in London, and lend funds to Japanese and non-Japanese firms overseas through other branches, especially in New York.

(4) The present phase of the internationalization of Japanese banking is the third or fourth phase (in which banks enlarge the number of their customers to include both Japanese and non-Japanese firms, and to diversify their business to include merchant banking, etc. By strengthening their branches and representative offices, they seek to globalize their profits by improving and extending capital participation, business affiliations, fund-raising and so on). The ratio of international business to total banking business for Japanese banks is considerably lower than that for major American and European banks (although the size of the international business carried out by Japanese and major European banks is similar).

(5) Some limitations and problems facing the development of the internationalization of Japanese banking exist. First, it will be necessary to train competent staff and establish an operational system to cope with increasingly diverse and complex international business. Second, the economic circumstances that fostered the development of the internationalization of Japanese banking will change, providing a bleaker environment with the prospect of problems such as friction over trade issues and increasing protectionism. Third, despite the liberalising of previous controls on international banking, which should stimulate the internationalization of the yen, the Japanese money and capital market and, consequently, Japanese banking, problems may arise as banks have to practise self-regulation. Fourth, despite liberalization, there are still some areas (such as the securities business) in which the domestic finance system takes precedence over standard international banking practice.

In summary, Japanese banks will face intense competition in international banking business in an economic environment which is at once more harsh and more liberalized. In order to survive in these conditions, Japanese banks will need to be self-reliant, which depends on their ability to acquire competent staff and establish an effective system of international operations.

General References

Arima, Toshinori, Kinyū no Kokusaika to Tokyo Offshore Market (Internationalization of Money and Banking and Tokyo Offshore Market), *Hikone Ronsō* (Shiga), No. 220, pp. 47–68, May 1983.

Bronte, Stephen, *Japanese Finance: Markets and Institutions*. London: Euromoney Publications, 1982.

Ekken, Sena, Integration of Domestic and International Financial Markets: The Japanese Experience, *International Monetary Fund Staff Papers* (Washington), Vol. 31, No. 3, pp. 499–548, September 1984.

Emery, Robert F., *The Japanese Money Market*. Lexington, Massachusetts: Lexington Books, 1984.

Fujita, Masahiro, Kokusai Kinyū Seisaku no Ichi Kousatsu (On the International Monetary Policy), *Kokumin Keizai Zasshi* (Kobe), Vol. 142, No. 4, pp. 35–68, October 1980.

Fujita, Masahiro, Internationalization of Japanese Commercial Banking—The Recent Experience of City Banks, *Kobe Economic & Business Review* (Kobe), No. 30, pp. 23–54, 1984.

Fujita, Masahiro, Honpō Ginko no Kokusaika no Jittai ni tsuite (Internationalization of Japanese Commercial Banking ––– Recent Example of Banks –––), *Kokumin Keizai Zasshi* (Kobe), Vol. 151, No. 2, pp. 1–21, February 1985.

Fujita, Masahiro, Niwa Noboru and Izawa Hideki, Australia eno Honpō Kinyu Kikan no Shinsyutsu ni Kansuru Ankēto Chousa Kekka (Fact-finding Research by the Questionnaire on the Bank Lending to Australia), *Kinyu Kenkyu* (Kobe Review of Monetary Economics) (Kobe), No. 6, pp. 163–201, July 1985.

Fujita, Masahiro, Gōsyu oyobi New Zealand ni okeru Honpō Kigyō Shinsyutsu no Kinyū-teki Sokumen no Jittai Kenkyu (Fact-finding research on the Enterprise Investment to Australia and New Zealand), *Kinyu Kenkyu* (Kobe Review of Monetary Economics) (Kobe), No. 6, pp. 1–24, July 1985.

Fujita, Masahiro, Honpō Kinyū Kikan no Kokusaika no Jittai (The Actual Conditions of Internationalization of Japanese Commercial Banks), *Nikkei Center Kaihō* No. 492, pp. 37–44, July 1985.

Fujita, Masahiro, and Kenichi Ishigaki, The Internationalization of Japanese Commercial Banking. In *Multinationals and the Restructuring of the World Economy* ed. by Michael Taylor and Nigel Thrift, pp. 193–227, London: Croom Helm, 1986.

Ginkō Mondai Kenkyū Kai, Kokusai Shinyō Seido no Shin Dankai to Nihon no Kinyū Jiyūka (International Credit System and Our Liberalization of Money and Banking), *Kinyū Zaisei Jijō*, pp. 18–63, Tokyo, October 1985.

Gyōten, Toyoo, Wagakuni Kinyū Kikan Gyōmu no Kokusaika to Shomondai (The Internationalization of Our Banking Business and Its Problems), *Finance* (Japan), Vol. 19, No. 9, pp. 50–58, December 1983.

Hayden, Eric, Internationalizing Japan's Financial System. In *Japan's Economy: Coping with Change in the International Environment*, ed. by Daniel I. Okimoto. Boulder, Colorado: Westview Press, 1982.

Hosomi, Takashi, Tokyo ni Offshore Banking Center o Tsukure (On the Proposal of Tokyo Offshore Banking Center), *Shūkan Kinyū Zaisei Jijō* (Tokyo), Vol. 31, No. 15, pp. 14–17, April 1980.

International Monetary Fund, Annual Report of the Executive Board for the Financial Year Ended April 30, 19––. Washington, various issues.

Iwata, Kazumasa, Japanese Financial System and Its Recent Changes, Seminar on Long-Term Economic Cooperation Between Mexico and Japan. Unpublished, Japanese Economic Planning Agency, 1982.

Japan Economic Institute, Capital Market Liberalization in Japan, *JEI Report* (Washington), No. 10A, March 9, 1984.

Kaizuka, Keimei, Kinyū no Kokusaika (Internationalization of Money and Banking), *Financial Review* (Japan), No. 3, pp. 1–8, December 1986.

Kawai, Masahiro, Kinyū Jiyūka to Kinyū Seisaku (Liberalization of Money and Banking and Monetary Policy), *Keizai Seminar* No. 373, pp. 34–41, February 1986.

Klein, *Kokusai Kinyū Kiki, (International Finance Crisis)*, translated by Ochi, 325p. Tokyo: Kinyū Zaisei Jijo Kenkyūkai, April 1985.

Kojima, Sachio (ed.), *Kinyū Kokusaika Michi eno Chōsen*, (New Challenge to the Internationalization of Money and Banking --- Political Economy of the Yen Problem), 203p. Tokyo: Toyo Keizai Shinposha, June 1983.

Komiya, Ryūtarō (ed.), *Postwar Economic Growth in Japan*. Selected papers of the first conference of the Tokyo Economic Research Center. Berkeley, California: University of California Press, 1966.

The Ministry of Finance, *Annual Report of the Bureau of the Ministry of International Finance*, Tokyo, 1982–86.

Matsukawa, Michiya, The Yen --- A Newly Emerging Reserve Currency. In *Reserve Currencies in Transition*, pp. 24–31. New York: Group of Thirty, 1982.

Morgan Guaranty Trust Company of New York, Japanese Exchange Control Liberalization and the Yen, *World Finance Markets*, pp. 5–11. New York, March 1981.

Nunome, Masao, *Euro Banking*, 249p. Tokyo: Nihon Keizai Shinbunsha, February 1980.

Organization for Economic Cooperation and Development, *Controls on International Capital Movements: The Experience with Controls on International Financial Credits, Loans and Deposits*. Paris: OECD, 1982.

Pigott, Charles, "Financial Reform in Japan," Federal Reserve Bank of San Francisco, *Economic Review*, pp. 25–46. Winter, 1983.

Rōyama, Shōichi, *Kinyū Jiyūka*, (Liberalization of Money and Banking), 246p. Tokyo: Tokyo University Press, September 1986.

Sakakibara, Eiji, "Kinyū no Kokusaika," (The Internationalization of Money and Banking), *Business Review* (Tokyo: Hitotsubashi University), Vol. 34, No. 1, pp. 28–33, August 1986.

Sakakibara, Eisuke, The Japanese Financial System in Transition. Unpublished, Japanese Ministry of Finance, n.d.

Sakakibara, Eisuke, and Robert A. Feldman, The Japanese Financial System in Comparative Perspective, *Journal of Comparative Economics* (New York), Vol. 7, pp. 1–24, March 1983.

Suzuki, Yoshio, Changes in Financial Asset Selection and the Development of Financial Markets in Japan, *Monetary and Economic Studies* (Tokyo), Vol. 1, pp. 29–53, October 1983.

Suzuki, Yoshio, *Money and Banking in Contemporary Japan: The Theoretical Setting and Its Application*. New Haven, Connecticut: Yale University Press, 1980.

12

Estimations of Self-Dual Demand Functions: An International Comparison

RYUZO SATO

The Center for Japan-U. S. Business and Economics
Graduate School of Business Administration
New York University
New York, New York

MASAHIRO MATSUSHITA

Department of Economics
Aoyama Gakuin University
Shibuya, Tokyo
Japan

1. Introduction

The primary purpose of this paper is to find systems of theoretically plausible demand functions which can be integrated into consumers' utility functions. In the traditional demand analysis for an individual consumer, a system of direct demand functions is derived from the assumption of rational behavior, given his preference ordering and the budget constraint. Here the type of observable market behavior manifested in the direct (or inverse) demand functions crucially depends on the type of preference ordering expressed in the form of his or her direct (or indirect) utility function. But since the preference ordering is subjective, we are not able to observe it directly. Therefore, we reverse the process of analysis by first studying observable market behavior and then inferring the underlying properties of the preference ordering.

Furthermore, from the direct utility function we obtain the inverse demand functions by the traditional methods. These inverse demand functions are invertible, but in general we cannot express the direct demand functions in explicit form. Similarly, from the indirect utility function we can derive direct demand functions, but we do not know the explicit form of the direct utility function. One convenient way to relate the direct utility function to the direct demand function explicitly is to introduce the concept of self-duality.

In this paper we adopt the Sato definitions of self-duality and apply them to linear and log-linear demand functions. We find one set of linear demand functions and ten sets of log-linear demand functions which satisfy the conditions of theoretical plausibility and self-duality. For each set of demand functions, the corresponding explicit form of the underlying utility function is derived.

One of the objectives of our empirical study is to examine the plausibility of these self-dual demand functions, and the other objective is to make an international comparison between American and Japanese consumption behavior.

We fit self-dual demand functions to United States and Japanese data and find that these functions, except the linear case, explain the U. S. and Japanese demand far better than expected. We also find that a system of nonhomothetic CES type demand functions is most plausible and practical among all sets of self-dual demand functions we have derived. This system of self-dual demand functions is very simple in that demands are functions only of their own real prices. Our study has demonstrated that U. S. data and Japanese data both yield good empirical estimation results. We can say with some conviction that this type of demand system would be a good predictor of actual consumption behavior.

2. Theoretically Plausible Demand Functions

A demand function is theoretically plausible only if it satisfies certain conditions which must hold if it is to be related to (or integrable into) a consistent preference ordering (or utility function). Consider the following utility function.

$$\phi = \phi(x_1, \ldots, x_n), \tag{1}$$

where $x_i (i = 1, \ldots, n)$, is a quantity of ith goods demanded.
Differentiating totally the utility function (1), we get

$$d\phi = \phi_1 \, dx_1 + \cdots + \phi_n \, dx_n, \qquad \text{where } \phi_i = \frac{\partial \phi}{\partial x_i}, \qquad i = 1, \ldots, n.$$

To depict movement along an indifference surface we set $d\phi = 0$, which gives us the following linear differential equations in n variables:

$$\phi_1 \, dx_1 + \phi_2 \, dx_2 + \cdots + \phi_n \, dx_n = 0, \tag{3}$$

or

$$\frac{\phi_1}{\phi_n} dx_1 + \frac{\phi_2}{\phi_n} dx_2 + \cdots + \frac{\phi_{n-1}}{\phi_n} dx_{n-1} + dx_n = 0. \tag{4}$$

Since this differential equation was derived from a utility function, it is obvious that we can integrate (3) or (4) into a well defined utility surface,

$$\phi(x_1, x_2, \ldots, x_n) = c. \tag{5}$$

However, suppose that we start the analysis without the presupposition of utility function but with only observations on price-quantity combinations chosen (by the individual), from which we estimate postulated demand functions,

$$x_i = f_i(y_1, y_2, \ldots, y_n), \qquad \text{where } y_i = \frac{P_i}{I}. \tag{6}$$

P_i is a price of ith goods and I is an income. If we are able to solve these demand functions for the n-relative prices we can get the inverse demand functions,

$$y_i = g_i(x_1, \ldots, x_n). \tag{7}$$

Now we can divide each of the first $n - 1$ functions by the nth to yield $n - 1$ functions in x_i.

$$\frac{P_i}{P_n} = \frac{y_i}{y_n} = \frac{g_i(x_1, \ldots, x_n)}{g_n(x_1, \ldots, x_n)} = R_i(x_1, \ldots, x_n), \qquad i = 1, \ldots, n. \tag{8}$$

Substitute (8) into (4) as follows;

$$R_1 \, dx_1 + \cdots + R_{n-1} \, dx_{n-1} + dx_n = 0. \tag{9}$$

We have a serious problem here. Since the $R_i(x_1, \ldots, x_n)$ were not derived from a utility function but were postulated independently, is it possible to integrate (9) into a utility surface? Or more generally, given a linear differential equation (9), with arbitrary functions $R_i(x_1, \ldots, x_n)$, is it always possible to integrate this function? This is primarily a mathematical problem. The answer, in general, is no. Samuelson proved that the necessary and sufficient condition for integrability is $K_{ij} = K_{ji}$, where

$$K_{ij} = \frac{\partial x_j}{\partial P_i} + x_i \frac{\partial x_j}{\partial I}, \qquad i, j = 1, \ldots, n.$$

That is, the symmetry conditions

$$\frac{\partial x_i}{\partial P_j} + x_j \frac{\partial x_i}{\partial I} = \frac{\partial x_j}{\partial P_i} + x_i \frac{\partial x_j}{\partial I}, \qquad i, j = 1, \ldots, n.$$

are equivalent to the integrability conditions.

In summary, when specifying the form of a demand function, we can ensure its theoretical plausibility by requiring that the function satisfies the constraints of (1) homogeneity, (2) additivity, and (3) integrability. Each of these constraints is attributable to the trait of consistency, or "rationality", which we require of our consumer. Homogeneity implies that the consumer is free from money illusion. The adding-up condition implies that the consumer chooses a collection of goods on the boundary of his or her feasible consumption set for all price-income situations, a necessary—though not sufficient—condition for utility maximization. Integrability implies that the consumer is able to compare different collections of goods and is consistent in his preference ordering of these different collections.

3.   Self-Dual Demand Functions

This paper examines the self-dual demand functions on which many economists began to focus their attention recently. Houthakker, Samuelson, and Hicks deal with the question of the existence of a nontrivial preference ordering which has the same mathematical properties in terms of both the direct and indirect utility functions. Sato extended the concept of self-duality recently and showed very interesting results. Therefore, we shall follow his formulations.

We know at least two concise ways of describing a consumer's preference ordering. One is the direct utility function, i.e., a function of all the elements of the commodity bundles $x = (x_1, x_2, \ldots, x_n)$, which is constant on any indifference surface. A consumer's behavior is regarded as maximizing his direct utility function ϕ subject to the budget constraint, i.e.,

$$\text{Maximize } \phi(x_1, x_2, \ldots, x_n)$$

$$\text{subject to } \sum y_i x_i = 1, \qquad \text{where } y_i = \frac{P_i}{I} \tag{A}$$

$$\text{for given } y_i = \bar{y}_i, \qquad i = 1, \ldots, n.$$

The other is the indirect utility function. Under the familiar convexity assumption of the preference ordering, the elements of x are completely determined by prices and total expenditure (or income) according to the demand functions

$$x_i = x_i(P_1, \ldots, P_n, I) = x_i\left(\frac{P_1}{I}, \ldots, \frac{P_n}{I}, 1\right) = f_i(y_1, \ldots, y_n).$$

The value of the direct utility function ϕ is indirectly a function of y_i. An alternative description of the consumer's behavior is that a minimization of indirect utility function $\psi(y_1, y_2, \ldots, y_n)$ subject to the budget constraint, i.e.,

$$\text{Minimize } \psi(y_1, y_2, \ldots, y_n)$$

$$\text{subject to } \sum y_i x_i = 1 \tag{B}$$

$$\text{for given } x_i = \bar{x}_i, \qquad i = 1, \ldots, n.$$

From a theoretical point of view the direct and indirect utility functions are equivalent descriptions of the underlying preference ordering. The programming (B) is a dual one of the programming (A). ϕ and ψ are completely dual functions, i.e., one possesses all the general properties of the other.

In solving program (A) we get the following relations as the necessary conditions:

$$\frac{\phi_j(x)}{\phi_i(x)} = \frac{y_j}{y_i}, \qquad i, j = 1, \ldots, n \tag{10}$$

$$\sum y_i x_i = 1. \tag{11}$$

From (10) and (11) we obtain

$$\frac{1}{y_i} = x_1 \frac{y_1}{y_i} + \cdots + x_i + \cdots + x_n \frac{y_n}{y_i}$$

$$= x_1 \frac{\phi_1(x)}{\phi_i(x)} + \cdots + x_i + \cdots + x_n \frac{\phi_n(x)}{\phi_i(x)}$$

$$y_i = g_i(x), \qquad i = 1, \ldots, n. \tag{12}$$

That is, from the direct utility function we obtain the inverse demand functions (12). The inverse demand functions are invertible, but in general we cannot express the direct demand functions in explicit form. Similarly, in solving program (B) we get

$$\frac{\psi_j(y)}{\psi_i(y)} = \frac{x_j}{x_i}, \qquad i, j = 1, \ldots, n. \tag{13}$$

$$\sum y_i x_i = 1. \tag{11}$$

From (13) and (11) we obtain

$$\frac{1}{x_i} = y_1 \frac{\psi_1(y)}{\psi_i(y)} + \cdots + y_i + \cdots + y_n \frac{\psi_n(y)}{\psi_i(y)}$$

$$x_i = f_i(y), \qquad i = 1, \ldots n. \tag{14}$$

Thus, from the indirect utility function we can derive direct demand functions. But, in general, we do not know the explicit form of the direct utility function.

One way of establishing a connection between the direct utility function and the direct demand function is to introduce the concept of self-duality. If we assume the weakly self-dual demand functions as defined below, the direct utility function is self-dual to the indirect utility function.[1] That is, the direct utility function has the same mathematical form as the indirect utility function. Therefore, from the demand functions which are observable through market behavior, we are able to ascertain the forms of the direct and indirect utility functions simultaneously.

Samuelson [1965], Hicks [1969] and Houthakker [1965] have dealt with the question of the existence of a nontrivial self-dual preference ordering which has the same mathematical properties in terms of both the direct and indirect utility functions. A preference ordering is self-dual if it has a direct utility function that can be written in the same mathematical form as the corresponding indirect utility function.[2] Samuelson showed that the Cobb-Douglas form of preference ordering is self-dual and asked if there were any other examples of self-duality. To answer this question, Houthakker modified the concept of self-duality as follows. Set x as the vector of quantities and y as the vector of prices (each divided by income), while ϕ and ψ denote a direct and indirect utility function, respectively.

Houthakker accepted a preference ordering as being self-dual if it has a $\phi(x)$ that is the same kind of function of x as at least one transformation of $\psi(y)$ is of y. That is, by $\phi S \psi$ we imply $F(\phi) S G(\psi)$ where F and G are monotonic transformations of ϕ and ψ.[3] If so, the demand functions $x = f(y)$ and the inverse demand functions $y = g(x)$ must also have the same form. More precisely, there must be a function F such that $x = F(y, A)$ and $y = F(x, B)$, where A and B are sets of m parameters; note that F is a single function, not a class of functions involving arbitrary parameters. Substituting the expression for y into that for x we get the functional equation

$$F\{F(x, B), A\} = x.$$

Houthakker argued that the self-dual addilog demand functions,

$$x_i = \alpha_i y_i^{\beta_i} T(y)^{1 - \delta + \delta \beta_i}$$

(where α_i, β_i, and δ are constants and π is a function of $(y_1, \ldots, y_n)$ further defined by substitution into the budget constraint $\Sigma x_i y_i = 1$) corresponds to a preference ordering which is self-dual in his sense. Houthakker's definition of self-duality includes Samuelson's as a special case. Houthakker

---

[1] See R. Sato [1972].

[2] Samuelson's [1965] original definition: S preference ordering is self-dual if the demand functions and their inverse demand functions are identically the same.

[3] We denote self-duality by the symbol S.

could not derive the explicit form corresponding to his self-dual addilog demand functions.

"The form of a function" is, however, an elusive concept. What we require is a more precise formulation of self-duality. This was provided by R. Sato [1972]. Sato extended the concept of self-duality and derived a more complete solution to the problem of self-duality. His definitions follow:

Self-Dual Preference Ordering

A preference ordering is self-dual if it has a $\phi(x)$ that is the same kind of function of x as at least one transformation of $\psi(y)$ is of y.

As the demand functions and the direct utility function are related by the duality property, it is more convenient to define self-duality in terms of the demand and inverse demand functions.

Strongly Self-Dual Demand Functions

Demand functions are said to be strongly self-dual if all of the demand functions and their inverse demand functions have the same mathematical form, i.e.,

$$f^i \mathscr{S} f^j, \qquad f^i \mathscr{S} g^i$$

and therefore,

$$g^i \mathscr{S} g^j, \qquad i \neq j, \qquad i,j = 1,\dots,n.$$

Weakly Self-Dual Demand Functions

If the demand function for each commodity $x_i = f^i(y)$ has the same mathematical form as its own inverse demand function $y_i = g^i(x)$, then the system of demand functions is said to be weakly self-dual.

$$f^i \mathscr{S} g^i, \qquad i = 1,\dots,n.$$

Note that the demand function for x_i need not have the same mathematical form as the demand function for x_j ($i \neq j$).

Since the notion of "a same mathematical form was ambiguous. Sato developed his definition in more precise terms. If the demand functions are given, we can always find n independent implicit functions, including the budget constraint relating the $2n$ variables x and y, such that F^i is monotone with respect to all elements in x and y and the Jacobian of the system of n implicit function is non-vanishing, i.e.,

$$F^i(x \cdot y) = 0, \qquad i = 1,\dots,n-1$$
$$F^n(x, y) = x'y - 1 = 0$$

or, more compactly,

$$F(x \cdot y) = 0$$

Strongly Self-Duality

The necessary and sufficient condition for a preference ordering to be strongly self-dual is that $F(x, y) = 0$ be set-symmetric in absolute value with respect to the quantity and (real) price vector, i.e.,

$$F(x, y) = \pm F(y, x).$$

Weak Self-Duality[4]

The System of demand functions is weakly self-dual if and only if there exist $F^i(x, y: a) = 0$, $i = 1, \ldots, n - 1$ and $F^n = x'y - 1 = 0$ such that $F^i(x, y: \bar{a}) = \pm F^i(y, x: J(\bar{a}))$

$$J: a \to b \qquad \text{and} \qquad J(\bar{a}) = \bar{a}.$$

The necessary and sufficient condition for the direct and indirect utility functions to be self-dual is that the demand and inverse demand functions are weakly self-dual [Sato, 1972]. Therefore, if we confine ourselves to the systems of weakly self-dual demand and inverse demand functions (f and g), we can explicitly relate observable market behavior with the direct utility function. The exact forms of f and g must be determined by observation of market behaviors. The problem of finding specific mathematical forms of f and g which are all weakly self-dual and warrant empirical considerations, can be more easily dealt with if we consider special cases of the systems of demand functions. Therefore, we shall examine some special cases of weakly self-dual direct and inverse demand functions as well as derive the underlying self-dual preference orderings.

4. Special Cases of Weakly Self-Dual Demand Functions

We shall analyze two special classes of weakly self-dual demand functions. The first special class consists of the system of linear demand functions. The second special class consists of the system of log-linear demand functions of

---

[4] Weak self-duality can be alternatively defined as follows: The system of demand functions is weakly self-dual if demand and indirect demand transformations can be arranged in pairs, the members of which are mutually inverse. That is to say, if corresponding to a set of values of the essential parameters $a = (a^1, \ldots, a^r)$ of the demand functions, there is another set $b = (b^1, \ldots, b^r)$ such that b is some function of a and the demand and indirect demand functions are mutually inverse. If there exists $J: a \to b$ such that $T_a: X_1 = f^i(y:a)$, $T_b: y_i = g^i(X:b) = f^i(X:b), i = 1, \ldots, n$, where $(T_a)^{-1} = T_b$, then the system of demand functions is said to be weakly self-dual.

which there exist several cases of weakly self-dual demand functions. First we examine the linear demand functions

$$X_i = \sum_{j}^{n-1} a_{ij} y_j + C_i, \qquad i = 1, \ldots, n-1 \qquad \text{where } y_j = \frac{P_j}{I}$$

$$X_n = \frac{1}{y_n} \left\{ 1 - \sum_{i}^{n-1} \left(\sum_{j}^{n-1} a_{ij} y_j + C_i \right) y_i \right\},$$

and find that only the following case satisfies the integrability conditions:

$$X_i = \sum_{j}^{n-1} a_{ij} y_j, \qquad i = 1, \ldots, n-1 \qquad \text{where } a_{ij} = a_{ji}$$

$$X_n = \frac{1}{y_n} \left\{ 1 - \sum_{i}^{n-1} \sum_{j}^{n-1} a_{ij} y_i y_j \right\}.$$

Substituting these demand functions into the differential equation

$$x_1 \, dy_1 + x_2 \, dy_2 + \cdots + x_m \, dy_n = 0$$

we have

$$\sum_{i}^{n-1} \sum_{j}^{n-1} a_{ij} y_j \, dy_j + \left\{ 1 - \sum_{i}^{n-1} \sum_{j}^{n-1} a_{ij} y_i y_j \right\} dy_n = 0. \qquad (C)$$

Solving this differential equation we get the indirect utility as the solution of (C)

$$\psi(y) = \frac{C y_n}{|1 - \sum_{i}^{n-1} \sum_{j}^{n-1} a_{ij} y_i y_j|} \qquad \text{where } C \text{ is a constant and}$$

$$a_{ij} = a_{ji}, \qquad i, j = 1, \ldots n-1.$$

Next we examine the log-linear type of demand functions:

$$x_i = \prod_{j=1}^{n-1} \alpha_i y_j^{\beta_{ij}}, \qquad i = 1, \ldots, n-1$$

$$x_n = \left[1 - \sum_{i=1}^{n-1} \left(\prod_{j=1}^{n-1} \alpha_i y_j^{\beta_{ij}} \right) y_i \right].$$

We have $(n-1)$ mutually independent demand functions with constant elasticities with respect to $(n-1)$ prices. The demand function for the nth commodity is determined by the budget constraint. Because of the integrability conditions on the Slutsky matrix and the second-order conditions for a maximum of ϕ, the parameters β_{ij}'s cannot take arbitrary values. We obtain the following results which can be shown to be self-dual.

(L1)   *Log-Linear Demand Functions Case 1*
                          (*Nonhomothetic CES Type Demand Functions*)

---

    demand functions   inverse demand functions

$$x_i = \alpha_i y_i^{\beta}, \quad i = 1,\dots,n-1 \qquad\qquad y_i = \alpha_i^{-1/\beta} x_i^{1/\beta}, \quad i = 1,\dots,n-1$$

$$x_n = \frac{1}{y_n}\left[1 - \sum_1^{n-1}\alpha_i y_i^{\beta+1}\right]^{1/(\beta+1)} y_n \qquad \phi(x) = \left[1 - \sum_1^{n-1}\alpha_i^{-1/\beta} x_i^{(1+\beta)/\beta}\right] x$$

    indirect utility function   direct utility function

$$\psi(y) = C_1\left[1 - \sum_1^{n-1}\alpha_i y_i^{\beta+1}\right]^{1/(\beta+1)} y_n \qquad \phi(x) = C_2\left[1 - \sum_1^{n-1}\alpha_i^{-1/\beta} x_i^{(1+\beta)/\beta}\right]^{\beta/(1+\beta)} x$$

(L2)   *Log-Linear Demand Functions Case 2* (*Bergson Family*)

---

    demand functions   inverse demand functions

$$x_i = \frac{\alpha_i y_i^{\beta}}{\sum_{j=1}^{n}\alpha_j y_j^{1+\beta}}, \quad i = 1,\dots,n \qquad y_i = \frac{\alpha_i^{-1/\beta} x_i^{1/\beta}}{\sum_1^{n}\alpha_j^{-1/\beta} x_j^{1+1/\beta}}, \quad i = 1,\dots,n$$

    indirect utility function   direct utility function

$$\psi(y) = C_1 \log \sum_1^{n}\alpha_j y_j^{1+\beta} \qquad\qquad \phi(x) = C_2 \log \sum_1^{n}\alpha_j^{-1/\beta} x_j^{1+1/\beta}$$

(L3)   *Log-Linear Demand Functions Case 3* (*Quadratic Type*)

---

    demand functions   inverse demand functions

$$x = \frac{(A + A')^{-1}y}{y'(A + A')y} \qquad\qquad y = \frac{(A + A')x}{x'(A + A')x}$$

where

$$x = (x_1,\dots,x_n)$$

$$y = (y_1,\dots,y_n)$$

    indirect utility function   direct utility function

$$\psi(y) = y'A^{-1}y \qquad\qquad\qquad \phi(x) = x'Ax$$

(L4)   *Log-Linear Demand Functions Case 4 (Cobb-Douglas Type)*

demand functions   inverse demand functions

$$x_i = \alpha_i y_i^{-1}, \qquad i = 1,\dots,n-1$$

$$x_n = \frac{1}{y_n}\left[1 - \sum_1^{n-1}\alpha_i\right]$$

$$y_i = \alpha_i x_i^{-1}, \qquad i = 1,\dots,n-1$$

$$y_n = \frac{1}{x_n}\left[1 - \sum_1^{n-1}\alpha_i\right]$$

indirect utility function   direct utility function

$$\psi(y) = C_1 \prod_1^{n-1} y_i^{\alpha_i} y_n^{1-\Sigma_1^{n-1}\alpha_i}$$

$$\phi(x) = C_2 \prod_1^{n-1} x_i^{\alpha_i} x_n^{1-\Sigma_1^{n-1}\alpha_i}$$

(L5)   *Log-Linear Demand Functions Case 5 (Homogeneous CES Type)*

demand functions   inverse demand functions

$$x_i = \frac{\alpha_i y_i^{-\beta-1}}{\sum_{j=1}^n \alpha_j y_j^{-\beta}}, \qquad i = 1,\dots,n$$

$$y_i = \frac{\frac{1}{\alpha_i}\cdot x_i^{-1/(\beta+1)}}{\sum_{j=1}^n \frac{1}{\alpha_j} y_j^{\beta/(\beta+1)}}, \qquad i = 1,\dots,m$$

indirect utility function   direct utility function

$$\psi(y) = \left[\sum_i \alpha_i y_i^{-\beta}\right]^{C_1}$$

$$\phi(x) = \left[\sum_i \frac{1}{\alpha_i}\cdot y_i^{-1/\beta}\right]^{C_2}$$

(L6)   *Log-Linear Demand Functions Case 6*

demand functions[5]

$$x_k = \alpha_k y_k^{-1}, \qquad \text{where } k \text{ can take any single value from 1 to } n-1.$$

$$x_i = \alpha_i y_k^{\alpha_k(\beta+1)/(1-\alpha_k)} y_i^{\beta}, \qquad i = 1,\dots,n-1, \qquad i \neq k$$

$$x_n = \frac{1}{y_n}\left[1 - \alpha_k - \sum_{\substack{i=1\\i\neq k}}^{n-1}\alpha_i y_k^{\alpha_k(\beta+1)/(1-\alpha_k)} y_i^{\beta+1}\right]$$

indirect utility function

$$\psi(y) = C\left[1 - \alpha_k - \sum_{\substack{i=1\\i\neq k}}^{n-1}\alpha_i y_k^{\alpha_k(\beta+1)/(1-\alpha_k)} y_i^{\beta+1}\right]^{-1/(\beta+1)} \cdot y_k^{\alpha_k/(1-\alpha_k)} y_n$$

---

[5] We show in cases (L6) to (L10) only demand functions and indirect utility functions. Direct utility functions can be easily derived by self-duality.

(L7)   *Log-Linear Demand Functions Case 7*

demand functions

$$x_i = \alpha_i \prod_{j=1}^{n-1} y_j^{\alpha_i(\beta+1)/\alpha_1} y_i^{-1}, \qquad i = 1,\ldots,n-1$$

$$x_n = \frac{1}{y_n}\left[1 - \prod_1^{n-1}\left(\sum_1^{n-1}\alpha_i\right)y_i^{\alpha_i(\beta+1)/\alpha_1}\right]$$

indirect utility function

$$\psi(y) = C\left[1 - \prod_1^{n-1}\left(\sum_1^{n-1}\alpha_i\right)y_i^{\alpha_i(\beta+1)/\alpha_1}\right]y_n^{-(\Sigma_1^{n-1}\alpha_i)(\beta+1)}$$

(L8)   *Log-Linear Demand Functions Case 8*

demand functions

$$x_i = \alpha_i y_i^{\beta} y_j^{\alpha_j(\beta+1)/\alpha_i}, \qquad i,j = 1,\ldots,n-1$$

$$x_j = \alpha_j y_i^{\beta+1} y_j^{\alpha_j(\beta+1)-1/\alpha_i}$$

$$x_k = \alpha_k y_k^{\beta\alpha_j(\beta+1)/\alpha_i}, \qquad k \neq i,j$$

$$x_n = \frac{1}{y_n}\left[1 - (\alpha_i+\alpha_j)y_i^{\beta+1}y_j^{\alpha_j(\beta+1)/\alpha_i} - \sum_{\substack{k=1\\k\neq i,j}}^{n-1}\alpha_k y_k^{(\alpha_i+\alpha_j)(\beta+1)/\alpha_i}\right]$$

indirect utility function

$$\psi(y) = C\left[1 - (\alpha_i+\alpha_j)y_i^{\beta+1}y_j^{\alpha_j(\beta+1)/\alpha_i} - \sum_{\substack{k=1\\k\neq i,j}}^{n-1}\alpha_k y_k^{(\alpha_i+\alpha_j)(\beta+1)/\alpha_i}\right]^{\alpha_i/(\alpha_i+\alpha_j)(\beta+1)} y_n^{-1}$$

(L9)   *Log-Linear Demand Functions Case 9*

demand functions

$$x_1 = \alpha_1 y_1^{-1}$$

$$x_i = \alpha_i \prod_{j=2}^{n-1} y_1^{\alpha_1/1-\alpha_1\Sigma_1^{n-1}\alpha_i(\beta+1)/\alpha_2} y_j^{\alpha_j(\beta+1)/\alpha_2} y_i^{-1}, \qquad i = 2,\ldots,n-1$$

$$x_n = \frac{1}{y_n}\left[\left(1 - \alpha_1 - \prod_2^{n-1}\sum_2^{n-1}\alpha_i\right)y_1^{\alpha_1/1-\alpha_1\Sigma_2^{n-r}\alpha_i(\beta+1)/\alpha_2} \cdot y_i^{\alpha_i(\beta+1)/\alpha_2}\right]$$

indirect utility function

$$\psi(y) = C\left[1 - \alpha_1 - \prod_2^{n-1}\left(\sum_2^{n-1}\alpha_i\right)y_1^{\alpha_1(\beta+1)\Sigma_2^{n-1}\alpha_i/(1-\alpha_1)\alpha_2}\right.$$

$$\left. \cdot y_i^{\alpha_i(\beta+1)/\alpha_2}\right]^{-\alpha_2/(\Sigma_2^{n-1}\alpha_i)(\beta+1)} y_1^{\alpha_n(\Sigma_1^{n-1}\alpha_i)/(1-\alpha_1)\alpha_2} \cdot y_n$$

(L10)   *Log-Linear Demand Functions Case 10*

---

demand functions

$$x_i = \alpha_i y_i^{-1}, \quad i = 1,\ldots,n-2$$

$$x_{n-1} = \alpha_{n-1} \prod_1^{n-2} y_i^{\alpha_i(\beta+1)/1 - \Sigma_1^{n-1}\alpha_i} \cdot y_{n-1}^{\beta}$$

$$x_n = \frac{1}{y_n}\left[1 - \sum_1^{n-2}\alpha_i - \alpha_{n-1}\prod_1^{n-2} y_1^{\alpha_i(\beta+1)/(1 - \Sigma_1^{n-2}\alpha_i)}y_{n-1}^{\beta+1}\right]$$

indirect utility function

$$\psi(y) = C\left[1 - \sum_1^{n-2}\alpha_i - \alpha_{n-2}\prod_1^{n-2} y_1^{\alpha_i(\beta+1)/1 - \Sigma_1^{n-2}\alpha_i}y_{n-1}^{\beta+1}\right]^{-1/\beta+1}\left(\prod_1^{n-2} y_i^{\alpha_i}\right)^{\beta+1/1 - \Sigma_1^{n-2}\alpha_i} \cdot y_n$$

---

5.   Empirical Evaluation of Self-Dual Demand Functions

Self-dual demand functions we have derived are fitted to Japanese data and U.S. data on per capita consumption expenditures.

Japanese Data. We have used two annual data reports on personal consumption expenditures in the *Annual Reports on the Family Income and Expenditure Survey* (published by the Bureau of Statistics Office of the Prime Minister, Japan). One is the annual data report on personal consumption expenditures of an *average* household (denoted as "All Household") for the period from 1963 until 1975. The other consists of similar data of an *average* household in cities with population, of 50,000 or more (denoted as "Household in Cities") for the period from 1947 until 1975. The expenditure data are classified into five commodity groups. Each of these groups represents an aggregation from a finer classification. The five commodity groups are: (1) food, (2) housing, (3) fuel and light, (4) clothing, and (5) miscellaneous. All of the data are in current yen. For prices, we have used the following indices (base: 1970 = 100): Consumer Price Index—All Japan, Subgroup Index, and Special Group Index, published by the Bureau of Statistics Office of the Prime Minister. We were able to obtain time series data for all households only back to 1963.

U.S. Data. We have used the annual data series on personal expenditures in the *Survey of Current Business and Statistical Abstracts of the U.S.* (both published by the United States Department of Commerce) for the period from 1956 until 1975. These data series usually appear in the July issue of the *Survey of Current Business.* We have mainly utilized the table of personal consumption expenditures, by type of product. Since the U.S. data are presented in twelve commodity groups (with finer classifications provided as well), it was necessary to collapse the U.S. data into the five commodity groups corresponding to the Japanese groupings. All of the data are in current dollars, and for price indices we have used the Consumer Price Index by Commodity Groups published in the *Statistical Abstract of the United States* (1957–59 = 100). (The price index for each commodity group could also be obtained by dividing the constant dollar figures into current dollar figures.) All series are also deflated by population.

First we estimated our demand functions by OLS and obtained the Durbin-Watson values (d). We tested the hypothesis of zero autocorrelation against the alternative hypothesis of positive first-order autocorrelations, using the Durbin-Watson test and the Henshaw's test. These tests show that the disturbance terms are autocorrelated in most cases. As OLS estimates are not unbiased, we need to turn to some other estimation method. As an alternative we have employed two methods. One is the Kadiyala and the other is the Beach-MacKinnon method. The Kadiyala method is the two-stage least square method of estimation. This is a very practical method and we can obtain good estimates. But these estimates are not unbiased and not consistent. We used the Beach-MacKinnon method which gives us much better estimates. These estimates are consistent.

Comparison of the estimated values of β_i in the log-linear case 1, using OLS, Kadiyala (K) and the Beach-MacKinnon (B-M) estimation techniques is presented in Tables 1, 2, and 3.

Thus, we compare the Beach-MacKinnon results with these three households (Table 5). We use the 95% confidence intervals of β_i and compared these estimated β_i (Table 4).

From the above results we can say the following.

Food. All own price elasticities are less-elastic ($|\beta| < 1$). We cannot find any significant differences between All Household and Household in Cities. That is, All Household and Household in Cities have almost the same demand pattern for food. Differences between the dietary life of U.S. households and that of Japanese households are reflected in the differences in these own elasticities. U.S. households are relatively less elastic than Japanese households. That is, Japanese households are more sensitive to the food price changes than U.S. households.

Housing. All own price elasticities are elastic ($|\beta| > 1$). U.S.A. and Household in Cities have almost the same demand patterns, though the confidence interval of Household in Cities is pretty wide. The own price elasticity of All Household is less elastic than in the U.S.A. All Household is least elastic

TABLE 1.
OLS Estimates

All Household

	α_i	β_i	$\bar{R}^2$	d
Food	0.3543	−0.5342	0.9944	1.3682
		(0.0116)		
		(−46.0847)		
Housing	0.1043	−1.2414	0.9607	0.7050
		(0.0723)		
		(−17.1622)		
Fuel & light	0.0393	−0.7667	0.9871	1.3252
		(0.0253)		
		(−30.3330)		
Clothing	0.1138	−0.7666	0.9583	0.8496
		(0.0461		
		(−16.6390)		
Miscellaneous	0.3813	−1.4001	0.9940	0.8795
		(0.0314)		
		(−44.6080)		

Household in Cities

	α_i	β_i	$\bar{R}^2$	d
Food	0.3619	−0.5257	0.9850	0.5811
		(0.0123)		
		(−42.8772)		
Housing	0.1104	−2.0029	0.9005	0.1941
		(0.1256)		
		(−15.9464)		
Fuel & light	0.0395	−0.7769	0.9705	0.4548
		(0.0256)		
		(−30.3115)		
Clothing	0.1199	−0.7886	0.9834	0.5152
		(0.0243)		
		(−40.7424)		
Miscellaneous	0.3832	−1.7673	0.9272	0.3552
		(0.0934)		
		(−18.9154)		

USA

	α_i	β_i	$\bar{R}^2$	d
Food	0.0197	−0.3506	0.9371	1.2375
		(0.0208)		
		(−16.8513)		
Housing	0.7181	−1.3287	0.9818	0.6978
		(0.0414)		
		(−32.0736)		
Fuel & light	0.0494	−1.0532	0.9426	0.4803
		(0.0595)		
		(−17.6864)		
Clothing	0.0234	−0.6261	0.8537	0.5066
		(0.0592)		
		(−10.5782)		
Miscellaneous	1.3752	−1.3067	0.9862	0.7906
		(0.0355)		
		(−36.8453)		

TABLE 2.
Estimates by Kadiyala Method

All Household

	α_i	β_i	γ
Food	0.3543	−0.5344	0.0227
Housing	0.1019	−1.1301	0.7066
Fuel & light	0.0394	−0.7696	0.1550
Clothing	0.1131	−0.7209	0.4864
Miscellaneous	0.3813	−1.4131	0.4096

where γ = estimated ρ in $u_t = \rho u_{t-1} + V_t$

Household in Cities

	α_i	β_i	γ
Food	0.3608	−0.5350	0.6899
Housing	0.0832	−1.4441	0.9278
Fuel & light	0.0397	−0.7903	0.7388
Clothing	0.1202	−1.0161	0.6529
Miscellaneous	0.3669	−1.6697	0.4935

USA

	α_i	β_i	γ
Food	0.0197	−0.3505	0.2799
Housing	0.6421	−1.3005	0.6462
Fuel & light	0.0331	−0.9470	0.8330
Clothing	0.0171	−0.5467	0.7733
Miscellaneous	1.3514	−1.3030	0.5308

TABLE 3.
Estimates by Beach-MacKinnon Method

All Household

	α_i	β_i	γ	$\bar{R}^2$
Food	0.3543	−0.5348	0.0569	0.9974
	(0.0018)	(0.0112)		
Housing	0.1020	−1.1317	0.7003	0.9818
	(0.0421)	(0.1522)		
Fuel & light	0.0394	−0.7696	0.1554	0.9941
	(0.0094)	(0.0267)		
Clothing	0.1128	−0.6974	0.6371	0.9807
	(0.0199)	(0.0811)		
Miscellaneous	0.3812	−1.4175	0.5384	0.9973
	(0.0107)	(0.0511)		

Household in Cities

	α_i	β_i	γ	$\bar{R}^2$
Food	0.3605	−0.5400	0.7764	0.9927
	(0.0278)	(0.0414)		
Housing	0.0761	−1.2988	0.9691	0.9508
	(1.0395)	(0.9438)		

TABLE 3 *(Continued)*

Household in Cities

	α_i	β_i	γ	$\bar{R}^2$
Fuel & light	0.0396	−0.7901	0.7702	0.9856
	(0.0758)	(0.0834)		
Clothing	0.1203	−1.0353	0.7972	0.9920
	(0.0867)	(0.0865)		
Miscellaneous	0.2796	−0.9256	0.9952	0.9643
	(4.4023)	(1.1276)		

USA

	α_i	β_i	γ	$\bar{R}^2$
Food	0.0197	−0.3510	0.3337	0.9697
	(0.1101)	(0.0292)		
Housing	0.6438	−1.3011	0.6418	0.9914
	(0.3415)	(0.0875)		
Fuel & light	0.0149	−0.7385	0.9690	0.9724
	(2.5094)	(0.6376)		
Clothing	0.0176	−0.5528	0.7464	0.9281
	(0.5751)	(0.1486)		
Miscellaneous	1.3430	−1.3016	0.6058	0.9934
	(0.2844)	(0.0723)		

TABLE 4.

95% confidence intervals of β_i

Food	$-0.6051 < \beta_1{}^A < -0.4645 \quad \hat{\beta}_1{}^A = -0.5348(0.112)$
	$-0.5560 < \beta_1{}^H < -0.5240 \quad \hat{\beta}_1{}^H = -0.5400(0.0414)$
	$-0.3645 < \beta_1{}^U < -0.3375 \quad \hat{\beta}_1{}^U = -0.3510(0.0282)$
Housing	$-1.2274 < \beta_2{}^A < -1.0360 \quad \hat{\beta}_2{}^A = -1.1317(0.1522)$
	$-1.6641 < \beta_2{}^H < -0.9335 \quad \hat{\beta}_2{}^H = -1.2988(0.9438)$
	$-1.3431 < \beta_2{}^U < -1.2591 \quad \hat{\beta}_2{}^U = -1.3011(0.0875)$
Fuel & light	$-0.7864 < \beta_3{}^A < -0.7528 \quad \hat{\beta}_3{}^A = -7696(0.0267)$
	$-0.8224 < \beta_3{}^H < -0.7578 \quad \hat{\beta}_3{}^H = -0.7901(0.834)$
	$-1.0445 < \beta_3{}^U < -0.4323 \quad \hat{\beta}_3{}^U = -0.7385(0.6376)$
Clothing	$-0.7844 < \beta_4{}^A < -0.6464 \quad \hat{\beta}_4{}^A = -0.6974(0.0811)$
	$-1.0688 < \beta_4{}^H < -1.0018 \quad \hat{\beta}_4{}^H = -1.0353(0.0865)$
	$-0.6242 < \beta_4{}^U < -0.4814 \quad \hat{\beta}_4{}^U = -0.5528(0.1486)$
Miscellaneous	$-1.4496 < \beta_5{}^A < -1.3854 \quad \hat{\beta}_5{}^A = -1.4174(0.0511)$
	$-1.3620 < \beta_5{}^H < -0.4892 \quad \hat{\beta}_5{}^H = -0.9256(1.1276)$
	$-1.3363 < \beta_5{}^U < -1.2669 \quad \hat{\beta}_5{}^U = -1.3016(0.0723)$

where hold

$\hat{\beta}_i{}^A$ = the estimated value of the coefficient $\beta_i{}^A$ of All Household
$\hat{\beta}_i{}^H$ = the estimated value of the coefficient $\beta_i{}^H$ of Household in cities
$\hat{\beta}_i{}^U$ = the estimated value of the coefficient $\beta_i{}^U$ of USA Household

TABLE 5.

Comparison

Food		(L1)	
All household	$x_1 = 0.3543$	$y_1 = -0.5348$	$\bar{R}^2 = 0.9974$
	(0.0018)	(0.0112)	$\gamma = 0.0569$
Household in cities	$x_1 = 0.3605$	$y_1 = -0.5400$	$\bar{R}^2 = 0.9927$
	(0.0278)	(0.0414)	$\gamma = 0.7764$
USA	$x_1 = 0.0197$	$y_1 = -0.3510$	$\bar{R}^2 = 0.9697$
	(0.1101)	(0.0282)	$\gamma = 0.3337$

where standard errors are in parenthesis under the estimated values of the parameters.

Housing		(L1)	
All housing	$x_2 = 0.1020$	$y_2 = -1.1317$	$\bar{R}^2 = 0.9818$
	(0.0421)	(0.1522)	$\gamma = 0.7003$
Household in cities	$x_2 = 0.0761$	$y_2 = -1.2988$	$\bar{R}^2 = 0.9508$
	(1.0395)	(0.9438)	$\gamma = 0.9691$
USA	$x_2 = 0.6438$	$y_2 = -1.3011$	$\bar{R}^2 = 0.9914$
	(0.3415)	(0.0875)	$\gamma = 0.6418$

Fuel & light		(L1)	
All household	$x_3 = 0.0394$	$y_3 = -0.7696$	$\bar{R}^2 = 0.9941$
	(0.0094)	(0.0267)	$\gamma = 0.1554$
Household in cities	$x_3 = 0.0396$	$y_3 = -0.7901$	$\bar{R}^2 = 0.9856$
	(0.0758)	(0.0834)	$\gamma = 0.7702$
USA	$x_3 = 0.0149$	$y_3 = -0.7385$	$\bar{R}^2 = 0.9724$
	(2.5094)	(0.6376)	$\gamma = 0.9690$

Clothing		(L1)	
All household	$x_4 = 0.1128$	$y_4 = -0.6974$	$\bar{R}^2 = 0.9807$
	(0.0199)	(0.0811)	$\gamma = 0.6371$
Household in cities	$x_4 = 0.1203$	$y_4 = -1.0353$	$\bar{R}^2 = 0.9920$
	(0.0867)	(0.0865)	$\gamma = 0.7972$
USA	$x_4 = 0.0176$	$y_4 = -0.5528$	$\bar{R}^2 = 0.9281$
	(0.5751)	(0.1486)	$\gamma = 0.7464$

Miscellaneous		(L1)	
All household	$x_5 = 0.3812$	$y_5 = -1.4175$	$\bar{R}^2 = 0.9973$
	(0.0107)	(0.0511)	$\gamma = 0.5384$
Household in cities	$x_5 = 0.2796$	$y_5 = -0.9256$	$\bar{R}^2 = 0.9643$
	(4.4023)	(1.1276)	$\gamma = 0.9952$
USA	$x_5 = 1.3430$	$y_5 = -1.3016$	$\bar{R}^2 = 0.9934$
	(0.2844)	(0.0723)	$\gamma = 0.6058$

among the three, which means that average households in Japan are not as sensitive to the price changes of housing, because most local households have their own houses and do not move. There are huge shortages of houses and housing facilities in big cities in Japan, and many urban people have to live in rented houses. The above results indicate that there is an enormous potential demand for housing, though Household in Cities cannot afford to buy. Thus, they are relatively responsive to price changes. An average U.S. person moves their residence from one place to another fairly often approximately every five years). Thus, they are relatively sensitive to the price changes in housing.

Fuel & Light. All own price elasticities are less elastic ($|\beta| < 1$), and all households have almost the same demand patterns, although the 95% confidence interval of the U. S. A. is pretty wide. This is a rather amazing result. Japanese energy consumption per capita is far behind that of U.S. households. Furthermore, we cannot find any significant differences between All Household and Household in Cities.

Clothing. The own price elasticity of All Household is slightly larger than that of the U.S.A. but the own price elasticity of Household in Cities is far larger than any others. Household in Cities usually follows the latest fashions and is strongly conscious of clothing. Therefore, the demands change drastically when the prices of clothing change. On the other hand, the U.S.A. is not also sensitive to the price changes of clothing. That means, the U.S.A. is rather more casual with respect to clothing.

Miscellaneous. The own price elasticity of Household in Cities is the smallest among the three, although the 95% confidence interval of Household in Cities is pretty wide. U.S.A. and All Household have almost the same demand patterns.

6. Concluding Remarks

In our theoretical analysis we derived one set of linear demand functions and ten sets of log–linear demand functions that satisfied the conditions of theoretical plausibility and self-duality. Making use of the self-duality property, the corresponding explicit utility functions were also derived. All of these functions had to satisfy stringent conditions placed on the parameters. It was a very difficult endeavor to apply these systems of self-dual demand functions in an empirical study.

One of the objectives of this empirical analysis was to examine the plausibility of these self-dual demand functions, and the other objective was to make an international comparison between American and Japanese consumption behavior.

As a first approximation, we used broadly classified time series data (five commodity groups). Thus, we did not make our comparison on the basis of a finely classified data set. We regarded the price index of the broadly classified commodity group as the price of that commodity. Some price indices were nearly the same because our groupings are too broad and the number of observations too small. Consequently, we confronted the problem of multicollinearity in much of our empirical result. In addition, since the ratio of prices was used in estimating the parameters of the Bergson type model (L2), the range of (relative) price variation became very narrow and the estimated values were not stable (i.e., we had fairly large standard errors of the estimates). Therefore, only the non-homothetic CES type demand functions (L1) results proved useful for comparing consumption behavior on an international basis.

If we chose a proper commodity group to be a basic commodity, the system of demand functions of the type (L6) would work out well. But as far as our data were concerned, there remained the possibility of multicollinearity.

Similarly, if we chose the proper pair of commodity groups in the system of demand function (L8), we could estimate the parameters without the annoying problem of multicollinearity. However, we could not succeed in finding such a proper pair and also failed to ensure that the symmetric condition placed on the parameters was fulfilled.

The other systems of demand functions are a kind of mixture of (L1), (L6), and/or (L7). Comparisons based on these results would not be particularly meaningful.

We would avoid the problem of multicollinearity by using more disaggregate data. But then the possible combinations become too large to handle in many cases.

Since the price of the basic good enters into all the other functions (except one) in the (L6) case, the plausibility of applying this system of demand functions to empirical study may diminish if we utilized more disaggregate data.

If we choose a pair of commodities that are (mutual) substitutes or complements, we can succeed in avoiding multi-collinearity and ensure the fulfillment of the symmetry condition. The remaining demand functions (except one) have the form of the non-homothetic CES type.

All prices except one are present in all demand functions (except one) in (L7), and the parameters have to satisfy the condition of integrability. Thus, it is very difficult to apply the (L7) case to empirical study even if we use more disaggregate data.

A system of non-homothetic CES type demand functions (L1) is the most plausible and practical among all eleven sets of self-dual demand functions. This system of self-dual demand functions (L1) is very simple in that demands are functions only of their own real prices. Our study has demonstrated that U. S. data and Japanese data both yield good empirical estimation results. We can say with some conviction that this type of demand system would be a good predictor of actual consumption behavior.

References

Hicks, J. R., Direct and indirect additivity, *Econometrica*, Vol. 37, 1969.

Houthakker, H. S., A note on self-dual preferences, *Econometrica*, Vol. 33, 1965.

Samuelson, P. A., Using full duality to show that simultaneously additive direct and indirect utilities implies unitary price elasticity of demand, *Econometrica*, Vol. 33, 1965.

Sato, R., On Self-Dual Preference, Department of Economics, Brown University, Discussion Paper, 1972.

Sato, R., Self-dual preferences, *Econometrica*, Vol. 44, 1976.

Matsushita, M., Estimations of self-dual demand functions: An international comparison, PhD Thesis, Brown University, 1982.

Index

275

U

Ultimate borrowers, 198
  in Britain, 201–205
Ultra-commodity bias, 67–68, 69, 72
  for nontradeables, 77
Ultra-Keynesian model, 32, 41
Uncontrollability, of public sector goods, 44–45, 55
Undervaluation, of exchange rate, 64–65
Unemployment, 31
  causes of, 44
  and price rigidity, 32
  and savings rate, 153–154, 175
Uniform national dividend, 47
  regional income redistribution and, 49
  and social optimization, 52, 54–55
Uniform quality, 199–201
Union(s)
  enterprise, 191, 193
  labor, 182–183, 187–188, 190
  trade, 186
United Kingdom
  balance of payments in, 204–205
  private savings rate of, 147, 155
United Nations Statistical Office, 100, 101, 102, 107
United Nations System of National Accounts, 99, 172
  Provisional International Guidelines on the National and Sectoral Balance-Sheet and Reconciliation Accounts of the System of National Accounts, 119
  revised, structure of, 102
  savings rate statistics, 155
United States
  aging population in, 166
  agricultural production, 68–69
  financial development in, 197, 199, 201, 205–207, 209, 214, 215, 235
  and labor market segmentation, 181–182, 183
  nineteenth-century land cultivation in, 68
  post World War II dollar shortage, 65
  private savings rate, 146, 147, 149, 150, 154, 155
Unit period
  cash balances per, 60
  contraction to zero, 5, 15, 21
  expectation sequences and, 19–20, 25–29

and investment allocation, 14
  see also Equiprofit curve, neighborhood
Utility
  equalization, 51–52
  functions, 253–254
  per capita income, 49–53
  public sector goods as, 54
Utilization rate, 141
Uzawa two-sector growth model, 4–11
  see also Models, growth

V

Valuation schemes, 102–103
Variable expenditure patterns, 90
  see also Expenditure(s)

W

Wage rate
  within booming sector, 79
  differential, 46
  seniority and, 182
  and unemployment, 44
  uniformity of, 5
Wage-rental ratio, 45
War(s)
  and financial developments, 201–202, 206–207, 211
  trade, 218–220
Watershed, financial, 206
Wealth
  comparisons of, 156
  domestic output and, 36
  effects, positive, 61, 74
  financial, stock of, 34
  household, 154, 165
  replacement, 152–153, 161–162
  savings rate and, 150–151
Weighted regressions, 174
Welfare maximization, 53
  see also Optimal condition; Social welfare
Workers
  Japanese, 184–185, 186, 187–188
  in manufacturing, 96
  propensity to consume, 88
  Quesnay's tableaé economique and, 87–94
  and savings rate, 151–155
  wage income of, 85
  see also Landowners

Working Group of Joint Japan-US Ad Hoc
 Group on Yen/Dollar Exchange Rate,
 Financial and Capital Market Issues,
 217–218
World Bank, 101
 dual sectoring, 105–107
World War I, 184
 foreign securities market during, 204
 US corporate bonds and, 207
World War II, 185, 187–188
 banking during, 204, 209

Y

Yasuda Corporation, 185
*Year Book of Coal, Petroleum and Coke Stat-
 istics*, 134
Year Book of Oil Statistics, 134

Yen
 appreciation of the, 38
 overvaluation of, 65
 undervaluation of, 65
 US/Japan commercial banking, and, 217–
 249
Yen-Dollar Committee, 217
Yokohama Specie Bank, 211
Yokonarabi ishiki, 247
Yugoslavia, private savings rate of, 147, 155

Z

Zaibatsu (family-owned conglomerate), 185,
 188
Zero autocorrelation, 266
Zigzags, Tableau, 91–94

DATE DUE